The Development of National Power

National Power
The United States, 1900-1919

The Development of National Power
The United States, 1900-1919

Richard L. Watson, Jr.
Duke University

Houghton Mifflin Company · Boston

Atlanta   Dallas   Geneva, Illinois
Hopewell, New Jersey   Palo Alto   London

Library of Congress Catalog Card Number: 75-31006

ISBN: 0-395-05522-9

To Ruth, for making it possible
for me to stay at it.

Contents

Foreword

This is the third of a series of volumes that together will cover the recent history of the nation. Since each author is a recognized authority on the period covered, no attempt has been made to order their contributions other than the setting of the time span and the maximum number of pages. And although it is expected that each will touch upon the major interpretations of their period, their own judgment will govern their selection of materials, the organization of the work, and finally the integrative principles or interpretation they wish to cast upon the complex number of historical forces emergent in any two or three decades of recent American history.

Readers will not go far in this splendid volume before they realize that Professor Watson is not completely content with any of the existing interpretations of the progressive movement, which he sees as an "almost infinitely complicated phenomenon" about which "no general theory works" to explain satisfactorily the sum of social movements. In fact, he almost concludes that in terms of one overriding sophisticated interpretation the past is probably unknowable. But in dealing with the years from 1900 to 1919 the author has rightly, I believe, seized upon the two major forces of internal reform and external war, or the threat of war, that altered the existing institutions and gave the period the identity that separated it from those that preceded and succeeded it. And more remarkably, he has combined the two as few other authors have in showing how each influenced the development of the other, and how the twain contributed to an almost inexorable concentration of power at the level of the national government. In fact, one of the major contributions of this volume is in its unified treatment of internal and external affairs.

Although the author states that the habit of increasing national power was a part of the "mood of the times" he also clearly demonstrates that nationalism was not an end in itself but rather utilized as an instrument in securing social objectives. Thus the local and state solutions to both the "trust" and the liquor problems were tried repeatedly without success on the local and state levels and the national government called in as a court of last resort. Professor Watson is probably at his best in discussing the contribution of military policy to the modern consolidated state. His description of the impact of technology as well as foreign threats on the changing nature of the federal bureaucracy and its relations to internal affairs is both fresh and challenging. As the author shows, a military-industrial complex clearly developed in the period and the war department underwent many of the changes that American industry had experienced and was experiencing.

The last third of this volume is almost entirely concerned with intelligent discussion of the enormous influence that foreign affairs and war mobilization had in reordering the division of powers between the various levels of the American government. The National Defense Act of 1916, as the author puts it, was one of "the most sweeping extensions" of power in American history. And in the distribution of that power he later cites the Overman Act of 1918 as a towering landmark in the swift development of executive supremacy over the legislative and judicial branches of the federal government. The usual treatment of the progressive period separates foreign and domestic affairs, resulting in a warped viewpoint that obscures the intimate and interdependent relationship of the two. In this volume Professor Watson has done a superb job of corrective refraction.

George E. Mowry

Preface

I have focused my attention in this volume on the national government from about 1900 to about 1919—a period in which an unprecedented growth of national power took place. I hope that my treatment will suggest a more than conventional logic in this periodization, even though it is obvious that the growth of power cannot be understood without recognizing the influence of factors rooted in earlier years. It must be recognized as well that these factors of industrialization, urbanization, migration, education, and technological invention, particularly in the field of transportation and communication, had a somewhat similar effect on developments in other countries. Nor can we isolate the first two decades of the century from the years that follow. Indeed, the origins of a number of the questions discussed in the United States after World War II regarding power—"corporate power," "federal power," the "power elite," and the "military-industrial complex"—are to be found in the Progressive Era and in mobilization for the First World War. It should be emphasized that neither the transition from the nineteenth century to the twentieth century nor from war to peace in 1919 was easy. For the first two decades of the twentieth century in the United States were characterized by confusion as to means and ends rather than unity and clarity of vision in the attempts to solve problems of modernization and waging war.

In my treatment of the development of national power in this volume, I have considered the growth of military power in response to a greater involvement overseas as well as the expansion of governmental controls and the inauguration of programs to aid individuals and specific groups. Utilizing a vast body of research by others, I have attempted to take into account those studies that have described factors influential in promoting change on the local as well as on the national level; those that have explained the motives and appraised the results of reform programs and overseas expansion; those that have stressed the importance of public and private bureaucracies and of groups and organizations as well as individuals; and those that have begun the investigation of twentieth-century military policy—particularly mobilization, rather than overseas operations, during the First World War.

I wrote on the premise that an understanding of the period requires a blend of both older and newer interpretations. While a focus on national power may overlook much about the way people lived and their contributions, changes in national power do indirectly or directly affect all the people. The American people's response to impersonal forces in peace and war are primary factors in the development of national power; the role of ideas in stimulating and accompanying action are significant; and roles of such national leaders as Theodore Roosevelt and Woodrow Wilson are important in relationship to their contemporaries, as well as to later generations. Although the language of the public champions of reform frequently exceeded actual accomplishment, many individuals and organizations were sincerely dedicated to making the world a better place in which to live. No radical changes in social and political structure occurred during the period, but numerous changes in institutions and practices did take place that merit itemization and that were to have considerable importance in the years to come.

As indicated above, I am deeply obligated to the numerous scholars upon whose research this book has drawn extensively. I am also indebted to my colleagues in the Department of History and the Duke University Library who have helped me in many ways throughout the years and especially to Robert F. Durden of Duke University, George E. Mowry of the University of North Carolina at Chapel Hill, and Allen Yarnell of the University of California at Los Angeles, who read critically substantial portions of this manuscript. Three of my former students, John M. Lindley, Winfred B. Moore, Jr., and Mark Stauter patiently checked statistics and bibliographical references. Elizabeth Foster, Vivian Jackson, Carolyn Morgan, Dorothy Sapp, and Judith Swimmer exceeded the call of duty in translating my handwriting and typing into a readable typescript. I am grateful as well to the Duke University Research Council for grants for this project. Obviously no one except the author should be blamed for factual errors or idiosyncracies of interpretations.

Richard L. Watson, Jr.

The Development of National Power

National Power
The United States, 1900-1919

1

The Setting

The Transportation Revolution

Wednesday, February 12, 1908, was a beautiful Lincoln's birthday. Early
in the morning people began to gather in Times Square in New York City,
and by eleven o'clock some fifty thousand people had assembled. This
crowd was awaiting the start of an automobile race whose destination
was Paris. The drivers planned to cross the United States, Alaska, the
Bering Strait when frozen, Siberia, Russia, and from there, on to Paris.
Six cars set out, a German *Protos,* three French cars (a *Sizaire et Maudin,*
a *Moto-Bloc,* and a *De Dion*), an Italian *Zust,* and an American *Thomas.*
All cars carried tools, chains, searchlight, wheels, springs, tires, inner tubes,
picks, shovels, block and tackle, camping gear and extra clothing, and an
arsenal of rifles and revolvers. On March 24, the *Thomas* reached San
Francisco, forty-one days, eight hours, and fifteen minutes after it had
left New York. By August 1, both the German car and the American car
had reached Paris. After crossing the Pacific by ship rather than driving
across the frozen Bering Strait, they then travelled through Manchuria,
and Siberia, which included bumping along the railroad ties of the Trans-
Siberian railroad, European Russia, and Germany on roads that at times
were "magnificent."

The purpose of this dramatic race was to show what the automobile
could do. At the time of the race, fewer than a dozen automobiles had
crossed the continent on their own wheels. Given the state of the roads in
the United States in the winter of 1908, the Thomas car had made remarkable time in reaching the coast in forty-one days. Many rivers were not
bridged except for railroads; service stations were virtually nonexistent;
roads were frequently no more than trails. Prior to the twentieth century
there had been various good-roads movements, partly concerned with
improving transportation facilities for the farmers, partly with encouraging

1

recreational riding particularly by energetic bicycling organizations. Some two million miles of roads existed, but they were unsurfaced and not always satisfactory even for the wagons and carriages for which they had been designed. In 1895, only four automobiles were registered in the United States, and hence it is understandable why their owners had little influence in agitating for good roads. However, by 1900, 8,000 motor vehicles were registered; by 1910, 468,500; by 1915, almost 2.5 million; and by 1920, more than 9 million.* Another transportation revolution was under way, one that would increasingly eliminate isolated communities and provide a new stimulus for the development of federal power.

Although the automobile revolution had thus begun before 1920, it had only begun. Road mileage in rural areas had increased to almost three million in 1920, but only a tiny percentage were made of concrete or of reasonably durable macadam. By the turn of the century electric cars had replaced horse cars in the cities, and subways were screeching through tunnels in New York and Boston. Twenty years later more than a million trucks were wearing down the comparatively few miles of paved roads; but buses were only beginning to compete with streetcars in the cities; and horses still clattered along delivering milk at the crack of dawn or hauling refuse to the city garbage dump.

At the same time that the internal-combustion engine was bringing the city closer to the country and the Atlantic closer to the Pacific, aeronautical designers were laying the groundwork for the next phase of the transportation revolution. In 1900, two courageous Frenchmen held the world's distance record for aeronautics. They had ridden a free spherical balloon from Vincennes in France to Korostychew in Russia, a distance of more than a thousand miles. Two Americans almost equaled that record in 1910. By that year, however, attention was being focused on the airplane. Two bicycle builders, the Wright brothers, had flown their fragile machine at Kitty Hawk, North Carolina, in 1903. Five years later, the Wrights kept a plane aloft for more than an hour. In 1908, Glenn Curtiss, a motorcycle builder, won a trophy offered by the *Scientific American* by flying 5,090 feet; a year later, he won the same trophy for a flight of 25 miles; and in 1910 won it again by flying from Albany to Camelot in New York state, a distance of 74 miles; he immediately took off for New York City and won a prize of $10,000 offered by the *New York World* to an aviator who would follow the route of Robert Fulton's *Clermont.*

By the time the war broke out in 1914, aviation enthusiasts were heralding the role of the "birdmen in battle," and prophesying a new day in strategy and tactics. For several years European governments had

*In 1900, approximately 4,000 new automobiles were sold; in 1910, 181,000; in 1915, 895,930; and in 1920, more than 1,900,000. *Historical Statistics,* p. 462; Faulkner, *The Decline of Laissez Faire,* p. 233ff.

been listening to these prophets and had subsidized aeronautical laboratories. Then in 1914, Congress, through the Naval Appropriations Act,
established an Advisory Committee on Aeronautics for the army and the
navy. Within a year both the navy and the Massachusetts Institute of
Technology had established wind tunnels, and the base for a thriving
industry had been founded. As recently as 1910 the "small, unreliable
flying machine" had been considered "good for exhibition purposes only,"
but now it had developed "by gigantic strides into a carrier of immense
power and promise."

Communication and Electricity

Although the transportation revolution may have been the most important
factor in providing a base for expansion of federal power in the twentieth
century, the revolutions in communication and electric power provide
close rivals. The electrical industry as it moved across state lines was in
itself a medium that called for federal control, but as the basic element
in the communication revolution it also helped strengthen the structural
framework of federalism. The late 1880s and early 1890s had seen a
sometimes bitter battle between Edison-sponsored direct current and
Westinghouse alternating current. Alternating current had distinct practical
advantages and, with the perfection of transformers and alternators, won
the battle. Indeed, the Edison Company merged with the General Electric
Corporation in 1892 and began to use alternating current. In the meantime, Westinghouse engineers were attempting to develop motors that
would use alternating current and replace steam engines for industrial
uses. Westinghouse proved his company's superiority when he used new
alternators and motors to light the Chicago World's Fair in 1893.

The electrical industry was still not ready to replace steam as the principal source of industrial power partly because of the need for a central
source for the generation of electricity. Niagara Falls was one obvious
source, and serious attempts were begun in 1886 to provide the necessary
facilities. The power was there, and the location, near centers both of
trade and population, was ideal, and by 1892 basic technical problems
had been solved. Again Edison and Westinghouse found themselves as
rivals in competing for a contract to provide generators for the Niagara
project. This battle was bitter, with charges of espionage, of theft of blue-
prints, and of conspiracies to defraud. Westinghouse won the initial contract in 1893, but as the years went by both companies shared, as did
some others, in providing generators, transformers, rotary converters,
and other equipment.

The success of the Niagara Falls project proved that a single, central
complex could generate and distribute power. Within a decade, when
again the ubiquitous George Westinghouse played an innovating role,

improved steam turbines had made possible the establishment of central power plants away from waterpower sites. These developments inspired the organization of utility companies which looked to the possibilities of a huge market for electricity if produced at low cost.

Electricity did not immediately capture the field. But "the total primary factory power applied through electric motors increased from 5 per cent in 1899 to 55 per cent in 1919." At the same time electricity was making life more pleasant for many city dwellers. Although gas still lit many urban homes as late as the 1920s, electricity was available in 1900 for those who could afford it. The electrical utilities, however, were unwilling to take a chance on a rural market, and in 1900 farmers still used candles and lamps. Indeed in 1920, fewer than 2 percent of the farm dwellings had electrical service. Telephone companies on the other hand, appeared more venturesome and seemed to trust to eventual demand to pay for initial costs. By 1900, well over 1 million telephones were in use, almost 18 for every 1000 persons, and Boston and New York had been connected. By 1920, there were more than 13 million telephones, 124 for every 1000 persons, and New York and San Francisco had been connected for 5 years. The communication revolution was under way.

The significance of the radio was less obvious in 1920. In 1895, Marconi succeeded in transmitting coded signals from one point to another. De Forest and Fessenden began experiments with voice "point-to-point" transmission after 1900, but not until 1906 or 1907 did they attempt to broadcast a program. The value of wireless telegraphy as a safety device for ships was soon recognized, and in 1910 federal regulation required that all passenger vessels install transmitters and receivers. As private operators increased in number, the need for some kind of regulation became obvious, and by the Radio Act of 1912 operators were required to register. The hams became increasingly active during the war years, and the federal government took over completely until 1919. The radio's principal use was still in point-to-point transmission, and commercial interests began to stake out their claims in what they envisaged as a major communications revolution. Westinghouse, General Electric, American Telephone and Telegraph—all the major companies became involved. Not until the 1920s, however, were the entertainment and advertising potentialities recognized.

The Railroad

In spite of the potential significance of the automobile, electricity, the telephone, the radio, and the airplane, the railroad continued to be the principal agent making possible a regional division of labor and the development of the country as a huge, free trade area. By the turn of the century, many of the early railroad builders such as Cornelius Vanderbilt, Jay Gould, and Collis Huntington had given way to less colorful figures such as J. P. Morgan, Edward Harriman, and James Hill who were interested not so much in building new lines as in consolidating those that already existed. The twentieth century had its share of stock watering, power grabbing, and a search for easy profits, but railroad men apparently believed that if the cutthroat competition of the nineteenth century were to continue it would destroy the railroads, and hence that consolidation was necessary.

The railroads had been seriously hurt by the Panic of 1893. However, they had recovered by the turn of the century, and expansion continued between 1900 and 1906 averaging more than five thousand miles of track built yearly, a rate of construction higher than any but the peak construction years in the 1870s and 1880s. At the same time, the lines were being consolidated. By 1906, perhaps two-thirds of the more than two hundred thousand miles of track in operation was controlled by seven groups, in which the names of Vanderbilt, Morgan, Hill, and Harriman figured prominently. The same interests were still dominant in 1920.

By that time, however, railroading was already beginning to show signs of having reached its peak. Construction declined after 1906 and mileage was being abandoned. Traffic continued to increase, but the financial condition of some railroads was deteriorating. For decades investors had considered railroads the principal field of investment; "their position was regal." By 1910, however, they had lost this priority and had given way to industrials. No one was probably aware at the time that this downward trend, spurred on by the automobile, the truck, the bus, and the airplane, would continue until the railroad industry would be on the brink of disaster by the middle of the century.

Although American economic growth may not have been solely dependent upon the railroad, American economic growth was sensational, and the railroad played an important part in it. National income had jumped from less than $7 billion in 1870 to more than $17 billion in 1900 to almost $89 billion in 1920. In terms of constant dollars, this represented an increase from $223 in per capita income in 1870 to $688 in 1920. Potential farm production seemingly became almost unlimited. In 1890, for example, American farmers grew about 449 million bushels of wheat. In 1900 that figure was 600 million, and it reached a peak of more than 1 billion bushels in 1915. American merchants engaged in a lively foreign commerce as both exports and imports increased markedly in value, and manufactured goods played an increasingly important part in exports, a development that undoubtedly is related to the fact that steel production, which had amounted to less than 20 thousand long tons in 1867, increased to more than 10 million tons in 1900 and to more than 42 million in 1920. Moreover, investments abroad which had totaled $684 million in 1897 had increased to almost $7 billion in 1919.

In considering the relationship among these economic developments, it is very easy to become involved in a chicken-and-egg discussion as to which led to what. Clearly farmers, merchants, and industrialists wanted the kind of quick, relatively inexpensive transportation that the railroad came to provide. Clearly, too, the growing urban areas required lumber and steel for construction, coal and oil for fuel, and agricultural products for clothing and food. The railroads not only transported these products but provided passenger service among the cities and changed the direction of the economic competition among them. At the same time, the railroads stimulated the economy by consuming enormous quantities of iron, lumber, and coal, encouraging technological development, and employing vast numbers of workers, one million in 1900 and two million in 1920. The railroad came to symbolize interstate commerce, and it touched the lives of all. It made both possible and necessary the increase of federal power.

The Industrial Bureaucracy

Equally important in explaining the development of federal power were changes that were taking place in the size and organization of business and industry. The period from the 1880s until the First World War saw the coming of big business. After the railroads, business became big in the manufacturing of consumer goods. Some of these large enterprises, making new products such as marketable meat, cigarettes, harvesters, and typewriters, not only manufactured the product but marketed it and purchased the constituent raw materials as well. Small enterprises, which had been manufacturing staples such as sugar, whiskey, and fertilizer, expanded by absorbing other small units and then created huge marketing organizations as the railroad and urban demand enlarged the market areas. As soon as the horizontal combination was completed, it became possible to concentrate manufacturing in more favorable locations, standardize manufacturing processes, and develop advertising, distributing, and purchasing departments. The producer-goods industries also developed combinations and consolidations and bureaucracies to run them, although usually somewhat later than did the manufacturer of goods for consumers.

Prior to 1890, the leading demand for steel and the products of heavy industry came from the railroads. Although this demand continued, the dynamic element in the economy increasingly became the cities whose growth in the late nineteenth and early twentieth centuries coincided with new inventions and new techniques of construction. Demand seemed unlimited for "electric lighting apparatus, telephones, copper wire, newsprint, streetcars, coal, and iron, steel, copper, and lead piping, structures and fixtures." By 1909 the new producer-goods industries, headed by such industrial giants as U.S. Steel and Amalgamated Copper, dominated the industrial scene.

No one factor explains the dynamic developments of industry in the late nineteenth century: the rapidly growing size of the home market fed by millions of European immigrants; the growth of scientific knowledge and technological innovation occurring in England, France, and Germany as well as in the United States; the availability of scientists, engineers, and other highly trained specialists as well as an improving quality of labor force all played their part. Perhaps the most historical controversy has buzzed around the role of the enterprising entrepreneur. The Vanderbilts, Goulds, Rockefellers, Huntingtons, and Carnegies were a remarkable group, whether by the standard of robber baron or of industrial statesman. The label assigned to them depends to some extent upon the standard of morality used to judge them and the weight given to their accomplishments as opposed to their methods or to their ruthlessness and dishonesty as opposed to their boldness, foresight, and resourcefulness. In any case, regardless of waste and frequently questionable practices, they led the way in developing the most dynamic economy in the world.

The battle over combination and consolidation had been fierce in the last part of the nineteenth century. Part of the battle took place within each industry as various elements struggled for control, but part was between the industries and the state and federal governments, which distrusted the power that the consolidations were acquiring. The battles had resulted in experimentation with various devices on the part of the promoters of the consolidations to find one that would work and pass inspection. The trust as technically defined had been rather effectively ruled out by state law and judicial action in the late eighties and early nineties, and the federal government had added the Sherman Antitrust Law in 1890.

In the meantime, an ingenious new device, the holding company, was making it possible for the combinations to operate across state lines and to avoid the regulations of those states that had taken legislative action to control the trusts. In 1889, the state of New Jersey put legislation on the statute books that made it possible for a corporation of New Jersey to purchase stock in other corporations for a fee. The holding company was thus legalized and promised low taxes and the right to operate in any state in the Union. A cartoon of the day showed New Jersey, a buxom female, observing corporations harried by other states and calling, "Come to Mother." The corporations heeded the call and flocked to New Jersey, New York, and Delaware, all of which were competing for the reputation of being most hospitable. A promoter of one of these holding companies could pay a comparatively small fee, charter his corporation, and then do business in any state of the Union. A great burst of consolidation activity occurred between 1895 and 1904. More than 300 firms "disappeared" into mergers each year, and such giants as U.S. Steel, American Tobacco, International Harvester, DuPont, and Amalgamated Copper Company were born.

As the process of consolidation continued, the role of the "finance capitalist" became greater. Perhaps the most important factor stimulating the merger movement, and the industrial economy in general, was the growing efficiency of mechanisms for borrowing, lending, and investing. Short-term arrangements gained remarkably in efficiency with an increasing number of banks and with more money in circulation. Many industries were becoming so large that the resources in individual banks or entrepreneurs were inadequate, and an investment house became a useful agent to handle the financing of the industrial establishments. Such firms as J.P. Morgan & Company and Kuhn, Loeb & Company helped refinance and reorganize old companies, bought and sold securities, and promoted new concerns. At the same time, the investment houses were further strengthening their resources by forming alliances with insurance companies, many of which were building up resources of millions of dollars which simply itched for investment. In this process, interrelationships developed among the financial powers. Representatives of the Rockefeller interests, for example, served on the Board of Directors of the U.S. Steel Corporation which was controlled essentially by the House of Morgan. The businessman seeking stability and concerned about the difficulty of protecting his profits in a highly competitive market saw salvation in the merger. The more efficient market mechanism and the promoters provided the means to construct the mergers and in turn offered further enticements in a rising stock market.

By 1903, when the first great merger period ended, the largest concerns had become bureaucracies. Most of them were divided into separate departments for purchasing, production, marketing, and finance. Increasingly, success in business depended upon the effectiveness of an accounting system which would keep accurate data. Increasingly, prices were determined by costs rather than competition, and competition took place more in advertising and changes in product than in price. Moreover, in a competitive situation where new products were important, industries, particularly those involved with chemicals, electricity, and machinery, added research and development departments that provided a new impetus to expansion. The complexity of the operation was so great that by 1909 the principal officers of the consolidation were themselves specialists in their industry. In short, these industries were "operating companies" rather than speculative "holding companies." Entrepreneurs, such as James B. Duke, John D. Rockefeller, Andrew Carnegie, and the various du Ponts, continued to make individual contributions. They were, however, experts in business statistics, and their decisions were dependent upon a large bureaucracy (increasingly held together by the typewriter and telephone) that was as much a civil service as that of the federal government.

Railroads, the large urban market, and the bureaucratic corporation were dynamic forces in the economy as the twentieth century opened. Electric power, the internal-combustion engine, research, and development provided additional stimuli. All transcended state lines and had profound effects on the way people lived. These forces added up to tremendous actual and potential centralized economic power and provoked a response in the political field.

Many viewed the process of consolidation with alarm. Consolidation had led to the passage of numerous state antitrust laws in the eighties and nineties and finally to the passage of the Sherman Antitrust law in 1890. It is not clear why this law was passed. Public clamor does not seem to have been the principal reason for congressional action. The final draft of the bill was drawn by conservative senators, mostly Republicans from the Northeast. The measure passed with only one dissenting vote in both houses. Its philosophy was that competition was in accord with natural law. It served as the rallying cry for those who fought the premise that combination was natural and that bigness was inevitable.

No clear-cut party line existed within the business community on the subject of consolidations. Writers in business publications praised the genius of management yet questioned whether size might not at some point unduly complicate operations. Fundamental differences existed among businessmen from the small town and from the large city, among businessmen from the Northeast, the South, and the West, and among those engaged in different types of business—the railroads against the shippers, foreign traders who favored a low tariff against manufacturers who favored protection. Obviously the stereotypes that developed as a result of these rivalries prevented any agreement as to the merits of the large combination.

The varying attitudes toward the combinations are further reflected in the way that the federal antitrust law was enforced. For more than a decade after the passage of the Sherman Act, no sustained efforts were made to enforce it. Congress provided no special appropriations; the administrations did not ask for funds. The Department of Justice simply assumed the additional responsibility for enforcement. However, the attorneys general, except for Judson Harman during the second Cleveland administration, were corporation lawyers who had little sympathy for the purposes of the act and provided little encouragement to local federal attorneys. Consequently many complaints containing substantial evidence of evasion of the law were ignored. During the entire decade, the Department of Justice prosecuted only eighteen consolidation cases under the Sherman Act, only three being large concerns; the department won only ten of these cases, none of them a major one, and four of the successful cases were against labor unions.

Although unwillingness to prosecute vigorously was probably the chief reason for the failure of the Sherman Act, an important contributory factor was the attitude of the majority of the Supreme Court. Justices led by Chief Justice Melville W. Fuller and Associate Justice Stephen J. Field accepted a constitutional interpretation that essentially incorporated the doctrine of laissez faire into constitutional law in a way that made it very difficult for any governmental authority to impose significant restraints upon the operations of business. This constitutional interpretation rested in part upon a traditional and rather vague concept of vested rights which had provided some protection of property against arbitrary legislation. More important, however, it rested upon an interpretation of the Fourteenth Amendment to the Constitution. One clause in that amendment, which had been designed to protect the civil rights of blacks, read that no state may deprive any person of life, liberty, or property without due process of law. By accepting the definition of a corporation as a "person," it was possible to say that in passing regulatory legislation a state was depriving a corporation of its property rights and was thus acting unconstitutionally. The Court accepted this interpretation, and in many cases declared unconstitutional such state laws as one setting a ten-hour limit on bakers in New York state on the grounds that it interfered with the employers' property rights without due process of law.

In spite of the tendency of the Supreme Court to use the new doctrine of due process, that Court could not ignore the historic principle of the police power of the states. Under that principle, many states had passed laws designed to protect the health and welfare of their citizens. Although the conservative Court vetoed several such ordinances in the early 1890s, in some instances the Court upheld them. In 1898, for example, the Court upheld the right of the state of Utah to limit the hours of workers in the mines.

The enforcement of the Sherman Antitrust Act was complicated because of differences of opinion regarding its constitutionality. In the first place those who had drafted the law had probably been intentionally vague as to its scope. The relevant section of the law read: "Every contract, combination in the form of trust or otherwise, or conspiracy, in restraint of trade or commerce among the several States, or with foreign nations, is hereby declared to be illegal. . . ." Initially, Sherman's proposal was that all consolidations manufacturing products for interstate commerce would be declared illegal. The statute as finally approved raised the fundamental question as to whether the law actually was designed to regulate manufacturing even if the product was designed for interstate commerce. Many believed that Congress had the right to regulate only those industries such as railroads which operated clearly in interstate commerce. Probably intentionally, the framers of the law left the decision up to the courts.

Equally controversial was the question as to whether the act unequivocally prohibited *all* combinations in restraint of trade. Senator George F. Hoar of Massachusetts, one of the principal authors of the measure, claimed that the bill had incorporated the principles of English common law on monopoly and thus implied that only those combinations which resulted in a substantial or unreasonable restraint of trade were illegal. The Supreme Court was not consistent in its decisions on these points, indicating that the presentation of the cases and the personal attitudes of the judges played a prominent role. Reasonableness and unreasonableness and goodness and badness became a part of the rhetoric as combinations and consolidations were subjected to scrutiny at the turn of the century. In 1898, Congress appointed an Industrial Commission to investigate industrial combinations, and in 1900 this commission arrived at a conclusion that would divide twentieth-century reformers. As the commission put it: "Experience proves that industrial combinations have become fixtures in our business life. Their power for evil should be destroyed and their means for good preserved." Unhappily, from the point of view of the "trust busters," the Supreme Court would adopt this "rule of reason" early in the twentieth century. In the Standard Oil case of 1911, Chief Justice Edward D. White stated clearly that the Sherman Act ruled out only "unreasonable combinations or contracts in restraint of trade."

In spite of continuing opposition to combination and consolidation of business from reformers, from politicians, and from worried businessmen themselves, big business continued to establish itself in the twentieth century, and this continued expansion provoked varied responses. For those who feared bigness, the response usually was simply to call for the breakup of the corporate giants. For those who accepted bigness, such as Theodore Roosevelt, the response was varied, but usually it included regulation; it might include, implicitly at least, the need to balance bigness in business with bigness in government and possibly with bigness in labor. Businessmen themselves increasingly talked in terms of the "new competition" in which stability, agreement, and negotiation with the blessing of government replaced the competitive ideal.

Organized Labor

Probably large labor organizations were regarded with as much suspicion as were the "trusts" at the turn of the century. The period from 1897 to 1904 was one in which labor union membership increased remarkably and when the American Federation of Labor emerged as the leading force in the labor movement. In 1897 total membership in trades unions was approximately 450,000, of whom 270,000 were in the American Federation of Labor. The AFL was a federation of approximately sixty unions ranging from carpenters, cigarmakers, and typographers, each having more than 28,000 members, to the broom makers and stoneware potters, numbering about 100 members each. Leading independent unions were the railroad brotherhoods and the bricklayers numbering more than 20,000 members. By 1904 total union membership had jumped to more than 2 million, of whom at least 1.5 million were in the AFL.

The AFL was a centrist force in the labor movement. By the 1890s, Samuel Gompers, its perennial leader, and his close associates had defeated the attempts of a socialist minority to sponsor a substantial program of public ownership. Gompers' position would continue to be practical, never looking for the "chimerical tomorrow," accepting the capitalist system, yet insisting that interests of workers and capitalists were "reconcilable only on a temporary basis" and rejecting the notion of a caste system into which labor was frozen. The failure of socialism in the United States rests to a considerable extent upon the inability of the socialist leadership to persuade the rank and file of American labor that each one of them did not have a chance to become a capitalist.

Gompers' apparent acceptance of the capitalist system led to another basic premise—that fundamental differences between labor and management should be settled by collective bargaining and, if necessary, the strike. The right to organize, the right to bargain collectively, and the right to strike were the irreducible minimum of the demands of the leading trade unions by the turn of the century. In general the AFL opposed legislation as the way to gain bread-and-butter aims of better hours, wages, or working conditions. In the minds of leaders like Gompers, legislation might be necessary to protect women, children, and government workers and to prevent the undermining of labor's standards by convicts and immigrants, but it was not necessary to protect able-bodied men.

This hardheadedness accounts to a considerable degree for the increased strength of labor between 1897 and 1904. Times had been difficult for labor unions during the eighties and nineties, but these hardships had developed discipline and dedicated leadership. With the return of prosperity, the unions tested their experience, became more aggressive, and were in general successful.* Membership burgeoned, particularly in the building trades and in the coal mines. The United Mine Workers, which in 1897 numbered fewer than 10,000 workers, jumped to 250,000 within six years. In this case, effective leadership in the person of John Mitchell, aggressive action in the shape of important strikes, statesmanlike action on the part of Mark Hanna and, in the anthracite strike of 1902, of Theodore Roosevelt, accounted for the UMW's success.

The rapid expansion in union membership stopped in 1904, and a period of decline began. Employer associations and citizens' alliances led by the National Association of Manufacturers, the Antiboycott Association, and numerous others launched a vigorous assault against the unions at a time when labor was weakened by a sharp depression. Labor spies, strike-breakers, antiunion books and periodicals, and vigilantism were a part of the antiunion campaign. Periodically such dramatic incidents as the assassination of Frank Steunenburg, a former antiunion governor of Idaho, in 1905, and the dynamiting of the *Los Angeles Times,* which killed twenty-one people in 1910, put the union movement under a serious cloud. At the same time the legal position of labor had become insecure.

*Between 1893 and 1898 there were about 7,000 strikes; between 1899 and 1904, there were 15,463; and in the whole period the workers considered about half the strikes to be victories.

The Supreme Court, which had already shown that it might consider labor unions to be conspiracies in restraint of trade, and therefore subject to the Sherman Antitrust Act, followed the same course in the twentieth century. Not only did the Court uphold employers who broke strikes by obtaining injunctions from local courts against strikers, but it made possible assessing damages against individual workers engaged in a strike.

Perhaps the most significant union failure during these years of labor decline was in the steel industry. The principal union involved here was the Amalgamated Association of Iron, Steel, and Tin Workers, a union of skilled workers associated with the AFL. Carnegie had defeated the union in the Homestead Strike of 1892 but allowed it to exist. Then in 1901 and again in 1909, strikes against U.S. Steel failed, and steel remained a stronghold for the open shop until the New Deal provided the protection for which unions had been fighting for more than a century.

The setbacks which organized labor experienced after 1904 caused a significant change in the attitude of the AFL toward politics. Officially the AFL favored campaigning by its membership but did not favor the leadership's taking any official position. Theoretically it stood on the principle of rewarding friends and punishing enemies, but it had done little in support of this principle. It engaged in vigorous lobbying activities, particularly against the use of the injunction in labor disputes, but by 1904 these lobbying activities had clearly failed. As the antiunion activities of employers became more blatant; as the socialists claimed that the AFL was selling the workers out; as membership and finances declined; as the antilabor bias of the courts seemed to offer no last resort, Gompers and his cohorts decided that they would turn to more vigorous political action. In 1906 they prepared a bill of grievances in which they demanded the elimination of the injunction in labor disputes, called for restrictions upon the use of convict labor and upon immigration, demanded protection for seamen, and expressed support for the eight-hour day for federal employees and for more stringent enforcement of the Sherman Antitrust Act. This bill was submitted to President Roosevelt and leading congressional officials, but it was not favorably received. At the same time Gompers urged an intensified campaign of rewarding friends and punishing political enemies.

In the course of these activities, the leaders of the AFL drew away from the Republican party. In 1908, they attempted to persuade the Republican platform committee to accept some of their proposals. They made similar attempts at the Democratic convention and were somewhat better received. As a result Gompers supported William Jennings Bryan in the presidential election and officially urged the membership of the AFL to support the Democrats. The result showed clearly that the AFL leadership was certainly not able to deliver the votes of any substantial group of union members.

In spite of the sometimes vicious labor conflicts, there were those on both sides who were paying at least lip service to the ideal of industrial democracy. This development was important, not because there was agreement as to what it meant, but because it gave some evidence of a recognition that big industry was leading to big labor and that without some means of working out differences, disastrous clashes were inevitable. The syndicalists might think that the only solution was revolutionary change toward a kind of government by the working class, and the National Association of Manufacturers might think that the employer should run his business as he saw fit, but the AFL worked for collective bargaining; and a growing number of employers accepted unionism or at least talked about cooperation, and the desirability of industrial peace as a part of "the new competition."

Many motives undoubtedly explain the new directions that management was taking: efficiency, stability, paternalism, or humanitarianism. In some instances employers negotiated alliances with labor unions in order to eliminate competition. In other instances, companies recognized the need for good public relations. Such enterprises as the Bell System with its increasingly national communications network, even U.S. Steel and Standard Oil, could not avoid a sense of social accountability. Popular favor as well as economic performance might determine the extent of government control.

Indeed the managerial professionalism required by the large enterprises led to increasing attention to ways of promoting industrial stability and efficiency. Perhaps the most important means to the end was the adoption of the techniques of Frederick W. Taylor who preached scientific management, the aim of which was "to simply and clearly define jobs, to improve the physical conditions of work . . . to minimize waste time and lost motions, and to provide an incentive for increased production through methods of pay based on worker productivity." Management increasingly accepted the premise that efficiency and productivity could be improved by greater comforts on the job such as bathing and recreational facilities, fringe benefits such as old-age pensions and profit sharing, and industrial safety campaigns.

The most serious effort to bring labor and industrial leaders together and to discuss contemporary issues of importance was the founding of the National Civic Federation in 1900 by Ralph M. Easley, a crusading newspaper editor from Chicago. The federation had an executive committee representing wage earners, employers, and the public. At one time or another it included politician-businessman, Mark Hanna, steelmen such as Elbert H. Gary and Charles Schwab, and labor leaders such as John Mitchell and Samuel Gompers. Gompers and Hanna seemed to think that "a mutual trust between the laborer and the employer" could be developed, but the rank and file of labor were not so sure. Too many employers such as Gary, Schwab, and Henry Phipps solemnly attended meetings of the federation and yet supported the antiunion policies of the U.S. Steel Corporation.

In spite of such ambivalence, however, after 1905 the National Civic Federation helped settle hundreds of strikes and began considering how the state and federal governments could be used to work out solutions to the problem of labor and capital and of the large corporation in general. Conferences, attended by businessmen and labor leaders, were held to study trust regulation, workers' compensation, and other questions that were to provide programs for social and economic reformers for many years to come.

Many industrialists, however, were horrified at the activities of the federation, an attitude increasingly manifested by antiunion organizations. Perhaps the most important of these was the National Association of Manufacturers founded in 1895 to promote foreign trade. By 1903 the NAM had taken as its goal the maintenance of the open shop, denounced members of the National Civic Federation as "industrial doughfaces," and led the way in forming such organizations as the Citizens Industrial Association in 1903 and the National Council of Industrial Defense in 1908 to combat unions and to lobby against labor legislation.

These antiunion activities held unionization down, but by 1910 membership began to increase again and continued to do so until 1920. Although the reasons for the advance after 1910 were complicated, one of the principal factors was the success of the International Ladies' Garment Workers organized in 1900. This union mobilized in 1909, and approximately twenty thousand women went out on strike in New York City. Cruel treatment against pickets by the police brought public sympathy and support; the net result was victory for the workers. A year later the United Garment Workers led by a young man with a long future, Sidney Hillman, won a partial victory in Chicago against Hart, Shaffner and Marx. These victories strengthened the cause of labor by incorporating women and Jewish and Italian immigrants into the labor movement. Significantly, these unions were affiliated with the class-conscious American Federation of Labor, which traditionally had been opposed to industrial unionism and had firmly opposed unrestricted immigration. A paradox about the increasing participation of the immigrant group is that a significant number of recent immigrants introduced ideals of European radicalism, social reform, even international socialism. At the same time, many of the newly arrived immigrants were Roman Catholic, a church which, though not averse to social reform, certainly used its influence in keeping the American labor movement divorced from the socialist cause.

In spite of the growth of American unionism during the first decades of the twentieth century, labor union membership was never more than a small fraction of total possible membership. In 1910, for example, slightly more than 10 percent of the possible membership belonged to unions. In general the unions won their greatest success among the manual workers in factories, mines, railroads, and buildings, and perhaps their greatest failures among the white-collar workers. Gompers took an ambivalent position on the role of unskilled workers, immigrants, and blacks in the labor movement. In theory he saw no difference between skilled and unskilled workers, and he insisted that special efforts be made to organize the unskilled. In theory, too, he favored accepting blacks on equal terms with whites. In both cases, however, he left it up to the local to make decisions, and rarely were black workers welcomed in a local of the AFL. In the case of immigration, he took a particularly hardheaded position, given the fact that he himself was a Jewish immigrant, and supported restriction on the grounds that immigrants undermined labor standards and were not interested in joining unions.

Immigration and Internal Mobility

Gompers' ambivalent attitude reflects the unsettling effect of immigration upon American culture. Few issues of the early twentieth century had so many emotional overtones, both from the point of view of the immigrants themselves and their children, "the uprooted," as Oscar Handlin aptly called them, and from that of the predominantly white, Protestant, Anglo-Saxon "native." The latter point of view was a composite of attitudes—the idealistic view of the United States as a haven for the oppressed or a melting pot, the more practical view of the effect of immigration upon economic and social conditions, and the nativistic view of simply not liking the "strangers in the land."

In spite of increasingly hostile attitudes toward immigration, no sweeping restrictions were imposed until after the First World War. In the nineteenth century, idealism combined with the demands for manpower to meet the needs of railroad building and expanding industry encouraged immigration rather than restricted it. After a century of unrestricted entry, restrictions were imposed in 1882 against certain types of "undesirables," and a temporary exclusion bill was enacted against the Chinese. Nonetheless, immigration rapidly increased, and that increase, together with a declining death rate aided by improved diets and medicines, resulted in a rapidly growing population. In 1890, the population was almost 63 million; ten years later it was approaching 76 million; and in 1910 it was almost 92 million, totals larger than any European nation except Russia, which had a population of 140 million in 1903. Between 1883 and 1900 more than 7 million immigrants came into the United States, and from then through 1914 at least 13 million more immigrants arrived.

By this time a change had taken place as to the countries from which immigrants came. Until the 1880s, the majority of the immigrants came from the countries of northwestern Europe, whose cultures were somewhat comparable to those from which most native-born Americans had sprung. In the decade of the 1890s, however, the percentage was shifting to the countries of southern and eastern Europe, and in the next decade a majority of new immigrants came from those sources. Most of these latter immigrants were Italians, Slavs, and Jews. Except for some of the Jews, most of the new immigrants were peasants, uneducated and poverty stricken; many had been forced from lands upon which their ancestors had toiled, and then were enticed by employment bureaus seeking to fill the need for unskilled labor in the United States.

Approximately 80 percent of the new immigrants employed in 1900 held industrial and commercial jobs. Some found themselves in small mill towns, but most swelled the population of the rapidly growing cities. Before the end of the first decade, a majority of the children in the schools of the leading cities had foreign-born fathers. Consequently, at a time when urbanism was becoming one of the most dynamic elements in American society, the character of the city was being modified by the increasing number of immigrants, predominantly Roman Catholic or Jewish, uneducated, poor, and mostly from a rural environment. Understandably they could afford only the poorest housing, in many instances owned by landlords interested only in getting as much rent as possible for it. Flats were crowded; garbage was rarely collected and streets rarely cleaned; vermin were endemic; sewage disposal was primitive with open drains common; water usually was available only in the street, and if piped to the one or two public toilets available in a tenement, it frequently froze in the unheated hallways or could not work its way through the stuffed-up commodes. It is perhaps understandable why labor unions, mostly consisting of skilled workers, saw immigration as a threat to their standards; and why some social workers, seeing the filth, disease, and poverty which seemed to revolve around the sections where the new immigrants lived, thought of immigration restriction as a progressive reform.

While immigration from without was increasing, the American people continued to move extensively from one part of the United States to another. Historically the reasons for internal migration had been economic, primarily the search for better farm lands. Until 1910, the same motivation predominated. From 1889, when the barriers went down in the Oklahoma territory, until the First World War, perhaps the most exciting migration was into Oklahoma. Texas, California, Washington, and Idaho also saw large increases. However, increasingly, country folk were pouring into the towns and cities. In 1890, out of a total population of 63 million, about 35 percent lived in communities larger than 2,500; by 1920 slightly more than half of the total population, which then reached 132 million, lived in such places, which the census office considered urban. The lake ports and industrial cities of Chicago, Milwaukee, Detroit, Toledo, and Buffalo boasted large gains. In the South, prior to the twentieth century, only three cities, Louisville, Memphis, and New Orleans, exceeded 100,000 in population. By 1901, although the South was still predominantly rural, Atlanta, Birmingham, Nashville, and Richmond had joined that 100,000 group, and within ten years Norfolk, and four Texas cities, Dallas, Fort Worth, Houston, and San Antonio, exceeded the 100,000 mark; towns such as Danville in Virginia and Greensboro, Greenville, and Gastonia in North Carolina were busily manufacturing textiles; Durham and Winston-Salem in North Carolina had become identified with tobacco.

A significant ingredient in these migrations, and one of particular concern to the South, was the black, the nation's largest racial minority. There were just under 7.5 million black people in the United States in 1890, approximately 12 percent of the total population. At the same time there were perhaps 250,000 American Indians, fewer than 100,000 Chinese, and no more than 2,000 Japanese. Although the black population declined to 10 percent in 1920, the percentage of those living in cities increased from about 23 percent in 1900 to 34 percent in 1920. Blacks, attracted by positions in the growing cities of the new South, streamed into New Orleans, Birmingham, and Atlanta and even more into the North during the First World War. Wages were higher there; cotton farming in the South was becoming increasingly uneconomical; and social disabilities in the North seemed to be fewer.

The blacks' plight was discouraging. In the North, they were usually second-class citizens. In the South their inferior position was explicit. Southern state after southern state had set up barriers against their voting, and segregation had become firmly established in the early years of the century. Recorded lynchings were running well over one hundred a year during the 1890s and through 1901. Few blacks found jobs which required a skill. They worked as unskilled labor in steel mills, foundries, and meat-packing houses. Many found work on the railroads as pullman porters. On the happier side, although the percentage of black people engaged in agriculture declined, the number of black farm owners increased significantly between 1910 and 1920, and illiteracy showed a sharp drop from 44.5 percent to 30.4 percent between 1900 and 1910.

Conditions of Labor and the Economy

Given the polyglot nature of the population, the internal migration, the immigration, and the geographical variations in standards of living, it is not surprising that conditions of labor varied widely throughout the country. To complicate the general status of the working class the number of women in the work force tripled between 1890 and 1920. Likewise the number of children between ten and fifteen years of age gainfully employed continued to increase until 1910 when it reached almost two million. However, child labor agitation then began to have a significant effect, and the percentage of child workers, 6 percent in 1900, had decreased to less than 3 percent in 1920.

To generalize about hours, wages, income, and standards of living is difficult. Hours of labor, for example, varied from one industry to another and were generally longer for recently arrived immigrants and blacks and where unions were weak. Many industries and occupations had achieved the ten-hour day by the 1890s; however, in textile plants, saw mills, steel mills, and bakeries, hours ran from eleven to thirteen. The most notorious case was the steel industry where the average work week was about sixty-five hours; while thousands working the blast furnaces and open hearths labored from seventy-two to eighty-four hours a week.

Although American wages certainly compared favorably with wages in other industrial countries, the average worker did not receive enough to live comfortably, and variations in income were embarrassing. Consumption was conspicuous among high society, and it may well have been widely known that Andrew Carnegie, one of the less conspicuous consumers of the upper crust, had had an income of 10 million dollars a year from steel alone between 1896 and 1900. And then there was no income tax. At the same time a good many Boston shop girls were getting from 5 to 6 dollars a week, and workers over sixteen years old in the southern cotton mills were earning less than that. Unskilled Italian workers in Chicago were getting between 4 and 5 dollars a week, and Jacob Riis testified that garment workers in New York were receiving from 30 to 40 cents a day finishing trousers. Average hourly earnings in all manufacturing in 1900 was 15.1 cents, and annual earnings $432; in 1914, corresponding figures were 22 cents, and $574. One estimate of the income of 11,156 "normal families (a wage-earning father, a mother, and not more than five children, all under fourteen)" in 1903 was $650.98 a year.

To place these figures in some kind of relationship to the cost of living is difficult given the inadequacy of the available statistics. It would appear, however, that real wages increased substantially between 1890 and 1914, perhaps as much as 40 percent. At the same time, few among the wage-earning group in the United States enjoyed a comfortable, even a subsistence, standard of living. Again, generalizations are dangerous in view of the different conditions in different parts of the country and because of the impossibility of evaluating supplementary sources of income. However, shortly after the turn of the century it probably cost the family of an urban worker between $650 to $800 to live, and this estimate would include little if anything for medical expenses, insurance, and recreation. Undoubtedly the struggle for subsistence was rendered even more bitter to those aware of the wide differences that existed in income. In 1896, for example, the richest 1.6 percent of the population received 10.8 percent of the national income, and in 1910 that percentage had risen to 19. Robert Hunter in his famous book *Poverty* published in 1904 estimated that there were at least ten million persons living in poverty in that year in the United States. A brilliant critic of the establishment, Thorstein Veblen, after surveying the period from 1873 to 1896 had concluded that depression was chronic in the "regime of the machine."

Conditions did improve, however, early in the twentieth century. An unusual demand in Europe for American wheat, a doubling of the world's gold production, national bank note inflation, the demands of the Spanish-American War all had helped restore the American economy after the depression of the 1890s. Prosperity in Europe further created a demand for American products, and American export trade hit new heights. In fact, having reached the billion mark in 1896, a figure achieved only twice before, in 1892 and 1894, it had almost exactly doubled by 1911. Confidence in the American economy then resulted in a doubling of foreign investments between 1897 and 1908. Two sharp panics occurred before 1914, one in 1903, largely confined to the stock exchange and dubbed a "rich man's panic," and the more serious one of 1907, which, although also associated primarily with the rich, reflected a worldwide economic decline. Business failures, crashing stocks, credit stringency, and a banking panic led to a sharp depression, and unemployment rose sharply to almost three million in 1908, about 8.5 percent of the labor force. It declined to about 4.4 percent in 1913, but the banking system remained chaotic, consumer purchasing power remained low, and a Balkan war upset European investment. Thus once more the United States experienced a serious economic decline, and unemployment had reached almost 10 percent in 1915 when war orders boomed. Chronic prosperity there might have been, but there was little job security: in general, joblessness was considered the fault or sin of the individual, and, except for an occasional bread line or soup kitchen, the public accepted no responsibility.

Agriculture

In the field of agriculture, the first two decades of the century were comparatively prosperous. Actually, farm income, though spotty, had been rising since the 1870s, and when the planners of the 1930s were working out the parity-price system to aid farmers, they decided that the period from 1909 to 1914 was the one in which the relationship between what the farmer had to buy and what he had to sell was most favorable. The war demands after 1914 carried the farmer to new heights. During the whole period, crops were excellent. Wheat and cotton production increased steadily between 1896 and 1920. Shifts in diets created new demands for citrus fruits, sugar, poultry, and eggs, but meat production remained "the most important branch of farm economy." More favorable farm prices, increased immigration, and lower interest rates combined to increase the demand for farm real estate, but the most desirable land was already gone. Thus the best lands were farmed more intensively, and land values increased. Farm income increased almost five times between 1890 and 1920. At the same time, the rate of growth of the agricultural population was slowing down. Farm population was only slightly larger in 1920 than what it had been in 1900.

Agriculture seems to have established at least a temporary stability in the decade before the First World War. The country had adjusted to the mechanical revolution that had taken place in the early nineteenth century. During the last part of the century, the huge trade in agricultural products, the large size of the farms, particularly in the West, and the scarcity of labor had encouraged the development of new devices to produce the crops that were needed. Reapers, binders, mowers, and innumerable other gadgets, even the combines, all pulled by horses and mules, were in existence before 1900. The result of such mechanization had helped to produce an oversupply and to a great extent explains the farm depressions after the Civil War. Then an increase in overseas demand, increased immigration and the growing city market, a greater diversification of agriculture, expansion of rural banks, together with the inflationary developments following the Spanish-American War created the demand that brought stability.

In spite of relatively favorable conditions, every generalization obscures troublesome details. One study made for the midwestern farmer in the year 1900, for example, concludes that about 90 percent of all farm operators received a below-subsistence income, and that in the South incomes were lower. A particularly discouraging factor was that 35 percent of the farms in 1900 and 38 percent in 1920 were operated by tenants, while in the South Atlantic and South Central states the respective figures increased from 47 percent to almost 50 percent.

However, another technological revolution was already beginning that would not reach its climax until after World War II. Government support in the form of land-grant colleges, the Department of Agriculture, and agricultural experimental stations led to "the flowering of agricultural research" in the late nineteenth century. Inventors did their share with such inventions as barbed wire, a cream separator, and most especially the gasoline tractor. Steam had failed to provide more satisfactory power, electricity did not seem any more promising, but by 1908 the internal-combustion engine showed real promise. Progress continued and by 1910 some 1000 tractors were in use. Within four years, there were 17,000. The tremendous demand of the war years for farm products and the lack of labor created a greater need, and by the end of the war some 158,000 tractors were on the farms. A revolution was under way.

Although evidence for Erskine Caldwell's novels of agrarian ignorance and decadence might have been found among the tenants and croppers of the early twentieth century, efforts were being made to break down barriers of illiteracy and tradition. More knowledge about crops, techniques, fertilizer, and improved marketing facilities was being made available and was reflected in the external appearance of farms: new barns, new granaries, new drainage systems, "better and more durable roads on the farm and between the farm and its market town." All these things made it possible to consider more amenities. In 1905, the *Yearbook of Agriculture* advised its readers that "with the advent of improved plumbing supplies and simple, yet effective forms of power it has become possible at a moderate cost to install in the country home every convenience now available in the city dwelling." The *Yearbook* deprecated the fact that so few farms took advantage of the possibilities—particularly when "the entire fixtures for a satisfactory bathroom" (tub, basin with hot and cold water, and flush commode) could be provided for $35.00.

Although the discontent reflected in the activities of the Farmers' Alliances and the Populists of the 1880s and 1890s had substantially diminished, organization was a part of the climate of the early twentieth century, and the farmers of the South and West contributed their share. The Farmers Union, emerging from Texas in 1902, for example, was particularly successful in its business activities. It established cooperatives dealing in livestock, grain, insurance, and farm and household items. It produced implements and fertilizers; it inspired programs to limit production or hold products off the market in order to support prices; and it built warehouses in cotton and wheat states to store surplus crops. Various equity organizations likewise attempted, rather unsuccessfully, to work out price-setting programs but had greater success in maintaining cooperatives to sell insurance and to operate warehouses, creameries, meat-packing plants, and flour mills.

The Federal Government: Agencies and Finances

The communications revolution, the concentration of industry, the crisis of urbanization, the plight of the farmer and the wage earner, overseas expansion, the Spanish-American War, and the acquisition of new territory, all of these things led to demands from different groups for the federal government to expand its activities. In the platforms of the political parties in the election of 1900, for example, the Democrats demanded more vigorous action in regulating interstate commerce and controlling "trusts" and called for a department of labor whose secretary should sit in the Cabinet, irrigation policies to restore arid western lands, and Chinese exclusion. The Republicans called for "monetary legislation" to meet "the varying needs of the season and of all sections," legislation to prevent the abuses of monopoly, "more effective restriction of immigration" in order to protect the American workman, a protective tariff, support for an American merchant marine, and reclamation of arid lands. The two People's parties ran candidates, both of whom advocated public ownership of the railroads and a graduated income tax. The new Social Democratic party demanded the public ownership of "industries controlled by monopolies," railroads, telegraphs, and telephones, public utilities, mines, and gas wells; labor legislation; and accident, employment, and old-age insurance.

Increasingly, the requirements of the city and the problems of industry and commercialized farming were resulting in demands that some official government body take action to meet these concerns. Americans seemed quite pragmatic, and, although laissez faire was undoubtedly a prevailing philosophy, the tacit acceptance of this philosophy did not mean that government action would not be taken, if it seemed the thing to do. State legislative action did not reflect an undeviating devotion to principles of laissez faire. The police power principle, by which courts had upheld the right of the states to legislate for the health and welfare of their citizens, had resulted in a wealth of statutes establishing and regulating corporations and business activities and supporting the building of railroads, canals, bridges, and public utilities.

Yet those who accepted the logic of the state's regulation or promotion of economic activity would not necessarily accept similar federal intervention. Again, however, opposition to federal action was probably in most cases theoretical and might depend upon the successes or failures of other elements in the federal system in solving problems.

At the turn of the century, the United States consisted of forty-five states and seven territories (New Mexico, Arizona, the Indian Territory and Oklahoma, the District of Columbia, Alaska, and Hawaii). Oklahoma was to become a state officially in 1907, New Mexico and Arizona in 1912. The United States was also responsible for an overseas empire consisting of the islands of Puerto Rico, Guam, Tutuila, Wake, and other small Pacific islands; was waging a nasty war to "pacify" the Philippines; and by the Platt amendment had established what amounted to a protectorate over Cuba. Congress had won a predominant role in the national government since the impeachment of Andrew Johnson, and the President, in the persons of the relatively strong Cleveland and McKinley, had only partly restored the prestige of that office. Even Cleveland, in his second inaugural address in 1893, had said that "while the people should patriotically and cheerfully support their Government its functions do not include the support of the people." The states were still jealous of their prerogatives, and Congress consisted of 90 senators and 356 representatives, many of whom seemed to consider themselves as little more than plenipotentiaries of their states.

In spite of apparent hostility, federal power was nevertheless increasing. There was a notable increase in the number of paid civilian employees of the federal government, from 157,000 in 1891 to 239,000 in 1901 to 396,000 in 1911. Moreover, the agencies of government were assuming added responsibilities. The Departments of Treasury, State, War, Navy, and the Post Office had remained relatively stable, carrying out their historic functions during the last part of the nineteenth century. Since its establishment in 1849, the Department of the Interior had come to be known as the "Great Miscellany." The department's principal responsibilities were centered in the Bureaus of Patents, Pensions, Lands, and Indian Affairs. In addition it included the Bureau of Education, the Commissioner of Railroads, the U.S. Geological Survey, the Census Office, the Government Hospital for the Insane, the Freedmen's Hospital, Howard University, six territorial governments, and four national parks. Within the Office of the Geological Survey, moreover, experiments were being made in reclamation and irrigation that had led to the conclusion that private capital could not provide the necessary funds for what had to be done.

Even more significant were the expanding activities of the Department of Agriculture. Organized as a department in 1862, it did not achieve cabinet status until 1889. It was the first federal department to help a particular group of Americans in that it was designed to aid the farmers by scientific research and suggestions for improved marketing and production. By 1913, in fact, it could legitimately be called "the world's greatest research organization." The department had dedicated and skillful leadership; in fact, only three secretaries, Jeremiah M. Rusk, J. Sterling Morton, and James Wilson, held the post from 1889 to 1913. In 1900, the various subdivisions of the department were engaged in studying the introduction of the planting of tea; the extent and character of food adulteration; wireless telegraphy for storm forecasts; the importation of various insects and fungus diseases to destroy locusts and olive scale and to fertilize fig blossoms; diseases of cereals; corn breeding; staple-cotton hybridizing; and the introduction of the Belgian hare "and what we may expect of it." The Office of Experiment Stations established in 1888 sought to promote agricultural education through cooperation with the state agricultural experiment stations; the Office of Public Roads provided advice on road matters and supervised some road construction; the Section of Foreign Markets sought to promote the demand for American agricultural products abroad; and the Bureau of Animal Husbandry, established in 1884, inspected meat in interstate and international trade and was trying to develop remedies for swine diseases, sheep scab, rabies, dips, and black leg. One of the researchers, Theobold Smith, and his associates spent $65,000 in discovering that the tick caused Texas fever. The department valued this discovery at $40 million a year.

Besides the regular cabinet departments, the federal government had few active agencies. One of these, the Civil Service Commission, was becoming increasingly important. Set up under the Pendleton Act of 1883, it had had a tough battle in making headway against an entrenched patronage system dominated by Congress. However, by the turn of the century, the commission had won several limited victories. Although evasion occurred, competitive examination for many governmental positions had become the rule; and the commission was exercising its investigatory function by giving wide publicity to blatant abuses of the patronage system which it otherwise could not control. In 1891, of approximately 157,000 civil service employees, approximately 34,000 were classified in the competitive civil service; by 1920, some 498,000 out of 655,000 were classified.

The two most important independent federal agencies touching the economic life of the nation were the Department of Labor and the Interstate Commerce Commission. The agitation for a department of labor had begun shortly after the Civil War. Both the National Labor Union and the Knights of Labor had urged the establishment of a responsible government agency designed to investigate labor conditions. Yet Congress delayed, fearing that such a bureau might delve into the private affairs of individuals and that it would lead to attempts on the part of Congress to legislate in matters of health, wages, hours, and working conditions. However, in 1884, Congress approved the establishment of a bureau within the Department of the Interior, and four years later it became an independent department, reporting directly to the president. The agency was largely designed to collect and publish information, but in 1888 Congress provided for a three-man commission designed to promote industrial peace on interstate railroads and carriers. The recommendations led to the passage of the Erdman Act in 1898 which provided for mediation machinery to be available in railway disputes. In 1903, the Department of Labor and Commerce was created, and ten years later, Labor was given a cabinet position of its own.

In the meantime, in 1887, Congress had established the Interstate Commerce Commission. Although the commission's effectiveness was debatable in 1900, its establishment was historically significant because it constituted the first of a series of important federal regulatory agencies. Appropriately this first agency regulated railroads, whose functions were so directly involved in interstate commerce that even die-hard advocates of laissez faire could hardly question the constitutionality of federal authority.

The business of the federal government was becoming bigger and more complicated, and thus more expensive. Until 1910, principal sources of revenue came from customs duties supplemented by the sale of public land and by excise taxes on such products as tobacco, liquor, oleo, and playing cards. Beginning in 1910, a corporation income tax began to play a prominent role, but not until 1918 did income tax collections exceed other revenues. Before 1921, no bureau of the budget or formal method of balancing income with outgo existed. Some reformers began to advocate budget procedures for individual states early in the century, and by 1919 at least forty-six states had adopted them. However, at the turn of the century, the presidents had little to do with government finance, either in making recommendations, estimating amounts for specific purposes, or the actual use of funds appropriated. Estimates of need usually came from the individual bureau chiefs, were perfunctorily approved by the department secretaries, and then passed on to congressional committees for action.

The presidents did recommend economy and Congresses were economy-minded. In extraordinary times such as years of depression and war, however, expenditures did exceed income. The national debt was well under $1.5 billion from 1891 through 1916; it rose sharply in 1918, reaching $25 billion in 1919, a peak that was not exceeded until 1934.

Expenditures, with occasional fluctuations, have generally increased since the founding of the Republic. From an average annual expenditure of approximately $4 million between 1789 and 1791, the figure had reached $63 million by 1860. It jumped quickly to more than $1 billion in 1865, declined to a low point of $237 million in 1878; rose to $521 million in 1900 and to $734 million in 1916; jumped to almost $2 billion in 1917, and reached a peak of $18.5 billion in 1919, a figure that was not surpassed until 1942. In spite of a substantial increase of federal expenditures between 1890 and the First World War, the percentage of these expenditures to the gross national product actually declined from more than 2 percent to below 2 percent.

National Defense

A significant fact about the expenditures of the federal government is that only rarely, even in peacetime, did expenditures for matters essentially civil exceed those for functions which related to the national defense. From 1891 to 1912, annual expenditures for national defense ran more than twice as much as civil expenses; and from 1912 to 1920 that percentage varied from 67.2 in 1915 to 97 in 1918.* This predominance of military expenditures does not prove an excessive interest in militarism but indicates simply that few other responsibilities were recognized as falling within the jurisdiction of the federal government. There was no argument that Congress had a responsibility for the common defense, maintaining the army, the navy, and the coastal fortifications.

The Spanish-American War had come at a time when our defense policy was being gradually modified, and war sped up the process. Since the days of President Chester A. Arthur in the early 1880s, the United States had been gradually building a modern navy. In 1885, Congress had authorized a board, headed by the Secretary of War, William C. Endicott, to study the seacoast fortifications and recommend improvements. The report had recommended a building program tremendous for the time, which would have cost $127 million. Congress did not approve this recommendation, but over a fifteen year period, it did authorize more than $60 million for concrete gun pits, 10- and 12-inch mortars, and huge disappearing guns to provide harbor defenses.

The army was small. It only once exceeded 28,000 men in the 1890s until the Spanish-American War, and total military personnel in the army, navy, and marines only once exceeded 43,000. In 1897, 28,000 troops

---

*These estimates include expenditures for international affairs, the War and Navy departments, veterans pensions, and the interest on the national debt. In view of the fact that the national debt was largely the result of war and preparation for war, it may be legitimately included. However, precise statistics must be used with caution. They vary in different sources. Moreover, some of the expenditures by essentially civic departments such as Treasury and State, can be related to defense. This fact is brought out in *Statistical Abstract,* 1921, p. 747. For other figures, see *Historical Statistics,* pp. 718–719.

were scattered among approximately eighty-five posts throughout the United States. Privates received pay of $13 per month, the commanding general, a major general, received $7,500 per year. American military policy still assumed that the militia would supplement this regular army in the event of an emergency, and the Militia Act of 1792 required that every able-bodied man between the ages of seventeen and forty-five should be available for service. In 1897 there were more than 10 million men eligible, but the effectiveness of the system was left to the several states, and the militia system as envisaged had given place to a volunteer system supported by a few states, and that not well. Consequently few more than 100,000 militiamen had any kind of training at all.

In defense of the system, it should be said that events had shown that no greater strength had been necessary. The army had defended the frontier, and the regulars and the militia, informally known as the National Guard, had kept domestic insurrection in the forms of strikes in hand. However, the lack of any real military policy was clear. The creation of the first advanced service schools, the publication of treatises by military men pointing to the poor morale, to the inadequacies of the regulars and the militia, to the evils of detached service, to bureaucratic red tape, and particularly to the lack of anything resembling a general staff corps to prepare plans for waging war suggested even before the Spanish-American War that changes to keep up with changing times might actually take place in military policy.

The ferment within the military establishment was partly in response to political and social changes at home and abroad. Technological developments in transportation and communication had encouraged the centralization process in industry, altered the lives of farmers and wage earners, revolutionized foreign commerce, and made possible the existence of huge metropolitan areas. These developments were taking place not only in the United States but also in Europe, Australia, New Zealand, Japan, and to a lesser degree in other areas. The centralization process did not take place without friction, friction within nations because of the effect of centralization upon people and established groups, and friction among nations as they jockeyed for position in the modernizing world. In response to these frictions, institutional changes were advocated in the public sector—in government and military organizations. At bottom the issue was usually one of national power, how powerful should the nation be, and how should that power be exercised.

Bibliography

Good general treatments of the subject of this chapter may be found in George E. Mowry, *The Era of Theodore Roosevelt, 1900–1912* (1958); Harold U. Faulkner, *The Decline of Laissez Faire, 1897–1917* (1951);

and C. Vann Woodward, *Origins of the New South, 1877–1913* (1951). Two richly interpretative studies are Robert H. Wiebe, *The Search for Order, 1877–1920* (1967) and Ray Ginger, *The Age of Excess; The United States from 1877 to 1914* (1965). For statistics, I have used *Historical Statistics of the United States, Colonial Times to 1957* (1960), the *Statistical Abstracts of the United States,* and the *World Almanacs.* For some notion of the historiography, see William H. Cartwright and Richard L. Watson, Jr., ed., *Interpreting and Teaching American History* (1961), and chapters by Walter T. K. Nugent, J. Carroll Moody, and Robert H. Wiebe in William H. Cartwright and Richard L. Watson, Jr., eds., *The Reinterpretation of American History and Culture* (1973).

Pages 1–2

The New York to Paris automobile race was reported almost daily in the *New York Times;* see also Erwin Lessner, *Famous Auto Races and Rallies* (1956). For statistics and accounts of the automobile and streetcar industries see Faulkner, *The Decline of Laissez Faire,* pp. 221ff.; see also James J. Flink, *America Adopts the Automobile, 1895–1910* (1970); and John A. Miller, *Fares Please: From Horse-Cars to Streamliners* (1941).

Pages 2–3

The treatment of early aviation was based on the *American Yearbook,* 1910, pp. 700–714, and 1915, pp. 575–580, and Elsbeth E. Freudenthal, *The Aviation Business From Kitty Hawk to Wall Street* (1940), pp. 1–18.

Pages 3–4

For my treatment of the electrical industry, see Harold C. Passer, *The Electrical Manufacturers, 1875–1900; A Study in Competition, Entrepreneurship, Technical Change, and Economic Growth* (1953), pp. 164–175, 276–293; Richard B. DuBoff, "The Introduction of Electric Power in American Manufacturing," *Economic History Review,* 20 (December 1967), 509–518.

Page 4

For the controversies over radio, see Gleason L. Archer, *History of Radio to 1926* (1938); Erik Barnouw, *A History of Broadcasting in the United States,* vol. I, *A Tower In Babel, to 1933* (1966).

Pages 4–6

For the data on railroads, see Faulkner, *Decline of Laissez Faire,* chap. IX. The champions of the new economic history have questioned the role of railroads in economic growth. See, for example, Robert W. Fogel, *Railroads and American Economic Growth: Essays in Econometric History* (1964); Paul D. McClelland, "Railroads, American Growth, and the New Economic History: A Critique," *Journal of Economic History* (March 1968), 102–123; Louis M. Hacker, "The New Revolution in Economic History . . .," *Explorations in Entrepreneurial History,* 3 (Spring–Summer, 1966), 159–175.

Pages 6-8

Alfred D. Chandler, Jr., has made several important contributions to understanding the development of big business. See particularly, *Strategy and Structure: Chapters in the History of the Industrial Enterprises* (1962); see also Douglass C. North, *Growth and Welfare in the American Past: A New Economic History* (1966).

Pages 6-7

On the robber baron legend, see David Chalmers, "From Robber Barons to Industrial Statesmen: Standard Oil and the Business Historian," *American Journal of Economics and Sociology,* 20 (October 1960), 47–58; Gabriel Kolko, "The Premises of Business Revisionism," *Business History Review,* 33 (Autumn 1959), 330–344; Thomas Cochran, "The Legend of the Robber Barons," *Pennsylvania Magazine of History and Biography,* 74 (July 1950), 307–321; Hal Bridges, "The Robber Baron Concept in American History," *Business History Review,* 32 (Spring 1958), 1–13.

Pages 7-8

On holding companies, see Faulkner, *Decline of Laissez Faire,* pp. 161–162; Ralph L. Nelson, *Merger Movements in American Industry, 1895–1956* (1959), pp. 59ff.

Page 8

For the philosophy of businessmen, see Marian V. Sears, "The American Businessman at the Turn of the Century," *Business History Review,* 30 (December 1956), 382–443; for the differences among businesses, see Robert H. Wiebe, *Businessmen and Reform: A Study of the Progressive Movement* (1962).

Pages 9-11

On antitrust policy, see Hans B. Thorelli, *The Federal Anti-Trust Policy; Organization of an American Tradition* (1954); Arnold M. Paul, "Legal Progressivism, The Courts, and the Crisis of the 1890's," *Business History Review,* 33 (Winter 1959), 495–509. Ralph H. Gabriel adds a dimension to the understanding of American constitutional law in *The Course of American Democratic Thought,* 2nd ed. (1956), chap. 21; see also Edward C. Kirkland, *Industry Comes of Age: Business, Labor and Public Policy, 1860–1897* (1961), pp. 319–324. *The Report of the Industrial Commission,* 19 vol. (1900–1902) is a mine of information.

Pages 11-13

On organized labor, see Philip Foner, *History of the Labor Movement in the United States,* vol. III, *The Policies and Practices of the American Federation of Labor* (1964); Philip Taft, *The A.F. of L. in the Time of Gompers* (1957) is a particularly sympathetic account. For Gompers, see particularly Bernard Mandel, *Samuel Gompers: A Biography* (1963), and Fred Greenbaum, "The Social Ideas of Samuel Gompers," *Labor History,* 7 (Winter 1966), 35–61; but cf. Ronald Radosh, "The Corporate Ideology of

American Labor Leaders from Gompers to Hillman," *Studies on the Left,*
6 (November–December 1966), 66–96.

Pages 13–16

For the IWW, see Foner, *History of the Labor Movement in the United
States,* vol. IV, *The Industrial Workers of the World, 1905–1917* (1965) and
Melvyn Dubofsky, *We Shall Be All: A History of the Industrial Workers
of the World* (1969). For the complex problem of attempting to integrate
the workers into the industrial system, see Milton Derber, *The American
Idea of Industrial Democracy 1865–1965* (1970); Morrell Heald, *The
Social Responsibility of Business: Company and Community, 1900–1960*
(1970); Norman J. Wood, "Industrial Relations Policies of American Manage-
ment, 1900–1933," *Business History Review,* 34 (Winter 1960), 402–420;
Milton J. Nadworney, "Frederick Taylor and Frank Gilbreth: Competition in
Scientific Management," *ibid.,* 31 (Spring 1957), 23–34. The controversial
role of the National Civic Federation is described by Marguerite Green,
*The National Civic Federation and the American Labor Movement, 1900–
1925* (1956); Philip S. Foner, "Historical Materialism and Labor History,"
Studies on the Left, 6 (March–April 1966), 71–75; and James Weinstein,
"Big Business and the Origins of Workmen's Compensation," *Labor
History,* 8 (Spring 1967), 156–174. On the role of Catholic workers, see
Marc Karson, *American Labor Unions and Politics* (1958); on blacks and
immigrants in the AFL, see Herman D. Bloch, "Labor and the Negro:
1866–1910," *Journal of Negro History,* 50 (July 1965), 163–184. Louis
Galambos argues that hostility of organized labor toward big business was
at a high point in the 1890s and declined only slightly prior to the First
World War. "AFL's Concept of Big Business: A Quantitative Study of
Attitudes Toward the Large Corporation, 1894–1931," *Journal of American History,* 57 (March 1971), 847–863.

Pages 16–17

On immigration, see chapters by Roger Daniels and Rudolph Vecoli in
Cartwright and Watson, eds., *The Reinterpretation of American History
and Culture;* see especially Oscar Handlin, *The Uprooted,* 2nd ed. (1973)
and John Higham, *Strangers in the Land; Patterns of American Nativism,
1860–1925* (1955).

Pages 17–18

For internal migration, I used Faulkner, *Decline of Laissez Faire,* pp.
94–97; and Woodward, *Origins of the New South,* chap. XI.

Page 18

Lynching statistics were regularly carried in the *World Almanac.* Harold
U. Faulkner, *The Quest for Social Justice 1898–1914* (1931) refers to
black workers. See also Kenneth K. Bailey, "Southern White Protestantism
at the Turn of the Century," *American Historical Review,* 68 (April 1963),
618–635. For women and children in the work force, I made use of
Faulkner, *Decline of Laissez Faire,* pp. 249ff.

Pages 18–20

F. L. Allen, *The Big Change: America Transforms Itself, 1900–1950* (1952) has some colorful detail on wages. For real wages see Paul Douglas, *Real Wages in the United States, 1890–1926* (1930) and Albert Rees, *Real Wages in Manufacturing, 1890–1914* (1961). Arthur S. Link and associates have an excellent analysis of income and income shares in *American Epoch: A History of the United States since the 1890's,* 3rd ed., vol. I (1963), pp. 21–23; for the discussion of the business cycle, see North, *Growth and Welfare,* pp. 145–147; Charles H. Hession and Hyman Sardy, *Ascent to Affluence: A History of American Economic Development* (1969) contains the Veblen quotation.

Pages 20–22

For the analysis of tenancy, see Fred A. Shannon, "The Status of the Midwestern Farmer in 1900," *Mississippi Valley Historical Review,* 37 (December 1950), 491–510. For bathroom facilities and amenities, see *Yearbook of the Department of Agriculture,* 1905, pp. 511–532, and *ibid.,* 1909, pp. 345–356. See also Wayne D. Rasmussen, "The Impact of Technological Change on Agriculture, 1862–1962," *Journal of Economic History,* 22 (December 1962), 578–591. For farm organizations, see Luther Tweeten, *Foundations of Farm Policy* (1970), pp. 67–70.

Page 22

Platforms of all the national political parties are in Kirk H. Porter et al., *National Party Platforms, 1840–1956* (1956).

Pages 22–26

See particularly Leonard D. White, *The Republican Era: 1869–1901: A Study in Administrative History* (1958), also William L. Wanless, *The United States Department of Agriculture, A Study in Administration* (1920); John Lombardi, *Labor's Voice in the Cabinet; A History of the Department of Labor, from its Origins to 1921* (1942).

Pages 26–27

For the military and naval forces, see the annual reports of the secretaries of the army and navy; Walter Millis, *Arms and Men: A Study of American Military History* (1956); and Russell F. Weigley, *History of the United States Army* (1967).

2

The Conflict in Ideas

The frictions, the struggles for power, the institutional changes of the late nineteenth and early twentieth centuries were accompanied by controversies among the intellectual elite. New ideas came as a reaction to new conditions by those who looked back to happier days; who resented the immigrants, the cities, the labor unions, the corporations, and the overseas interests; and who saw all these things as signs of the imminent destruction of society. Or the new ideas were developed by those who were critical of conditions but who considered them a challenge, and who had confidence in people's abilities to improve them and build a better society. How much these ideas developed in a vacuum, or stimulated change, or replaced old ideas in popular acceptance are questions which are not easy to answer with assurance. By the end of the nineteenth century, however, intellectual rebels were not satisfied with any deterministic system of thought that held that people could not take a hand in shaping their future. They were rebelling against those theologians who saw the world governed by a "changeless plan," God's law; against the scientists whose "changeless plan" consisted of the laws of nature; or against the classical economists who set up the hypothetical economic person responsive in predictable ways to pleasure, pain, supply, or demand.

The Impact of Darwin

Paradoxically, the concept of organic evolution, which at first seemed upsetting to the establishment in church and society, soon became a leading support for conservative thought. The evolutionary hypothesis was particularly upsetting to those who had accepted the literal interpretation of the Biblical story of creation. To them the thought of the origin of species through the struggle for existence was sacrilegious and psychologically shattering. The hypothesis was equally shattering to those who saw the universe and society subject to a changeless plan. The knowledge-able had discussed evolution, however, long before the publication of Darwin's *Origin of Species* in 1859, and Darwin had supplied the mass of evidence which, to the scientific mind, seemed irrefutable. The compara-tively few scientists who disputed it were dead by the end of the century. Moreover, while the evolutionary hypothesis was revolutionizing theology and revising scientific theory, it was also making sense to those who believed that life was a struggle for existence, that poverty was inevitable because of the basic inequality of human beings, and that disaster would follow if individuals attempted to interfere with the natural course of this struggle.

Those who so believed found support in the writing and teaching of Herbert Spencer (1820–1903). Both Spencer and Darwin had seen a struggle for existence in the industrial towns of England. Both of them were influenced by Malthus, who had found the evidence for his *Essay on the Principle of Population* in the misery of early English industrialism. Spencer aimed at finding a synthesis of the latest scientific discoveries. In his search, he had, in fact, arrived at an evolutionary hypothesis before the publication of the *Origin of Species,* and he had become convinced that the hypothesis could be applied to society. In his devotion to science and his conviction that the evolutionary principle obtained in the bio-logical, physical, and social spheres, his ideas conformed with the natural-istic thought characteristic of at least some intellectuals of the late nineteenth and early twentieth centuries.

Like the naturalists, Spencer grappled with the problem of the part the individual might play in society. In his first book, *Social Statics,* published in 1850, he seemed to be pleading for almost complete freedom of the individual to act as he chose; he was clearly endorsing laissez faire and branding any interference with the individual by the state as the courting of disaster. He opposed state regulation of any kind and state support of anything, including education. The struggle would lead to perfection: "The poverty of the incapable, the distresses that come upon the impru-dent, the starvation of the idle, and those shoulderings aside of the weak by the strong . . . are the decrees of a large, farseeing benevolence."

Spencer became popular. Between 1860 and 1903, more than 350,000 copies of his books sold in the United States. One of Spencer's most enthusiastic disciples, Edward Livingston Youmans, founded *Popular Science Monthly* in 1872, and it became "little more than a vehicle for the dissemination of Spencer's thought." The jargon of evolution became popular, particularly for those who found it a bulwark for their own version of laissez faire. To those who were patient, Spencer's was a hope-ful philosophy. To Henry George, who queried what a Spencerian would do about the evils of the day, Youmans replied, "Nothing! You and I can do nothing at all. It's all a matter of evolution. . . . Perhaps in four or five thousand years evolution may have carried men beyond this state of things. But we can do nothing."

Although Youmans and the prolific writer and speaker, John Fiske, were probably the leading publicists of Spencerian ideas in the United States, the chief intellectual proponent of Social Darwinism was undoubtedly that toughminded, controversial yet popular Yale professor, William Graham Sumner (1840–1910). Sumner absorbed nineteenth-century ideals of frugality from a hardworking father and even before matriculating at Yale in 1859 had become a convert to British classical economics. He studied theology at Yale, then secured a substitute in the Union Army, and went abroad to study classics and theology. Although he spent a short time as rector of an Episcopal church, his life's work was at Yale, first as a tutor in 1868, and then as the first professor of political and social science in Yale College. From the point of view of the ecclesiastically dominated Yale corporation, Sumner with a background in theology and classics was an ideal appointment. Almost immediately, however, he accepted Spencer, hung a picture of Darwin over his desk, and later was supposed to have said that one day he had put his religious beliefs in a drawer, returned sometime later to retrieve them, and found that they were no longer there. Although the delight of Yale's business alumni when he endorsed their version of laissez faire, he was considered a traitor by the same following when he showed the incompatibility of the concept of laissez faire with the practice of tariff protectionism.

To Sumner, as to Spencer, the evolutionary hypothesis could be applied to society. Life was a struggle for existence. People were not created by God; they were thinking mammals who had appeared through evolution; they were not characteristically good; and they had to fight to survive. Being physically weak, they used their brains in order to create institutions which helped them in the struggle for existence. Government and society thus resulted from evolutionary forces, but government should limit itself to basic functions such as the preservation of order and the protection of property. Sumner attacked several theoretical tenets of democracy. He did not believe that people had *natural* rights to life, liberty, or property. They had to fight for these rights. People were not born equal. The survival of the fittest meant inequality in strength and brains, and thus, Sumner concluded, inequality of possession followed inequality of talents, and legislative attempts to eliminate poverty or protect certain groups would lead to disaster. Said Sumner: "If we do not like the survival of the fittest, we have only one possible alternative, and that is the survival of the unfittest. The former is the law of civilization; the latter is the law of anti-civilization."

Although Sumner's hero was the self-reliant individual, his later work indicated that he had modified his earlier views somewhat. In *Folkways,* published in 1907, he argued that in the last analysis individuals would not act according to their reason but that their actions would be shaped by the accumulated customs of their society. Moreover, Sumner identified his protagonists with the middle class, "the forgotten ones" frequently squeezed between "mobocracy" on the one hand and "plutocracy" on the other. Even in his earlier years, he had expressed concern lest burgeoning business combinations might make government regulation necessary. By the end of the first decade of the century, he acknowledged that "the evils of monopoly" required some sort of governmental action.

Sumner's thought was pessimistic and deterministic. Theoretically a believer in democracy because of its encouragement of individual initiative, he saw democracy as only one landmark in the evolution of society. Democracy could work when the population was small and the food supply large, but as the food supply decreased in proportion to the population, the result would intensify the struggle for existence and end in imperialism and war.

The evolutionary hypothesis strengthened the convictions of those who saw their economics through the eyes of the classical economists. At the end of the nineteenth century, the classicists dominated colleges and universities. Francis Bowen at Harvard, J. Laurence Laughlin at Harvard, Cornell, and Chicago, Amasa Walker at Amherst, Arthur T. Hadley and Sumner at Yale preached the doctrines of the unchanging nature of economic laws, the importance of self-interest, the merits of competition, the sacredness of the law of supply and demand, and the inefficiency of government.

Critics of Laissez Faire

The defenders of laissez faire, however, did not have the field to themselves. Practices on the state level did not always conform to these theories. Throughout the century state legislatures assumed their right to legislate for the health and welfare of their citizens. Agrarian unrest produced leaders who sought solutions for the problems of the farmer on the national level if the states did not meet the farmers' demands. Popular writers began to question laissez faire. Henry George, noting the paradox of poverty in the midst of plenty, insisted that poverty was brutalizing the human spirit, that industrialism could lead to despotism. Optimistically he concluded that people by using their brains could promote progress. In *Progress and Poverty* (1879) he advanced a hypothesis that the government could help by imposing a single tax on land. His solution was not so important as his conviction that an individual was not helpless in confronting impersonal forces.

Actually, George departed only in one small particular, the single tax, from classical laissez faire. But others favored more radical solutions. One of these was Laurence Gronlund, an immigrant from Denmark, who in *The Coming Revolution* (1878) and *The Cooperative Commonwealth* (1884) produced what were among the earliest tracts on socialism in English. He attacked the wage and profit system, called for a classless society and the establishment of a cooperative commonwealth whose basic function was to maintain the general welfare. First a utopian socialist, by the 1890s he had become "the intellectual founder of the American Fabian Movement" and was advocating working for reform through existing institutions.

Gronlund's works had considerable circulation but were by no means so popular as a leading seller of all time, Edward Bellamy's *Looking Backward* (1888). Bellamy, an obscure writer from Massachusetts, had traveled in Europe where he had been upset by industrial conditions and had decided to write about them. No crusader, he apparently was converted by his own writings. He took direct issue with the classicists by calling competition "the application of the brutal law of the survival of the strongest and the most cunning." He believed that human nature was basically good and generous, that with wholesome conditions a freer and nobler individual would emerge. His solution was to endow the state with complete control of production and distribution and to guarantee every person economic security and an income capable of providing all needs.

Bellamy claimed that people did not need the incentive of the profit motive to make an economic system work. Incentives in his utopia were provided by promotions to positions of prestige, by ribbons and medals awarded for special service, by shorter hours for the more difficult tasks, by the realization that an ideal system could be maintained only by cooperation, and especially by the stimulation of working for others—the principle of human fellowship. Bellamy justified what was essentially a totalitarian state by arguing that with such obvious benefits not even token opposition would exist. The transition to the utopia, he thought, would develop peaceably and would grow out of the trend toward private monopoly. In *Equality,* sequel to *Looking Backward,* he showed how the obvious efficiency of big enterprise led to an ever more concentrated industry, and at the same time how the greed of the private owners made continuing private control unacceptable to the overwhelming majority. The solution then was clear—simply permit concentration to continue until there was one huge monopoly and put it under public control.

Although thousands read *Looking Backward,* and 150 or more Nationalist clubs were formed based on its principles, the clubs disappeared in the 1890s. The nationalists did not seem to frighten the pillars of society, perhaps because Bellamy envisaged a peaceable transition to utopia, perhaps because the plan was merely considered utopian. However, society was sensitive to radical movements. The Illinois governor, John Peter Altgeld, lost his political life in 1893 by pardoning the anarchists convicted of involvement in the Haymarket Square explosion seven years earlier. Anyone belonging to an offshoot of the International Workingmen's Association, the First International, which Karl Marx had moved to the United States in 1872, was usually assumed to be an alien determined upon violent revolution. A Socialist Labor party was breaking up into factions, with one faction following Daniel De Leon, doctrinaire Marxist favoring "uncompromising revolutionary tactics," and another faction willing to support peaceful institutional change. At almost the same time, in the late 1890s, Eugene Debs was organizing a Social Democratic party willing to accept socialism through evolution. Thus Bellamy's writings appeared when American socialism was at a crossroads, and both Debs and De Leon acknowledged their debt to Bellamy. At the very least he had made Socialism respectable. Those who read Bellamy knew that all socialists did not believe that socialism's fundamental tenet, the public ownership of the principal means of production and distribution, had to be brought about by violent revolution.

Nonetheless, it was equally clear that socialism had made little headway in the United States. Political democracy partially answered the demands of the wage-earning class to be heard; it was difficult to find ideological support for the idea of the class struggle in the United States which boasted of the equality of all people and lacked the feudal base for social classes. Even though justifiable cause for complaint about economic hardship existed, living standards were higher than anywhere else in the world, and if practice did not always match theory, hope existed that it would in the future. Moreover, as the ideas and practices of a welfare state evolved, solutions which seemed more in the American tradition than those of the socialists were being found; thus capitalism would be retained though modified.

Ideas from Abroad

By the time socialism began to gain a following in the United States, a firmer intellectual base than George and Bellamy was in existence for revolts against the status quo, and in many instances young men occupying new posts in the colleges and universities supported this base. These scholars found many flaws in the creeds of classical economics and social Darwinism. Some pointed out that, paradoxically, unrestricted competition could lead to monopoly, the antithesis of competition; others questioned whether the survival of the fittest, if this were to mean the survival of the strongest and most cunning, was indeed necessarily desirable; still others pointed out that it was ironic for the people to oppose granting increased powers to a democratic government, the government of the people; some inquired whether it was consistent for the social Darwinists to support social evolution only to the point of the laissez faire state; why could they not accept the possibility of the continuation of evolution to the welfare state; and in any case, they inquired, was not the individual, by using reason, capable of shaping the course of evolution?

Although these questions might logically have been raised as a result of circumstances within the United States, an infiltration of ideas from Europe undoubtedly had as great a stimulating effect as had Spencer and the classicists upon the American advocates of laissez faire. English novelists such as Disraeli, Dickens, and George Eliot, widely read in the United States, attacked the ugliness and immorality in the capitalistic system. Scientists such as Alfred Russel Wallace and Thomas Henry Huxley attacked the Spencerian conclusions of societal evolution. Huxley, for example, insisted that people could shape the course of evolution by using their intelligence, and that if society were to evolve, it would require "a mind to think for it," which could be supplied by the state.

Americans were also interested in practical experiments in social reform which were taking place in England. In spite of the apparent predominance of laissez faire thought, reform legislation had been passed, and Americans were quite aware of it. They were aware also of the conscious efforts made in England to investigate social problems, the concern of English upper-class reformers to improve the lot of the less fortunate. Numerous Americans studied settlement work in England, visited Toynbee Hall, the most famous of the British settlement houses, and several of the visitors, such as Robert A. Woods, Vida D. Scudder, and Jane Addams were inspired to establish similar houses in the United States. At the same time other Americans, such as Albert Shaw, author of *Municipal Government in Great Britain* (1895), and Frederic C. Howe, close associate of Robert La Follette in Wisconsin and author of *The British City: The Beginning of Democracy* (1907), were advocating municipal home rule and public ownership of the utilities.

It is impossible to measure the extent of foreign influence. Experiments in Australia, New Zealand, and in continental Europe were probably as important as those in England. Certainly the influence of German economic thought in the 1880s and 1890s was substantial. In Germany there was little willingness to accept British classical economics, perhaps on the theory that laissez faire and free trade were devices to maintain Britain's economic predominance in the world. In any case, a galaxy of economists appeared in the German universities and civil service among whom there were many differences but who had enough in common to be called the "German Historical School." Economists such as Bruno Hildebrand at Jena and Karl Knies at Heidelberg denied that economic laws were unchanging and insisted that history was constantly presenting new facts, new conditions, and a new environment and that theory must be equally flexible. They criticized the classicists for their reliance upon the deductive method and for their assumption that their hypothetical economic individual was stimulated only by the profit motive. Other incentives, such as service to humanity, they insisted, were important too. Younger German economists, such as Gustav von Schmoller and Adolf Wagner at Berlin, saw possibilities in using statistics to determine laws of causation. At the same time, they stressed the need for a greater emphasis on ethical and humanitarian motivation in any economic hypothesizing and urged the use of state power to bring about a more equitable distribution of wealth and improved working conditions.

These German ideas began to infiltrate the United States shortly after the Civil War. English and French journals had a considerable circulation in the United States and carried articles preaching the ideas of the historical school. Americans interested in the study of statistics attended international congresses and were impressed by the progress made by German statisticians. Henry Carter Adams who had studied with Ernest Engel in the Royal Statistical Bureau of Prussia became the first statistician of the Interstate Commerce Commission. Caroll D. Wright, also influenced by Engel, became a pioneer student of labor statistics, and gave Massachusetts a lead in this field as chief of the Massachusetts bureau in the 1870s. Then he became United States Commissioner of Labor and developed the Bureau of Labor Statistics into one of the most important offices of the federal government.

Reform Economics

The emigration of American students to Germany for graduate training was most important, however, in bringing the influence of the German Historical School to the United States. From perhaps 109 students in the decade of the 1840s, the number increased to more than 2,000 in the 1880s. Although some of these young students undoubtedly went to Germany to earn what could be a relatively easy degree, others were interested in the rigorous training also available, received the Doctor of Philosophy and returned to the United States as crusaders for the new economics. They were not all well received in the United States. Academic doors were sometimes closed to them or, if they obtained posts, they sometimes found the atmosphere inhospitable. Little academic freedom existed, as those with unacceptable views discovered when they lost their jobs, found their teaching loads increased, and their promotions blocked.

These young economists knew that they were engaged in a revolution and that organization was necessary. Thus in 1885 a number of them, including Richard T. Ely, Edmund W. James, John Bates Clark, Simon Patten, and Edwin R. A. Seligman met at Saratoga, New York, to form the American Economic Association. They compromised with the conservatives by electing Francis A. Walker of Amherst president of the new association, but Richard Ely, almost a symbol of the rebellion, was elected secretary-treasurer, and the constitution adopted was a clarion call for reform. Perhaps in response to this meeting, Sumner, who had refused to attend, penned a famous essay, "The Absurd Effort to Make the World Over."

The statement of principles, which were apparently the work of Ely, roused considerable discussion. Some favored modifying them. Several wanted it clearly brought out that they respected the work of the British classicists and their American counterparts. All agreed that any economist of whatever persuasion should be welcomed into the association, and Ely denied that it was a German movement. "Nothing about it was more marked than its American character," he insisted. "It had sprung up almost spontaneously in answer to felt needs."

Those conservatives who joined the association must have done so with intellectual trepidation. Its principles included the flat statement that "we regard the state as an agency whose positive assistance is one of the indispensable conditions of human progress"; it acknowledged that "political economy as a science" was "still in an early stage of its development," and urged less emphasis on "speculation" and more on the "historical and statistical study of actual conditions" in the development of political economy as a science; it pointed to the social problems that had resulted from the conflict of labor and capital and called for the "united efforts . . . of the church, of the state, and of science," in the solution of these problems.

The statement was accepted "as a general indication of the views" of the founders even though it was not looked upon as binding upon individual members. Certainly the umbrella of these principles covered a multitude of views. One of the vice presidents, for example, was John Bates Clark (1847–1938), whom some regarded as the greatest American theoretical economist and others as orthodox and too mechanical. Clark, like the classicists, saw competition as the ideal state of economic activity, but at the same time, he realized that unrestricted competition could lead to monopoly. To him, the monopolist was the bogy, and thus the economist should find out what made monopoly possible, support legislation that would protect competition, and authorize the state to punish those who would engage in monopoly practices.

Richard T. Ely (1854–1943) was more of a reformer. An undergraduate at Dartmouth and Columbia where he graduated in 1876, he studied in Germany, receiving a Ph.D. at Heidelberg in 1879. He finally found a teaching position at Johns Hopkins in 1881, but promotion was slow; he moved to the University of Wisconsin in 1892 where he stayed for thirty-three years as director of the School of Economics, Political Science, and History. A profoundly religious man, Ely, unlike the classicists, stressed ethics. To him low wages were unethical and he denied that the individual need be a slave to economic laws. He saw no need to fear the state since the state now represented the people; in fact the state through its institutions would be the means by which the economy and the welfare of the individual could be brought about. He opposed socialism but he sought the golden mean between socialism and unrestricted capitalism. This golden mean permitted natural monopolies, such as the telegraph, telephone, water works, and electric power plants to be publicly owned; it accepted big business as the result of free play of economic forces; and it otherwise favored ethical regulation such as health and sanitary legislation, the eight-hour day, public housing, and social insurance.

The roll call of the reform economists became longer in the twentieth century. It included E. J. James and Simon Patten of the University of

Pennsylvania, Henry C. Adams of Michigan, E. B. Andrews of Brown, Edwin R. A. Seligman of Columbia, Davis R. Dewey of Johns Hopkins, and that colorful and complex figure, Thorstein Veblen. Veblen was a particularly biting critic of late nineteenth- and early twentieth-century American capitalism and orthodox economic theory. His *The Theory of the Leisure Class* (1899) and *The Theory of Business Enterprise* (1904) satirized the hypothetical economic man reacting in foreordained ways to pleasure and pain. Listening to him, said Wesley Mitchell, a brilliant institutional economist of the next generation, was like "vivisection with an anaesthetic."

Veblen insisted upon the changing nature of human beings who in turn could create changing institutions. He developed the thesis that the conflict between industry and business was essentially a conflict between production for use and production for profits. On the one hand, he seemed to be saying that people were bound by the habits of the social group in which they found themselves; on the other hand he was saying that the ideal of good workmanship, concern for community welfare, and natural curiosity to find other ways of doing things would lead, as one historian has put it, to "the development of the Christian tradition" at the expense of the competitive system. In any case classical economics was never the same after *The Theory of the Leisure Class.*

Reform Sociology

Although Veblen's contributions are properly placed principally in the field of economic theory, he made use of contemporary scholarship in anthropology, psychology, and sociology. In all of these fields, new approaches were being tried. In sociology, for example, vigorous assaults were being made on social Darwinism and laissez faire. So characteristic were these attacks by the sociologists that Sumner disassociated himself from them by calling his work the science of society rather than sociology. In the first issue of the *American Journal of Sociology* which appeared in July 1895, Albion Small, its editor and head of the first department of sociology in the United States at the University of Chicago, called his lead article "The Era of Sociology." Small claimed that diversification of industry, division of labor, speed of transportation and communication all combined to make "human association . . . more influential than in any previous epoch." He claimed that people were "socially self-conscious" and that popular plans for institutional reform were being formulated without sufficient consideration of human limitations. These plans, according to Small, were based upon the premises that relationships among people were not what they should be, and that something should be done "directly, systematically, and on a large scale to right the wrongs." However, a danger existed, warned Small, that the reform proposals might have a political effect before scholars had a chance to verify them.

One of the scholars to whom Small no doubt referred was the great pioneer sociologist, Lester Frank Ward (1841–1913). Like Sumner, a confirmed evolutionist, he was unlike Sumner in his belief that man could shape the course of evolution. Ward came from poverty on the Illinois frontier. Largely self-educated, he was particularly interested in birds, flowers, and plants; but he also managed to learn French, German, and Latin. He was wounded in the Civil War and then became a federal civil servant, working in numerous government agencies. From first hand, he became convinced that bureaucrats were not necessarily stupid and inefficient. He went to night college for five years while with the government and received diplomas in arts, law, and medicine. In 1883, his first book, "the first comprehensive sociological treatise written in the United States," appeared. It was entitled *Dynamic Sociology* in contrast perhaps to Spencer's *Social Statics.* Numerous books and articles followed, showing great erudition but written in a pompous style filled with words such as *synergy* and *anpheclexis.* Perhaps because of such obscurities, he gained recognition slowly. However, in 1906, he was elected the first president of the American Sociological Association and received his first academic appointment at Brown University where he characteristically offered a survey course entitled "Of All Knowledge."

Like Spencer and Sumner, Ward's social philosophy began with evolution. However, he concluded that a change had taken place in the nature of evolution, once the mind of the human being had evolved. Prior to that time, the principle of the survival of the fittest had prevailed; yet, Ward pointed out, natural forces are blind; the survival of the fittest is extremely wasteful—millions of fish eggs are needed to produce comparatively few fish. Indeed, he suggested, the fittest frequently is not the most useful; how much more useful are cultivated crops and domesticated animals than are those which survive through the struggle for existence? Here Ward broke clearly from Sumner and Spencer and insisted that with the development of the human mind, human progress became dependent upon an intelligence able to create an environment hospitable to the individual.

Ward identified the school and the state as institutions essential for the improvement of the human environment. Universal public education, he thought, would not only stimulate individuals' intelligence but would also make them receptive to new ideas and social legislation. With the state now controlled by popular majorities, he saw no reason for fear of the state; it would in fact not only be responsible for maintaining public education but would also support sociological laboratories in which specialists could work out solutions to the problems of society. Legislatures would still exist, but their function would be largely to put "the final sanction of society" on decisions of the specialists. In short, evolution would have gone somewhat past "democracy" to a "sociocracy," a thoughtful version of the welfare state and a planned society.

By the twentieth century, the reform scholars had made quite clear some of the issues separating them from the Social Darwinists and the advocates of laissez faire. If Ward's writings were too obscure for the uninitiated to understand, he had disciples who were more successful in reaching the less well informed. Albion Small, while editor of the *American Journal of Sociology,* became a scholarly popularizer of Ward's views and of the concept of "sociological ethics," which set standards valid only in reference to the conditions of a given time or place. Edward A. Ross (1866–1951), like Small, a Hopkins Ph.D. and with German postgraduate training, named one of his children Lester Ward and to the horror of the administrative authorities at Stanford assigned *Dynamic Sociology* as a text. Ross lost his position there but was welcomed at the University of Wisconsin in 1906, where he remained for thirty years, a humanitarian, optimistic, egalitarian, and moderate reformer. The point is that teachers in colleges and universities were taking new ideas seriously and it may be that as many students were being exposed to them as to Sumner's doctrine by the turn of the century.

Channels of Communication

It is impossible to conclude to what extent the conflict struck a responsive chord among the students of the day. They were increasing in number. Between 1870 and 1900 the number of institutions of higher learning had increased from 563 to 977; college students from 52,000 to 238,000; graduate students numbered 6,000 in 1900, a threefold increase in ten years; and the total number of college degrees conferred, 29,375, was not quite 13,000 more than in 1890. Many of these students doubtless attended college because of the environment of friendships, social development, fraternity houses, good sportsmanship, athletic teams. Yet in the 1890s the elective principle in choosing courses was common, and although it had its weaknesses, it did permit the addition of the new disciplines and "permitted the American university to enter into a vital partnership with the society of which it was a part." Moreover, the universities were determined to improve the quality of research and educational standards in general.

This spirit manifested itself in many ways. In some colleges, student clubs were founded that reflected the students' interest in various reforms. Harvard, for example, had its Social Politics Club; Good Government Clubs and Sociology Clubs were epidemic. Moreover, students in almost all the large urban areas participated in settlement work, actually establishing college settlements. Stanton Coit, an Amherst graduate, established the first settlement in New York in 1886; several Smith College graduates opened the New York College Settlement three years later, in the same year that Jane Addams and Ellen Starr founded Hull House in Chicago, the most famous of them all. These settlements attempted to resolve the problems of the slums and the newly arrived immigrant. First and foremost, however, they were educational enterprises.

To some extent then the scholars were spreading their doctrines through their teaching. The enthusiasm for science so characteristic of the late nineteenth century had spread to the study of society, and a conviction that in no field had "scientific progress been more real than in the field of economic, social, and political studies" resulted in a determination to see that the findings of this research should be made more widely available. Within a comparatively short space of time, the *Political Science Quarterly* (1886), the *Quarterly Journal of Economics* (1886), the *American Journal of Sociology* (1895), *The Annals of the American Academy of Political and Social Sciences* (1890), and *The American Historical Review* (1895) were founded, and the media were available for the communication of ideas at least to other scholars.

Reform Religion

If the conflict in ideas was making itself felt on the college campuses and in the scholarly world of the late nineteenth and early twentieth centuries, the stirrings of the time were also upsetting orthodox religion and the organized churches. The organized churches, predominantly Anglo-Saxon and Protestant, found themselves on the defensive on numerous fronts. Every month, thousands of immigrants who could not speak English were coming into the United States, and an increasing number of them were Roman Catholic and Jewish. They crowded the cities and intensified the battle with the slums. The Roman Catholic church, with its historic interest in ministering to the poor, set up missions in the slums, but found its resources strained, as perhaps five-sixths of the Roman Catholic communicants in 1900 were urban immigrants.

At the same time, other factors were weakening the nation's religious structures. Particularly disturbing was the growing secularization of American life. Sunday newspapers and sports, the availability of inexpensive transportation—bicycles, electric cars, and finally the automobile—competed with the churches for the Sunday congregation. Perhaps most important of all, the hypothesis of evolution and scholarly critics raised questions about the Creation, Noah and the flood, and other sacred Biblical stories upon which many denominations based their faith. The battle was joined between those who endorsed the new scholarship and those who fought for the old beliefs either as scholars who defended certain principles of fundamentalism or revivalist preachers such as Dwight L. Moody or Billy Sunday who usually combined simple preaching about sin and salvation with the denouncement of liquor, dancing, and tobacco.

While the modernists and fundamentalists brought out their differences, another controversy was developing over whether the organized church was sufficiently responsive to the evils that came with urbanism and industrialization. Edward A. Ross, the pioneer sociologist, shocked the readers of one of his most effective tracts, *Sin and Society* (1907) in a colorful paragraph: "They chastise with scorpions the old authentic sins, but spare the new. They do not see that boodling is treason, that blackmail is piracy, that embezzlement is theft, that speculation is gambling, that tax-dodging is larceny, that railroad discrimination is treachery, that the factory labor of children is slavery, that deleterious adulteration is murder." One question was whether the church should pay any attention to these new sins. Equally important, however, was the question of why so few laboring men attended well-established urban churches. Attempts to find the answers were illuminating. Some workers complained that they were not able to dress well enough; others claimed that the churches were "chiefly attended and controlled by the capitalist and employing classes"; other complaints criticized the ministry for being either ignorant of economic questions, unwilling to discuss them, or fearful of positively taking labor's side.

This criticism of the church was somewhat ironic in view of the fact that historically religious impulse had been one of the stimulating factors in reform movements in the United States. Works of charity, support for the antislavery, temperance, and hospital reform movements all seemed to indicate a direct relationship between the church and reform. At the same time, there were other aspects of Protestant orthodoxy that were less compatible with movements for economic and social reform. One of these was the belief that the primary role of the church must be upon individual conversion. Life on this earth, went this view, was a period of testing; the reward would be received in Heaven. Fortunate individuals should be imbued with Christian charity and the wealthy should be stewards of their wealth and use it to help others. These attitudes tied in closely with, but in some ways seemed contradictory to, the Protestant ethic that sanctified thrift and urged people to "Work, for the Night is Coming." Russell Conwell, an eloquent Baptist minister, in a famous lecture, "Acres of Diamonds," assured his listeners in 1890 that "to secure wealth is an honorable ambition, and is one great test of a person's usefulness to others," and Bishop Lawrence of Massachusetts in 1900 stated simply that "Godliness is in league with Riches." These doctrines of the calling and of stewardship constituted what Andrew Carnegie called the Gospel of Wealth, although no nineteenth-century code of ethics clearly imposed sanctions on economic behavior.

The self-satisfied acceptance of the doctrines of the Gospel of Wealth did not go unchallenged. Some simply advocated more charitable generosity, whereas others found that capitalism and Christianity must inevitably be at war. Judaism was perhaps less plagued with conflict over the social question than either Roman Catholicism or Protestantism. The Jews had an unusual sense of community based upon the biblical injunction to help *"thy needy brother."* The founding in 1895 of the Associated Jewish Philanthropies of Boston symbolized this historical concern. Moreover, the Conference of Reform Judaism which met in Pittsburgh in 1885 took note of the social problem. Its platform asserted that "the great task of modern times" was "the contrasts and evils of the present organization of society" and that Judaism had the duty to help solve this problem.

Roman Catholicism was dominated in the post-Civil War period by those hesitant to become involved in social and economic problems. A change came in 1891, however, with the encyclical, *Rerum Novarum,* of Pope Leo XIII on conditions of the working class. This encyclical had inspired campaigns for social reforms by European Catholics, and in the United States the priests who had previously been inclined to take up the cudgels for the workers now in some instances received encouragement from their superiors. Archbishop John Ireland of St. Paul, Minnesota, for example, approved reform efforts so long as these efforts did not jeopardize property rights; at the same time he was decidedly suspicious of unions and strikes; Cardinal James Gibbons of Baltimore, on the other hand, had consistently supported the cause of the organized worker, even before *Rerum Novarum.* At the turn of the century, Bishop George Montgomery of Monterey–Los Angeles, California, went so far as to favor compulsory arbitration, income taxes, and the nationalization of railways and telegraphs as a means of solving the labor problem.

Even more important for the future was the scholarship of a young Catholic priest at the Catholic University of America, John A. Ryan (1869–1945). Ryan, born on a Minnesota farm, had read Henry George and knew some of the local populist leaders. His doctoral dissertation, published in 1906, was entitled *A Living Wage: Its Ethical and Economic Aspects.* By 1909, he was proposing a comprehensive plan for social reform: a minimum wage law, the eight-hour day, the abolition of child labor, conciliation and arbitration boards, regulation of public utilities, monopolies, and speculation, and the taxation of incomes and inheritances.

An important factor in determining the role of Catholics in social reform was *Der Deutsche Romisch-Katholische Central-Verein Von Nord-Amerika,* a federation of German Catholic Mutual Aid Societies founded in 1855. Although this organization had supported some social activities in the nineteenth century such as the creation of employment bureaus, its position was generally considered conservative, fearful of undue Americanization and especially fearful of socialism. Actually the fear of socialism, however, became a factor leading to an endorsement of a program for social reform. Many Germans were socialists, and with the organization of the socialist party in the United States in 1901, the Central-Verein saw the need of providing a program that would rival that of the socialists. Under the dynamic leadership of Frederick P. Kenkel, a complex, religiously conservative, devoted, but somewhat autocratic former newspaper editor, the Central-Verein by 1909 had adopted a program calling for support by Roman Catholics of labor organizations, safety regulations, and restrictions upon women's and child labor.

Not until 1919, however, did the Catholic hierarchy give significant support to an organized campaign for social justice. In that year Ryan produced the "Bishop's" Program for Social Reconstruction which called for a comprehensive program of government action, including minimum wage laws and social insurance. This program, however, went too far for Kenkel and the conservative reformers who feared state socialism and probably saw in the Middle Ages the kind of Christian community they were seeking.

The Protestant response to the problems of industrialization was known as the social gospel. The social gospel, like so many other phenomena of the late nineteenth and early twentieth centuries, cannot be summarized adequately because it consisted of the ideas and actions of different individuals belonging to different denominations. The social gospelers did have in common an unwillingness to accept the Gospel of Wealth and a conviction that man could mold his environment and create a Kingdom of God on earth. They saw Jesus as a "Prophet of social righteousness" and they almost completely abandoned the concept of God as the Judge. Above all, they insisted that the clergy could legitimately deal with questions other than spiritual.

By the turn of the century, the battle had already been joined in several Protestant denominations. Washington Gladden, a Congregationalist of Springfield, Massachusetts, began his campaign in the 1870s; Josiah Strong, another Congregationalist, denounced the corrupting power of money in his book, *Our Country*, in 1885. The Brotherhood of the Kingdom, an association of those who favored the social gospel, was founded in 1893 and met annually until 1915. The Protestant Episcopal church played a leading role in the movement. Episcopalian clergymen founded the Church Association for the Advancement of the Interest of Labor (CAIL) in 1887. CAIL fought for the right of labor to organize, furnished arbitration and mediation personnel for strikes and lockouts, and set up sweatshop and tenement committees. In 1891, the Christian Social Union, with Bishop F. D. Huntington of New York and Richard Ely as secretary was founded. This organization was considered as a research organization to publish tracts and to furnish speakers.

Many social gospelers wrote tracts in support of their position, but not until the publication of Charles M. Sheldon's *In His Steps* in 1898 did any of their writings reach the mass market. Millions of copies of this book were sold. It was a rather sentimental tale of a portion of a congregation which elected to do what Jesus would have done in every circumstance. In general, it concluded that problems could be solved by personal sacrifice.

Sheldon's social gospel was rather bland, and perhaps many read *In His Steps*, as they did Bellamy's *Looking Backward*, without taking it very seriously. At the same time, however, the movement had followers who were clearly quite ready to upset the status quo. George D. Herron achieved prominence by preaching a sermon entitled "The Message of

Jesus to Men of Wealth" at a Congregational conference in Minnesota in 1891. He became one of the most popular preachers in the Midwest and used his popularity to support the Populists. A chair of Applied Christianity was created for him at Iowa College (later Grinnell) in 1893. He soon was vigorously denouncing the capitalistic system as being contrary to the principle of fellowship among people, and admitted that "the doctrines of property which I hold are subversive to the existing industrial and political order." Such views led to his resignation from Iowa College and shortly thereafter, in 1900, he became associated with Eugene Debs. Herron, like other social gospelers, was convinced that the kingdom of love could be created in the foreseeable future. In his case he saw populism or the Socialist party as agents. Through his powerful preaching, he spread the principles of the social gospel through the Midwest and gave theological support to profit-sharing schemes, rural cooperatives, and the aims of organized labor.

The development of the institutional church was somewhat less controversial than the activities of Herron yet one of the most practical manifestations of the social gospel. A number of these had been founded in the late nineteenth century with the express purpose of ministering to those who considered the church hospitable only to the wealthy. These churches added athletic programs, classes in industrial education, sewing schools, and employment bureaus. St. George's Episcopal Church in New York, the Berkeley (Congregational) Temple in Boston; Russell Conwell, the author of the "Acres of Diamonds," at the Baptist Temple in Philadelphia; S. Parkes Cadman at the Methodist Metropolitan Temple in New York; and Charles H. Parkhurst at the Madison Square Presbyterian Church in New York were among the leaders. In 1894, the organization of the Institutional Church League, designed to coordinate the activities of such churches, encouraged their growth at the turn of the century.

If the effectiveness of the social gospel had depended only upon the mild reforms of Charles Sheldon, the fiery attacks of George Herron, and the institutional organizations of some of the big city churches, it might never have been intellectually respectable. However, Walter Rauschenbusch, whose religious publications were among the most significant in the English language in the first two decades of the century, provided this respectability.

Rauschenbusch was born in Rochester, New York, of German parents who had immigrated to the United States after the revolutions of 1848. He returned to Germany for schooling, but received the Bachelor of Arts at the University of Rochester Theological Seminary in 1886. He became pastor of a Baptist church in New York City where he ministered to German immigrants during the hard times of the 1890s. He read Henry George, Tolstoy, Bellamy, Ruskin, and Marx. He studied economics and theology at the University of Berlin in 1891 and 1892 and observed the social conditions in English industrial towns, where he was impressed by the work of the Fabian socialists, Sydney and Beatrice Webb. Appointed to a chair of church history at Rochester in 1902, he determined to bring about reform in Christian theology.

His first book, entitled *Christianity and the Social Crisis* (1907), set the stage for a later vigorous attack upon capitalism. From the beginning, according to Rauschenbusch, the fundamental aim of Christianity had been to reform society according to the will of God, but medieval monasticism and asceticism had obscured that aim. Then, in the eighteenth and nineteenth centuries rapid industrialization, the development of political democracy, and study of the social sciences had come almost simultaneously. Industrialization produced the worldly goods necessary for the good life; the development of political democracy was the secular equivalent of the principle of brotherly love; and knowledge of the social sciences contributed the scientific knowledge necessary to combine all these into the heavenly city on earth. Unfortunately, according to Rauschenbusch, defenders of the institution of private property were threatening the proper working out of these possibilities. A single, economic class was gaining wealth and power. The working class suffered the most within this social structure; through labor unions the working class would be the instrument to bring about social reforms such as a guaranteed annual wage, old age pensions, and medical care, and thus prevent a bloody destruction of the social order. A religious revival, he argued, was necessary to encourage the individual to use the social sciences to promote social reform.

Five years later, in *Christianizing the Social Order* (1912), he attacked capitalism. Optimistic about the current of reform sweeping the United States, he concluded that the capitalistic economy was the only "institutionalized aspect of the United States not Christianized," and he warned that if capitalism were not converted to Christianity, it would destroy Christianity. Again he insisted that industrialization had created the foundation for the good society, that people, with divine inspiration were able to change their institutions with the help of the social sciences, and that if people made the right choice, Christianity would triumph.

How significant was the social gospel? Certainly its analysis of the social problems of the day was not always profound; at times it accepted too unquestioningly the characteristic belief in progress of the nineteenth century; its advocates seemed to believe that a quick change of heart could create the kingdom of God on earth.

Among the most complex questions of all are the relationships between the laborer and social Christianity and the role of labor leaders and local churchpeople in working-class areas in the social gospel movement. Undoubtedly suspicion and distrust of the church existed among labor leaders; yet religion had played a powerful role in pre–Civil War America, and religion undoubtedly continued to be an influential factor with workers on the railroads or in factories or mines. The ideas of human fellowship, of Christ's mission to the poor, and of Christian perfectionism in general were pervasive in labor periodicals and in the writings and speeches of labor leaders in the last part of the nineteenth century. With apparent sincerity they professed that Christ was on their side, and Christianity became both a unifying and a motivating factor.

After the turn of the century, however, suspicion and distrust apparently began to undercut confidence in Christian perfectionism, and the religious tone of the labor rhetoric declined. Although this change may have been simply typical of the increased secularization of American society, Herbert Gutman has suggested that the twentieth century brought in a new generation of workers and leaders. He described the post–Civil War generation as transitional, carrying "with them meaningful and deeply felt traditions and values rooted in the immediate and even more distant past." The new labor leaders may have been increasingly disillusioned by seeing social Christianity frequently fought by business interests and by revivalists who linked the social gospel with modernism. At the same time, they were probably not impressed by the rather detached reform programs supported by intellectuals such as Rauschenbusch who recognized the needs of laboring people, saw what had to be done, but could not inspire confidence among the rank and file of workers. His remedies were appeals to Christian sympathy; he seemed to be trying to impose middle-class, American values on a working-class, immigrant culture, and he appeared to think that leadership had to come from a kind of religious elite.

In spite of the opposition, however, the leading denominations had almost officially accepted the aims of the social gospel by the first decade of the century by adopting statements of social principles and appointing agencies to carry them out. Perhaps the symbol of the official attitude of the churches was the social creed adopted in 1908 when the Federal Council of Churches was organized. This creed endorsed social justice reform and called for child labor laws, old age pensions, shorter working hours, protection of labor strikes, minimum wages, and temperance legislation. In short, although it is debatable how many churchpeople of the early twentieth century accepted the ideas of the social gospel, it had had an important effect in changing the direction of theological thought and in forcing the institutions to face up to the challenges of industrialization and the city.

Pragmatism

Although the prophets and institutions of the social gospel may have touched more individuals in the late nineteenth and early twentieth centuries, it is probable that the ideas of an intellectual triumvirate, Charles S. Peirce, William James, and John Dewey, had a greater effect in the long run in undermining the concept that the world and its inhabitants are governed by a changeless plan.

Charles Peirce (1839–1914), an inconsistent, brilliant, tragic mathematician, was never able to hold an academic job for long. He spent much of his lifetime in trying to work out a new philosophical system that was based upon scientific methodology, emphasized chance rather than certainty, and recognized change as a leading characteristic. Although he failed to create a philosophical structure that others could easily understand, he did succeed in showing how scientific methodology could be applied in the realm of philosophy and ideas. He insisted that hypotheses be "experimentally verifiable," that hypotheses and concepts be made clear, and that they be formulated in a way that would promote rational behavior.

Peirce belonged to a famous Metaphysical Club at Harvard in the 1860s, which included among its members Oliver Wendell Holmes, Jr., and William James. William James (1842–1910) credited Peirce with the founding of pragmatism, and Peirce in his later life recalled that it had resulted from the arguments in the club at Harvard. "The members of the club," as Paul Conkin described it, "were interested . . . not only in scientific methodology but in semantic clarity, in the new theory of evolution, in physiology and a new psychology, and in moral and ethical problems." William James was certainly interested in all of these. The son of one Henry James and the brother of another, widely traveled and German-educated, a Harvard doctor of medicine, the author of a mighty two-volume *The Principles of Psychology* published in 1890, he was appointed to the department of philosophy at Harvard in that same year. Although converted to the scientific method, he distrusted science and would not concede that it had a monopoly on truth. James himself was not entirely consistent in developing his ideas, because on the one hand he put a great deal of emphasis on actual experience in verifying a concept while at the same time he emphasized that what one wanted or needed was an essential ingredient in formulating a philosophical concept; to him faith was a fact of life.

Although his ideas were contradictory, they were so in part because to James, like Peirce, change was fundamental. And in change the free individual, never clearly defined, was paramount. The mind of each individual was engaged in the process of choosing both individual goals and means to achieve these goals. To James this testing process was the essence of the pragmatic methodology because only by testing could the truth or falsity of an idea be determined. As James put it, "the truth of an idea is not a stagnant property inherent in it. Truth happens to an idea." Pragmatic methodology led directly to a very toughminded position called radical empiricism which insisted that concepts were only the beginning of wisdom, that actual sensations and feelings were equally important, and that nothing could be assumed to be fixed or permanent. People were not caught up in some predetermined plan; they had to be willing to take a chance and to test the results of their ideas through experimentation.

The third member of the triumvirate, John Dewey (1859–1952), was even more of a radical empiricist. Dewey remained a profound influence on American thought and action for nearly seventy years. From his youth in Vermont, through graduate experiences at Johns Hopkins and years of teaching and research at Michigan, Chicago, and Columbia and in retirement, he was developing a philosophical system. Similar to Peirce and James in his resentment of deterministic philosophy, or for that matter of anything repressive, and in his belief that nothing should be complacently accepted as good without being tested for its contemporary usefulness, his philosophical system grew out of his own experiences more than theirs.

Dewey's intellectual philosophy became one of social reform. At Michigan, from 1884 to 1894, in the days of populism, depression, and strikes, he met two brothers, Franklin and Corydon Ford, who were proposing a social revolution leading to an industrial system ruled by trades unions. From Michigan, Dewey moved to Chicago where he immediately found himself associated with Hull House "among the new army of Chicago's poverty-stricken, immigrant workingmen." Here he met the inspirational Jane Addams, Florence Kelley, the first labor inspector in Illinois under Governor John P. Altgeld's exciting administration, and Henry Demarest Lloyd. More important, he taught and argued with "anarchists, single taxers, and socialists." In Chicago, too, he served as director of the Laboratory School of the University of Chicago from 1896 to 1904, working with brilliant scholars in philosophy and psychology and gifted and dedicated public school teachers. With them he developed a school designed both to experiment with innovative teaching methods and to work for "a new society where cooperation rather than competition should rule." To Dewey the destruction of "undemocratic forms of social organization" were as much the function of philosophy as of politics.

Dewey's technique of problem solving is normally called instrumentalism: the problem exists; it is investigated; a method of solving the problem is worked out; it works. "Would it not hold," said Dewey, ". . . that observations are pertinent and ideas correct just so far as, overtly acted upon, they succeed in removing the undesirable, the inconsistent?" The idea became the instrument which led to the solution of the problem. Every plan must be flexible, however, since a rigid plan assumes a fixed world and a static individual, neither of which, according to Dewey, exists.

By the outbreak of the First World War, Ely, John Bates Clark, Veblen, Lester Frank Ward, Albion Small, E. A. Ross, and most of the social gospelers were of an older generation. William James was dead and even he and John Dewey, as Henry May has put it, "had their roots firmly in the nineteenth century." They represent what May has described as the paradox of the progressive era: the curious combination of "Wilsonian moral idealism and Deweyite relativism." They believed in progress, and, in spite of their relativism, their standards for truth and for the ideal society were not far removed from those of the nineteenth-century's moral order. "In one combination or another," concluded May, "morality and progress together ruled the American scene."

The Dimension of Race

May's conclusion, however, does not apply to at least one dimension of American culture. One of the many unanswered questions about the intellectual elite is the extent to which their attitudes toward race and other cultures colored their thought. Few Americans no doubt would have admitted to being racist. At the same time many, probably most, white, Anglo-Saxon Protestants openly accepted the premise that certain racial or ethnic groups possessed superior characteristics that no change in environment could alter. The revival of genetic studies around the turn of the century with emphasis on Mendelian laws taught the genetic transmission of characteristics, and the fetish for organization led to the establishment of such groups as the American Breeder's Association and the Committee on Human Heredity. Those who gave intellectual support to theories of racial superiority undoubtedly dominated the field until Franz Boas in the first decade of the twentieth century, as Eric Goldman has put it, "trained his anthropological guns on Americans who assigned inherent inferiority to the Negro, and in 1911 ... launched a massive assault on the detractors of the new immigrants." His position was a relatively simple one that "culture was a cumulative evolutionary product, not a function of racial heredity."

Racism in the United States knew no regional barriers. It was intensified by the flood of immigrants which poured into the United States after 1900, the migration of black people from South to North and into the cities, the confrontation of Americans overseas with the peoples of Africa and Asia. Radical nativism led to such organizations as the American Protective Association which saw Roman Catholicism as a menace and the Immigration Restriction League which prophesied the death of New England culture if unlimited numbers of "inferior" peoples were allowed to contaminate white, Protestant, Anglo-Saxons.

In the South, racism smothered the promise of emancipation by a pattern of disfranchisement and segregation ordinances. The millions of black people found themselves poverty stricken and without essential ingredients for a counterattack. They were not entirely leaderless, however, and new organizations responding to new conditions grew out of conventions of intellectual blacks which met annually from the 1830s to about 1890.

Although differences in means led at times to bitter clashes among the black leaders in the twentieth century, the basic aims of virtually all of them were the same. In one way or another, they were primarily concerned with developing racial pride and removing the barriers to economic, social, and political justice. Some saw the need for reminders of the black heritage, and such writers as George Washington Williams in his *History of the Negro Race in America* (1882) provided a base for the founding by Carter Woodson of the Association of Negro Life and History and the *Journal of Negro History* in 1916. Others saw the need for developing a greater economic foundation upon which to build pride in race and joined a general movement to provide blacks with agricultural and industrial education. The manual labor colleges, Samuel Chapman Armstrong at Hampton Institute founded in 1868, philanthropic foundations such as the General Education Board and the John F. Slater Fund all endorsed the principle that to earn respect one had to possess a desire and an ability to earn one's livelihood.

From the widespread acceptance of this principle grew a fundamental conflict symbolized by the relationship between Booker T. Washington and W. E. B. Du Bois. Washington, a student of Armstrong's at Hampton Institute, and the founder of Tuskeegee in 1881, worked on the premise that by "thrift, industry, and Christian character, Negroes would eventually attain their Constitutional rights." He was equally convinced that black advancement was dependent upon harmonious relationships; thus in a famous speech at the Atlanta Exposition in 1895 he said that "in all things that are purely social we can be as separate as the five fingers, yet one as the hand in all things essential to mutual progress." At the same time behind the screen of accommodation, he secretly fought against disfranchisement and for racial justice in the courts.

W. E. B. Du Bois at first accepted Washington's program. By the turn of the century, however, Du Bois became increasingly irritated at growing discriminations, criticized the emphasis on industrial education, and, himself a Harvard Ph.D., saw the need for college education for at least a "talented tenth." In 1903, he launched a full-scale attack on Washington and denied that a black could achieve respect by accepting discrimination. As he put it in *Souls of Black Folk*, "one feels his two-ness—an American, a Negro, two souls, two thoughts, two unreconciled strivings, two warring ideals in one dark body."

These conflicting approaches were to some extent reflected in two important organizations designed to improve the lot of the black people in the early twentieth century, the National Urban League and the National Association for the Advancement of Colored People. The Urban League, founded in 1911, grew out of earlier committees designed to improve opportunities for blacks in industry. Washington had given his blessing to this organization before he died and had worked with the philanthropist Julius Rosenwald and the Columbia economist E. R. A. Seligman in establishing it. Du Bois, on the other hand, had been instrumental in launching the Niagara movement in 1905, which aimed at openly protesting against the abridgment of rights of black people. In the meantime, some whites, disturbed at lynchings, race riots, and overt racism, joined with Du Bois in founding the NAACP. As director of publicity and research and editor of the association's journal *Crisis,* he increasingly denounced the emphasis on industrial education without political rights and trumpeted that no square deal was possible where segregation existed.

The struggle for the rights of racial and ethnic minorities joined that for the goals traditionally associated with progressivism at only a few points, and there is no positive way to measure the contribution of educated elites, black or white, to political and social change. However, it would be difficult to deny the proposition, as Edward Purcell has put it, "that ideas have practical significance as they subtly interplay with human hopes and values, social institutions, and important historical events."

Bibliography

Pages 32–33

Before finishing this chapter, a reader should peruse Paul K. Conkin, "American Intellectual History," chap. 10 in William H. Cartwright and Richard L. Watson, Jr., eds., *The Reinterpretation of American History and Culture* (1973). Useful general works are Sidney Fine, *Laissez Faire and the General Welfare State: A Study of Conflict in American Thought, 1865–1901* (1956); Ralph Henry Gabriel, *The Course of American Democratic Thought,* rev. ed. (1956); Richard Hofstadter, *Social Darwinism in American Thought,* rev. ed. (1955); Eric F. Goldman, *Rendezvous with Destiny; A History of Modern American Reform* (1953); Stow Persons, *American Minds; A History of Ideas* (1958); Morton G. White, *Social Thought in America; The Revolt Against Formalism* (1949). Henry May finds the beginning of a cultural revolution before the First World War in *The End of American Innocence; A Study of the First Years of Our Own Time, 1912–1917* (1959). Critical of the optimistic thinkers is David Noble, *The Paradox of Progressive Thought* (1958). Pessimists are studied in Frederic Cople Jaher, *Doubters and Dissenters; Cataclysmic Thought in America, 1885–1918* (1964).

Pages 34–35

For John Fiske, see Milton Berman, *John Fiske; The Evolution of a Popularizer* (1961); for a novel slant on Sumner, see Bruce Curtis, "William Graham Sumner 'On the Concentration of Wealth,' " *Journal of American History,* 55 (March 1969), 823–832, and Robert C. Banister, Jr., "William Graham Sumner's 'Social Darwinism': A Reconsideration," *History of Political Economy,* 5 (Spring 1973), 89–109. Paul F. Boller, Jr., *American Thought in Transition: The Impact of Evolutionary Naturalism, 1865–1900* (1969).

Pages 35–37

For socialist and utopian thought, see Steven B. Cord, *Henry George: Dreamer or Realist?* (1965); Solomon Gemorah, "Laurence Gronlund, Utopian or Reformer," *Science and Society,* 33 (Fall–Winter 1969),

446–458; Sylvia E. Bowman, *The Year 2000: A Critical Biography of Edward Bellamy* (1958); Howard H. Quint, *The Forging of American Socialism; Origins of the Modern Movement* (c. 1953); Stow Persons and Donald Drew Egbert, eds., *Socialism and American Life,* 2 vols. (1952). See also Ira Kipnis, *The American Socialist Movement, 1897–1912* (1952); Chester M. Destler, *Henry Demarest Lloyd and the Empire of Reform* (1963).

Pages 37–39
For European influences, see Arthur Mann, "British Social Thought and American Reformers of the Progressive Era," *Mississippi Valley Historical Review,* 42 (March 1956), 672–692; Goldman, *Rendezvous with Destiny;* Fine, *Laissez faire and the General Welfare State;* Jurgen Herbst, *The German Historical School in American Scholarship, A Study in the Transfer of Culture* (1965); Joseph Dorfman, "The Role of the German Historical School in American Economic Thought," *American Economic Review,* 45 (May 1955), 17–28; Charles F. Thwing, *The American and the German University; One Hundred Years of History* (1928).

Pages 39–41
For the economists, see Goldman and the work by Joseph Dorfman, *The Economic Mind in American Civilization, 1865–1918,* vol. III (1955). For the principles of the American Economic Association see *Publications of the American Economic Association,* I (1886–1887), 23; see also John R. Everett, *Religion in Economics; A Study of John Bates Clark, Richard T. Ely, and Simon N. Patten* (1946); Sidney Fine, "Richard T. Ely, Forerunner of Progressivism, 1880–1901," *Mississippi Valley Historical Review,* 37 (March 1951), 599–624; Benjamin G. Rader, *The Academic Mind and Reform; The Influence of Richard T. Ely in American Life* (1966); Daniel M. Fox, *The Discovery of Abundance; Simon N. Patten and the Transformation of Social Theory* (1967); for Veblen, see Abram L. Harris, "Veblen as Social Philosopher, A Reappraisal," *Ethics,* 63 (April 1953), 1–31; David Noble, "Veblen and Progress: The American Climate of Opinion," *ibid.,* 65 (July 1955), 271–285; Helen P. Liebel, "Thorstein Veblen's Positive Synthesis," *American Journal of Economics and Sociology,* 24 (April 1965), 201–216; The standard biography would still probably be Joseph Dorfman, *Thorstein Veblen and his America* (1934).

Pages 41–43
For the sociologists, see Gabriel; Goldman; Henry Steele Commager, *The American Mind: An Interpretation of American Thought and Character since the 1880s* (1950); Hofstadter, *Social Darwinism;* Albion Small, "The Era of Sociology," *American Journal of Sociology,* 1 (July 1895), 1–15; Samuel Chugerman, *Lester Frank Ward, The American Aristotle; A Summary and Interpretation of His Sociology* (1939); Julius Weinberg, *Edward Alsworth Ross and the Sociology of Progressivism* (1972).

Pages 43–44

For education, see Frederick Rudolph, *The American College and University; A History* (1962); Lawrence A. Cremin, *The Transformation of the School; Progressivism in American Education, 1876–1957* (1961); *The Annals of the American Academy,* 1 (July 1890), 132.

Pages 44–47

For the religious controversies, see Clifton E. Olmstead, *History of Religion in the United States* (1960); G. H. Hopkins, *Rise of the Social Gospel in American Protestantism, 1865–1915* (1940); Henry F. May, *The Protestant Churches and Industrial America* (1949); Aaron I. Abell, *The Urban Impact on American Protestantism, 1865–1900* (1943) and *American Catholicism and Social Action* . . . (1960). For fundamentalism, Ernest R. Sandeen, *The Roots of Fundamentalism* . . . (1970); Robert R. Roberts, "The Social Gospel and the Trust Busters," *Church History,* 25 (September 1956), 239–257. See also Beryl H. Levy, *Reform Judaism in America* (1933), and Moshe Davis, *The Emergence of Conservative Judaism: The Historical School in 19th Century America* (1963); for Catholic reform, see Robert D. Cross, *The Emergence of Liberal Catholicism in America* (1958); Francis L. Broderick, *Right Reverend New Dealer, John A. Ryan* (1963); Philip Gleason, *The Conservative Reformers; German-American Catholics and the Social Order* (1968).

Pages 47–50

The literature is extensive on the social gospel. In addition to the general works above, see Jacob Henry Dorn, *Washington Gladden; Prophet of the Social Gospel* (1967); Lionel L. Mitchell, "The Episcopal Church and the Christian Social Movement in the Nineteenth Century," *Historical Magazine of the Protestant Episcopal Church,* 30 (September 1961), 173–182; John W. Ripley, "The Strange Story of Charles M. Sheldon's *In His Steps,*" *Kansas Historical Quarterly,* 34 (Autumn 1968), 241–265; H. R. Dieterich, "Radical on Campus: Professor Herron at Iowa College, 1893–1899," *Annals of Iowa,* 37 (Fall 1964), 401–415; Noble, *Paradox of Progressive Thought,* has an excellent chapter on Rauschenbusch. See also John R. Aiken and James R. McDonnell, "Walter Rauschenbusch and Labor Reform: A Social Gospeller's Approach," *Labor History,* 11 (Spring 1970), 131–150; Robert T. Handy, "Christianity and Socialism in America, 1900–1920," *Church History,* 21 (March 1952), 39–54; Fred Nicklason, "Henry George: Social Gospeller," *American Quarterly,* 22 (Fall 1970), 649–664; John F. Piper, Jr., "The Formation of the Social Policy of the Federal Council of Churches," *Journal of Church and State,* 11 (Winter 1969), 63–82. An unusually perceptive article is Herbert G. Gutman, "Protestantism and the American Labor Movement: The Christian Spirit in the Gilded Age," *American Historical Review,* 72 (October 1966), 74–101.

Pages 50–53

For a brilliant, somewhat technical, but precise study see Paul K. Conkin, *Puritans and Pragmatists: Eight Eminent American Thinkers* (1968). There are numerous biographies of William James. See, for example, Ralph Barton Perry, *The Thought and Character of William James,* 2 vols. (1935), and Edward C. Moore, *William James* in the Great American Thinkers series (1965). For Dewey, I also used Lewis S. Feuer, "John Dewey and the Back to the People Movement in American Thought," *Journal of the History of Ideas,* 20 (October–December 1959), 545–568; E. Darnell Rucker, *The Chicago Pragmatists* (1969); Edward C. Moore, *American Pragmatism; Peirce, James, and Dewey* (1961). The quotations from May are in *End of American Innocence,* p. 164.

Pages 53–55

For a sampling of studies on racism and on anti-Catholicism, see Thomas F. Gossett, *Race; The History of an Idea in America* (1963). A sociologist's treatment of the principal views toward immigration is Milton M. Gordon, *Assimilation in American Life; The Role of Race, Religion, and National Origins* (1964), Richard Weiss, "Racism in the Era of Industrialization," in Weiss and Gary B. Nash, eds., *The Great Fear; Race in the Mind of America* (1970), pp. 121–143. Donald L. Kinzer, *An Episode in Anti-Catholicism; The American Protective Association* (1964); S. Lipset and Earl Rabb, *The Politics of Unreason; Right Wing Extremism in America, 1790–1970,* Patterns of American Prejudice series, vol. 5 (1970); Paul M. Gaston, *The New South Creed; A Study in Southern Mythmaking* (1970), and Lawrence J. Friedman, *The White Savage; Racial Fantasies in the Post-Bellum South* (1970). A comprehensive survey of black thought is August Meier, *Negro Thought in America, 1880–1915: Racial Ideologies in the Age of Booker T. Washington* (1963), which can be complemented by I. A. Newby, *Jim Crow's Defense; Anti-Negro Thought in America, 1900–1930* (1965). Louis Harlan is the leading authority on Booker T. Washington, see especially *Booker T. Washington: The Making of a Black Leader, 1856–1901* (1972), the first of two volumes. Other useful volumes on the black experience are Elliott M. Rudwick, *W.E.B. Du Bois; A Study in Minority Group Leadership* (1960); Emma Lou Thornbrough, *T. Thomas Fortune: Militant Journalist* (1972); Guichard Parris and Lester Brooks, *Blacks in the City; A History of the National Urban League* (1971), and Charles Flint Kellogg, *NAACP, History of the National Association for the Advancement of Colored People* (1967).

Page 55

The final quotation is from Edward A. Purcell, Jr., *The Crisis of Democratic Theory; Scientific Naturalism and the Problem of Value* (1973), p. ix.

3

Progressivism

The Problem of Definition

Between the 1890s and the First World War, important changes took place in almost every phase of American life: In the economy, industry became paramount; labor unions achieved greater prominence; and agriculture enjoyed greater prosperity than in many years. In society, although rural America still predominated, community isolationism broke down and urbanization increased dramatically at the same time that increased tension developed among ethnic and racial groups. In politics, the balance of power that had existed from the Civil War to the mid-1890s between the Democratic and Republican parties gave way to Republican predominance except in the South. On the diplomatic front, the United States participated as never before in overseas activities and by the end of the Spanish-American War had to administer an overseas empire. In the intellectual sphere, more people attended school at all levels, and writers and scholars in various disciplines and professions questioned beliefs and values. In almost all of these areas at the turn of the century, there was a sense of dissatisfaction with things as they were, and many of those seeking solutions to new problems were turning to government on either the local or national level as the logical agent to bring about certain changes.

The period is called the Progressive Era, and many leading reformers of the period called themselves progressives apparently because they assumed they could remove the causes for dissatisfaction and assure human progress. Yet the term is a trap if it is used to force a hypothetical unity onto a period that was unusually complex. An initial question, for example, is whether there was a relationship between the increasingly dynamic foreign and military policy of the United States and the expanding role of the federal government on the domestic scene. At almost any given time after the turn of the century, issues of both foreign policy and domestic policy clamored for solution almost simultaneously. The same executive and the same congressmen had to deal with them. The same taxes, tariffs, and other revenues had to finance them. Headlines in the same newspapers on the same day might give almost equal stress to issues at home and abroad. It is historically dangerous to compartmentalize foreign and domestic policy, as is customarily done in teaching or writing about this period, unless one is constantly aware of the ways in which one impinged upon the other.

There is no clear-cut relationship, however, between progressivism in general and any particular position on foreign policy. Some of those known as progressives supported American expansion and militarism and seemed to have had "an exaggerated concern with manliness . . .[,] power, and activity." Yet progressives moved in and out of every divergent position on foreign and defense policy in the early twentieth century. Nationalists such as Theodore Roosevelt and Albert Beveridge, internationalists such as Woodrow Wilson, pacifists such as William Jennings Bryan dealt extensively with foreign policy and considered themselves progressives. It is not surprising that advocates of a vigorous foreign policy, such as Roosevelt, supported the development of the power of the central government at home. There were, however, enough exceptions to the Rooseveltian model to suggest that there was no rule. More intriguing is the thesis that enlightened businessmen, in cooperation with governmental officials, promoted order and stability both at home and abroad by encouraging government support for a vigorous policy of foreign trade and overseas investment.

Yet this hypothesis applies only to one sector of early twentieth-century progressivism, which was an almost infinitely complicated phenomenon. Instead of a single movement there was a complex of local, state, and national movements aiming at political, social, and economic reforms of different kinds and supported by diverse individuals and groups. Historians themselves have not agreed upon a definition. In 1951, for example, Daniel Aaron designated progressives as a "moral and righteous minority" who were "riveted to principles" and demanded "real social equality"; they included Ralph Waldo Emerson, Theodore Parker, Henry George, and Henry D. Lloyd. Theodore Roosevelt and Woodrow Wilson were, to Aaron, opportunistic and politically ambitious, and thus "pseudoprogressives." In the 1960s Gabriel Kolko, looking at progressivism from a different perspective, insisted that corporate business promoted the reforms of the era, at least on the national level, as a means of maintaining order and stability, and he called the period "an era of conservatism." Kolko's label, however, should not be accepted. The term *progressive* is firmly attached to that era. Even though there were radicals who were not progressives and progressives who might be conservatives, the term itself was too widely used in the first two decades of the century to abandon it.

Yet historical analysis has brought out aspects of progressivism that would probably not have been recognized by the progressives themselves. One of the approaches was that advanced by George Mowry and Richard Hofstadter. Mowry and Hofstadter, while recognizing connections with late nineteenth-century populism, saw progressivism as "concerned with urban problems" and the leadership drawn from the upper middle class; "the Mugwump type," Hofstadter called them. They were businessmen, merchants, lawyers, preachers, and teachers, the type that had held positions of prestige and influence throughout the nineteenth century. However, as Hofstadter saw it, their status was being threatened by the Johnny-come-latelies—the new industrialists and political bosses of the late nineteenth and early twentieth centuries. The old elites "found themselves checked, hampered, and overridden by the agents of the new corporations, the corrupters of legislatures, the buyers of franchises, the allies of the political bosses." Thus, Hofstadter concluded, a revolt occurred, not so much because of "economic deprivation" but because of a loss of status to the new businessman and political boss. Frustrated and anxious, these old elites turned to reform to restore their lost status.

The Timing of the Progressive Era

Since similar social and economic conditions and an urban middle class had existed decades earlier, Hofstadter had to show why the progressive revolt occurred in the twentieth century rather than in the 1870s and 1880s. His explanation is complex but persuasive. Actually there were reformers in those earlier years, the patrician reformers known quite commonly as mugwumps. The mugwumps, born before the Civil War, had been concerned about dishonesty in government but opposed to fundamental change in the economic and social system. The postwar generation, however, had a different perspective. Its members had grown up while big business was developing and while labor was consolidating. After 1897 increasing prices were pinching the consumer. New businesses were profiting from the growth of the cities, and demands for utilities, buildings, streets, and sanitation were creating ties between city bosses and these new businesses. Joining the Populists had been an alternative for the middle-class reformer in the 1890s, but undoubtedly a patrician distaste for the lack of sophistication and for the apparent radicalism of the Populist leaders ruled that out. At the same time scholars were questioning conventional economic and sociological theory, and a new generation of journalists were reaching out to more people and describing conditions in popular prose.

The new journalism appealed to the mass market, to the many consumers rather than the few producers. Between 1870 and 1909, the number of daily newspapers increased from 574 to 2,600, circulation from 2,600,000 to 24,200,000. The more dignified journalism of Joseph

Pulitzer on the *St. Louis Post Dispatch* and the *New York World* gave way to the tough yellow journalism of William Randolph Hearst in the *New York Journal.* Pulitzer himself succumbed to some extent, and his competition with Hearst in extravagant reporting of the Cuban crisis in the 1890s helped create support for the war with Spain. More importantly, perhaps, they championed the laboring man and various reform causes.

In the meantime technical changes were making possible the modern magazine. After 1886, a geometrical increase of printing speed resulted when rotary presses replaced the flat-bed press. In the nineties the new Hoe rotary art press made possible the printing of pictures at much less cost. In the 1870s the government introduced low-cost mailing for periodicals, and rural free delivery began in the 1890s. Too, the growing literacy of the American people provided a market that had not existed before. Soon the cultivated, literary magazines such as *Harper's, Scribner's,* the *Century,* and the *Atlantic Monthly* at twenty-five or thirty-five cents an issue saw their supremacy in the field challenged. Samuel McClure, Frank A. Munsey, and John B. Walker of *Cosmopolitan* saw the possibility of cutting the price below cost in order to increase circulation, and then recouping losses through advertising. *McClure's* at first sold for fifteen cents and then followed *Munsey's* to ten cents in 1895.

At first these new periodicals featured literature such as the works of Robert Louis Stevenson, Rudyard Kipling, Thomas Hardy, and Stephen Crane. Only Benjamin O. Flowers in the *Arena* was consciously battling for social reform. By the turn of the century, however, Samuel McClure had decided that he would publicize the facts of corruption that were coming out in investigations of city and state government, and in 1901 he published stories about corruption on Wall Street and a series on the underworld. He then drew into his orbit a galaxy of colorful writers including Ida Tarbell, Ray Stannard Baker, and Lincoln Steffens. In 1902, Tarbell, inspired by McClure, began a history of the Standard Oil Company; Steffens was engaged in a study of municipal corruption; and Baker completed research for an article on labor unions. By coincidence each of these authors had an article ready for publication in the issue of January 1903.

Although Theodore Roosevelt did not use the phrase *the man with the muckrake* to describe these writers until 1906, the term *muckraking* is frequently dated from that famous issue of *McClure's* in 1903. Between then and 1912, more than 2,000 muckraking articles appeared in the cheap magazines, most of them by about a dozen writers including Samuel H. Adams, Baker, Burton J. Hendrick, Thomas Lawson, David G. Phillips, Charles E. Russell, Upton Sinclair, Steffens, and Tarbell. In most instances these writers were sophisticated reporters who did not start out with a philosophy of reform, but they seemed to agree that "business and the big businessman were at the root of the corruption." On the other hand, they did not blame specific businessmen but perhaps implied, as David

Chalmers put it, that the development of the corporation "had outstripped our legislative and moral awareness." The muckrakers hoped for more responsive democracy and the elimination of corruption. Few favored extreme solutions, but Baker, Phillips, and Steffens were attracted by socialism, and Sinclair and Russell actually were socialists.

Another factor in explaining the timing of progressivism was the woman's rights movement. Long before the twentieth century, American women had joined in various reform crusades. Dorothea Dix in exposing the horrors of the insane in the 1830s and the Grimké sisters in attacking the institution of slavery in the years before the Civil War were at the same time helping to build the platform from which women launched a campaign for their own rights. Indeed the progressive era brought to at least one high point a complex movement which included a cluster of drives for humanitarian reform and especially for women's suffrage.

Changes in the status of women were in turn brought about by a considerable variety of economic and cultural factors. Changes occurred in the nature of the family as men, women, and children became factory workers, as the invention of the telephone and typewriter attracted women to offices and switchboards, as knowledge of contraception increased, and as attitudes toward divorce became more liberal.

A particularly important stimulus to the growing independence of women was the increasing acceptance of the desirability of education in a democratic society. State after state was expanding its educational system, and, to meet the demand for teachers, women in growing numbers attended summer institutes and teacher training schools. Between 1880 and 1901, the number of teachers in elementary schools increased from about 287,000 to about 432,000, and of this number the proportion of women increased from 57 to 71 percent. At the same time, more women were going to college. Before the end of the century, such colleges as Oberlin, Mount Holyoke, Vassar, Smith, Goucher, Wellesley, Harvard Annex (Radcliffe), and Cornell, were turning out well-educated women. The numbers of women graduates were still small, only 25 percent of a total of 23,000 graduates in 1901, but an increasing number of them were to be found as newspaper editors, novelists, physicians, and social workers.

Yet there was really no such thing as the "new woman," as her culture varied from that of the rural black or newly arrived immigrant to the contented or discontented women of leisure publicized in the novels of the day. No doubt the great majority of women consisted of those who of economic necessity were teaching in schools, typing letters, engaging in prostitution, staying on the farms, or otherwise working for pay or keeping the home fires burning with very little thought given to their rights as women. A growing number, however, were openly rebelling against the point of view that a woman's mission was in the home where they would "by their blandishments and their lives . . . assuage the passions of men as they come in from the battle of life."

The rebellious yearning for independence was frequently channeled into organization to achieve specific goals as women like other groups— farmers, wage earners, and businessmen—recognized that in unity there was strength. Even women's missionary societies sometimes became concerned with problems of housing and unemployment. The origins of the settlement houses, made famous by Jane Addams and Lillian Wald, for example, can be found in the 1880s in the Methodist Home Missionary movement in Georgia, South Carolina, and Alabama. The settlement houses provided useful employment for those women who yearned to be of service yet who did not necessarily wish to revolutionize the society from which they came. Closely associated with religious organizations was the Women's Christian Temperance Union, founded in 1874, which provided an acceptable platform from which women could support other reform crusades and become involved in politics. Concurrently, clubs were being organized that had goals varying from self-education to social reform. Federations came into existance in many states, and in 1889 the General Federation of Women's Clubs was organized. By 1896, there were "495 clubs and 21 state federations, the latter including over 800 clubs."

In the background of these organizational activities was the intensification of the women's suffrage movement. The women's rights movement that had stemmed from the women's declaration of independence at Seneca Falls, New York, in 1848 at first had stressed "complete sexual equality." Such an apparent frontal attack on the family, however, led to so much hostility that the new organizations which emerged emphasized the suffrage as the principal goal. By 1890, the National American Woman Suffrage Association had absorbed two associations which had been competing for twenty-one years, and its members were campaigning to make women's suffrage a means for social change. They acknowledged that women were different from men but that these peculiar feminine qualities would help cleanse public life and at the same time justify special protective legislation. Local suffrage groups became numerous and respectable in the South as well as in the North, and men's leagues supported the women as the suffragists joined in crusades to improve working conditions, housing, and public health. Organizations such as the National Consumers League, organized in 1899 and led by women such as "the indomitable Florence Kelley," and the Women's Trade Union League, founded in 1903 and combining settlement house workers with "compassionate women of wealth and trade union leaders," began their long campaign for social justice. By the turn of the century the women's rights movement provided a stimulating ingredient for progressive reform.

Numerous factors do add up, therefore, to explain why the early twentieth century witnessed a flowering of reform impulses without resorting to the status-anxiety thesis. Indeed sociological and psychological theorists do not appear to be agreed as to the applicability of a status-anxiety thesis to reform movements, and certainly alternate hypotheses are available to explain motivation. Moreover, such a thesis requires that progressives must have a status to be threatened and that the status of all progressives should be the same and significantly different from the status of the Republicans or Democrats who were not progressives. The fact is, however, that although many progressive leaders were from the middle or upper classes, there were many exceptions, and usually their opponents were drawn from about the same economic background.

Robert M. La Follette in Wisconsin

The example of Wisconsin and its experience with progressivism points to the impossibility of explaining what happened there by any sociological or psychological generalization, and, at the same time, helps to explain why progressivism arose when it did. Here there were unusual ethnic factors, as well as the impact of an outstanding individual. Robert M. La Follette emerged from a political situation that was more complex than a confusion of ethnic groups. In the early 1890s, foreign-born voters, mostly Scandinavian and German, outnumbered natives. A Republican political machine had controlled the state since 1855. Although the Grangers had had some success in organizing the farmers, the state had never gone Populist, and conservatives such as the veteran Senator, John C. Spooner, the lumberman, tough Philetus Sawyer, and the railway magnate and later postmaster general, Henry C. Payne, were at one time or another the political powers. Even Bryan could carry only three of the seventy counties of the state in 1896. Although the state was predominantly rural, the city of Milwaukee had grown from 204,000 to 285,000 between 1890 and 1900; lumbering, railroads, flour-milling, and even the manufacturing of automobiles were important occupations.

Wisconsin had produced its share of reformers in the decades after the Civil War. Local communities fought the battles for temperance, against prostitution, and for Sunday blue laws. In the eighties suffragists won the right for women to vote in school board elections, and civil service reforms and the secret ballot won substantial victories in the state legislature. The real nudge for wide-scale reform came in the communities as a result of the depression in the 1890s. Like an even greater crisis forty years later, this depression resulted in unrest that united hitherto feuding religious, ethnic, and social groups. In the atmosphere of the depression the agitation of women's and municipal reform organizations, the preaching of social gospelers, the teaching of social scientists (Richard Ely was by this time at the University of Wisconsin), and the complaints of interests such as the farmers and the wage earners took on a new meaning.

In this crisis, problems that had come with industrialization and urbanization now attracted widespread attention. The self-centeredness of the corporations, ties between these corporations and local government, inequitable tax laws, tax evasion on the part of corporations and men of wealth, and the lack of responsiveness of local government to the popular will, all these created a conviction that the consuming public was the victim of producers in league with complacent if not corrupt politicians.

Robert M. La Follette emerged from this complicated mixture of complaints, crusading individuals, and pressure groups. La Follette was undoubtedly influenced by the poverty of his boyhood, the idealistic influence of his teachers at the University of Wisconsin, and the discovery that breaking into politics was not easy. At the same time he was energetic, had many friends, could recognize issues which had wide popularity, could translate these into simple questions of right and wrong, and then use oratorical skill to dramatize them.

Wisconsin had had its reformers before La Follette. In community after community, corporate regulation, tax reform, and a higher level of political responsibility had antedated the conversion of La Follette to the Cause. But by 1897 he had been converted, and he was calling for the direct primary and tax reform. In the meantime, taking advantage of a deteriorating Republican machine, he had made political alliances with the disaffected, including a wealthy lumberman, Isaac Stephenson. Finally, after two previous failures, he won the governorship in 1900.

As governor, finding the legislature still controlled by the stalwarts, he threw himself in 1902 into the legislative campaign and gained majorities in both houses. He organized carefully, appointed his friends to positions of influence, and consulted a brain trust of professors at the University of Wisconsin, many of whom he appointed to government posts. His program included direct primary laws and the initiative; laws to clean up political and legislative procedures; expert commissions to regulate industry, utilities, taxation, banks, insurance companies, and the stock exchange; restrictions on child and female labor; a pure food law, workman's compensation laws, improved educational systems, and conservation.

All these proposals did not become law while La Follette was governor, but many did, and most were put on the books before 1912. Unquestionably, the depression of the 1890s had forged a coalition of representatives of virtually all consumer interests, except upper-class businessmen, that focused on the sources of social, political, and economic ills. Railroad interests were late converts to the usefulness of railroad regulation. Tension existed between La Follette and some of the reformers who had engaged in local battles before La Follette had been converted, but his ability to combine what David Thelen called the old politics with the new politics enabled representatives of consumers to push through the new program designed to give power to the people. Like Franklin Roosevelt, La Follette may have taken advantage of the depression, followed public opinion as much as he led it, and gained support by judicious use of patronage. But he gave Wisconsin distinction and deserves the title of "Mr. Progressive."

Reform in the States

In the meantime progressives had carried other states. Hazen Pingree in Michigan, Albert B. Cummins in Iowa, Samuel Van Sant and John A. Johnson in Minnesota, Joseph Folk in Missouri, John Burke in North Dakota, Coe Crawford in South Dakota, and George Sheldon in Nebraska put the progressive mark on the Middle West. In the far West, Hiram Johnson battled the railroad interests in California, and in Oregon William S. U'Ren organized the Direct Primary League and the Peoples Power League. In the East, Theodore Roosevelt returned in triumph from Cuba to win the New York governorship in 1899. The influence of George Record and Mark M. Fagan in Jersey City and Everett Colby in Essex County had shaken up the state legislature in New Jersey, which by 1906 had approved laws regulating railroads, insurance companies, and public utilities.

The City

Progressivism in the states conformed to no clear pattern, and probably, as in Wisconsin, the patterns depended upon the ways in which reform movements developed in the cities and towns. The leaders, more often than not, do seem to have been drawn from the urban middle class, but many urban reformers grew up in the country, and a factor in stimulating progressive reform was undoubtedly the clash of rural values with the concentrated vice, corruption, and despair of the twentieth-century city, an institution that was both loved and hated. On the one hand there were those who saw the city as "an organism which, if properly directed, would enable men to attain the good life." These visionaries saw the need for services, the conglomerate population, the faltering governments, and the corrupt political machines as challenges; to them the cities were laboratories for social experimentation in welfare legislation and public ownership. They studied European experience, concluded that the European cities that had been most successful in solving their problems had relied upon science and administrative skill and that the complexity of the American metropolis required an equal reliance upon experts, not only because they were well trained but because they would be sufficiently disinterested to do the job properly.

To some, the city typified the nouveau riche, those entrepreneurs who had recently gained wealth and power. To others, the city meant the new immigrants, uneducated, predominantly Jewish or Roman Catholic, unable to assimilate easily into the Anglo-Saxon, Protestant culture of nineteenth-century America and largely responsible for commercialized vice. Historically, the humanitarian liberal had supported the traditional immigration policy of unrestricted entry. The Statue of Liberty with its inscription

"Give me your tired, your poor,
Your huddled masses yearning to breathe free"

symbolized a welcome to those seeking liberty and opportunity. By the twentieth century, however, many reformers were no longer hospitable. Those who sympathized with organized labor were aware that the AFL favored a restriction on the grounds that low immigrant wages were undermining the standards of American workers; those who were trying to improve conditions in filthy slums found themselves torn between sympathy for the unfortunates who lived there and the thought that if immigrants were kept out slum conditions could be improved.

Regardless of attitudes, varied problems grew with the city in the mid-nineteenth century and led to gestures of reform. By the 1890s, municipal reform became both more popular and better organized. By 1898, some seventy Good Government Clubs, Municipal Leagues, Taxpayers Associations, and other groups concerned with urban reform had combined into the National Municipal League. Professional journals as well as the popular periodicals joined in the crusade and sought to itemize the problems and propose solutions.

One of the basic difficulties in the federal system made cities subject to state legislatures that in turn were usually controlled by representatives of small towns and rural areas. An initial step in municipal reform, therefore, was to win independence for the city in order to carry out local reforms. In 1898, the California legislature granted San Francisco a charter authorizing home rule, apparently the first city so blessed. By 1900, California, Minnesota, Missouri, and Washington had general home-rule statutes, and by 1914 eight more states were added to the list.

That municipal home rule was not essential for municipal reform, however, is indicated by the example of Ohio, which did not attain that goal until 1912. That state, however, was blessed with another ingredient in a recipe for municipal change, a number of intelligent and dedicated leaders. One of these was Samuel M. "Golden Rule" Jones, who was elected mayor of Toledo in 1897. An immigrant from Wales, he worked in the Pennsylvania oilfields, moved to Toledo where he established a company to produce oil-well machinery. The company prospered, and Jones granted all the right things to his workers—an eight-hour day, a minimum wage, paid vacations, and profit sharing. Elected mayor of Toledo in 1897, he broke with the political professionals, set a city minimum wage of $1.50 a day, and advocated public ownership of utilities. He drew his chief support from organized labor and wage earners in general. He was opposed by a curious coalition of political organizations, the Antisaloon League and the churches, some of his opposition insisting that he did not adequately enforce the law. The opposition could not defeat him. After his fourth successive election, he died in office in 1904, whereupon the electorate voted in an equally determined reformer and Jones' close personal friend, Brand Whitlock.

Such leaders as "Golden Rule" Jones, Tom Johnson in Cleveland, Hazen

Pingree in Detroit, and Mark M. Fagan in Jersey City bear out the traditional picture of the progressive era—the battle for social justice against entrenched forces of graft and corruption. There is, however, another side to the story of urban reform which adds a dimension to the thesis of middle-class leadership, raises questions about the aims of some of the reformers and the sources of support for reform drives, and requires a second look at the traditional picture.

Among the most important urban reforms, for example, were those establishing the city manager or commission forms of government. In September 1900, a hurricane hit Galveston, Texas, and created such destruction that the city government was unable to cope with it. The state legislature, responding to requests for help, appointed five commissioners to govern the city. The system worked, and by 1910 at least a hundred cities had adopted modified forms of the commission, and by 1914 that number had quadrupled. In the meantime, other cities, led by Staunton in Virginia and Dayton in Ohio, wishing more concentration of authority and at the same time a nonpolitical administration had adopted the city manager type of government.

A number of factors explain the drive for these new reforms. One aim was to curb the corruption that seemed to accompany the conventional form of mayor, city council, and wards. More important, however, as Samuel P. Hays has shown, was the concern felt over the complexity and expense of government that resulted from motor vehicles, electricity, harbor facilities, and public utilities in general. The model of city government became the corporation. The watchwords became economy and efficiency, and the advocates of municipal reform became chambers of commerce, commercial clubs, and boards of trade. Members of these groups were generally businessmen who wanted well-educated men with business experience in office. They wanted to concentrate decision making in few hands. Perhaps of most importance, they advocated citywide elections of political representatives rather than elections by the local ward in order to undermine the local bosses.

These aims frequently brought the reformers into conflict with the lower- and middle-class groups that had controlled ward politics. Ward politics in Pittsburgh, for example, were dominated by small businessmen (grocers, saloon keepers, druggists), white-collar workers, and workmen. These men opposed reform drives led by larger businessmen and the professions. They sensed that the new forms of government would not adequately represent them. In some instances at least, those advocating reforms such as the city manager and commission form of government wished to restrict the influence of lower-class groups and were not enthusiastic for democratic reforms such as the initiative and referendum. They feared a tyranny of ignorance.

Although the aim may have been for a businessman's government, the actual results depended upon the managers or those who influenced the management. In some instances economy meant reduced services and incomes for city workers. Managers might have little concern save for the budget. On the other hand, efficiency might mean municipally operated public services, as at Dayton, Ohio, where John H. Patterson of the National Cash Register Company, the power behind the management movement, saw to it that many services were publicly owned and that a comprehensive welfare department was established. Patterson supported reform not merely for humanitarian motives but because, as he frankly put it, "it pays."

Thus urban reform resulted from a complex interrelationship between the promotion of efficiency and social justice. Within the same administration might be found the traditional crusade for reform and the efficiency expert. Furthermore, as Joseph Huthmacher has pointed out, reform legislation required the votes of the "urban lower class." To point out that certain progressives favored immigration restriction might obscure the fact that much progressive legislation was approved by immigrant voters. Immigrants undoubtedly differed according to ethnic origins as well as according to their generation, but they reacted to living in slums and working for low wages in insanitary conditions, and they were concerned by the unrepresentative characteristics of political institutions. They were not involved in any status revolt. They did not consider their aspirations limited by any philosophy of laissez faire; indeed, they probably were conditioned to think of government as a principal source of help. They wanted legislation that would regulate wages and hours and working and living conditions and provide help for the injured and aged. The recommendations of the New York State Factory Investigating Commission, for example, resulted in some fifty labor laws within a four-year period and the commission's effectiveness resulted from close collaboration among such people as Alfred E. Smith and Robert Wagner, state senators who sprang from the urban lower class, Frances Perkins, a trained social worker who served as investigator, and Samuel Gompers, the president of the AFL.

Most of those who supported this type of legislation were interested in urban problems and usually had little use for some of the other reform crusades that were simultaneously taking place in the more rural areas. They fought immigration restriction; they were skeptical of Bible Belt morality and sabbatarianism; they had little use for temperance reform and flatly opposed prohibition. Yet prohibition was frequently one of the most hotly contested issues of the day. Usually it was involved with the increasing conflict that seemed to be developing between urban and rural cultures and at times was the one issue that was persistent in dividing parties at the grass roots.

Prohibition

Prior to 1900, the temperance movement had been dominated by Frances Willard and the Women's Christian Temperance Union (WCTU). Willard believed that crime, prostitution, and intemperance were the results of harsh social conditions, and she advocated such reforms as a minimum wage and the collective ownership of the means of production. At the same time the WCTU pointed to habits of industry and thrift as necessary to prevent urban unemployment, claimed that temperance was necessary for economic success, and, between 1882 and 1902, succeeded in getting passed in every state laws which would require temperance instruction in public schools.

By the turn of the century, however, the temperance reformers had turned to prohibition, and the Antisaloon League had become the dominant temperance organization. The league, founded in 1893, called for "the extermination of the beverage liquor traffic." It insisted upon nonpartisanship in politics and upon maintaining "strict neutrality on all questions of public policy not directly and immediately concerned with the traffic in strong drink." Essential in its technique was a close alliance with religious denominations. It claimed to be "the Church in action against the Saloon."

To many persons in the cities and towns the saloon was a necessary social institution. It served as a club, labor exchange, union hall, game room, and political headquarters. In the unlovely environment of the New York slums, the saloon held "the monopoly up to date of all the cheer of the tenements." In the saloon occurred workers' parties, weddings, dances, meetings of singing societies, and other social functions. It was the spot where the immigrant was able to make some adjustment to alien customs and where he was introduced to the politics of the political machine.

To the reformer, on the other hand, the saloon was a different institution. It was the place where saloonkeepers enticed the worker to deprive his family of his weekly pay. It was the hangout of pimps and prostitutes. It was the center where the corrupt political boss purchased votes. The liquor interests were suspected of being responsible for bribery and rigged elections. Thus some urban reformers formed a link with the advocates of temperance; their common aim became the abolition of the saloon. It was a weak link because the urban leadership was not so much interested in prohibition as in temperance, and the rural constituents distrusted an urban culture consisting partly of high society and partly of the newly arrived foreigner.

Perhaps the most effective strategist for the league was James Cannon, Jr. A Methodist preacher from Virginia, Cannon began his fight with the liquor interests in the 1890s. He not only held prominent positions in the Antisaloon League but for many years chaired the Committee on Temperance of the Virginia Annual Conference of the Methodist Episcopal Church, South, a position which he held until elected bishop in 1918. He was largely responsible for the techniques employed by the Antisaloon League in winning victories for prohibition on the local level before the Eighteenth Amendment was ratified. He described the program of the league as consisting of agitation, legislation, and law enforcement. Agitation included the use of posters, sermons, campaign speeches, and control of local newspapers. Legislation meant exposing the position of legislators or candidates for political office on the prohibition question, advancing if necessary one step at a time by taking what could be obtained and making alliances with whatever political groups were necessary in order to obtain the objective.

By 1919, thirty-three states had prohibition laws. Except for Ohio and Michigan, the dry states were predominantly rural. In Ohio, a continual battle went on between the rural voters and the rural-dominated legislature on the one side and several of the city machines, particularly those in Cleveland and Cincinnati, on the other. The league hired professional workers to concentrate on the issue of prohibition. By taking one step at a time, the league succeeded in drying up the rural areas by local-option elections, but it could not gain sufficient support to overcome the anti-prohibition voters in statewide referenda until 1918. In that year, it worked out a detailed organization through the counties and down to the precincts. It organized every imaginable group—laborers, women, blacks, the industrialists, and the farmers. The prohibition amendment passed, but it probably would have been defeated had it not included a provision permitting manufacture and importation for home use. Urban Ohio never approved prohibition, nor did New York, Pennsylvania, Massachusetts, California, and several other states in which many foreign voters found the idea of prohibition inconceivable.

Although the evidence seems conclusive that the prohibition crusade intensified antagonisms between country and city folk, it is possible to exaggerate the rural origins and characteristics of the prohibition movement. Many cities, particularly in the South and Middle West, supported prohibition, and it may be that a class-ethnic factor in both rural and urban areas was more important than mere geographic location in determining support for prohibition. It did appear that native, old-stock Protestant individuals, largely of the lower middle class, seemed to support prohibition while working-class elements, largely immigrants and Roman Catholics, were inclined to oppose it. There were some nativistic, anti-Catholic, anti-immigrant, even anti-black implications to it, and, as James Timberlake has put it, "to the old-stock, middle-class progressive, prohibition was a way of uplifting . . . the lower classes; to the urban masses, it was an intolerable interference with their personal liberty." In the early twentieth century temperance, if not prohibition, was a middle-class, white, Protestant, Anglo-Saxon value and perhaps had become a kind of cultural symbol; to those who identified temperance with efficiency and industry and liquor with drunkenness and absenteeism, prohibition did become a symbolic crusade.

Thus prohibition is another question which complicates defining twentieth-century progressivism: to many thoughtful, sincere individuals prohibition was a reform. Some of its advocates may have been fanatics; yet suffering resulted from the excesses of alcohol. Scientific evidence seemed to show a baneful relationship between the alcoholism of parents and the health of children; corruption and vice frequently did accompany the saloon; liquor interests did intervene in politics; and economists could show how drunkenness affected labor productivity. To a relatively unsophisticated people, the solution to these ills was to eliminate the cause in the most obvious way, and thus many progressives such as Jane Addams, Walter Rauschenbusch, Gifford Pinchot, and Hiram Johnson were prohibitionists. At the same time, others were not. Jonathan Dolliver of Iowa, for example, although sympathetic to temperance, endorsed prohibition in Iowa hesitantly and probably because of the political power of the Methodists, and Robert La Follette seems to have been equally ambivalent. On the other hand, except for Frances Willard, few of the most famous prohibitionists were progressives. Although prohibition may have been a symbolic crusade, its devoted supporters probably considered it the most important reform of the twentieth century.

Conservation

Another crusade which rivaled prohibition in its popularity and which also shows the danger of generalizing as to the meaning of progressivism was the drive for the conservation of natural resources. Almost equally with prohibition, conservation had its prophets, its devils, and its propagandists to the extent that the nature of the controversies is easily obscured.

Gifford Pinchot, the energetic Pennsylvanian who in many ways personified conservation, claimed to have been a cofounder of the conservation movement. He reminisced, some thirty years after the event, that while riding his "old horse Jim" through Rock Creek Park in the nation's capital, perhaps in 1907, it occurred to him that natural resources should not be studied in isolated, "watertight compartments" but as "one united problem" in order to make "use of the earth for the permanent good of man." Such a concept was then so new, Pinchot thought, that it did not have a name until his "little inside group" called it "the conservation movement."

Actually, the origins of conservation were considerably more complicated than Pinchot's recollections. In a brilliant book published in 1864, George Perkins Marsh clearly foresaw one facet of twentieth-century conservation when he warned of "the power of man irreparably to derange the combinations of inorganic matter and of organic life." Marsh represents the strand of conservation which favored the preservation of wilderness areas and wildlife refuges.

When Marsh wrote in 1864, the American government had already made a pregnant decision. In a series of enactments, it had made it possible for private individuals to acquire public lands for little or nothing without imposing restraints over how these lands would be exploited. By so doing, Congress had abandoned its control over these private lands and could consider only the remaining public domain as legitimate areas for federal conservation practices. By 1912, some 600 million acres remained in the public domain. In addition to these acreages, large areas were controlled by the individual states.

A dynamic element in the conservation movement consisted of dedicated individuals who formed the National Conservation Association in 1909. This association included people such as Jane Addams and Samuel Gompers as well as real publicists of conservation such as Pinchot, Harry Slattery, the amiable but keen secretary of the association, and W. J. McGee, one of the principal theorists of the movement. These men were determined to prevent wasteful exploitation, yet they did believe in the development of resources "for the benefit of the many and not merely the profit of the few." They might misinterpret the role of monopolistic corporations and at times imagine conspiracies against the public interest, but they were seriously concerned about waste, dishonesty, and lack of planning. Although their rhetoric in pleading for economic justice and for democratizing the use of resources was sometimes emotional, they were not talking in terms only of preservation but of efficient use for the best interests of all.

Thus equally important with the conservationist demands for social justice were the hardheaded pleas for efficiency and planning. This aspect of the movement was not dramatic or popular but was in accord with an increasing interest in science and efficient management in business and government. Undoubtedly, for example, an initial stimulus for conservation came as early as 1888, as hydrographers with the U.S. Geological Survey studied the uses of water. Other scientists trained in such fields as forestry and geology were horrified at the lack of centralized planning and expertise that had characterized the disposition of the public domain. Undoubtedly, too, Theodore Roosevelt's interest in the outdoors combined with his own disposition toward efficient management helps to explain his identification with the conservation crusade. At the same time, the plea of efficiency rallied businessmen to the cause, and big business on occasion endorsed sound conservation practices in opposition to local citizens (the people) who were interested in lumbering or grazing or moving onto neighboring lands.

Conservationists at times found themselves at odds with one another not only over broad goals but over means to reach these goals. One issue which again illustrates the complexities of the movement developed between the advocates of multipurpose river development and the army engineers. Multipurpose development had become a basic premise of conservationist thought by 1907. It assumed that preserving the forests was an effective means of preventing disastrous floods. The army engineers, who had developed techniques of their own after years of experience with floods on navigable rivers, fought the new theory. Their principal champion was Lieutenant Colonel Hiram Martin Chittenden, a dedicated public servant who had joined the engineers in 1884. In a paper, prepared in 1908, on the relationships between forests and stream flow, he raised questions that the conservationists could not answer, which insisted that their assumption, that deforestation was a major cause of floods, had not been proved, and which even suggested that forests might create conditions which would encourage flooding. The conservationists certainly considered Chittenden their enemy, but in fact he promoted the cause of conservation by his own studies of how to control large rivers more effectively.

Thus with conservation, as with such questions as state and local government and prohibition, it is difficult to explain the relationship to progressivism. No general theory works. The vastness of the area involved, the varied conditions, and the federal system all required a hierarchy of leadership which showed significant differences at different levels within the same geographical area and which almost certainly varied markedly in different geographical areas.

Progressivism in the South

Developments in the southern region further demonstrated this complexity and variety. Southerners played an active role in the farmers' revolt of the late nineteenth century. The Southern Farmers Alliances campaigned strenuously against the railroads, crop lien laws, contraction of currency, the protective tariff, and "trusts" in fertilizer, tobacco, jute bagging, and cottonseed oil. Attempts to establish cooperative exchanges in Florida, Georgia, and Texas to cut out the profits of intermediaries seemed to flourish for a while but then overexpanded and collapsed. Southern farmers pioneered the subtreasury plan, an ingenious proposal championed by Dr. C. W. Macune for crop storage and agricultural credit. The farmers' rebellion against the ruling Democrats of the new South; the willingness of some of them to organize all farmers, black and white; and the threat of fusion with the Republicans to gain political power threatened the dominant position of the Democrats. The plight of the party in power was the greater because of the depression of the 1890s which was as intense as in other parts of the country. Labor difficulties and continuing crises on the farm rocked the South. The southern Democrats turned to the Cleveland administration for aid, which was not forthcoming. Indeed Cleveland's conservative economic policies made it difficult for the southern Democrats to hold the section for their party.

Events of 1896 threw southern politics into confusion but in the last analysis saved the Democratic party in the South. The triumph of Bryan and the silver wing of the party over the unpopular Cleveland and the "Gold" Democrats was an essential ingredient in this salvage operation. The swift decline of the Populist party after the election of 1896 was equally essential since it left southern white farmers no place to go except to one of the old parties. The Democratic accusation that Republican or

Populist success at the polls would lead to black domination resulted in a revival of Democratic strength among white supremacists. The issue was most clearly drawn where Populists made local alliances with Republicans, many of whom were black, in order to achieve their political objectives. Only in North Carolina, however, was such fusion dramatically successful. In other states where black people were voting in large numbers, widespread corruption and intimidation helped maintain the Democrats in power.

The decline of the Populist party after 1896 did not signify the disappearance of issues which had led to the rise of that party in the South. Although the silver issue virtually disappeared with the gradual inflation at the turn of the century, the issues of the railroads and the trusts still remained. In the South these issues had a unique quality, for, in spite of notable exceptions, the new South was to a considerable degree a colony of the Northeast. Railroads, steel manufacturing, oil wells, and the mining of iron, sulphur, manganese, phosphate, and bauxite were largely controlled by the Morgans, Rockefellers, Mellons, DuPonts, and others like them in the North.

Colonialism was less characteristic of the textile and tobacco industries. New England textiles experienced hard times in the 1890s, and entrepreneurs from that area looked into conditions in the South. Here proximity to the raw material, favorable tax rates, cheap power, and, especially, a cheap, unorganized, and available labor supply had unusual attractions. Between 1890 and 1920, the number of cotton spindles in New England increased from almost 11 million to slightly over 18 million, but in the South they increased from about 1.5 million to more than 15 million. Yet Southern capital controlled 84 percent of the southern spindleage, even though much of the cloth had to be shipped north for processing and there was substantial dependence upon northern commission houses for selling.

In the meantime, big business had come to the tobacco industry. Pre–Civil War beginnings were expanded as the reputation of southern chewing and smoking tobacco of the new bright-leaf variety was carried throughout the United States by returning veterans. By the 1880s the Blackwell factory in Durham, North Carolina, manufacturing Bull Durham tobacco had become the largest tobacco factory in the world. Almost simultaneously Winston, with Pleasant Henderson Hanes and Richard Joshua Reynolds leading the way, was becoming a ranking tobacco town.

Perhaps the most important decision in the history of the tobacco industry occurred when James Buchanan Duke and his partners came to the conclusion that the future of tobacco lay in cigarettes. The Duke family had been moderately successful in tobacco in the 1870s but rose to rank among the top four or five cigarette manufacturers in the country in the 1880s. The Dukes transformed cigarette manufacturing by cutting prices drastically, engaging in high-pressure advertising, gambling on the use of the most modern machinery to make cigarettes (which had been hand-rolled), and using no-holds-barred competition.

The American Tobacco Company was incorporated under the laws of New Jersey in 1890 by James B. Duke and his leading competitors. By 1910, it controlled more than 80 percent of the tobacco industry. It had become a virtual monopoly, and it was hated as such by many. Competitors envied its power; union organizers denounced it for being open-shop; investors accused it of stock manipulation; farmers claimed that it controlled the tobacco market and dictated below subsistence-level prices. So convinced were tobacco farmers that American and other large tobacco companies were responsible for low prices that they formed cooperatives such as the Mutual Protective Association of the Bright Tobacco Growers of Virginia and North Carolina. In Kentucky and Tennessee, from about 1905 to 1908, the American Tobacco Company fought a veritable war, the Black Patch War, against farmers attempting to organize independently. Intimidation and murders characterized this war which ended when federal suits broke up both the anti-American Tobacco Company night-riders and the American Tobacco company.

Such conditions in the southern states created continuing demands for reform. After Populism declined, it appeared that conservatism controlled the state machinery, but in fact the Populists had forced party reorientation, and many of the old Populist demands found a ready following among the Democrats. Trust busting, bank and railroad regulation, the graduated income tax, expansion of departments of agriculture, all these and other reforms were frequently demanded. In addition there was a growing interest in public education and in the political reforms that were identified with progressivism outside the South, the secret ballot, the direct primary, and the commission form of government.

Indeed, at an earlier date southern states launched some of the reforms that are associated with states in the North or the West. Wisconsin adopted the statewide nominating primary in 1903, but by then it was being used in South Carolina, Arkansas, Georgia, Florida, Tennessee, Alabama, and Mississippi, and by 1915 all southern states had adopted it. States and communities in the South experimented with the initiative, referendum, and recall, and passed corrupt practices enactments. Georgia's railroad commission established in 1879 ranked with California's as one of the earliest effective laws dealing with the railways. Safety laws, prison reforms, and pure food bills were passed in various southern states.

At the same time, there was no necessary continuity between Populists and twentieth-century progressives. Indeed in Alabama, as Sheldon Hackney has suggested, they were quite different. Populists fought the establishment but seem to have held a Jeffersonian suspicion of positive government. The progressives, on the other hand, were more urban, more interested in industrial development, and willing to form political alliances with planters to defeat their mutual foes. Yet the Alabama progressives were irritated at the same abuses that had disturbed the Populists and supported "increased governmental services to stimulate growth and enable individuals to take advantage of the greater opportunity." They were more like the eastern progressives than those Populists and Democrats who followed William Jennings Bryan. In Mississippi, the 1890s witnessed the development of increasing opposition to the elitist politics of state and county committees. By 1900 James K. Vardaman, a lawyer and newspaper editor who had twice lost the nomination for governor in convention, had joined Edmund F. Noel, perhaps the state's leading reformer, in proposing a statewide primary. They battled the veteran politicians of the delta where black population was high and succeeded in getting the direct primary in 1902, a full year before Wisconsin's much publicized primary. In the next election, Vardaman won the governorship and put through an extensive program of social reform. He ended the convict-leasing system, increased school appropriations, regulated insurance companies, railroads, banks, and utilities, and advocated aid to cripples, child labor legislation, and a state school for the deaf and dumb.

Racism, Disfranchisement, and Segregation

Yet the Vardaman reform campaigns, like most of the reform campaigns in the southern states at the turn of the century, revealed another paradox of progressivism. They were reforms for whites only, and the campaigns were frequently charged with the emotionalism of white supremacy. The direct primary encouraged such mass appeals, and the real or imagined fear of black domination increasingly characterized political campaigns of southern Democrats after 1890. Until then, even though sympathetic understanding of the black question rarely existed, there had been little talk of disfranchisement. Blacks voted, and party organizers made good use of them. Indeed some Populist leaders at first promoted cooperation between black and white farmers, but as the Democrats saw their control threatened by the Populists and their allies, they started to use the white supremacy issue to stimulate racial antagonisms and thus split the opposition. As Populists saw apparent victories vanish owing to corruption at the polls and as they watched white leaders in the Black Belt march blacks to the ballot box and vote them, Populists fell prey to the argument that the black was in some way responsible for such abuses. Eliminate the black voter became the rallying cry, and you eliminate the basis for corruption. Under these circumstances, there were those who seriously considered black disfranchisement as a reform.

Thus began a parade as one southern state after another approved statutes or constitutional provisions that effectively disfranchised the black voter. By 1910, the process was completed. Mississippi had been among the leaders in 1890; Oklahoma was the last to succumb in 1910. Property qualifications, literacy tests, poll taxes, and "understanding" clauses effectively cut down the number of potential voters. To protect the illiterate, propertyless, white voter, "grandfather clauses" were sometimes included which made the restrictions not applicable to voters or descendants of voters who had had the ballot before 1867. Presumably the literacy test and understanding clauses were not discriminatory; however such provisions left much to the discretion of the registrars of voters, and these registrars saw to it that very few black people were registered to vote. Moreover as a final protection against black voting, Democratic organizations in the southern states described themselves as private political clubs whose membership could be restricted to whites only. Since most officials were actually chosen in the Democratic primary, blacks could be effectively excluded from participating in the election process.

Southerners were not alone in their endorsement of white supremacy. Organized labor throughout the nation not only opposed unrestricted immigration of foreigners on the grounds that they would undermine labor standards but discriminated against blacks in union membership. At the turn of the century, Maine, Michigan, Minnesota, Mississippi, Montana, Nevada, and Washington had restrictions on the voting of American Indians, and Nevada, California, and Oregon excluded Chinese from the suffrage. Federal statutes and judicial decisions had made clear that Asiatics were not eligible for naturalization. In California in 1906, a vigorous anti-Japanese campaign developed which included the segregation of all Oriental school children in San Francisco. The resulting storm of indignation in Japan was so great that President Theodore Roosevelt skillfully worked out an informal gentleman's agreement to restrict Japanese immigration, but he persuaded San Francisco to repeal its segregation ordinance. The issue persisted, however, and in 1913, despite objections from President Wilson, the California legislature passed a measure that prevented persons "ineligible" for citizenship, that is Orientals, from owning land. Much of the support for overseas expansion came from those who were convinced of the superiority of the white race. The idea of civilizing the "little brown brother," humanitarian though it might be, smugly judged that little brown brother inferior to his white brethren.

By the first decade of the twentieth century, the institutionalization of racial segregation had taken place, largely in the South, where about 90 percent of the blacks remained. The process began during the 1890s. In almost every conceivable way, state laws, city ordinances, or local regulations required that the white and black races carry on their public activities separately. The Supreme Court, more often than not, upheld this institutionalization under the guise of "separate but equal" arrangements. Blacks, to be sure, found it difficult to make a good legal case. Even if a black dared to bring a case before a court, lawyers were frequently not available; local courts were hostile; and appeals were expensive. Not until the founding of the National Association for the Advancement of Colored

People did an organization exist that had the resources to support any significant legal assaults on local law. The blacks themselves were torn between the view of Booker T. Washington who believed that "the agitation of questions of social equality is the extremist folly" and W. E. B. Du Bois who supported a demand for "every single right that belongs to a freeborn American, political, civil and social."

The founding of the National Association for the Advancement of Colored People was one of the few points where the progressive impulse worked for the improvement of race relations. The first decade of the twentieth century saw continual violence against black people. More than one thousand blacks were known to have been lynched between 1900 and 1914. Rioting increased. In Lincoln's home town of Springfield, Illinois, in 1908, a white mob roared through a black section, attacking the inhabitants and destroying businesses and residences. Roused by such wanton acts, W. E. B. Du Bois and other young blacks organized the Niagara movement in 1905–1906. They demanded the suffrage, freedom of speech and the press, and complete equality of treatment. The movement met annually for four years.

In the meantime, an increasing number of social workers and others were becoming aware of the plight of black people in northern cities. Local organizations in New York, for example, established settlement houses and playgrounds for blacks, worked for improved housing, and fought to remove discrimination and to obtain better employment opportunities. Thus the publicity given to the Springfield riot struck a responsive chord in those who already had black people on their consciences. The answer to the need, so characteristic of the early twentieth century, was organization, and several whites including Mary White Ovington, a New York social worker, and Oswald Garrison Villard, grandson of William Lloyd Garrison and editor of the *Nation,* issued a call for a national conference in 1909. Du Bois and others from the Niagara movement were invited, along with such whites as Jane Addams, William Dean Howells, and John Dewey. By May 1910, they had launched the National Association for the Advancement of Colored People with Moorfield Storey as president and Du Bois as director of publicity and research. The NAACP pledged itself to protect the civil rights of the blacks and to eliminate discrimination wherever it could be found. It established a periodical, *Crisis,* and the Legal Redress Committee. Under the editorship of Du Bois, *Crisis* campaigned against lynching and discrimination; while the committee, led by Arthur B. Spingarn, a white man, mobilized white and black lawyers to defend black people in the courts.

Undoubtedly the most important decision upholding segregation was in the case of *Plessy* v. *Ferguson,* decided in 1896. The *Plessy* case was a sequel of the civil rights cases of 1883, when the Supreme Court had declared the Civil Rights Act of 1875 unconstitutional. This act had attempted to establish the right of all persons regardless of race to "the full and equal enjoyment of the accommodations, advantages, facilities and privileges of inns, public conveyances . . . theaters and other places of public amusement." A majority of the Court had ruled this law unconstitutional on the grounds that the Fourteenth Amendment prohibited only state abridgment of privileges and immunities but did not prevent discrimination by private individuals. Implicitly segregation required by state law might therefore be considered unconstitutional. In *Plessy* v. *Ferguson,* however, the Court upheld a Louisiana law requiring separate railway coaches for blacks on the grounds that the Fourteenth Amendment had not "been intended to abolish distinctions based upon color, or to enforce . . . a commingling of the two races upon terms unsatisfactory to either. Laws permitting and even requiring, their separation in places where they are liable to be brought into contact do not necessarily imply the inferiority of either race . . ." and, according to Justice Brown for the majority, plainly came within the exercise of the states' police power.

Justice John M. Harlan vainly dissented. "What can more certainly arouse race hate," argued Harlan, "what more certainly create and perpetuate a feeling of distrust between these races, than state enactments which, in fact proceed on the ground that colored citizens are so inferior and degraded that they cannot be allowed to sit in public coaches occupied by white citizens?" The principle of separate but equal, however, had been established and would continue to be the law until 1954 when the Supreme Court reversed itself in *Brown* v. *Board of Education.* Clearly the position that progressive reform was for whites only met with little disapproval regardless of geographical section.

Socialism

The complexities of progressivism were made the more complex by the ingredient of socialism. Prior to the organization of the Socialist party of America in 1901, American socialism consisted of little more than anti-capitalistic splinters: immigrants who might have been followers in Europe of Karl Marx or Ferdinand Lassalle, an injection of anarchism in the 1880s, the utopian socialism of Edward Bellamy, Christian socialists who helped preach the social gospel, and various other groups and individuals. Prior to 1900, the Socialist Labor party provided some unity to these miscellaneous groups, but even that party had little influence until 1890 when it came under the direction of Daniel De Leon a brilliant authoritarian Marxist who preached revolution leading to a syndicalist society. De Leon, hostile to collaboration with existing trades unions, alienated some of his most able associates and usually stimulated discord rather than unity. In the meantime, Eugene Victor Debs, strong advocate of industrial unionism and founder of the American Railway union, had converted himself to socialism and had founded the Social Democratic party in 1898. Nominated for president by his party in 1900, Debs ran a vigorous race and won the support of a fraction of the Socialist Labor party which could not tolerate De Leon's authoritarianism. In 1901, dissidents from the Socialist Labor party, Debs's associates from the Social Democratic party, Bellamy Nationalists, industrial unionists, and a variety of the otherwise-minded gathered in convention to form the Socialist party of America.

The Socialist party made a greater appeal to minority groups than did other parties. It was perhaps the first political party to endorse women's rights. Frances Willard, long-time leader of the Women's Christian Temperance Union, was a socialist before the party existed. The same was true of Florence Kelley who was active in the National Consumers' League, and Margaret Sanger who used the *New York Call,* a leading socialist newspaper, as a mouthpiece for her first articles on birth control. The party was less hospitable to the blacks, but even on racial issues its position reflected less prejudice than other overwhelmingly white organizations of the early twentieth century. Although Victor Berger talked about the "yellow peril," W. D. Haywood denounced racism; Debs fought against discrimination; and William Walling was a leading organizer of the NAACP. Yet questions of minority rights became caught up in the factionalism of American socialism to such an extent that the party did not provide unrestricted welcome to "homeless" blacks.

Indeed inability to agree became one of the tragedies of American socialism. Some socialists were ideologically oriented and believed in the economic interpretation of history, the class struggle, and the inevitability of revolution, yet leftists such as Debs and W. D. Haywood, always an advocate of direct action, did not think that the revolution would be violent, and "few had more than the haziest intellectual acquaintance with theoretical Marxism." A strong faction, represented by Victor Berger endorsed a doctrine of gradualism; saw municipal reform as a move in the right direction; favored cooperation with unions, the farmers, and even middle-class intellectuals; and lacked confidence in the proletariat. They all seemed to agree on the evils of capitalism and the desirability of a political party and of industrial unionism.

Although factionalism characterized American socialism throughout its history, several historians associated with the so-called "New Left" argue that factionalism prior to the First World War was submerged in an optimistic assurance among party members that the demise of American capitalism was inevitable. They point to an apparent increase of socialist strength at least until 1912. A number of the leading muckrakers—Gustavus Myers, Upton Sinclair, Charles Edward Russell, among others—were socialists. Sinclair led in organizing the Intercollegiate Socialist Society in 1905 with the purpose of attracting college-educated men and women. The initial organization included intellectuals such as Charlotte Perkins Gilman, writer and lecturer, Clarence Darrow, lawyer and reformer, and Jack London, controversial novelist, and it was financed by George

Strobel, a jewelry manufacturer, and Rufus W. Weeks, a vice president
of the New York Life Insurance Company. By 1915, the society was
flourishing with sixty chapters in universities and colleges. Socialist
literature also flourished during this period. By 1912 there were at least
13 dailies and 262 English and 36 foreign language papers; one of these,
The Appeal to Reason, had a circulation of 761,747. In addition to the
newspapers there were more than 100 socialist periodicals. Although these
publications represented widely varied attitudes, they united in calling
for "tearing down the walls of capitalism."

One of the difficulties in accepting this optimistic picture of socialism
during the progressive era is that it seems to overlook the failure of the
party to win the support of the labor unions. Socialist influence probably
did increase in the established unions until 1912 and most socialist officials
were former laborers. Yet by favoring political action and insisting upon
industrial unionism, the socialists came into direct conflict with the
hierarchy of the AFL, which opposed a separate labor party and favored
craft unionism. In this conflict, the AFL won out. In some unions at least
they won out not because the workers expressed a theoretical preference
for that type of organization, but because their leaders, who initially had
been inclined toward socialism, finally rejected it. The leaders had become
convinced that it was too impractical, and that "pure and simple trade
unionism" would better provide material gains for the worker.

Not only did the socialists fail with the established unions, but they
failed in attracting those workers left outside the labor movement. Even
Debs, in 1904, agreed that the Socialist party had fallen down in this
respect and called for a "new revolutionary industrial union." The Industrial Workers of the World, launched in 1905, was an answer to this
plea. This new organization was designed as a union which would organize
all workers in an industry with the aim of eventually controlling that
industry. It opposed traditional politics as a means of gaining power, and,
in accord with the views of revolutionary syndicalism, believed that as
the misery of workers increased, they would engage in more strikes and
would finally seize power as established government became helpless.

Although the socialists and IWW's were in fundamental agreement on
certain basic ideas, they disagreed on too many practical details. They
agreed, as James Weinstein has put it, "that the industrial working class
was to be the key agent of revolutionary change, and that the experience
of unionism was the primary path to a socialist consciousness." The IWW,
however, refused both to cooperate in any way with the AFL and to
consider gaining power through electoral or parliamentary tactics. Many
socialists, on the other hand, were willing to use unions of the AFL,
opposed setting up rival unions, and were exceedingly flexible in their
politics.

Ironically, although the IWW preached a creed of labor solidarity, its
call was increasingly to forgotten workers: the millions of migrants,

"wifeless, homeless, semi-skilled or unskilled," living and working under horrifying conditions; the immigrant workers of the East and Midwest, repudiated by the AFL. The blacks, the Hindus, the Japanese, Chinese, and Filipinos, were welcomed by the IWW organizers who saw "no race problem," only "a class problem." The principle was the same when applied to women. If they were a "part of the army of labor," they were to be organized "with the men, just as they work with the men." "To the submerged millions of unskilled wage slaves," said Mr. IWW, Big Bill Haywood, "the Industrial Workers of the World makes its appeal, fully realizing that within this mass of despised humanity there is a latent force, which if exerted by themselves, will arouse their consciousness, their love of liberty . . . and lift their faces toward the sunlight of a new life of industrial freedom."

Where do the socialists and the IWW fit into the pattern of progressivism? Perhaps the only safe answer to that question is that there is no clear-cut answer. Progressives generally feared radicalism and the direct action of the IWW; yet many were seriously concerned about the plight of the down-trodden. Leaders such as Roosevelt, Wilson, and Brandeis had studied socialism and had rejected it as an alternative to capitalism; indeed they used socialism as a menace and a goad to promote progressive reform. Historians of these radical movements such as James Weinstein and Christopher Lasch have argued that the movements were viable alternatives which the majority of the middle class and the established wage earners unfortunately refused to adopt. Others such as Michael Bassett insist that the failure to make headway in the labor movement and the increasing factionalism were basic weaknesses. He shows that reformers, who had turned to socialism when the two political parties rejected them, found a more compatible home later in the Progressive party of Theodore Roosevelt or the Democratic party of Woodrow Wilson. Bassett argues that the war and postwar development hastened a decline that was already well under way. He would question the theory that the Socialist party and the IWW were actually viable alternatives for the great mass of Americans.

Progressivism in all its complexities may never be fully understood. The beginning of wisdom is to recognize how pluralistic that movement really was. It involved localities, states, regions, and the national government with hierarchies of leaders at every level. It involved leaders who were individualists and leaders who were playing roles shaped by their origins, training, and the groups with which they were associated. It involved professionalization, local, state, and national bureaucracies, and scientific management. It involved the country and the city, racial and ethnic minorities, religious denominations, socioeconomic classes, corporate structures, and lobbying organizations of an infinite variety. It involved coalitions, indeed different and changing coalitions depending upon what issue was at stake. Even if the status-anxiety thesis is used as a legitimate psychological interpretation, and there is even some question as to whether it is valid as a hypothesis, it has to be applied more specifically to different areas and to different groups and should be supplemented with other explanations.

Perhaps an explanation of progressivism does not require probing so deeply into human motivation. The confluence of such powerful factors as industrialism, urbanization, populism, human mobility, and scientific and technological development naturally promoted conflict and change. Although the most emotional issues of the day may have been local issues such as prohibition or blue laws that affected everybody, technological change and economic crises combined with political propaganda brought other issues such as railroad regulation and social reform home to others and resulted in the tendency to look for help at the next higher governmental level. The creation of new social structures does not necessarily require, although it may be enriched by, the explanations of a psychologist. It is perhaps significant that Richard Hofstadter himself did not include the status-anxiety thesis in an analysis of progressivism published eight years after the *Age of Reform.*

Undoubtedly motives of those who considered themselves progressives were mixed, and undoubtedly reforms were carried out by those whom reformers of a later day would hardly brand as progressives. At the same time only the cynic can fail to recognize the side of progressivism that was working for constructive change and social justice. The fact that reforms were sometimes supported by businessmen make them no less reforms. An increasing number of college-educated women, moreover, seemed inspired to right wrongs that a masculine society had created. Jane Addams at Hull House, Lillian Wald on Henry Street, Grace Abbott, directing Chicago's Immigrant Protective League, Julia Lathrop of the Children's Bureau, and many others gave a new tone to American reform. [As another dedicated settlement worker, Vida Scudder, put it, "Any woman feels restless unless she is taking care of somebody." And the women were not always alone!]

Bibliography

Page 59

For a stimulating interpretation of the historiography of progressivism, see Robert Wiebe, "The Progressive Years, 1900–1917," in William H. Cartwright and Richard L. Watson, Jr., eds., *The Reinterpretation of American History and Culture* (1973); David Kennedy's introduction to *Progressivism; the Critical Issues* (1971). Straightforward accounts of the era are George Mowry, *The Era of Theodore Roosevelt, 1900–1912* (1958) and Arthur S. Link, *Woodrow Wilson and the Progressive Era,*

1910–1917 (1954). A colorful account is Ray Ginger, *Age of Excess; the United States from 1877–1914* (1965); an excellent brief interpretation is Samuel P. Hays, *The Response to Industrialism, 1885–1914* (1957). Commentaries on important issues are in Otis L. Graham, Jr., *The Great Campaigns: Reform and War in America, 1900–1928* (1971). An unusual synthesis is Robert H. Wiebe, *The Search for Order: 1877–1920* (1967).

Pages 59–60

For the relationship between progressivism and "imperialism" or foreign policy, see, for example, William E. Leuchtenburg, "Progressivism and Imperialism: The Progressive Movement and American Foreign Policy, 1898–1916," *Mississippi Valley Historical Review,* 39 (December 1952), 483–504; John P. Mallon, "Roosevelt, Brooks Adams, and Lea: The Warrior Critique of the Business Civilization," *American Quarterly,* 8 (Fall 1956), 216–230; Barton J. Bernstein and Franklin A. Leib, "Progressive Republican Senators and American Imperialism, 1898–1916: A Reappraisal," *Mid-America,* 50 (July 1968), 163–205; John M. Cooper, Jr., "Progressivism and American Foreign Policy: A Reconsideration," *Mid-America,* 51 (October 1969), 260–277; Thomas J. McCormick, *China Market; America's Quest for Informal Empire, 1893–1901* (1967).

Page 60

For Daniel Aaron's unique definition of progressivism, see *Men of Good Hope; A Story of American Progressives* (1951), and for Gabriel Kolko, see *The Triumph of Conservatism: A Reinterpretation of American History, 1900–1916* (1963). See also Christopher Lasch, *The New Radicalism in America, 1889–1963; The Intellectual as a Social Type* (1965).

Page 61

For the middle class, status-anxiety thesis, see George Mowry, *The California Progressives* (1951); Alfred D. Chandler, Jr., "The Origins of Progressive Leadership," in Elting E. Morison, ed., *The Letters of Theodore Roosevelt,* vol. VIII (1954), pp. 1462–1465; and Richard Hofstadter, *The Age of Reform; From Bryan to F.D.R.* (1955).

Pages 61–62

For newspapers and periodicals, see W. A. Swanberg, *Citizen Hearst, A Biography of William Randolph Hearst* (1961); Lloyd R. Morris, *Postscript to Yesterday; America: The Last Fifty Years* (1947); Frank Luther Mott, *A History of American Magazines, 1885–1905,* vol. IV (1957); Theodore Bernard Peterson, *Magazines in the 20th Century* (1956).

Pages 62–63

For the muckrakers, see Louis Filler, *Crusaders for American Liberalism* (1950); Cornelius C. Regier, *The Era of the Muckrakers* (1932); David Chalmers, *The Social and Political Ideas of the Muckrakers* (1964);

Harold S. Wilson, *McClure's Magazine and the Muckrakers* (1970); Robert S. Maxwell, "A Note on the Muckrakers," *Mid-America*, 43 (January 1961), 55–60; Stanley K. Schultz, "The Morality of Politics: The Muckrakers' Vision of Democracy," *Journal of American History*, 52 (December 1965), 527–547. A classic is J. Lincoln Steffens' *The Autobiography of Lincoln Steffens* (1931), but sample Ella Winter and Granville Hicks, eds., *The Letters of Lincoln Steffens*, 2 vols. (1938); and then read Justin Kaplan, *Lincoln Steffens, A Biography* (1974).

Pages 63–64

For the history of women, first consult Anne Scott's chapter in Cartwright and Watson, eds., *The Reinterpretation of American History and Culture.* For individuals, see the impressive *Notable American Women, 1607–1950; A Biographical Dictionary*, 3 vols. (1971) edited by Edward T. James, Janet Wilson James, and Paul S. Boyer. I have used principally Eleanor Flexner, *Century of Struggle; The Woman's Rights Movement in the United States* (1959); Aileen S. Kraditor, *The Ideas of the Woman Suffrage Movement, 1890–1920* (1965); Anne Firor Scott, *The Southern Lady; From Pedestal to Politics, 1830–1930* (1970); and William H. Chafe, *The American Woman: Her Changing Social, Economic, and Political Roles, 1920–1970* (1972). See also James M. McGovern, "The American Woman's Pre-World War I Freedom in Manners and Morals," *Journal of American History*, 55 (September 1968), 315–333. The contribution of the social workers is well brought out in Allen F. Davis, *Spearheads for Reform; The Social Settlements and the Progressive Movement, 1890–1914* (1967). For "The Woman as Alien," see Christopher Lasch, *The New Radicalism in America*, pp. 38–68.

Page 64–65

For criticism of the status-anxiety and middle-class origins theses, see David Thelen, "Social Tensions and the Origins of Progressivism," *Journal of American History*, 56 (September 1969), 323–341; Robert W. Doherty, "Status Anxiety and American Reform: Some Alternatives," *American Quarterly*, 19 (Summer 1967), 329–337; William T. Kerr, Jr., "The Progressives of Washington, 1910–1912," *Pacific Northwest Quarterly*, 55 (January 1964), 16–27; E. Daniel Potts, "The Progressive Profile in Iowa," *Mid-America*, 47 (October 1965), 257–268; Richard B. Sherman, "The Status Revolution and Massachusetts Progressive Leadership," *Political Science Quarterly*, 78 (March 1963), 59–65; Jorgen Weibull, "The Wisconsin Progressives: 1900–1914," *Mid-America*, 47 (July 1965), 191–221; Wayne E. Fuller, "The Rural Roots of the Progressive Leaders," *Agricultural History*, 42 (January 1968), 1–13.

Pages 65–66

One of the most important books on progressivism is David P. Thelen's, *The New Citizenship; Origins of Progressivism in Wisconsin, 1885–1900*

(1972). For La Follette, see Thelen, *The Early Life of Robert M. La Follette, 1855-1884* (1966); Robert S. Maxwell, *La Follette and the Rise of the Progressives in Wisconsin* (1956); Belle C. and Fola La Follette, *Robert M. La Follette*, 2 vols. (1953).

Page 67

For a sampling of reform in other northern and western states, see Carl H. Chrislock, *The Progressive Era in Minnesota, 1899-1918* (1971); Agnes M. Larson, *John A. Johnson; An Uncommon American* (1969); Mowry, *The California Progressives;* Ransom E. Noble, *New Jersey Progressivism Before Wilson* (1946); Spencer C. Olin, Jr., *California's Prodigal Sons; Hiram Johnson and the Progressives, 1911-1917* (1968); Michael P. Rogin and John L. Shover, *Political Change in California; Critical Elections and Social Movements, 1890-1966* (1970); Thomas Richard Ross, *Jonathan Prentiss Dolliver; A Study in Political Integrity and Independence* (1958); A. Bower Sageser, *Joseph I. Bristow, Kansas Progressive* (1968); Walter I. Trattner, *Homer Folks, Pioneer in Social Welfare* (1968); Hoyt Landon Warner, *Progressivism in Ohio, 1897-1917* (1964); Robert F. Wesser, *Charles Evans Hughes; Politics and Reform in New York, 1905-1910* (1967); G. Wallace Chessman, *Governor Theodore Roosevelt; The Albany Apprenticeship, 1898-1900* (1965); Irwin Yellowitz, *Labor and the Progressive Movement in New York State, 1897-1916* (1965); Richard M. Abrams, *Conservatism in a Progressive Era; Massachusetts Politics, 1900-1912.*

Pages 67-70

For progressivism in the city, see Wayne Fuller, "The Rural Roots of the Progressive Leaders" (cited above); Roy Lubove, "The Twentieth Century City: The Progressive as Municipal Reformer," *Mid-America,* 41 (October 1959), 195-208; Lubove, *The Progressives and the Slums; Tenement House Reform in New York City, 1890-1917* (1962); Egal Feldman, "Prostitution, The Alien Woman, and the Progressive Imagination," *American Quarterly,* 19 (Summer 1967), 192-206; Julius Weinberg, "E. A. Ross: The Progressive as Nativist," *Wisconsin Magazine of History,* 50 (Spring 1967), 242-253; Peter J. Schmitt, *Back to Nature; The Arcadian Myth in Urban America* (1969).

For the urban reform organizations, see Frank M. Stewart, *A Half Century of Municipal Reform; The History of the National Municipal Reform League* (1950); and *Annals of the American Academy,* 4 (March 1894), 850-856, and *World Almanac, 1898,* p. 75. See especially the thesis of Samuel P. Hays in his "The Politics of Reform in Municipal Government in the Progressive Era," *Pacific Northwest Quarterly,* 55 (October 1964), 157-169, a thesis supported by James Weinstein in "Organized Business and the City Commission and Manager Movements," *Journal of Southern History,* 28 (May 1962), 166-182. For a different view, see J. Joseph Huthmacher, "Urban Liberalism and the Age of Reform,"

Mississippi Valley Historical Review, 49 (September 1962), 231–241, and *Senator Robert F. Wagner and the Rise of Urban Liberalism* (1968), supported by John D. Buenker in *Urban Liberalism and Progressive Reform* (1973); cf. Otis A. Pease, "Urban Reformers in the Progressive Era: A Reassessment," *Pacific Northwest Quarterly,* 62 (April 1971), 49–58. Studies of particular cities provide variations of the Hays-Huth-macher views: See James B. Crooks, *Politics and Progress; The Rise of Urban Progressivism in Baltimore, 1895–1911* (1968); Bonnie R. Fox, "The Philadelphia Progressives: A Test of the Hofstadter-Hays Theses," *Pennsylvania History,* 34 (October 1967), 372–394; Melvin G. Holli, *Reform in Detroit: Hazen S. Pingree and Urban Politics* (1969); Roy Lubove, *Twentieth Century Pittsburgh: Government, Business, and Environmental Change* (1969); Arthur Mann, *Yankee Reformers in the Urban Age* (1954); Zane L. Miller, *Boss Cox's Cincinnati; Urban Politics in the Progressive Era* (1968); Michael Rogin, "Progressivism and the California Electorate," *Journal of American History,* 55 (September 1968), 297–314; Arnold S. Rosenberg, "New York Reformers of 1914: A Profile," *New York History,* 50 (April 1969), 187–206; Jack Tager, *The Intellectual as Urban Reformer; Brand Whitlock and the Progressive Movement* (1968).

Pages 70–73

On the importance of prohibition as a social and political issue, see references for Paul Kleppner and Richard Jensen in chap. 4 below. Joseph R. Gusfield, *Symbolic Crusade; Status Politics and the American Temperance Movement* (1963); Richard L. Watson, Jr., ed., *Bishop Cannon's Own Story; Life as I Have Seen It* (1955); Robert A. Hohner, "Prohibition and Virginia Politics, 1901–1916," unpub. doctoral diss., Duke University, 1965, and "The Prohibitionists: Who Were They?" *South Atlantic Quarterly,* 68 (Autumn 1969), 491–505; Peter H. Odegard, *Pressure Politics, The Story of the Anti-Saloon League* (1928); James H. Timberlake, *Prohibition and the Progressive Movement, 1900–1920* (1963); Ross, *Jonathan Prentiss Dolliver;* David P. Thelen, "La Follette and the Temperance Crusade," *Wisconsin Magazine of History,* 47 (Summer 1964), 291–300; S. J. Mennell, "Prohibition: A Sociological View," *Journal of American Studies,* 3 (December 1969), 159–175.

Pages 73–75

The Gifford Pinchot quotations on conservation are from Grant McConnell, "The Conservation Movement—Past and Present," *Western Political Quarterly,* 7 (September 1954), 463–478. Note Thomas LeDuc's words of caution in "The Historiography of Conservation," *Forest History,* 9 (October 1965), 23–28, then compare J. Leonard Bates, "Fulfilling American Democracy: The Conservation Movement, 1907–1921," *Mississippi Valley Historical Review,* 44 (June 1957), 29–57, with Samuel P. Hays, *Conservation and the Gospel of Efficiency; The Progressive*

Conservation Movement, 1890–1920 (1959). See also Elmo R. Richardson, *The Politics of Conservation; Crusades and Controversies, 1897–1913* (1962); John R. Ross, " 'Pork Barrels' and the General Welfare: Problems in Conservation, 1900–1920," unpub. doctoral diss., Duke University, 1969; and Gordon B. Dodds, "The Stream-Flow Controversy: A Conservation Turning Point," *Journal of American History,* 56 (June 1969), 59–69. See especially Samuel Haber, *Efficiency and Uplift; Scientific Management in the Progressive Era, 1890–1920* (1964).

Pages 75–76

Samuel Hays stimulates all sorts of ideas about localities and regions with his "Political Parties and the Community-Society Continuum," in William N. Chambers and Walter Dean Burnam, eds., *The American Party Systems; Stages of Political Development* (1967); C. Vann Woodward's *Origins of The New South, 1877–1913* (1951) remains a masterful synthesis. On Populism and the election of 1896, see Robert F. Durden, *The Climax of Populism: The Election of 1896* (1965); for fusion in North Carolina, see Helen Edmonds, *The Negro and Fusion Politics in North Carolina, 1894–1901* (1951). For the statistics on cotton, see Harold U. Faulkner, *The Decline of Laissez Faire, 1897–1917* (1951). On tobacco, see Joseph C. Robert, *The Story of Tobacco in America* (1949); Nannie Mae Tilley, *The Bright-Tobacco Industry, 1860–1929* (1948); Harry H. Kroll, *Riders in the Night* (1965).

Pages 77–78

Sheldon Hackney's important book discusses the transition from *Populism to Progressivism in Alabama* (1969).

A seminal article was Arthur S. Link's, "The Progressive Movement in the South, 1870–1914," *North Carolina Historical Review,* 23 (April 1946), 172–195. Since then, books and articles have multiplied: A. D. Kirwan, *Revolt of the Rednecks; Mississippi Politics, 1876–1925* (1951); Keith L. Bryant, Jr., "Kate Barnard, Organized Labor, and Social Justice in Oklahoma During the Progressive Era," *Journal of Southern History,* 35 (May 1969), 145–164; Dewey W. Grantham, Jr., *Hoke Smith and the Politics of the New South* (1958); William F. Holmes, *The White Chief: James Kimble Vardaman* (1970); Raymond H. Pulley, *Old Virginia Restored; An Interpretation of the Progressive Impulse, 1870–1930* (1968); Jack Temple Kirby, *Darkness at the Dawning; Race and Reform in the Progressive South* (1972).

Pages 78–79

For racism and progressivism, see Paul Gaston, *The New South Creed; A Study in Southern Mythmaking* (1970); Lawrence J. Friedman, *The White Savage; Racial Fantasies in the Postbellum South* (1970); Hugh C. Bailey, *Liberalism in the New South: Southern Social Reformers and the Progressive Movement* (1969); and especially Bruce L. Clayton, *The Savage Ideal: Intolerance and Intellectual Leadership in the South, 1890–1914* (1972).

Pages 79–80

For black disfranchisement and the institutionalizing of discrimination in the South, see C. Vann Woodward, *American Counterpoint: Slavery and Racism in the North-South Dialogue* (1971); Rayford W. Logan, *The Negro in American Life and Thought: The Nadir, 1877–1901* (1954); Loren Miller, *The Petitioners; The Story of the Supreme Court of the United States and the Negro* (1966).

For organized labor and the black, see Herman D. Bloch, "Labor and the Negro: 1866–1910," *Journal of Negro History,* 50 (July 1965), 163–184; for state restrictions on voting, see the *World Almanac* for appropriate years; for the Japanese issue in California see Thomas A. Bailey, *Theodore Roosevelt and the Japanese American Crisis: An Account of the International Complications Arising From the Race Problem on the Pacific Coast* (1934); Raymond A. Esthus, *Theodore Roosevelt and Japan* (1966); Charles E. Neu, *An Uncertain Friendship: Theodore Roosevelt and Japan, 1906–1909* (1963); Arthur S. Link, *Wilson, the New Freedom* (1956). More generally, see Leon Wolff, *Little Brown Brother; How the United States Purchased and Pacified the Philippine Islands at the Century's Turn* (1961).

Pages 80–81

For the NAACP, see Charles F. Kellogg, *The NAACP, A History of the National Association for the Advancement of Colored People* (1967). For special studies on the city, see Gilbert Osofsky, *Harlem, The Making of a Ghetto 1890–1930* (1966) and Allan H. Spear, *Black Chicago: The Making of a Negro Ghetto, 1890–1920* (1967). See also Gilbert Osofsky, "Progressivism and the Negro: New York, 1900–1915," *American Quarterly,* 16 (Summer 1964), 153–168. A stimulating article on *Plessy* v. *Ferguson* is Barton J. Bernstein, "Plessy vs. Ferguson: Conservative Sociological Jurisprudence," *Journal of Negro History,* 48 (July 1963), 196–205.

Pages 81–84

An excellent one-volume survey of American socialism is David A. Shannon, *The Socialist Party of America; A History* (1955). The controversy over the "viability" of socialism can be followed in John Laslett, *Labor and the Left; A Study of Socialist and Radical Influences in the American Labor Movement, 1881–1924* (1970); D. H. Leon, "Whatever Happened to An American Socialist Party? A Critical Survey of the Spectrum of Interpretations," *American Quarterly,* 23 (May 1971), 236–258; James Weinstein, *The Decline of Socialism in America, 1912–1915* (1967); Michael Bassett, "The Socialist Party Dilemma, 1912–1914," *Mid-America,* 47 (October 1965), 243–256; Sally M. Miller, *Victor Berger and the Promise of Constructive Socialism* (1973). The quotations on the IWW's are taken from Philip S. Foner, *History of the Labor Movement in the United States; The Industrial Workers of the World, 1905–1917,* vol. IV (1965), pp. 114–129, 171; and Melvyn Dubofsky, *We Shall Be All; A History of the Industrial Workers of the World* (1969).

Pages 84-85

For Hofstadter's revised version of progressivism, see his introduction to a collection of documents, *The Progressive Movement, 1900-1915* (1963); see particularly David Thelen's review article "Modernization and Reform in the Progressive Era: An Essay Review," *Wisconsin Magazine of History*, 52 (Autumn 1968), 62-65; for an attempt at a synthesis, see John D. Buenker, "The Progressive Era: A Search for a Synthesis," *Mid-America*, 51 (July 1969), 175-193. Vida Scudder's comment is in Allen Davis, *Spearheads for Reform . . .*, p. 37. For a final note, see Peter J. Filene, "An Obituary for 'the Progressive Movement,' " *American Quarterly*, 22 (Spring 1970), 20-34.

4

National Government and National Power: The Era of Theodore Roosevelt, 1900-1909

To include the name of Theodore Roosevelt in a label descriptive of the first decade of the twentieth century is to raise questions about hero worship and exaggerating the role that any individual can play in a nation's life. Yet Roosevelt's significance makes it worth taking the risk of raising such questions, even though it should be obvious that numerous factors were at work in the late nineteenth and early twentieth centuries broadening the horizons of countless Americans and requiring them to look beyond their local communities. Concern about expanding industry, labor unions, periodic depressions, and urbanization developed, even as technological and scientific changes in transportation, communication, bookkeeping, and construction provided the means to find solutions to problems that these new developments posed. At the same time, social scientists were preaching people's ability to shape human progress, and researchers and planners were staffing bureaucracies in government, business, labor unions, farm organizations—indeed in all manner of reform and interest groups. A pervasive theme throughout the period was that problems that might have been considered local in the nineteenth century could be solved by referring them to a higher level of government. In the case of foreign policy, there was no question where responsibility lay.

Foreign and Military Policy

During the nineteenth century, the United States had enjoyed largely free military security. Except for the Indians and minor episodes with Mexico, there had been no serious external threat since the War of 1812. Nonetheless, certain principles of foreign policy attained the authority of doctrine. One of these principles, sometimes rather inaccurately called isolationism, included the "avoidance of permanent alliances" and the "abstention from the *ordinary* vicissitudes and the *ordinary* combinations and collisions of European politics and wars." Another principle, sometimes called freedom of the seas, involved the right of a neutral to trade with other neutrals or even belligerents in time of war while permitting vaguely defined restrictions by blockading powers. In foreign trade the United States had stood on the most favored nation principle, popularly known as "the open door," which called for "reciprocal equality of treatment without discrimination against the subjects or ships of any nation" anywhere. The United States opposed the transfer of "any European colonial dominions in the New World from one European sovereign to another" and, since President Monroe's famous message in 1823, opposed further colonization in the western hemisphere and intervention in the internal affairs of other nations.

That these principles had rarely been challenged during the nineteenth century resulted from the weakness of neighboring nations, the geographical isolation of the United States, and the world political situation. Partly through good fortune, partly through skillful politics and economic ingenuity, Great Britain maintained a predominant influence in world politics with its industrial supremacy, merchant fleet, financial resources, and navy. Even though British policy makers were unhappy about the developing power of the United States, goals of the two countries coincided at important points. They both favored a Europe balanced in power, that is, one not dominated by any one continental power, and most favored nation privileges in trade throughout the world. So long as these goals remained the same, the British fleet was serving, however accidentally, as the first line of the defense of the United States, while upholding Britain's position.

Behind this shield, the United States developed guidelines for its own defense. In the first place, only a tiny army was necessary, sufficient to maintain order, protect the frontier, keep up with military doctrine, and be ready to provide cadres for expansion if war should occur. In the second place, according to the militia act of 1792, every able-bodied man between the ages of eighteen and forty-five should be in the militia and prepared to spring to arms in an emergency. In the third place, a navy should be maintained to protect the seacoast and should be supplemented by seacoast fortifications manned by the army and the militia. Such a military policy put few demands upon resources, did not require a large military budget, did not interfere with the accumulation of capital, permitted light taxes, and encouraged a permissive government. Under the circumstances, the United States needed few professionals in either the military or the diplomatic service.

Throughout the nineteenth century, the United States was a world power only in the sense that it had the resources necessary to make it a world power and that it produced as much power as was needed. Yet events at the end of the century destroyed the "free security" which the nation had hitherto enjoyed. The world of the late nineteenth century was filled with tensions. In Europe armaments and nationalistic rivalries were building up, and the struggle for colonies and markets increased the tensions. Shifting alliances threatened the balance of power which had been one of the factors providing international stability. Three essentially new powers, Germany, Japan, and the United States, with overseas interests and dynamic economies, challenged British hegemony at different points throughout the world.

The United States with no significant overseas possessions before the turn of the century suddenly found itself with an overseas empire. In the light of its traditional policies of diplomacy and defense, it is difficult to explain why the United States acquired such colonies as Samoa, Wake, Hawaii, Guam, Puerto Rico, and the Philippines. The Marxist interpretation that explains imperialism in terms of a search for markets, raw materials, and opportunities to invest capital needs to be inspected in each case. The tremendous agricultural and industrial expansion of the late nineteenth century had altered the nation's place in world economic affairs. For seventy-five years after 1896 its balance of international payments was constantly favorable, and before the end of the nineteenth century it was recognized as a rival of Britain in the world market of manufactured goods. American overseas investment, less than $1 billion before 1900 had increased to $2.5 billion in 1908. The American economy needed markets, but not necessarily colonies, and businessmen could think up many economic reasons for avoiding war.

Yet it would be a mistake either to exaggerate the economic argument or to deny its validity too hastily. The economic motive might have been at the root of that vague concept, "manifest destiny," which had justified continental expansion in the middle of the nineteenth century. This concept included ideas of racial superiority and a conviction that American Protestantism and political institutions were superior, and thus that they should be extended throughout the continent, perhaps throughout the hemisphere. As westward expansion came to an end, the popularity of Darwinian notions of the struggle for existence and survival of the fittest and the evangelistic fervor of Protestant missionary societies made overseas expansion seem not only desirable but at least, to some, inevitable, particularly as other nations seemed to be gaining great prestige in the process.

Tied in with the complexity of the idea of mission, according to Richard Hofstadter, may have been a kind of "psychic" crisis for which jingoism gave relief. Frustrations and emotions generated through years of depression, agrarian unrest, and fear of the trusts on the one hand and anarchists on the other might have created an aggressiveness that could find an outlet in overseas conflict. These attitudes might have been stimulated by the journalism of publishers such as Willian Randolph Hearst who saw in jingoism a chance to increase the circulation of his newspapers. At the same time, a small group of intellectuals, including Admiral Alfred Thayer Mahan, Senators Henry Cabot Lodge and Albert Beveridge, Secretary of State John Hay, Whitelaw Reid, editor of the *New York Tribune,* and Theodore Roosevelt advocated an aggressive commercial policy carried out by an American merchant fleet, protected by an American navy with bases strategically located, particularly at Pearl Harbor and in the Caribbean, where they could protect an Isthmian canal. If attitudes become sufficiently pervasive, the politician sees his chance, and the entire paraphernalia of the American election process becomes involved. Foreign policy is a traditional way to distract attention from the domestic scene, and expansion can be an exciting issue.

Strategy is another ingredient that must be added to economic motivation, the idea of mission, the psychic crisis, and political opportunism. In the last analysis, Mahan and his cohorts were talking about security. A great nation takes bases to provide protection to either territory or trade routes or to prevent other nations from getting them. Certain strategic areas in another nation's control might be a threat to the United States, and the acquisition of Pago Pago, Pearl Harbor, and the Philippines could be explained almost entirely for reasons of strategy. Yet strategic motivation could easily be obscured by the rhetoric of manifest destiny and by party considerations and at the same time could be used as an excuse for economic expansion.

The same confused motivation underlay the extension of American influence into East Asia and into Latin America at the turn of the century. In East Asia, traditional American commercial policy was that of the most favored nation; during the closing years of McKinley's administration the name "open door" was applied to this policy, and in 1900, Secretary of State John Hay attempted to restate this policy in terms much more sweeping than other nations were willing to endorse and the United States was willing to enforce. In addition to the traditional demand for equality of commercial opportunity, Hay had attempted to put the prestige of the United States behind the principle of the territorial integrity of China. Thus the United States found itself in the midst of a game of power politics in which so far Great Britain, Russia, and Japan were playing the leading roles.

The Monroe Doctrine too was in the process of undergoing modification. In 1895 a boundary dispute between Venezuela and Great Britain had drawn in the United States, ostensibly to uphold the principles of the Monroe Doctrine but also to protect possible American commercial interests there. In stating the position of the United States, Secretary of State Richard Olney broadened the traditional concepts of nonintervention and noncolonization. As he put it, "The United States is practically sovereign on this continent, and its fiat is law upon the subjects to which it confines its interposition." Olney's statement described a policy of unilateral power, and with the end of the Spanish-American War this policy expanded. Not only did the United States retain Puerto Rico, but it compelled Cuba to include in her constitution, adopted in June, 1901, certain provisions that Senator Orville Platt had added as an amendment to the Army Appropriation bill of the same year. These provisions included an authorization for the United States to maintain law and order in Cuba and to preserve Cuban independence and an agreement on the part of Cuba to provide the United States with a coaling station or naval base, thus making possible the building of the naval base at Guantanamo. Actually the policy of the Monroe doctrine was being converted into a Caribbean policy, which had as its aim the construction of a canal, owned, operated, and defended by the United States.

Political Parties and Congress

The increasingly dynamic nature of these domestic and foreign problems, interrelated and increasingly materialistic in character, called for new approaches on the part of political parties and of the governing elites who would occupy the two houses of Congress and the executive branch of the federal government. A big question became, therefore, which political party would persuade the voters that it could best confront the new problems of American society. Professional politicians were aware that fundamental changes had been taking place in the political system. They were seeing new, principally economic issues breaking down party differences which locally had frequently been based on ethnic, religious, and cultural questions such as prohibition. The trick of stimulating party loyalty by bands, torchlight processions, and emotional orations was giving way to finding and capturing the wavering voter by polls, persuasive literature, and discussion groups. From the end of Reconstruction to the 1890s the faithful of the two parties had battled it out on almost equal terms. In the elections of 1890 and 1892, however, the Democrats, seeming to grasp the essentials of the new politics first, overwhelmingly carried Congress and elected Cleveland president.

Then the depression of 1893 hit. Within a year the Democratic party was in a shambles, and the Republicans carried out one of the most sensational political turnovers in history. In 1894, they packed the House with 244 representatives to only 104 Democrats, more than reversing the previous House, and in 1896, Republican McKinley was overwhelmingly elected President of the United States. From then until 1911, except in the South, Republicanism dominated. Few states, outside of the South, went Democratic in presidential elections. Republicans controlled both houses of Congress with fifteen states having solidly Republican delegations, while only nine southern states had solidly Democratic delegations. The principal northern cities (Chicago, Philadelphia, Pittsburgh, Detroit, Cleveland, Baltimore, St. Louis, Boston, Milwaukee, San Francisco, Los Angeles, and New York) went almost overwhelmingly Republican in all four elections, although Baltimore went Democratic in one, while New York went Democratic in 1896 and Boston in 1896 and 1908.

Somehow the Republicans, taking advantage of depression conditions in the mid-1890s and the split between gold and silver Democrats, had succeeded in building a successful coalition. They had retained the basis of their post–Civil War strength, the veterans who "voted as they had fought," and the white, Anglo-Saxon, evangelical Protestants of the North and West. More importantly they had cut into the Democratic party by offering, as Richard Jensen has put it, "pluralism to the American people. . . . Every occupation, every religion, every industry, every section would receive fair treatment, with the protective tariff serving as an umbrella for all." in 1896 Bryan appealed to the farmers, the workers, the small businessmen to support him in a fight against immorality and the money trust and for free silver and other reforms. In spite of an unprecedented campaign, his moralistic crusade failed to convince the workers that he understood their problems, and the economic radicalism with which he surrounded himself frightened not only businessmen but farmers almost everywhere except on the great plains and in the South. In the meantime, McKinley's well-financed campaign had produced literature for everyone and even attracted votes from ethnic groups, such as the Germans, which had hitherto been strongly Democratic. Democratic strength was ominously sectional—in the South and in the plains and mining states west of the Missouri River.

McKinley won overwhelmingly, and his victory was one of brilliant party organization and brilliant campaign techniques. Yet paradoxically that victory marked the end of a half-century or more when party loyalty was perhaps the most important ingredient in electioneering. Unlike other organizations, political parties did not become more centralized in the early twentieth century. Moreover, with the sectional orientation of the parties, local competition and voter participation declined. Twentieth-century politics was less democratic, in the sense of the percentage of voter participation, than the nineteenth had been. It showed less respect for the party boss and more for the independent voter. Even McKinley, by appealing to all groups regardless of party, encouraged a decline in party loyalty. At the same time, the campaign that Mark Hanna planned succeeded in convincing people of wealth that protection against alleged economic and social radicalism lay in Republicanism.

The political changes of the 1890s provided the base for development of national power in the twentieth century. To a considerable extent congressmen remained the plenipotentiaries of their local constituencies, and these remained largely controlled by rural voters. The candidate for the presidency, on the other hand, appealed to the national electorate and emphasized his stand on national issues. A presidential candidate who committed himself on issues in order to convince a national electorate might find himself at odds with congressmen of his own party who came from quite different constituencies. At the same time, the war with Spain, the acquisition of an overseas empire, and the concern over overseas trade introduced issues which the executive was particularly qualified to exploit.

The parties were forced to take a stand on issues, but actually the platforms of the parties were more an indication of what issues were deemed important than of how presidential candidates stood on them. The platform was designed to alienate as few party men as possible and to attract as many independent votes as possible. In the period between 1900 and 1908, the platforms pointed to issues of foreign policy, of the tariff, of trusts, and of conservation as being important. They grappled increasingly with labor problems, the Democrats even proposing in 1908 a National Bureau of Public Health to regulate conditions in factories, mines, and tenements. For the farmers, tariff tinkering was a favorite device, but good roads and rural free delivery were likewise considered important.

These platforms were not dynamic documents and were probably not intended to be. That lack of dynamism, in fact, was quite in accord with the views of those who held the principal positions of power in Congress during much of the opening decade of the century. The Republicans were safely in control until 1911. In 1901, they had a safe margin in the House and a two-to-one margin in the Senate. The great majority of the congressmen were born in communities of fewer than 2,500 in population. They were well educated, approximately 70 percent of the representatives had gone beyond high school, about that many had been admitted to the bar, and most of them had held an elective office before coming to Congress. The Senate showed the same kind of distribution in relationship to the population. Of the eighty-two members, twenty-six came from places with fewer than 2,500 in population, fifty-four were lawyers; thirty-two of them were under sixty years old, but ten were between seventy and eighty. Although fifty-two of them were in their first term, fourteen had served more than eighteen years, and five more than twenty-four. In short, the principal legislative branches of the government contained men of education and experience, who spent little more than half their time at the job of legislating. Because Washington was exceedingly hot in the summer, Congress was rarely in session from the first of July to December. From 1899 to 1909, it met only nine or ten months out of the twenty-four that made up a session.

By the late 1890s, a pattern had emerged in the organization of Congress.

Legislative leadership rested in the Senate, largely because of the retirement of colorful Thomas B. Reed, who as Speaker of the House in the 1880s and 1890s, had given the House as much prestige as the Senate. The recognized leader of the Senate was Nelson W. Aldrich, who in 1899, at the age of fifty-eight, became head of the prestigious Committee on Finance. Aldrich divided his time between his numerous business and banking interests and politics. Supported by the Rhode Island Republican machine, he served a term in the House in 1879 and then in 1881 was elected to the Senate. He was an impressive six-footer, persuasive on the floor and in committee, skillful in debate when necessary, and thoroughly familiar with the details of industry and finance. A millionaire businessman himself, he believed firmly in Darwinian natural selection and was convinced that the future of the United States depended upon "the progress and prosperity of our manufacturing."

Aldrich's closest associates were William B. Allison of Iowa, John C. Spooner of Wisconsin, and Orville Platt of Connecticut. The "father of the Senate," chairman of the Republican caucus, of the Steering Committee, and of the Committee on Committees, the seventy-year-old Allison had moved into the Senate in 1872 after ten years in the House. For years he had dominated politics in Iowa. A suave man of "easy manners but positive convictions," few had more friends in Congress. Spooner, formerly active in lumbering and as a railway counsel, was chairman of the Rules Committee. A brilliant debater and hard worker, he had influence with his colleagues because of his knowledge of the law. The oldest of the four was Platt of Connecticut. He was seventy-three in 1900 and had entered the Senate in 1879. A high protectionist and expansionist, he opposed legislation that might "hamper business in any way" or anything that smacked of radicalism.

By 1900, Aldrich, Allison, Spooner, and Platt had been associated for fifteen years, and they were to be associated for five more. Young Albert J. Beveridge, elected to the Senate in 1900, marveled at the way in which "the Four," as they were called, dominated the Senate machinery. They and other committee chairmen were men of power, and not a single one of them could by any stretch of a definition be considered a progressive or a reformer. It would be difficult to identify any member of the Senate, Republican or Democrat, who had that kind of reputation in 1901.

Enter Theodore Roosevelt

And certainly, the president-re-elected would not be inclined to stir Congress out of its accustomed ways significantly. Even though McKinley had controlled his party and had cut loose from traditional foreign policy, he represented caution and conservatism and was a much-loved president rather than an imaginative one. At this point, those who like to speculate on the role of chance in history can have a field day: how McKinley's first-term vice president died in office, making a replacement on the ticket in 1900 necessary, how a combination of circumstances put Theodore Roosevelt on the ticket, and how an assassin's bullet cut McKinley down before his second term had been launched. No anarchist, presumably a foe of governmental restraints, ever made a greater mistake. Although few presidents have stirred up more controversies than the Republican Roosevelt, there can be little disagreement that his presidency immeasurably strengthened the power of that office and that national power grew in giant steps during his tenure.

At forty-three, Roosevelt was the nation's youngest president. He had come from a family of wealth and position, one proud of the nation's heritage and steeped in a tradition of public service and noblesse oblige, yet one also blessed with a sense of cosmopolitanism based upon an ancestral diversity of blood, religious denomination, and of occupation.

Sixteen years before, after completing two terms in the New York State Legislature, Roosevelt had written, "I have very little expectation of being able to keep on in politics. . . . I will not stay in public life unless I can do so on my own terms; and my ideal, whether lived up to or not is rather a high one." He was then all of twenty-five years old. By the time he was forty-two, he had written approximately twenty full-length books, innumerable articles, editorials, and book reviews on a wide variety of subjects. He had been defeated in a campaign for mayor of New York, served three years in the state legislature, six years as civil service commissioner (1889–1895), two as New York police commissioner (1895–1897), one as assistant secretary of the navy, fought in the Spanish-American War, and returned in time to be elected governor of the state of New York in the fall of 1898. He had spent spare moments reading books on subjects that ranged from Kipling to Brooks Adams, in body-punishing exercises to keep fit, and in relaxing in the Dakota territory by hunting bear. He was a historian and a naturalist.

But in spite of his intellectual interests, the fact remains that by profession Roosevelt was a politician. He entered politics upon graduating from Harvard in 1880. He joined the Republican party because, as he said in his autobiography, "at that day, in 1880, a young man of my bringing up and convictions could join only the Republican party." Attention to political facts of life proved to be one of the most consistent yet controversial aspects of his career. Although it kept him in hot water with the reformers and good government clubs, he was convinced that it accounted for many of his constructive achievements. As he saw it, a person should "gladly do the thing that is next, when the time and the need come together." He frequently assailed those who thought of the future without considering what was actually attainable. A position, such as the governorship or the presidency, he insisted, was a party position and thus required working with the organization and occasional compromise with principle.

When Roosevelt looked back at the period of his governorship from the vantage point of the postpresidential years, he concluded that his principal concerns had been morality and honesty but that he had not really been aware of the complexities and inequalities of late nineteenth-century America. Certainly his campaign in 1900 bore out his own conclusion. He did not give the impression of being particularly concerned with problems of labor and capital and of unemployment. When he referred to these subjects, his approach seemed to be either that of the social Darwinian, who saw such conditions as inevitable, or that of a paternalist who blamed the individuals concerned for hardships suffered. He expressed hatred for anything that smacked of radicalism, and he denounced as "crude and vicious" any theories that might lead to class conflict. He admitted the existence of some evils, but he gave the impression that most of these could be removed "only through that capacity for steady, individual self-help which is the glory of every true American, and can no more be done away with by legislation than you could do away with the bruises which you receive when you tumble down, by passing an act to repeal the law of gravitation." Yet he was concerned with conditions that he saw around him. Disease-ridden tenements, poverty, alliances between politicians and wealthy businessmen puzzled and infuriated him.

He groped for solutions. By 1894 he was denying that state legislation on economic and social matters would necessarily result in a diminution of "vigorous originality" or "speculative thought." Although theoretically having little sympathy with organized labor, he met informally with labor leaders while he was police commissioner and sought their advice while governor. His love for the outdoors early converted him to state support of conservation, and as governor of New York he was able to put some of his ideas into practice. In 1900 he made his position clear to the National Irrigation Congress, assuring them that "storing the floods and preserving the forests" were vital necessities. Private enterprise, he said, probably could not do the job, and even if it could, he added, the task should not be trusted to private hands. As governor he grappled with the "trust" problem. In 1899, he considered agitation against trusts "largely unreasonable." Existing misery and injustice, he had concluded, resulted from human failure or the "operation of nature's laws." Yet he saw "a very unpleasant side to this overrun trust development."

In his last years as governor he tried to explain his sentiments to the Platt machine which was alarmed by Roosevelt's "impulsiveness and . . . alliance with labor agitators, social philosophers, taxation reformers and the like":

> I want to be perfectly sane in all of these matters but I do have a good deal of fellow feeling for our less fortunate brothers, and I am a good deal puzzled over some of the inequalities in life, as life now exists. I have a horror of hysterics or sentimentality, and I am about

the last man in the world who sympathizes with revolutionary tactics, or with the effort to make the thrifty . . . go down to the level of the unthrifty. . . . All I want to do is cautiously to feel my way to see if we cannot make the general conditions of life a little easier.

As with most public figures, it is difficult to get beneath the surface of Roosevelt. How much of the thousands of speeches that he made and of the thousands of letters that he wrote was just rhetoric? Yet his political success was based upon much more than rhetoric and political maneuverings—it was based largely upon the enthusiasm that he inspired in people as varied as the man from the slums, Jacob Riis, and the fastidious New Englander, Henry Cabot Lodge. Roosevelt had some qualities that were unattractive. He blustered. He could see little good in those with whom he disagreed, whether Democrat, socialist, mugwump, anti-imperialist, or Henry James. He denounced them as traitors, cads, snobs, hypocrites, and scoundrels. He was egotistical. He was convinced that he deserved a congressional Medal of Honor. But he was aware of many of these foibles. He was humble about some things, and he had an appealing habit of enjoying jokes at his own expense.

But such characteristics add to the caricature. They hide qualities that must have been sensed by those who heard what he said, read what he wrote, and voted for him. One of these qualities has to do with his attitudes toward other people. Although he was intolerant of those who disagreed with him, he was equally intolerant toward discrimination based upon race or creed. On one occasion he boiled over at a man who by implication objected to Roman Catholics on the New York police force:

> You complain that we keep a lot of "drunken Roman Catholics" on the Police Force. As fast as I can I will turn them out, because they are drunkards, not because they are Roman Catholics; and at the same time I will turn out the drunken Protestants. You can guarantee that just as long as I have any say in the Board, the Catholic who does his duty will stand on precisely the same level with the Protestant or Jew or agnostic who does his duty.

In theory his attitude toward racial problems was much the same as that toward creed. He believed that every individual should be treated with the respect due a fellow human being. His children went to school with black children; he believed that blacks should have "an exact equality of right with their white neighbors," and as governor he appointed them to positions of trust. At the same time, he was firmly convinced of the superiority of the white race and especially of that part of it which spoke English and believed that it should be dominant in the Western Hemisphere.

The determination that the "English-speaking race" should be supreme helps to explain Roosevelt's belligerent concept of foreign policy. He much preferred dabbling in foreign policy to coping with problems of franchises, police departments, and sewers. He was working for a war with Spain a year before it happened. To him pacifists were at the very least decadent idealists, if not traitors.

Even though there was a boyish enthusiasm for matters that had to do with war or foreign policy, it is hardly accurate to refer to his ebullience as delayed adolescence. He showed too much understanding of wars and their results, of power politics, and of the balance of power. Except in his emotional public utterances, he demonstrated an understanding of world problems that could hardly be matched by any president including Wilson and FDR.

Roosevelt: Party Leader and Administrator

Roosevelt's succession to the presidency led to consternation in the minds of those who had adjusted themselves to the stability and conservatism of McKinley: the new president gave assurances that he would continue his predecessor's policies, and the leading newspapers approved of such a procedure. Moreover, even those who distrusted Roosevelt must have wondered what even such an unconventional president could do. The Republican party seemed in safe hands. Mark Hanna had developed a superb organization, and Hanna himself was now in the Senate. No legislation could be passed without the consent of Congress; the "Four" were in charge there; and it must have seemed inconceivable that a forty-three-year-old New Yorker would have a chance of doing very much that the congressional leadership disapproved.

No summary can adequately treat the complexities of a presidential administration. Yet if there is to be any understanding of decision making, it must be remembered that many things were going on at the same time, that some decisions were made after much more study than others, and that issues which may seem important after the event may have seemed of little if any importance at the time to the rancher in Wyoming, the tobacco-grower in Virginia, or the millworker in Massachusetts.

Yet the diversity of the problems with which the young president was concerned as he moved into the White House gave some indication of what he considered the scope of national power to be: immigration, business ethics, labor legislation, Merchant Marine, currency, the tariff, railroad regulation, conservation of natural resources, Cuba, the Philippines, China, the Isthmian Canal, a trans-Pacific cable, and the armed services.

No president, except one with supreme self-confidence, could confront such diverse problems with equanimity. Roosevelt had the self-confidence. He considered himself engaged in a fight for morality, and he was satisfied with his own definition of morality. At the same time he admitted that he would attempt only what was both right and feasible, and would plan, as he put it, "to go a little ahead of my party in the right direction, but not so far ahead that they won't follow me."

To a professional politician with presidential ambitions such as Roosevelt, at least two political facts of life must have been perfectly clear. Although he had a party majority in Congress, he would have to reassure the leadership, at least at first, in order to get a program through. At the same time, if he were to put his own program through, he would have to be elected president in his own right, and that would mean obtaining control of the machinery of the national party.

Perhaps nothing so well demonstrates the typical Roosevelt as his techniques in becoming party leader. He believed in civil service reform. Indeed, as civil service commissioner he had turned a moribund office upside down and made a record which, according to one assessment, "would have perpetuated his memory as a secondary figure of substantial accomplishment" even if he had performed no "other service to the American nation." As a professional politician, however, he was willing to use whatever means were available to make himself actual as well as titular leader of his party. Within hours of McKinley's death, he wrote to Booker T. Washington about appointments in the South, and before a month was out, he was deep in the politics of Colorado and New York. "Every day or two," as the *Detroit News* put it, "he rattles the dry bones of precedent and causes sedate Senators and heads of departments to look over their spectacles in consternation." He consulted the professionals, both local and congressional, but he appointed whom he pleased. In the South, he appointed a good many blacks to office, thus enraging some of the southerners, but most of his appointments there were white, some of them "gold" Democrats whom he thought might be lured into the Republican party. Some of his appointments made advocates of "good government" cringe. In Pennsylvania, he supported the friends of Senator Matthew S. Quay, a notorious boss, rather than those thought to be more in the traditions of the civil service, thus gaining support from the strongest organization in that overwhelmingly Republican state. He was almost equally successful in an even more difficult situation in his own state of New York.

Yet the Roosevelt haters could not obscure what Roosevelt actually accomplished in the way of improved administration. Although Roosevelt's position on some phases of the reform movements, such as tariffs, taxes, banks, and even trusts, may have been uncertain, he was unquestionably on the side of efficiency, scientific management, and cost accounting. Such goals were not ideological, but they could be interpreted as moral, and Roosevelt may have recognized that he could go all out to obtain them and retain the support of liberals and conservatives alike who were against sin.

Roosevelt's contributions as an administrator may have exceeded those of all other presidents: his Civil Service Commission was a strong one and, perhaps because it consisted of his friends, the members found it "an unalloyed delight" to serve under him. The quality of his appointments was, in general, high. He appointed some political hacks for political reasons, it is true, but these were overwhelmed by other "eager, high-minded, and efficient . . . public servants." When Roosevelt came into office, there were approximately 240,000 federal workers with fewer than one-half under the merit system. By the time he left the presidency, there were approximately 357,000 federal workers, and approximately 60 percent were under that system.

He was determined to make government service both more attractive and more productive. One of the most important moves in this direction was his appointment of a Committee on Department Methods in 1905, known as the Keep Committee, charged with finding out "what changes are needed to place the conduct of the executive business of the Government in all its branches on the most economical and effective basis in the light of the best modern business practice." He encouraged the development of a career foreign service, reformed the consular service and the forest service, developed meat inspection, and significantly strengthened the administrations of the army and the navy.

These impressive accomplishments in administration and party organization provided only a base for actions in domestic and foreign affairs upon which the reputation of an administration rests, in the last analysis. An extrovert, Roosevelt sometimes complained mightily at being limited by others in his performance as president, but he knew the limitations imposed by Congress and the committee chairman in getting legislation passed. In spite of his restiveness, he respected power and thus turned to the "Four" for advice shortly after McKinley's death. He grew to have increasing respect for Aldrich, Allison, Spooner, Platt, Lodge, and Hanna, as well as for the rather tough-talking, cigar-chewing Joe Cannon, Speaker of the House. Much as he differed with them on specific questions, he considered them the leaders, and, as he put it "their great intelligence and power and their desire . . . to do what is best for the government, make them not only essential to work with, but desirable to work with."

Establishing control over his party and a working relationship with Congress were only elementary requirements for a positive administration. Equally important was the understanding that the United States was divided up into governmental units not only of states and territories but also of interests and that these interests frequently were represented by pressure groups. These pressure groups were becoming increasingly numerous and influential—the National Association of Manufacturers, the American Federation of Labor, the Grange, the Antisaloon League, the Grand Army of the Republic, the American Woman's Suffrage Association, and many others were essential ingredients in the legislative process and, what is more, every prominent issue such as roads, labor legislation, foreign trade, and national defense created additional organizations which in some instances might be more influential than a political party at a given time.

Roosevelt: Business and Labor

The relationship between business and government was of particular importance during the age of Roosevelt. In the minds of business leaders, Robert Wiebe has suggested, American society consisted of various semi-autonomous power blocs. The business world itself included many groups, depending upon size, product, and geographical location. There were also labor blocs and farm blocs. The federal government was one of these blocs and necessarily had to negotiate with the other power blocs while they lobbied for political preferment. When Roosevelt came to office, Wiebe concluded, "Wall Street's leaders ranked the government among the second-rate powers."

Roosevelt changed this relationship, although the new relationship was tricky and not subject to easy interpretation. The term *trust buster* obscures Roosevelt's attitude. Certainly from the time that he became president, he accepted the idea that large business combinations might be desirable so long as they were regulated for the public welfare. His initial program as president included establishing a Department of Commerce and Labor, giving priority in the Department of Justice to cases relating to the antitrust laws, and prohibiting railway rebates by statute. Of these the most controversial proved to be the establishment of the Department of Commerce and Labor because of the provision to include in the department a Bureau of Corporations designed to accumulate information about interstate corporations. Roosevelt's idea was that the president would use this information to curb the "bad trusts," but that otherwise the information would be confidential. Opposition in the Senate from those who feared the power of the bureau came from business interests led by Senator Matt Quay of Pennsylvania. At the same time, smaller business represented in the National Association of Manufacturers lobbied for the bill. Roosevelt skillfully made use of these differences and the distrust of the Rockefeller interests, which opposed the bill, to rally popular support, and both houses of Congress passed the measure as the president wanted it.

The Bureau of Corporations met with mixed success. Publicity did not always work, and the interpretations of the data were at times open to question. Nevertheless corporate abuses were publicized; data accumulated by the bureau was used in moving against the trusts; and on the whole the staff was able and efficient. At the same time, some of the biggest businesses found it possible to work with Roosevelt and the bureau. George Perkins, a friend of Roosevelt and a partner in the House of Morgan, had supported the bureau from the beginning. Perkins also worked closely with Judge Elbert Gary, chairman of the Board of United

States Steel, one of Morgan's principal business interests. Gary was able
to work out an agreement with Roosevelt to the effect that the files of
the corporation would be turned over to the bureau, but that the president
would "arbitrate any differences between U.S. Steel and the bureau." A
similar agreement was worked out with International Harvester, a corporation organized by George Perkins.

By these agreements, Roosevelt worked himself into a position that
was easily misunderstood. The businessmen involved interpreted them as
meaning that, in return for the information, the bureau would alert them
to wrongdoing and permit changes in procedures, so that court action
would not be necessary. In short, the agreements would serve as buffers
between the businesses and the courts. Roosevelt never accepted this
interpretation and always considered that the government must be stronger
than private business. However, by trusting his own judgment in his
negotiations with these power blocs, he laid himself open to legitimate
charges of favoritism and bad judgments in his relations with J. P. Morgan
and Company.

At the same time that the legislative battles over the bureau were taking
place, the Roosevelt administration had launched a frontal attack at one
of the pillars of Morganism. The essence of Morganism was devotion to
"free" competitive enterprise. Among his favorite expressions on matters
of business policy were "unification," "peace," "order," "stabilization,"
and "centralized control." Such ideas undoubtedly explained his part
in creating the Northern Securities Corporation, a railroad corporation
which might have dominated the transportation of the Northwest. The
other creators of this holding company were James J. Hill and Edward H.
Harriman. Such was the reputation of this trio that the question was
raised as to whether such a combination might eventually control the
entire United States.

In the meantime, Roosevelt groped for a sensible antitrust policy. He
knew that the attitude and power of Aldrich, Spooner, and company in
the Senate, made it unlikely that legislation more elaborate than that
creating the Bureau of Corporations would be passed. Yet he had the
machinery in his Department of Justice to move against combinations,
and he knew enough of previous Supreme Court decisions to sense that a
vigorous prosecution might be successful. Moreover, from the point of
view of the practical politician, Northern Securities made an attractive
victim because of its unpopularity in the West.

The decisive issue may well have been a question of power. Roosevelt
was convinced that an industry should not be stronger than the United
States government, and he proposed to find out whether big business
could be controlled. He later said, "It was useless to discuss methods of
controlling big business by the National Government until it was definitely
settled that the National Government had the power to control it."
Northern Securities was big business personified. Thus the Department

of Justice launched a suit against it on March 2, 1902, and two years later, the Supreme Court upheld a decree of the Circuit Court which declared that the Northern Securities Corporation was in constraint of trade and therefore illegal.

The significance of this decision went far beyond the legal intricacies of the case. The year 1903 marked an end to a six-year period of rapid incorporation of large holding companies. In the same year Congress provided unprecedented appropriations for antitrust enforcement; it provided, in the Expediting Act, special procedures which would give antitrust action preference; and with the Bureau of Corporations it provided an institution charged with gathering data which could be used to launch cases. Following the E. C. Knight case, in the late nineties, a series of cases had provided the base for most of the antitrust activity of the twentieth century: the constitutionality of the Sherman Act itself, the expanding interpretation of the commerce clause, and the significance of the reasonableness of restraints on trade. The Northern Securities case climaxed these cases. Although it was legally not so significant as the others, it popularized the antitrust question; it showed that the Roosevelt Administration was willing to enforce the law and that the government could successfully confront the Morgans, Hills, and Harrimans; it received dramatic treatment in the press and by the president; and Congress gave its support. In short, "anti-trust was institutionalized."

The Northern Securities case had no more than been launched in the spring of 1902 when a crisis developed in the coal fields of Pennsylvania. As in the question of business consolidation, Roosevelt was grappling for a solution to the problems of labor, particularly organized labor. He disliked labor's becoming involved in politics, opposed violence in strikes, and talked about the open shop. Yet he insisted on labor's right to organize "without illegal interference from either capitalists or nonunion men." He believed that the growth of labor unions was just as inevitable as growth in industry. He consulted labor leaders, saw the need of constant study, and feared that if labor policy were left to reactionaries, disaster would result. Roosevelt's position was, as he put it in the campaign of 1904, to give labor a "square deal."

The crisis of 1902 occurred after several years of significant development in labor-management relations in the coal fields. Early in 1898 a conference system of settling labor differences had succeeded years of labor strife in the bituminous fields of the Midwest. Later that year, an attractive young miner, John Mitchell, had become persident of the United Mine Workers. Mitchell had perhaps undue faith in the reasonableness of the world of big business and concluded that a peaceful settlement of the issues in the concentrated anthracite coal fields in Pennsylvania, where the influence of J. P. Morgan was strong, might be possible. Mitchell may have been right with regard to the attitudes of a few farsighted executives such as Morgan. The operators of the mines in Pennsylvania, however, were intolerant of the notion that they should bargain peacefully with any labor leader. George F. Baer, spokesman of the operators, was not expressing any extraordinary doctrine when he said, "The rights and interests of the laboring" would be protected "not by the labor agitators, but by the Christian men to whom God, in His infinite wisdom, has given control of the property interests of the country."

Efforts to prevent a strike broke down, and the workers went out in April 1902. Many issues were involved—the consumers' need for coal, the hours and wages of the workers, the recognition of the union, the public's attitude toward unions and big business, the effect of the strike on national politics. But in perspective the principal importance of the strike may have been in the precedents that it set for federal action in industrial disputes. Roosevelt probably did not understand all the implications of the issues involved. In other labor disputes, he showed little sympathy with labor's position, but in this case he substantially added to his popularity by his part in ending the strike. He set precedents by calling a conference of labor and management, threatening the taking over of an industry by federal troops, persuading management to accept arbitration; and in general establishing the principle that labor as well as management would receive fair treatment from the government.

While the Northern Securities case was moving through the courts and the crisis in anthracite was coming to a climax, even more significant developments were taking place on the foreign scene. Here Roosevelt moved with more assurance than he did in most domestic affairs where he felt bound more by public opinion and congressional attitudes. Even though concepts of morality crept into his diplomatic negotiations, he considered himself a realist and realized the need to have military strength to back up policy. He believed that geography and the potential power of the United States made inevitable a prominent role on the world scene, that the President had to provide dynamic leadership, and that he was limited only by what the Constitution said that he might not do, not by what it said he *might* do. In spite of the faithful service of John Hay, who served as secretary of state from 1898 to 1905, Roosevelt was his own foreign minister.

Caribbean Policy

During Roosevelt's first administration, Anglo-American relations almost jelled into an entente, German-American relations deteriorated, and significant modifications developed in traditional American foreign policy. In these developments, the clarification of Caribbean policy played a significant role. Roosevelt was too good a student of naval policy, and of Alfred Thayer Mahan, not to recognize the importance of the control of the Caribbean for the security of the United States. A sixty-eight-day voyage of the battleship *Oregon* from Puget Sound around Cape Horn to reinforce the Atlantic fleet at the start of the Spanish-American War had illustrated one of Mahan's main points: the need for an interoceanic canal. For such a canal to be secure, the approaches to the canal had to be secure, and the eastern approaches to all possible routes were in the Caribbean. So great was the importance of the Caribbean, therefore, that any sort of foreign intervention in that area was open to suspicion.

An essential ingredient in the development of American Caribbean policy was an acceptance by Great Britain of American power there. By late 1903, even the traditionalists in the British government, Admiralty, and War Office had accepted the realities of the situation and were eliminating from their planning the possibilities of a war with the United States. In 1902, for example, a crisis involving Germany, Great Britain, Italy, and Venezuela developed. The issue was one of compelling a completely irresponsible dictator to arrange for payment of legitimate debts recently incurred by Venezuela. During this episode, the three European powers decided to enforce the collection of the debts by bombarding Venezuelan territory. Roosevelt at first acquiesced in the forcible collection of the debts, but rather clumsy diplomacy on the part of Germany led to misunderstanding; talk about possible acquisition of territory as compensation for the debts began to arouse American opinion and led to Roosevelt's threatening to intervene if Germany did not agree to an arbitration of the difficulties. Unlike Cleveland in the Venezuela episode of 1895, Roosevelt mobilized strong naval forces in the Caribbean to back up his threat, and Germany agreed to the arbitration.

The same vigor and self-assurance characterized another of Roosevelt's accomplishments, the acquisition of the Panama Canal Zone. Probably no action of the early twentieth century was more important in the development of national security, and yet perhaps no action in American foreign policy is less defensible on any other grounds. Up to a point, American negotiators met reasonable diplomatic standards: they worked out a treaty with Great Britain which authorized the United States to build a canal and which nullified a previous agreement that neither power would fortify such a canal. They agreed to purchase the rights of a French company which had a concession to construct a canal; and they negotiated a treaty with Colombia, the owner of the Isthmus, which authorized the United States to construct the canal.

At this point, the mood changed. The Senate of Colombia refused to ratify the treaty, and Roosevelt called them "dagoes" and "jackrabbits." Convinced that an inferior government was preventing progress, he indirectly encouraged a revolution in Panama and arranged for an American cruiser to prevent Colombian reinforcements from putting the revolution down. He immediately recognized the revolutionary government in Panama and saw to it that a treaty giving to the United States a zone ten miles wide "in perpetuity," was negotiated with embarrassing haste. The United States in turn was to pay Panama $10 million together with an annual fee of $250,000. The United States had acquired Panama. Although the immediate reaction in Latin America was not entirely hostile, the losses to the United States in friendship were incalculable.

The acquisition of the Panama Canal Zone with the treaty provisions permitting the United States to control and fortify the future canal was the most important development in the nation's Caribbean policy. The question still remained, however, as to how the United States would attempt to protect the approaches to the canal. The acquisition of potential bases at Pearl Harbor (1882) and eastern Samoa including the harbor of Pago Pago (1879–1899) partly secured the western approaches, and the acquisition of Puerto Rico and of the right to a naval base in Cuba as a result of the Spanish-American War provided some protection from the east. Governments were notoriously unstable in the Caribbean, however, a fact that might threaten the canal if this instability were to invite foreign intervention.

In spite of Roosevelt's strong reaction to German intervention in Venezuela in 1902, he thought that investors might legitimately expect some support from their government in collecting defaulted debts. In February 1904, the Permanent Court of Arbitration at The Hague brought the issue to a head by ruling that claims would be paid first to those powers that had used force to collect the debts. In that same month insurgents in Santo Domingo were threatening the lives and property of foreigners, and the Dominican government had defaulted. That government, in fact, was bedeviling the Roosevelt administration "to establish some kind of a protectorate over the islands." In spite of TR's usual belligerence, he hesitated to become involved. "I have been hoping and praying for three months that the Santo Domingans would behave so that I would not have to act in any way," he wrote. "I want to do nothing but what a policeman has to do. . . . As for annexing the island, I have about the same desire to annex it as a gorged boa constrictor might have to swallow a porcupine wrong-end-to."

Throughout his campaign for reelection, the Dominican pot was boiling. Rumors envisaged European powers, particularly Germany, intervening to protect nationals and collect debts, and then possibly remaining. Within a month of his triumph in the fall of 1904, he made clear what his position was:

> Chronic wrongdoing . . . may in America, as elsewhere, ultimately require intervention by some civilized nation, and in the Western Hemisphere the adherence of the United States to the Monroe Doctrine may force the United States, however reluctantly, in flagrant cases of such wrongdoing or impotence, to the exercise of an international police power.

This statement, which was the thesis for the "Roosevelt Corollary" to the Monroe Doctrine, began a new phase in the relationship of the United States with the Caribbean countries. The statement was a corollary to the

Monroe Doctrine only in the sense that it was a policy of American security with regard to the Western Hemisphere unilaterally determined by the government of the United States. It was used, however, to justify actual intervention and control over customs collections. Thus it represented a new position because it contemplated action to eliminate conditions that might invite intervention by other powers. Although private American interests were somewhat involved, the corollary's main justification was to achieve hegemony in the Caribbean and to keep threats away from the Panama Canal. Great Britain reacted significantly to these developments: between 1904 and 1906, while the great Admiral John Fisher was first Sea Lord, the North American and West Indies squadrons were virtually dissolved, and their units transferred to the Mediterranean and the English Channel.

The withdrawal of the British fleet from the Caribbean was undoubtedly predicated on at least two facts. One of these was that the similarity of interests of the United States and Britain was leading to an increasing collaboration between the two powers. The other was that Great Britain had a growing confidence in the power of the United States to defend its interests. Although his famous quotation of a West African proverb, "Speak softly and carry a big stick," may have been uttered in connection with domestic politics, Roosevelt also applied it to foreign policy. He had been only too aware of the weaknesses of the armed services during the Spanish-American War. As President, he was determined to eliminate those weaknesses. In trying to produce greater efficiency, however, Roosevelt seemed to fluctuate between willingness to defy military procedure and tradition and conviction that military policy was best determined by military experts. One of the main problems at the turn of the century was that technological developments made possible a revolutionary change in weapons and in turn called for fundamental changes in tactical and strategic doctrines. Even though there were intelligent officers and civilians connected with the Departments of War and Navy, those in the upper echelons tended to be conservative and satisfied with things as they were.

The Navy and the Army

The organization of the army and the navy encouraged neither flexibility nor coordinated action. The navy was administered by eight bureaus, and the army by ten. Each bureau chief, an admiral or general who frequently held the position longer than a president or Cabinet secretary, considered his bureau his private preserve, and few attempts were made to synchronize the various bureaus' activities. Expert as each naval bureau chief might be, only the secretary of the navy had the power to coordinate the bureaus and to make strategic decisions. The secretary, however, rarely had the knowledge, and no institutional arrangement existed for him to obtain that knowledge.

The Spanish-American War had demonstrated the need for coordination, and a temporary policy board for the navy was established. When it was dropped at the end of the war, the need for such an institution became so apparent that Secretary of the Navy John D. Long created the General Board, consisting of the admiral of the navy (in 1900 George Dewey), the chief of the bureau of navigation, the chief intelligence officer, and the president of the Naval War College. Although presumably this board was to advise the president on such matters as war plans, naval defense, and coastal and overseas defense, the advice did not have to be taken. Moreover, the board was obviously concerned with creating the strongest possible defense, and complicating factors of economics and politics played a very small part in their deliberations.

A case in point was a program proposed by the General Board in 1903, known as the forty-eight-battleship program. In that year the board considered Germany the enemy most to be feared. The German naval building program called for the construction of forty-one battleships and twenty large cruisers by 1920. Thus the board, basing its deliberations upon what it considered to be traditional requirements of American foreign policy—the Monroe Doctrine, the Open Door in the Far East, and control of the Caribbean—called for a balanced fleet with forty-eight battleships by 1920. At no time did this proposal receive the kind of consideration that would bring about consistent implementation. Instead battleships were built sporadically, depending upon particular crises, the recommendations of the president in response to diplomatic and political conditions, and the attitude of the congressional committees on naval affairs.

A power to be reckoned with in naval affairs during the Roosevelt years, for example, was Senator Eugene Hale of Maine. A close associate of the Big Four, he had been in the Senate since 1881 and on the Senate Committee on Naval Affairs since 1883. He became its chairman in 1897 and remained in that post until 1909. In the nineteenth century, he had fought to modernize the navy, but he was inherently conservative and had confidence in the bureau system. Thus in the twentieth century he opposed significant changes in naval administration as well as in naval construction. The bigger ships would cost money and might encourage aggression. Moreover, any coordinating board would centralize power now diffused among the bureau chiefs and might threaten civilian control.

Although the alliance between naval and congressional conservatism prevented any fundamental change in administrative structure, Roosevelt made possible other changes that justify ranking him as the president most important in the development of the modern navy. Although lacking technical knowledge, he knew that revolutionary technical developments were taking place, and he backed those naval officers who did have the know-how. One of these was the unconventional William S. Sims, who as a young intelligence officer and naval attaché in the late nineties had channeled an amazing number of penetrating intelligence reports back to the navy department where they had come to the attention of Assistant Secretary Roosevelt.

During the early years of Roosevelt's administration, numerous important technical improvements were introduced: the time required to build a ship was decreased; the introduction of steam turbines increased the speed of naval vessels; in 1903 wireless sets were added to naval equipment. Of most importance was authorization for the construction of the first big ship to match the heavily gunned, heavily armored, speedy British *Dreadnaught.* Sims had succeeded in getting advance information on this magnificent British man-of-war in December 1906 and promptly informed Roosevelt. It took all Roosevelt's political wiles to obtain authorization for the construction of one of these vessels, *The Delaware,* early in 1907. Not until 1910 would that vessel join the fleet. Ironically, then, even though the strength of Roosevelt's fleet had increased from seventeen to twenty-seven battleships during his eight years in office, the coming of the *Dreadnaught* made that fleet obsolete.

When Roosevelt became president, there were other questions about the navy that called for immediate attention. In spite of the smashing of the Spanish fleet, the embarrassing fact was that the navy had not performed efficiently. Maneuvers were not well carried out, and gunnery was miserable. Remarkable improvements in equipment, techniques, and tactics took place during the Roosevelt administrations. An improvement in gunnery was considered in some quarters to be "the most striking feature in the history of the navy" in the early years of the century. Probably more important, however, in the field of national policy was the success of experiments in 1902 to transform naval vessels from coal burners to oil burners. Naval vessels were tied down to their fuel supply and sophisticated bases were necessary, quite different from the days of sail. In the nineteenth century, the custom had been to scatter ships around in various positions at home and abroad, and fleet maneuvers were rarely held. New strategic considerations led Roosevelt to initiate large-scale maneuvers and to concentrate the principal naval forces in an Atlantic fleet and a Pacific fleet.

Although the Roosevelt navy was much more efficient than had been that of the Spanish-American War, he failed to push one reform, that of establishing a single Chief of Staff to coordinate the work of the bureaus. A general concern about irresponsible navalism warned Roosevelt that such a reform was politically impossible. Alarmed about the increasing power of Germany and Japan, he preferred to push an enlargement and modernization of the fleet rather than a much needed administrative reorganization.

Unquestionably Roosevelt considered the United States an essential element in the world power structure. He was convinced, moreover, that the nation's interests could be affected by changes in this structure no matter where they might take place. He was concerned about the Philippine Islands, particularly concerned that Germany had taken the Caroline and Mariana islands from Spain, thus threatening communications with the Philippines. He watched the course of the Russo-Japanese War in 1904 and helped bring it to an end in 1905, fearing that if it continued the balance of power might be upset in Asia. Concerned about how a European war might affect American commerce, he reluctantly called a conference at Algeciras in Spain in 1906 to try to resolve great power differences over Morocco and to assure the equal right of the United States to trade in the Mediterranean.

He tried all sorts of approaches in these controversies. He used personal diplomacy to assure friendly relations with Japan and with Britain, two countries that formed an alliance in 1902. He also prepared for war. Aware of the inept collaboration between the army and navy during the Spanish-American War, he authorized the establishment of a joint Army-Navy Board in 1903. The board promptly turned its attention to the possibility of war with Japan and prepared the first of many "color" plans which were to be the basis of American military planning until the entry of the United States into World War II. War Plan Orange was designed to provide the basis for American strategy in the event of a war with Japan. It assumed that the Philippines would be the first Japanese objective, that the battle fleet would fight its way across the Pacific via an incomplete base at Pearl Harbor and an undeveloped base at Guam, that it would relieve the Philippine garrison within four months, and bring in troops for an offensive while the fleet was defeating the Japanese fleet.

A weakness of the plan was the inability to determine where a naval base in the Philippines should be constructed. Differences developed between the army and the navy which were not ironed out until 1909. In that year the board decided that the major base should not be in the Philippines at all but at Pearl Harbor, that only minor repair facilities should be established in the Philippines at Subig Bay where the navy wanted a base, and that the army base at Corregidor in Manila Bay could serve to protect a coal pile and magazine. By that time appropriations of $900,000 to begin work on the base at Pearl had been made.

Roosevelt recognized the delicacy of the American position in the Pacific. He believed that a war would not be in the best interests of the United States; and he was equally certain that a balance of power in both Europe and Asia would best ensure future American interests. He knew that economic interests in East Asia were minuscule as compared with those of Britain, Japan, Russia, and even France and Germany. His attitude toward the different powers depended upon the particular situation. He favored Japan so long as Japan seemed to be needed to balance Russian influence. However, when relationships degenerated over discrimination against the Japanese in California, over Japanese immigration into the United States, and over the Philippines, he made two signficant moves. After battling with California hotheads, he managed to work out a gentlemen's agreement (1907-1908) with Japan, in which that country agreed to prevent its laborers from migrating to the United States. At the height of this crisis, he sent sixteen battleships from the Atlantic into the Pacific, and then around the world, a voyage which lasted from December 1907 to February 1909. This voyage was designed to impress Japan, stimulate an interest in the navy among the American people, give the navy experience, and test its resources. At the same time it probably gave support to German and Japanese militarists who were campaigning to build up their nation's fleets and may have upset the balance of power in a new way by at least temporarily bringing Japan and Russia together.

The East Asian policy of the Roosevelt administration was a curious combination of realism and idealism mixed with uncertainty. The efforts of Roosevelt and his secretary of state, Elihu Root, had promoted friendlier relations between Japan and the United States in 1905 and 1906, and their goals continued to be shaped by a sensitivity toward Japan's position in Manchuria. At the same time a variety of American economic interests were urging a stronger policy in the Far East. Official naval policy had been to maintain sufficient strength so that the United States would rank as an Asian power—economically and politically. Yet such goals were not in accord with the political situation in the United States. Probably by 1903, Roosevelt and Hay had concluded that public opinion in the United States would support little more than defense of the nation's possessions in the Pacific. By 1907 Roosevelt was feeling insecure even on that policy when he described the Philippine Islands as our "heel of Achilles," and indicated that under the circumstances, he would be "glad to see the islands made independent."

At the same time, younger men associated with the State Department who were strongly anti-Japanese were advocating more positive policies toward China. In 1907 and 1908, men such as Willard Straight, consul general at Mukden, and Huntington Wilson, third assistant secretary of state, supported not only the ideas of equality of commercial opportunity and the territorial integrity of China but also equal opportunity for investment. Later, during the Taft administration, such policies were to be pushed by Secretary of State Philander Knox. Such economic penetration had various motives: strategic, to prevent other countries from gaining predominance; economic, to give our businessmen a share in the potentialities of the China market; and humanitarian, to achieve the progressive goals of efficiency and stability and thus promote the well-being of the Chinese people.

While the acquisition of overseas territory focused attention on the navy, changes were also being made to modernize the army. William McKinley made one of his most important decisions when he unexpectedly appointed Elihu Root to the position of secretary of war in 1899. Root had the reputation of being an honest and successful lawyer, but he admitted that he knew nothing about the army. McKinley hoped that Root as secretary would develop a procedure for administering the new American colonies. When Root assumed his duties, however, he found a more chaotic administration than that in the Navy Department. The various bureau chiefs and their staffs were completely out of touch with the line of the army and not in any way responsible to the commanding general. They reported to the secretary, but because of their long tenure they were able to ingratiate themselves with veteran chairmen of congressional committees with whom they worked year after year, and thus the power of the secretary, whose tenure was short, was more apparent than real. No institution existed for making policy, planning, or coordinating the various bureaus. The regular army was tiny, and the old militia system quite outmoded.

Roosevelt as a lieutenant colonel in the Rough Riders had written numerous insubordinate letters to his friend Henry Cabot Lodge criticizing the army during the Spanish-American War and may have wanted to be secretary of war himself when McKinley appointed Root. Yet he respected Root, and when Roosevelt became president, he and the secretary worked together to put into effect a far-reaching program for army improvement.

Root's first problem was to mobilize forces to end the fighting in the Philippines. Prior to the Spanish-American War, the regulars had numbered about 28,000 officers and enlisted men. About 225,000 men were called to the colors for the war. Most of these had been mustered out after the war, but a new measure authorizing a regular army of 63,000 and 35,000 additional volunteers had passed in March 1899. To get this new army ready for fighting in the Philippines was difficult enough, but Root soon concluded that the real problem was more than simply training troops. What was needed, he thought, was an acceptance of the principle that the function of the War Department was to prepare and plan for war. In addition to a regular army, adequate in size, he emphasized the need for a planning agency, a weapons evaluation agency, an improved training system, and a system of reserves to reinforce the regulars in time of emergency.

The size of the regular army was promptly settled. An enactment of 1901 provided for an aggregate strength of between 60,000 and 100,000 men. Much more controversial was the establishment of the army General Staff, undoubtedly Root's most significant reform. The concept of such a staff conflicted with the tradition of the bureau chiefs with its entrenched support in the army and in Congress. In addition, the model came from abroad, and the phobia against Prussian militarism ran deep in the United States. Yet Root did not possess this phobia. He concluded that a staff similar to that of Germany was what the United States needed.

Recognizing that it might be a long pull to get a General Staff bill through Congress, he approached the issue somewhat circuitously by strengthening the army's educational system. He established new schools at military posts. He refurbished the advanced schools for special services such as the cavalry and engineers. Most important, in November 1901 he established by executive order a War College Board later to be known as the Army War College. The purpose of this college was to study such questions as military organization, administration, arms, transport, supplies, mobilization, and plans and to provide military information to the War Department.

During the next two years, Root patiently laid the basis for getting congressional approval for the General Staff. When Roosevelt became president, he threw his influence behind the concept, and in February 1903 the General Staff bill was passed in spite of strong opposition from the military hierarchy. The bill set up a General Staff corps under a chief of staff responsible to the secretary of war and the president. The theory of this relationship was perfectly clear; the military, represented by the chief of staff, was subordinate to the civilian commander in chief. The office of commanding general was abolished. The staff corps was freed from routine administrative duties and charged with planning and policy making. Rather vaguely, and perhaps surreptitiously, Root had left the door open for the staff to assume responsibility for field operations.

On a final issue of importance, that of how the regular forces would be supplemented in an emergency, Root was forced to compromise. His preference was for some system of organized federal reserves, and he was supported by reform-minded army officers. Here, however, he was faced with entrenched state militia units which were unofficially organized under the name of National Guard. Root's position was that the Militia Act of 1792 had never worked satisfactorily, and that the militia companies were suitable only for holding fortifications and training officers for volunteer units. A strong enough National Guard lobby existed, however, to prevent the passage of a measure which would undermine the Guard and had a strong representative in General Charles Dick of Ohio, chairman of the House Committee on Military Affairs. The bill which Dick presented was actually similar to one which the National Guard Association had been promoting since the 1870s. The most serious opposition came from organized labor, which was aware that the Guard had been used to break strikes in the past, but labor lacked the votes and the Militia Act, more frequently called "The Dick Bill," was passed. The bill's passage was a victory for the National Guard, but the bill did recognize certain realities. It maintained the fiction that the militia would consist of every able-bodied man between eighteen and forty-five, but it designated the organized militia as the National Guard, and provided that, within five years, the National Guard would be organized, equipped, and disciplined according to the standards of the regular army.

The Root reforms did not solve all problems of the army. The battle with the bureaus was not completely resolved. Insufficient funds prevented regular maneuvers, although the need was recognized. Desertion rates were high, and some efforts were made to meet this by moderate increases in pay scales. The private, for example, had been receiving $13 per month; this amount was raised to $15 in 1908. With comparable civilian wages running from $1.75 to $2.00 per day, that raise seemed minimal, but desertion rates did drop. Considerable confusion still remained about whether the National Guard could be used outside of the continental limits of the United States, and a militia act of 1908 attempted to establish the principle of federal service anywhere up to the term of enlistment of personnel in the guard, but even these provisions did not completely resolve these problems. Yet there is little question that key issues had been confronted, and that the army was quite a different organization at the end of the first decade of the twentieth century from what it had been before.

Domestic Program: 1904–1906

The election of 1904 occurred while the Russo-Japanese War was still being fought and while disorder in the Caribbean was inspiring Roosevelt to develop the corollary to the Monroe Doctrine. Roosevelt claimed to be surprised at the extent of his victory. He had won by more than two and a half million votes and carried all states except thirteen from the south and the border. After his triumph, he made an announcement, long planned, but which he later would regret, that "under no circumstances will I be a candidate for or accept another nomination." On March 4, 1905 when he delivered his inaugural address, a huge crowd "gave forth a mighty roar—the first display of an enthusiasm that eclipsed all previous inaugurations save Andrew Jackson's first."

Before he had delivered his inaugural address, and in less than a month after his election, he delivered his fourth annual message to Congress. In that message he outlined what would be pervading themes in his future annual messages as well as in numerous special messages and public addresses. In foreign policy, he stressed the world responsibilities of a great power, which he insisted had to be backed by "the force necessary to back up a strong attitude." At the same time he declared that "the steady aim of this Nation . . . should be to strive to bring ever nearer the day when there shall prevail throughout the world the peace of justice." In domestic policy he delineated more clearly and emphatically his views on capital and labor. Over and over in his messages to Congress and elsewhere he repeated that "great corporations are necessary," that bigness in itself was not necessarily bad, but "that these corporations should be managed with due regard to the interest of the public as a whole."

On this last point, the president became increasingly outspoken as the years went by. His concern was with good conduct, rather than size, on the part of business organizations or labor organizations alike. When it came to business, he was becoming increasingly irritated with those who took the attitude of "the public be damned." By 1906 he advocated that all corporations engaged in interstate commerce should come under government regulation. When it came to labor, he was becoming less sympathetic with the use of the injunction to break strikes. He was horrified at the annual carnage in industry and at the inadequacy of workmen's compensations laws; in 1900, he pointed out, more than ten thousand persons were killed as a result of accidents in railroad work alone. He saw the need for hour laws on interstate railways, restrictions upon child labor, and controls over the sale of drugs, drinks, and food. Perhaps most far-reaching of all, in his annual message of 1906 he came out in favor of a graduated inheritance tax and a graduated income tax.

By the time Roosevelt began to deliver these rather advanced requests for congressional action, the situation in Congress was in a state of flux. Time had undermined the dominating influence of the "Four." Orville Platt, the able Connecticut Yankee, tired of the political wars, died in 1905. By that time the unrest among Iowa Republicans had reshaped Allison's course, and he was becoming increasingly sensitive to the demands of the reformers. Thus encouraged, Allison's colleague, Dolliver, as well as Moses Clapp of Minnesota reacted more quickly to the demands of western radicalism. In the meantime Beveridge of Indiana, whose eloquence had supported Roosevelt enthusiastically in his overseas ventures, more and more turned his attention to reform at home. Even Aldrich must have had moments of uncertainty, as the Democrats, supported by some antimachine Republicans, won the governorship of Rhode Island in both 1902 and 1903. And finally what in the long run would be the most significant event of all, upon the death of Senator Quarles of Wisconsin, the legislature chose as his successor Governor Robert La Follette.

If the unbroken front of the Aldrich organization was showing a few chinks, there still were no more than half-a-dozen senators who could be considered really infected with the reform virus. The House remained an even greater block to the development of national power, largely because of the succession of Joseph Gurney Cannon of Illinois to the speakership in 1903. Cannon, witty, profane, frank, had served in the House since 1873 except for one two-year term. He had been a power behind the throne during the speakership of "Czar" Reed. He believed that the federal government should "afford protection to life, liberty, and property under the Constitution, and when that is done by a wise legislature, then let every tub stand on its own bottom, let every citizen root hog or die."

Within the House, he exerted his control through appointments to strategic committee positions and through his chairmanship of the Rules Committee which in turn decided what and how issues would be debated on the floor. His lieutenants in 1903 included such stalwarts as Sereno Payne, a twenty-year veteran from New York, chairman of Ways and Means and James A. Tawney of Minnesota, in Congress for ten years and chairman of Appropriations. They and others in strategic positions were in most instances small businessmen or lawyers who had grown up on the farm. They were conscientious, honest, small-town people who distrusted big government. Undoubtedly they were at various times inspired by the wishes of their constituents, their philosophical opposition to the extension of federal power, and their loyalty to Uncle Joe Cannon.

Although Speaker Cannon was able to put up numerous roadblocks to Roosevelt's legislative program, Roosevelt could legitimately boast of the legislative record made by Congress in the nineteen months that it was in session during his second administration. It included increased appropriations for agricultural experimental stations; consular reorganization; employers' liability in the District of Columbia, the territories, and in interstate and foreign commerce; important amendments to the Militia Act; increased powers to the Interstate Commerce Commission (the Hepburn Act); the establishment of a Bureau of Immigration and Naturalization; the authorization of a lock canal through the Isthmus; regulations on the sale of foods, drugs, and meat; compulsory education and limitations on child labor in the District of Columbia; an act limiting to sixteen the number of consecutive hours that a railway worker could work; and workers' compensation for workers on public works.

Although many of these measures were landmarks in principle, the Hepburn Act, the Pure Food and Drug Act, and the Meat Inspection Act were perhaps the most important. All three of these enactments were noteworthy in their specific accomplishments, in substantially widening the area of federal action, and in illustrating the procedures by which such significant laws were passed through an essentially conservative Congress. Roosevelt was convinced that the clause in the Constitution which authorized Congress to regulate interstate commerce could be extended to justify the control not only of the actual process of commerce across state lines but also of those industries manufacturing products which were to move in interstate commerce. The principle of the Hepburn Act was to give to the Interstate Commerce Commission the right to regulate railway rates, a right already upheld by the Supreme Court. Thus constitutionally this act did not represent a particularly new development. More touchy, however, was the question of whether the government could find constitutional justification for inspecting the production of meat or regulating the sale of food and drugs. The antitrust laws had been upheld on the grounds that the commerce clause justified keeping "interstate commerce free from the obstacles and interferences resulting from monopoly and other combinations and conspiracies designed to destroy free competition and restrain trade." The question remained whether Congress could constitutionally impose restrictions upon an industry by barring its products from interstate commerce. In 1903, the Court gave a partial answer to this question by upholding the right of Congress to ban the shipment of lottery tickets in interstate commerce. The decision, however, was by a five-to-four margin, and Associate Justice Harlan for the majority made it clear that he was not establishing a principle, but that every case would have to be decided as to whether it came within the proper limits of Congress.

Even though there seemed a good chance for the Supreme Court to uphold a well-written law regulating the sale of meats or food and drugs, a fundamental obstacle to all of these laws was the seemingly overwhelming opposition in Congress to an extension of national power. It is unlikely that a measure could have been passed had the business community been united in opposition. In fact, however, that community was divided. At one extreme was Thomas E. Wilson, general manager of Nelson Morris & Company, who appealed to Congress for protection against "a bill that will put our business in the hands of theorists, chemists, sociologists" rather than "the men who have devoted their lives to the upbuilding and perfecting of this great American industry." On the other hand, the National Board of Trade consistently supported federal regulation of the trade in food and drugs, and, to the surprise of the top leadership, the National Association of Manufacturers in its convention of 1906 unanimously adopted a report of its Pure Food Committee supporting the passage of a federal law.

Business attitudes toward the regulation of railroad rates were equally complicated. Since 1900 the Interstate Commerce Law Convention, organized by Edward P. Bacon, a dynamic member of the Milwaukee Chamber of Commerce, had been lobbying for a law that would authorize the Interstate Commerce Commission to regulate rates. Grain dealers, millers, and other shippers, mostly midwesterners, consistently gave their support to such a measure. Even some of the railroad leaders such as Alexander J. Cassatt, president of the Pennsylvania Railroad in 1901, favored passing a "reasonable measure now than to have a more drastic and perhaps a seriously injurious one forced upon us by public clamor." The net result of this initial agitation was the Elkins Rebate Bill of 1903.

However, this mild measure hardly satisfied the clamorers, and the differences among businessmen grew more raucous. Increasingly the eastern railroad interests supported by lumbermen, coal operators, and manufacturers of railroad equipment denounced rate regulation. These groups were well organized and overwhelmed congressmen with petitions and telegrams. On the other hand, a poll of the membership of the NAM showed that it favored a strong commission by a large majority. Even the steel men, Henry Clay Frick and Andrew Carnegie, went against the House of Morgan by coming out in favor of rate regulation. Times were prosperous for most of these businessmen, and when profits were good, the fair-minded might recognize that abuses existed and could provide moderate support for reform. At the same time motives were undoubtedly mixed, and some businessmen probably promoted federal regulation as a means of stabilizing conditions in an industry, perhaps even of eliminating certain kinds of competition.

The year 1906 saw an opinion-making crusade come to a climax. One of the factors that had kept the articulate public interested in many of the legislative reforms of the day were the articles and books written to expose injustice and corruption. Roosevelt was aware of the importance of public opinion. In February 1906 he prophesied "I shall get rate legislation of some kind this winter because the public mind is aroused on the subject." Yet he had mixed feelings about the journalism of the day. He concluded that "corruption in business and politics" had produced "a very unhealthy condition of excitement and irritation in the popular mind" and an "enormous increase in socialistic propaganda." He was equally critical of the "outpourings" of such writers as Tom Lawson, David Graham Phillips, and Upton Sinclair, whom he saw as "building up a revolutionary feeling which will most probably take the form of a political campaign." He was particularly irritated at William Randolph Hearst, editor of, as he put it, "sensational, scandal-mongering newspapers." By April 1906, Roosevelt had read both Phillips' *Treason of the Senate,* which Hearst's *Cosmopolitan* had just begun to serialize, and Upton Sinclair's recently published *The Jungle,* a colorful indictment of the meat packers and a plea for socialism.

Unquestionably the bill that Roosevelt wanted most was the bill to regulate railroad rates. In order to get this measure passed, he engaged in an unusually complicated series of maneuvers in Congress which involved the Democrats, the comparatively few progressives, Joe Cannon in the House, and the Senate leadership still dominated by Allison and Aldrich. Anything might upset these maneuvers, especially articles such as Phillips' which called the roll of the Senate—Aldrich, Spooner, Allison, and so on— and labeled them traitors. Perhaps Roosevelt sensed this danger when he used the figure from *Pilgrim's Progress,* "the Man with the Muck-Rake," to denounce the writers in colorful speeches in January and April. At the same time he carefully praised authors who attacked evil and guarded against "indiscriminate assault" and concluded that "to denounce mud-slinging does not mean the endorsement of whitewashing."

Representative William P. Hepburn of Iowa who had introduced a bill more than a year before to amend the Interstate Commerce Act of 1887 would hardly have recognized the measure which the President signed on June 29, 1906. It extended the jurisdiction of the Interstate Commerce Commission to activities such as express and sleeping car companies and oil pipe lines; it authorized the commission to require standard bookeeping methods and to examine the books; and it gave the commission the power to investigate complaints concerning rates and to prescribe maximum rates. Although judicial review was authorized, the authorization in the measure was skillfully cloaked in obscurity.

The Hepburn Act was a Roosevelt victory and a major step in the development of national power. Even the South Carolina demagogic Democrat, Senator Ben Tillman, admitted that Roosevelt had almost "unhorsed" Aldrich. Roosevelt knew that the act did not solve all the problems of railroad transportation, but it gave aid and comfort to those who saw commission government as a logical midpoint between government ownership and unbridled competition. "For an orderly administrative system, for the right of efficient federal controls, for the positive government of an industrial society," as John Blum put it about Roosevelt, "he mobilized in a crucial first skirmish the full powers of his office."

On the day after Roosevelt's signature of the Hepburn Act, both the Pure Food and Drug Act and the Meat Inspection Act became law. A fight for a federal pure food and drug bill had been under way for many years. In 1883 the most important event in the history of the enactment occurred, the appointment of Harvey W. Wiley as chief chemist in the Department of Agriculture. Wiley, largely self-educated with some training in medicine, came to Washington from Purdue University. He soon became interested in food adulteration. Beginning in 1887, his office published a series of bulletins analyzing in detail techniques of adulteration. Boards of trade, grocers' associations, and farm interests became alarmed about the adulteration of their products and began to propose controls. Although Congress approved several limited measures, really effective laws, introduced after 1886, failed to pass. In the meantime, some of the large cities were attempting through boards of health to prevent traffic in adulterated foods, and most states, pressured by industries complaining of unfair competition, put laws on their books which dealt with both food and drugs. Danger from the uncontrolled sale of the latter was becoming horrifying as proprietary medicines, those protected by trademark, multiplied, and claimed cures for everything from colds to cancers.

After 1895, the campaign for food and drug legislation in Congress increased in intensity. The National Pure Food and Drug Congress, organized in 1898, in which Wiley became a central figure, was one of the most effective lobbyists. Additional support came from a wide variety of organizations including the American Medical Association and the National Retail Liquor Dealer's Association. Difficulties arose, however, as interests that were being hurt introduced objections. By 1903 new controversies developed as attention focused on proprietary medicines. Edward Bok, editor of the *Ladies' Home Journal,* sponsored numerous exposés, which among other things brought out that such popular medicines as Lydia Pinkham's Vegetable Compound was 20.6 percent and Hostettar's Stomach Bitters 44.5 percent alcohol. Fearful that regulation might get out of hand, the Proprietary Association of America and other drug organizations moved into the opposition camp. In Congress, Representative Adamson from Georgia and Senator Money from Mississippi constantly raised the issue of constitutionality and called for state control, and it seemed clear that Allison, Spooner, Platt, and Aldrich were using delaying tactics.

Gradually, however, the opposition in Congress was worn down. Wiley persuaded various groups to put pressure on their congressmen: the National Pure Food and Drug Congress, the Association of Manufacturers and Distributors of Food Products, the National Retail Grocers Association, the National Grange, the American Medical Association, and others complied. He threw "a fresh army, the club women of America, into the assault." The battle in the journals rose in intensity. A young lawyer, Mark Sullivan, wrote a series of careful legal studies on proprietary medicine for the *Ladies' Home Journal* and for *Colliers* in 1905 and 1906.

Samuel Hopkins Adams, in the same year, wrote an even more dramatic series for *Colliers.*

The Senate capitulated in February and passed the measure. Four southern Democrats opposed; twenty-two senators, including Aldrich, who inscrutably withdrew his opposition, did not vote. Included among the supporters were such diehard conservatives as Foraker, Penrose, Gallinger, and Money—testimony to the differences within the business community and to the power of public opinion in getting a popular bill passed. In the meantime, the House of Representatives which had previously passed the bill was now dragging its feet. The liquor and food preservative interests and the drug companies were fighting delaying actions, and Speaker Cannon at the very least was not pushing the measure.

At this point, two legislative battles converged and supported one another. The secretary of agriculture had been inspecting meat for foreign commerce to a limited degree since at least 1891. Allegations that canned spoiled meat had been given troops during the Spanish-American War publicized the issue. In January 1905, a British Medical Journal, *Lancet,* began a series of articles claiming that the Chicago meat-packing houses were insanitary, and articles by Upton Sinclair on the same subject began to appear in a Socialist journal, *Appeal to Reason.* After five tries, Sinclair persuaded Walter Hines Page of Doubleday, Page & Company to publish these articles as *The Jungle.*

The book was sensational. It described in lurid detail the filth, disease, and deception that went into meat packing and came to a climax in describing how men sometimes fell into vats and were overlooked until "all but the bones of them had gone out to the world as Anderson's Pure Leaf Lard." Disturbed by these revelations, President Roosevelt launched several investigations of the meat-packing industry which toned down the Sinclair finds somewhat, but supported him on the main points.

Clearly legislation was in order, and Senator Albert Beveridge worked out a measure in collaboration with representatives from the Department of Agriculture and those whom Roosevelt had delegated to make a study of the industry. Beveridge presented the measure on May 21, 1906 and four days later added it as an amendment to the Agricultural Appropriations Bill. Opposition developed in both houses, and the interests mobilized. The Illinois Manufacturers' Association, the Chicago Commercial Association, and the Chicago Board of Trade attacked the proposed legislation. The National Association of Manufacturers claimed that the charges against the packing companies had been "the result of a conspiracy." In Congress, James W. Wadsworth, with cattle interests in upstate New York, Speaker Joe Cannon, looking over his shoulder at his home of Illinois, and Senator Francis Warren, a sheep raiser from Wyoming, did their best to delay and modify the bill.

At this point the Hepburn Railway Rate Bill, the Meat Inspection Act, and the Pure Food and Drug Law were at about the same stage. Roosevelt was now determined that all of them would be passed. He pointed out to

Cannon the importance to the Republican party of the passage of the Pure Food Bill. He engaged in as skillful maneuvering with congressional leaders on the meat inspection measure as he had on the Hepburn Act. He argued with Wadsworth that it was to the interest both of the stock growers and packers to be able to give assurances that meat would be properly inspected. He compromised at significant points.

The Meat Inspection and the Pure Food and Drug acts became law on June 30, 1906, one day after the Hepburn Act. The Senate had passed the Meat Inspection Act without dissent. On the Pure Food Bill only 4 in the Senate and 17 in the House opposed, all those recorded in the negative were southerners, but 22 in the Senate and 121 in the House did not vote. Both of these enactments, the one designed to prevent the manufacture or sale of "adulterated or fraudulently labeled foods and drugs sold in interstate commerce," and the other to provide for federal inspection of meat packing industries and the elimination of insanitary conditions in these industries, represented, according to Beveridge, "the most pronounced extension of federal power in every direction ever enacted." Even the courts approved. In 1911 and again in 1913 the Court affirmed that Congress had the right to ban "adulterated and misbranded food and drugs from interstate commerce." In 1917, the Court upheld the right of Congress to delegate authority to the secretary of agriculture to make administrative rules concerning inspection of the meat, and in the following year a unanimous court upheld the right of Congress to prevent "interstate and foreign shipment of impure and adulterated meat-food products."

The Last Two Presidential Years: 1907–1909

Although Congress passed these enactments by lopsided votes, the following two years witnessed a complex struggle for power that culminated in the splitting of the Republican party and the victory of Woodrow Wilson in 1912. These years also witnessed Roosevelt's abandonment of a position in which he seemed to be compromising with conservative business interests and their congressional supporters and the assumption of a position that was about as far out as the Democratic Roosevelt would take twenty-five years later. Like that later Roosevelt, Theodore found his legislative program shackled by a conservative Congress.

It is perhaps understandable why Congress should rebel against the increasingly popular and outspoken Roosevelt. He made no secret of his belief that the presidency was more powerful than the executive in any other Republic or Constitutional monarchy of the day. As he put it, "I have not cared a rap for the criticisms of those who spoke of . . . 'usurpation of power.' " Moreover in his last years in office he demonstrated how that power could be used.

Roosevelt had very positive views about the need for firm executive control over the use of the nation's natural resources. In 1902 he had pushed through Congress the Newlands Act setting up the reclamation service and providing for the construction of dams for irrigation purposes financed by the sale of lands in certain western states; he set up the forest service in the Department of Agriculture with Gifford Pinchot at its head, and he withdrew from private exploitation 150 million acres of the public domain. Roosevelt was no "preservationist," and supported Gifford Pinchot in developing with lumber companies efficient programs of cutting and reforestation. But Roosevelt vigorously prosecuted lumbermen, ranchers, miners, and power companies that ignored the law. Congressmen, roused by such constituents, managed in 1907 to put through Congress a rider that would prevent the creation of additional forest reserves without the consent of Congress; whereupon Roosevelt promptly withdrew seventeen million acres without the consent of Congress before he signed the bill with the attached rider. Furthermore, within a year, he stirred up enthusiastic public support for his conservation program by calling a National Conservation Congress consisting of governors, congressmen, justices, and experts from numerous disciplines. This congress led to the setting up of conservation commissions in more than forty states, and providing the base for future ecological programs.

Roosevelt likewise used his executive power to restore economic stability in the panic of 1907. He had become irritated at accusations from businessmen that his antibusiness rhetoric had led to this panic. He refused to issue reassuring forecasts as Hoover was to do twenty-two years later, but he did support national banks throughout the country and New York banks by various types of financial transactions to the amount of more than $200 million. Moreover he gave implicit support to a controversial deal by which J. P. Morgan Company and the U.S. Steel Corporation prevented a key brokerage firm on the New York Stock Exchange from going bankrupt while at the same time making possible a significant expansion of the coal and iron holdings of U.S. Steel.

Throughout these years, Roosevelt became more and more critical of "malefactors of great wealth" and determined to promote new reforms. He wished particularly to see the Sherman Antitrust Law revised to make large business combinations legal but subject to federal control, and up to a point he worked with representatives of business to promote such a revision. He would not tolerate, however, any bill that would amend the act to permit the combinations but not to authorize the executive to regulate them.

More upsetting to the business establishment was the increasing radicalism of the president's messages to Congress. Resulting partly from his irritation at the complaints and actions of the businessmen, partly from a fear that a socialist revolution might well occur if reforms were not carried out, and partly from a realization that serious reforms were necessary, he outlined a program for the development of national power that foreshadowed the New Deal: income and inheritance taxes, regulation of stock exchanges, sweeping extension of federal regulation of railroads, labor legislation that would include limitation of the use of injunctions, the eight-hour day, workmen's compensation, and a federal agency to control corporations engaged in interstate commerce. All this was accompanied by colorful attacks on conservative courts and selfish individuals of wealth.

Undoubtedly as Roosevelt found himself against a high congressional wall of opposition to these advanced proposals, he bemoaned the day when he had counted himself out as a candidate in 1908. Now with his patronage exhausted and in fact almost a lame duck, his powers to persuade Congress were almost nonexistent. Actually of the reforms he advocated, Congress passed only two—moderate bills for employers' liability for injuries to workers on interstate railways and government compensation for injuries to workers in public projects. Nonetheless, in spite of pressures to the contrary, he stood firm on that pledge not to run in 1908, secure in this theory that the tremendous power of the presidential office could not be abused so long as "the holder does not keep it for more than a certain, definite time."

Bibliography

Page 93

For general coverage, see the volumes listed for Chapter 3. On Theodore Roosevelt, see Dewey W. Grantham, Jr., "Theodore Roosevelt in American Historical Writing, 1945–1960," *Mid-America,* 43 (January 1961), 3–35; the most comprehensive biography is William Henry Harbaugh, *The Life and Times of Theodore Roosevelt,* rev. ed. (1963); John Blum provides stimulating essays in *The Republican Roosevelt* (1954); sample Elting E. Morison, et al., eds., *The Letters of Theodore Roosevelt,* 8 vols. (1951–1954). A starting point for considering the foreign policy of this period is Daniel M. Smith, "Rise to Great World Power, 1865–1918," in Cartwright and Watson, eds., *The Reinterpretation of American History and Culture.*

Page 94

The "principles of foreign policy" were taken directly from Samuel F. Bemis, *A Diplomatic History of the United States,* 5th ed. (1965). See also Richard W. Leopold, *The Growth of American Foreign Policy: A History* (1962) and compare Lloyd Gardner, Walter LaFeber, and Thomas McCormick, *Creation of The American Empire: U.S. Diplomatic History* (1973) because of its self-styled revisionist approach to diplomatic history.

Page 94

For Anglo-American relationships, see Kenneth Bourne, *Britain and the Balance of Power in North America, 1815–1908* (1967); Bradford Perkins, *The Great Rapprochement; England and the United States, 1895–1914* (1968); Richard A. Preston, *Canadian Defence Policy and the Development of the Canadian Nation, 1867–1917* (1970); Charles S. Campbell, *Anglo-American Understanding, 1898–1903* (1957).

Pages 94–95

For American military policy, see Walter Millis, *Arms and Men; A Study in American Military History* (1956). On the significance of military security, see C. Vann Woodward, "The Age of Reinterpretation," *American Historical Review,* 66 (October 1960), 1–19. On the idea of the United States as a world power, see Thomas A. Bailey, "America's Emergence as a World Power: The Myth and the Verity," *Pacific Historical Review,* 30 (February 1961), 1–16. Cf. Richard W. Leopold, "The Emergence of America as a World Power: Some Second Thoughts," in John Braeman, et al., eds., *Change and Continuity in Twentieth Century America* (1964).

Pages 95–97

On overseas expansion, see Edward M. Burns, *The American Idea of Mission; Concepts of National Purpose and Destiny* (1957); Walter LaFeber, *The New Empire* (1963); David F. Healy, *U.S. Expansionism; The Imperialist Urge in the 1890's* (1970); Jerry Israel, *Progressivism and the Open Door; America and China, 1905–1921* (1971). Richard Hofstadter, "Cuba, the Philippines, and Manifest Destiny," *The Paranoid Style in American Politics* (1965); Ernest R. May, *American Imperialism: A Speculative Essay* (1968); Thomas J. McCormick, *China Market: America's Quest for Informal Empire, 1893–1901* (1967); Marilyn Blatt Young, *The Rhetoric of Empire; American China Policy, 1895–1901* (1968); Paul S. Varg, *Missionaries, Chinese, and Diplomats; The American Protestant Missionary Movement in China, 1890–1952* (1958).

For a beginning on a topic almost ignored in my treatment, see Robert L. Beisner, *Twelve Against Empire; The Anti-Imperialists, 1898–1900* (1968); John W. Rollins, "The Anti-Imperialists and 20th Century American Foreign Policy," *Studies on the Left,* III, no. I (1962), 9–23; E. Berkeley Tompkins, *Anti-Imperialism in the United States: The Great Debate, 1890–1920* (1970).

On Caribbean policy, see Samuel F. Bemis, *The Latin American Policy of the United States, An Historical Interpretation* (1943); and for quite different views, see Walter LaFeber, "The Background of Cleveland's Venezuelan Policy: A Reinterpretation," *American Historical Review,* 66 (July 1961), 947–967; David F. Healy, *The United States in Cuba, 1898–1902: Generals, Politicians, and the Search for Policy* (1963).

Pages 97–99

On the politics of the late nineteenth century, see Walter T. K. Nugent, "Politics from Reconstruction to 1900," in Cartwright and Watson, eds., *The Reinterpretation of American History and Culture.* For comprehensive surveys, see John A. Garraty, *The New Commonwealth, 1877–1890* (1968) and H. Wayne Morgan, *From Hayes to McKinley; National Party Politics 1877–1896* (1969); for the party structure, I have drawn on Paul Kleppner, *The Cross of Culture; a Social Analysis of Midwestern Politics 1850–1900* (1970); Robert D. Marcus, *Grand Old Party; Political Structure in the Gilded Age 1880–1896* (1971); Richard J. Jensen, *The Winning of the Midwest: Social and Political Conflict, 1888–1896* (1971); Carl N. Degler, "American Political Parties and the Rise of the City: An Interpretation," *Journal of American History,* 51 (June 1964), 41–59. For voting statistics, see Edgar E. Robinson, *The Presidential Vote, 1896–1932* (1934). E. E. Schattschneider has concluded that by 1905 there was little political competition in twenty-nine states, and in only six were the political parties about equal in strength. "United States: The Functional Approach to Party Government," in Sigmund Newmann, ed., *Modern Political Parties* (1956).

Pages 99–100

For a comprehensive treatment of the "Big Four" and national congressional politics, see Horace S. Merrill, *The Republican Command 1897–1913* (1971); cf. Lewis Gould, "New Perspectives on the Republican Party, 1877–1913: A Review Article," *American Historical Review,* 77 (October 1972), 1074–1082. See also Leland L. Sage, *William Boyd Allison; A Study in Practical Politics* (1956); Dorothy Canfield Fowler, *John Coit Spooner: Defender of Presidents* (1961); John A. Garraty, *Henry Cabot Lodge, A Biography* (1953); John Braeman, *Albert J. Beveridge; American Nationalist* (1971); Belle and Fola La Follette, *Robert M. La Follette* (1953).

Pages 100–101

Recent studies of William McKinley are Margaret Leech, *In the Days of McKinley* (1959), and H. Wayne Morgan, *William McKinley and His America* (1963). See also Herbert Croly, *Marcus Alonzo Hanna; His Life and Work* (1912); Thomas Beer, *Hanna* (1929).

Pages 101–107

For Theodore Roosevelt, see references above. Some of the present text is taken almost verbatim from the author's essays on Roosevelt in the *South Atlantic Quarterly* 51 (April 1952), 301–315, and 53 (January 1954), 109–129. See also Howard K. Beale, "Theodore Roosevelt's Ancestry: A Study in Heredity," Edward N. South, ed., *American History and the Social Sciences* (1964). On patronage, see especially, Blum,

The Republican Roosevelt, pp. 36–54; Harbaugh, *Life and Times,* pp. 209–210; *Detroit News* quoted in *Literary Digest,* 23 (November 30, 1901), 669; and Morison, ed., *Roosevelt Letters,* III, 149 et seq. For Civil Service Reform, see Paul P. Van Riper, *History of the United States Civil Service* (1958); Harold T. Pinkett, "The Keep Commission, 1905–1919: A Rooseveltian Effort for Administrative Reform," *Journal of American History,* 52 (September 1965), 297–312. See Roosevelt to Spooner, September 30, 1901, in Morison, ed., *Roosevelt Letters,* III, 155–156, and Roosevelt to Taft, *ibid.,* p. 450 for comments on congressional leadership.

Pages 107–109

For Roosevelt's public attitude toward business and his early antitrust policy, see his annual messages printed in James D. Richardson, ed., *A Compilation of the Messages and Papers of the Presidents,* 20 vols., XV (1917); Arthur M. Johnson, "Theodore Roosevelt and the Bureau of Corporations," *Mississippi Valley Historical Review,* 45 (March 1959), 571–590; Robert M. Wiebe, *Businessmen and Reform: A Study of the Progressive Movement* (1962) and "The House of Morgan and the Executive, 1905–1913," *American Historical Review,* 65 (October 1959), 49–60. Hans B. Thorelli, *The Federal Anti-Trust Policy; Organization of an American Tradition* (1954) is the standard work. See also Roosevelt to Joseph B. Bishop, February 17, 1903, Morison, ed., *Roosevelt Letters,* III, 429, and n. 3; John Garraty, *Right Hand Man; The Life of George Perkins* (1960).

Pages 109–110

For Roosevelt's attitudes toward labor, see Roosevelt to Root, June 2, 1904, Morison, ed., *Roosevelt Letters,* IV, 811. On the coal strike, I have relied upon Robert H. Wiebe, "The Anthracite Coal Strike of 1902: A Record of Confusion," *Mississippi Valley Historical Review,* 48 (September 1961), 229–251. See also Robert J. Cornell, *The Anthracite Coal Strike of 1902* (1957).

Pages 110–111

For United States and Britain in the Caribbean, see Bourne, *Balance of Power.* On the Venezuelan episode, see Howard K. Beale, *Theodore Roosevelt and the Rise of America to World Power* (1956); Seward W. Livermore, "Theodore Roosevelt, the American Navy, and the Venezuelan Crisis of 1902–1903," *American Historical Review,* 51 (April 1946), 452–471; John G. Clifford, "Admiral Dewey and the Germans, 1903; a New Perspective," *Mid-America,* 49 (July 1967), 214–220; Ronald Spector, "Roosevelt, the Navy, and the Venezuela Controversy: 1902–1903," *American Neptune,* 32 (October 1972), 257–263.

Pages 111–112

For the Canal issue, see Beale, *Theodore Roosevelt;* Harbaugh; Bourne; Mowry, *The Era of Theodore Roosevelt;* Charles D. Ameringer, "The

Panama Canal Lobby of Philippe Buneau-Varilla and William Nelson Cromwell," *American Historical Review,* 68 (January 1963), 346–353. On Roosevelt's choice of the Panama route, see Roosevelt to John Hay, August 19, 1903, Morison, ed., *Roosevelt Letters,* III, 567, also n. 2. John Patterson, "Latin-American Reactions to the Panama Revolution of 1903," *Hispanic American Historical Review,* 24 (May 1944), 342–351; Charles D. Ameringer, "Philippe Buneau-Varilla: New Light on the Panama Canal Treaty," *Hispanic American Historical Review,* 46 (February 1966), 28–52.

Pages 112–113

For the quotation on Santo Domingo, see Roosevelt to Joseph Bucklin Bishop, February 23, 1904, Morison, ed., *Roosevelt Letters,* IV, 734; see also Dana G. Munro, *Intervention and Dollar Diplomacy in the Caribbean, 1900–1921* (1964), but contrast Gardiner, LaFeber, and McCormick, *Creation of the American Empire,* pp. 275–279.

Pages 113–115

On the navy, I made extensive use of Elting E. Morison, *Admiral Sims and the Modern American Navy* (1942); see also Leonard D. White, *The Republican Era, 1869–1901* (1958); Albert C. Stillson, "Military Policy without Political Guidance: Theodore Roosevelt's Navy," *Military Affairs,* 25 (Spring 1961), 18–31; Gordon C. O'Gara, *Theodore Roosevelt and the Rise of the Modern American Navy* (1943); and for Roosevelt's concern about irresponsible navalism, see Morison, ed., *Roosevelt Letters,* VI, 891–892, 980, n. 1; Seward W. Livermore, "The American Navy as a Factor in World Politics, 1903–1913," *American Historical Review,* 63 (July 1958), 863–879, and Richard D. Challener, *Admirals, Generals, and American Foreign Policy, 1898–1914* (1973).

See a thought-provoking chapter, Peter Karsten, "Armed Progressives: The Military Organizes for the Twentieth Century," in Jerry Israel, ed., *Building the Organizational Society: Essays on Associational Activities in Modern America* (1972). See also Edward B. Parsons, "Roosevelt's Containment of the Russo-Japanese War," *Pacific Historical Review,* 38 (February 1969), 21–43. Raymond Esthus questions points made by Beale, *Theodore Roosevelt* on the development of agreements with England and Japan. Raymond A. Esthus, "The Taft-Katsura Agreement— Reality of Myth," *Journal of Modern History,* 31 (March 1959), 46–51. See also Ralph E. Minger, "Taft's Missions to Japan: A Study in Personal Diplomacy," *Pacific Historical Review,* 30 (August 1961), 279–294.

Pages 115–116

For Pacific planning, start with Seward W. Livermore, "American Strategy Diplomacy in the South Pacific, 1890–1914," *Pacific Historical Review,* 12 (March 1943), 33–51, and "American Naval Base Policy in the Far East," *ibid.,* 13 (June 1944), 113–135. See also Louis Morton,

"War Plan Orange: Evaluation of a Strategy," *World Politics,* 11 (January 1959), 221–250. William R. Braisted, *The United States Navy in the Pacific, 1897–1909* (1958) and *The United States Navy in the Pacific, 1909–1922* (1971).

Pages 116–117

For East Asian policy, a still useful survey is A. Whitney Griswold, *The Far Eastern Policy of the United States* (1938); see particularly Beale, *Theodore Roosevelt;* Stillson, "Military Policy without Political Guidance." For the "Achilles Heel" quotation, Roosevelt to Taft, August 21, 1907, Morison, ed., *Roosevelt Letters,* V, 762. See also Raymond A. Esthus, "The Changing Concept of the Open Door, 1899–1910," *Mississippi Valley Historical Review,* 46 (December 1959), 435–454. Jerry Israel sees an aggressive interest in exploiting China, *Progressivism and the Open Door: America and China, 1905–1921.* Useful in explaining the Japanese position is Akira Iriye, *Pacific Estrangement and American Expansion, 1897–1911* (1972).

Pages 117–120

For the army reforms, see Russell F. Weigley, *History of the United States Army* (1967); Philip C. Jessup, *Elihu Root,* 2 vols. (1938); Richard W. Leopold, *Elihu Root and the Conservative Tradition* (1954); Philip L. Semsch, "Elihu Root and the General Staff," *Military Affairs,* 27 (Spring 1963), 16–27; Elbridge Colby, "Elihu Root and the National Guard," *Military Affairs,* 23 (Spring 1959), 28–34; Graham A. Cosmas, "Military Reform after the Spanish-American War: The Army Reorganization Fight of 1898–1899," *Military Affairs,* 35 (February 1971), 12–17. See also Louis Cantor, "The Creation of the Modern National Guard: the Dick Militia Act of 1903," unpub. doctoral diss., Duke University, 1963.

Pages 120–127

On Roosevelt's domestic policy, I sampled extensively Morison, ed., *Roosevelt Letters,* IV and V, and used Harbaugh; Blum; and Mowry, *The Era of Theodore Roosevelt;* for Roosevelt's annual messages, see Richardson. For the organization of the House, see Blair Bolles, *Tyrant from Illinois; Uncle Joe Cannon's Experiment with Personal Power* (1951). For the Pure Food and Drug Act, see Oscar E. Anderson, *The Health of a Nation; Harvey W. Wiley and the Fight for Pure Food* (1958). For meat inspection, John Braeman, "The Square Deal in Action: A Case Study in the Growth of the 'National Police Power,' " in John Braeman, et al., eds., *Change and Continuity in Twentieth Century* (1964). The position of Gabriel Kolko, *The Triumph of Conservatism, A Reinterpretation of American History, 1900–1916* (1963), and James Weinstein, *The Corporate Ideal in the Liberal State, 1900–1918* (1968), is challenged by Braeman and by Fred Greenbaum, "The Progressive World of Gabriel Kolko," *Social Studies,* 60 (October 1969), 224–228. See also Robert W. Harbeson,

"Railroads and Regulation, 1877–1916: Conspiracy or Public Interest?" *Journal of Economic History,* 27 (June 1967), 230–242; Richard Lowitt, *George W. Norris; The Making of a Progressive, 1861–1912* (1963).

Pages 127–128

For conservation, see Samuel P. Hays, *Conservation and the Gospel of Efficiency; the Progressive Conservation Movement, 1890–1920* (1959); Harbaugh; M. Nelson McGeary, *Gifford Pinchot, Forester-Politician* (1960); Elmo Richardson, *The Politics of Conservation; Crusades and Controversies, 1897–1913* (1962). See also William L. Bowers, "Country Life Reform, 1900–1920: A Neglected Aspect of Progressive Era History," *Agricultural History* 45 (July 1971), 211–221.

Pages 128–129

For Morgan and the antitrust laws, see Harbaugh; Garraty, *Right Hand Man;* Wiebe, "The House of Morgan and the Executive"; James C. German, Jr., "Taft, Roosevelt, and United States Steel," *Historian,* 34 (August 1972), 598–613. For financial moves to meet the economic crisis, see Morison, ed., *Roosevelt Letters,* V, 848–849, n. 1, and Roosevelt to Low, April 1, 1908, *ibid.,* VI, 986; Arthur M. Johnson, "Anti-Trust Policy in Transition, 1908; Ideal and Reality," *Mississippi Valley Historical Review,* 48 (December 1961), 415–434.

5

Republican Collapse, 1909-1912

Although Congress could block Roosevelt's legislative program during his last two years in office, it could not block his choice of successor. Roosevelt effectively demonstrated his political know-how by securing the nomination and election of his close friend William Howard Taft.

Active in politics since his graduation from the Yale Law School, Taft had never held an elective political office before becoming President. Although he believed that political parties were absolutely necessary to make popular government work, he lacked the political touch. He served on both state and federal courts, made a great success as governor general of the Philippines, and served competently as secretary of war. He had a high sense of public duty, was refreshingly frank about his own idiosyncrasies, and possessed about all the personal qualities that might typically be expected of a 300-pounder. He enjoyed food, jokes, and leisure. Unfortunately he came to office at a time when more and more was being demanded of the federal government. The Republican party was being torn apart over local and national issues and ideologies that upset traditional notions about the role of government and the courts, the status of organized labor, and the relationship between business and government. Taft had ideas about all of these issues, but he was not able to put up an umbrella under which all Republicans of whatever region or philosophical persuasion could happily take refuge.

Taft was inherently conservative. Yet that conservatism illustrates the complexity of progressivism since he conscientiously and seriously supported many progressive reforms. Few could have been more determined to enforce the antitrust act; actually his Department of Justice instituted more cases than that of Roosevelt in half the number of years. As governor general of the Philippines and a secretary of war, he had known federal administration at first hand, and he was just as devoted an advocate of efficiency in government as the most ardent reformer. As president he stressed this goal, including the appointment of a Committee on Economy and Efficiency which prepared at least eighty-five useful reports.

Moreover Taft had no need to be ashamed of the accomplishments of Congress during his administration. They were hardworking Congresses, with sessions lasting for about thirty months during the four-year period. In contrast, Congress remained in session for only thirty-eight months during Roosevelt's eight years in office. Many of the key issues embodied in federal statutes during Roosevelt's presidency were expanded under Taft. The principle of consumer protection, which had produced the Pure Food and Drug and Meat Inspection acts led to statutes preventing the manufacture and sale of adulterated Paris Green, lead arsenates and other insecticides (1910), and white phosphorous matches (1912), the importation of adulterated seeds (1912), and the misbranding of drugs (1912). The control of interstate and foreign commerce was also extended to prohibit the importation of prize fight films (1912) and the white slave-traffic (1910).

Railroad legislation during the Taft administration matched that under Roosevelt. In 1910, railroads were ordered to use automatic couplers, continuous brakes on cars, and driving wheel brakes on locomotives; a year later, they were told to equip their engines with "safe and suitable boilers." Moreover the Mann-Elkins Act of 1910 significantly amended the Interstate Commerce Act of 1887 and the Hepburn Act of 1906. It provided for a Commerce Court to hear rate appeals from the Interstate Commerce Commission. At the same time that commission was given the authority to initiate rate changes, and the carrier had to prove that the rate established by the commission was not fair. The enactment also placed telephone, telegraph, cable, and wireless companies under the authority of the commission. At that time, the progressives were not able to get approval for one of their favorite devices, authorizing the commission to investigate costs and property values of the railroad and thus determine rates on the basis of "physical valuation." Two years later, however, just before Taft left office such a bill was passed. Taft's administration also saw Congress require wireless telegraphy on "certain ocean steamers" (1910) and a rule that radio operators be federally licensed by the secretary of commerce if their operations should extend beyond state lines.

The Taft administration witnessed a substantial improvement in the federal status of industrial labor. A Bureau of Mines was established in the Department of the Interior with the aim of improving safety conditions in the mines (1910). An act passed in 1912 established an eight-hour day for federal workers and workers in the territories and in the District of Columbia and was extended a year later to workers on rivers and harbor projects. In 1912, an industrial relations commission was created to investigate conditions of labor in the principal industries of the United States including agriculture, and on the eve of his handing over the presidency to Woodrow Wilson, Taft signed a measure symbolizing labor's new status which set up the cabinet post of the Department of Labor.

Various conservation measures were passed. One authorized the federal government to contract for impounding and storing water and to cooperate in constructing reservoirs; another authorized the president to withdraw public lands from entry, sales, or settlement while at the same time making possible future arrangements for mining all products but coal, oil, gas, and phosphates on the lands withdrawn. Another permitted state cooperation in the preservation of watersheds and authorized a commission to study the retaining of the navigability of rivers. A third provided for the protection of the seal fisheries of Alaska.

Numerous other significant acts characterized Taft's administration. The controversial Payne-Aldrich Tariff was passed during the special session of Congress called immediately after his inauguration. Congress shortly thereafter imposed a tax on corporations. In 1910, a postal savings bank system was established, and statehood was provided for New Mexico and Arizona. In 1911, a reciprocity agreement for trade with Canada was approved by both Houses, reapportionment for the House of Representatives was approved, a Children's Bureau was established in the Department of Commerce, and in 1912 an act was passed for the "opening, maintenance, protection, and operation" of the Panama Canal, and, not so incidentally, quite contrary to the Hay-Pauncefote Treaty, exempting American coastwise shipping from paying the canal tolls.

Taft's most important legislative contribution was a rather delicate maneuver, almost matching Roosevelt's wiles, which resulted in the adoption of a joint congressional resolution calling for the submission to the state legislatures of a constitutional amendment legalizing a tax on incomes. This intricate maneuver took advantage of the fact that on this issue it was possible to combine enough progressive Republicans with the Democrats to outvote the Aldrich-managed Republicans. Aldrich and his allies succumbed, hoping no doubt that the states would not approve the amendment. By February 1913, however, the requisite number of states had approved, and the Sixteenth Amendment was declared adopted. Congress could now "lay and collect taxes on incomes, from whatever source derived, without apportionment among the several States, and without regard to any census or enumeration."

The approval of this amendment was perhaps the most far-reaching action of any Congress between Reconstruction and the New Deal. Although many progressives claimed to be devoted to economy in government, any philosophy that called for more positive state activity inevitably led to greater governmental expenditure. As the *Philadelphia Ledger* put it, "The days of low expenditures and low taxes have disappeared." Yet traditional governmental revenues from customs, sales of public lands, and even excise taxes were reaching a ceiling. Only the income tax provided the base for the kind of governmental activity that progressivism encouraged. Yet few at that time apparently realized the significance of the Sixteenth Amendment as Taft's part in originating the resolution and in encouraging its ratification by state legislatures was lost in the overwhelming progressive complaints over the passage of the tariff.

While Congress and the executive were formulating this constructive program of domestic policy, they were engaged in a far less effective foreign policy. In East Asia, Taft and his secretary of state, Philander Knox, strongly stimulated by younger men in the State Department developed a policy of dollar diplomacy. In the Caribbean, business enterprise was encouraged to strengthen the economies of several states, notably Santo Domingo, Honduras, and Nicaragua, as a means of maintaining the stability of states bordering on the Panama Canal. An incidental result of this policy was the dispatch of marines to Santo Domingo and to Nicaragua in 1912, where a small detachment remained until withdrawal began in 1925.

Although Taft at one point had been dubious about the usefulness of the Monroe Doctrine, his views changed as president. He seemed at times torn as to what his government's policy should be. Although he attempted to be correct in his negotiations with the Latin American countries, at times he privately exploded. He was aware that instability in the Caribbean might result in a threat to the United States. The case of Mexico was a particularly complicated one. Since 1880 the neutral dictator of that country had been Porfirio Diaz, who had maintained friendly relations with the United States. He had encouraged American investment, and by 1900 American interests controlled 80 percent of the railroads and most of the mining industry. An American oil leader, Edward Doheny, Standard Oil, and certain British interests were battling for control of Mexican Oil, while the dictatorship and foreign rivalries at first obscured the poverty and discrimination which finally led to the emergence by 1910 of such revolutionary heroes as Francisco Madero, "Pancho" Villa, and Emiliano Zapata. In spite of pressures to intervene to prevent the disorder, murders, and property damage that were epidemic, Taft patiently remained aloof.

Origins of the Progressive Party

The above recital of data, though dry and factual, serves the purposes of demonstrating not only the accomplishments of the Taft administration but also the variety of activities in which the federal government was becoming involved. At the same time, it obscures the basic weaknesses of Taft's presidency: his inability to steer a course between the various elements in his party and at the same time preserve party unity. In fact, the party tore itself apart over passing the Payne-Aldrich Tariff; changing the parliamentary rules of the House of Representatives, which led to undermining the influence of the Speaker; and resolving a conservationist dispute over coal lands in remote Alaska, which led to Taft's firing his chief forester, Roosevelt's close friend Gifford Pinchot. The splintering of the Republican party in turn led to the resurgence of the Democrats so that they carried the House of Representatives in 1910 and elected Woodrow Wilson in 1912.

While the Republicans were tearing their party apart, the fifty-two-year-old ex-President was always in the background. "Shades of Theodore Roosevelt," editorialized the *Des Moines News.* "May the ghosts of the wild animals he has killed in Africa ever haunt him for having foisted onto the country this man Taft!" And Taft's peace of mind was not soothed by cartoons that portrayed TR's supposed reaction to what he was learning as he proceeded through Africa. After Africa, he made a triumphant tour of the European capitals. "The glory of Halley's comet was eclipsed on the landing of Washington's successor," wrote the *Paris Intransigeant* upon Roosevelt's appearance in France. By late 1909, as editorial writers and reporters contemplated the growing differences within the party and followed Roosevelt's triumphant travels in Africa and Europe, they increasingly referred to him as a twentieth-century Napolean temporarily in exile and about to return from Elba.

On June 18, 1910, Roosevelt landed in New York. An enormous crowd greeted him including the mayor of the city, bands, and a delegation of Rough Riders. "I am more glad than I can say to get home," he told them. "And I am ready and eager to be able to do my part so far as I am able in helping solve problems which must be solved if we of this, the greatest democratic republic, are to see its destinies rise to the high level of our hopes and its opportunities."

The elections of 1910 constituted a disaster for Taft. In states where primaries were held, progressive Republicans usually overwhelmed the regulars. In the fall elections, progressive nominees had the greatest success against Democratic candidates, but 24 of the 46 states, including the strongly Republican states of Maine, Connecticut, Massachusetts, New Jersey, and Taft's own Ohio, elected Democratic governors. The 62nd Congress had 228 Democrats and 160 Republicans in the House, and 51 Republicans and 40 Democrats in the Senate, but with Poindexter of Washington, Bourne of Oregon, La Follette of Wisconsin, Dixon of Montana, Brown of Nebraska, Gronna of North Dakota, Works of California, Borah of Idaho, Crawford of South Dakota, Cummins and Kenyon of Iowa, Bristow of Kansas, Clapp of Minnesota, and possibly Townsend of Michigan quite willing to defy the party caucus on certain issues, even the Senate could not be counted for the Republicans. The election suggested that the first significant shifts in party control since 1894 might be taking place. What is more the days of the Big Four were gone, its last remaining member, Nelson Aldrich, now seventy years old, seeing his base in Rhode Island being undermined, shocked by the trends in Congress, had not run for reelection.

Any assessment of these results would have to take into account the age and fatigue of the regular Republicans and the appearance of a new breed of Democrat. Perhaps of most importance, however, the progressive Republicans displayed an increasing sense of confidence and unity. La Follette was convinced that the election was not a victory for the Democratic party, but "a defeat of reactionary Republicanism."

It is not surprising that a mighty struggle for political power developed in the two years between the off-year elections and the presidential election of 1912. This struggle for power was more than the relatively simple one of whether "progressives" or "conservatives" were going to control the Republican party, and whether Democrats or Republicans were going to control the national government. An always increasing number of organized interest groups and of groups interested in specific reforms were getting in on the act. For the first time, perhaps, there was something resembling a progressive movement. True, this progressive movement did not encompass all progressives. There were still progressive southern Democrats who differed from progressive northern Democrats, all of whom differed from progressive Republicans. There were progressives in the urban East who were not really a part of what La Follette described as "this great progressive movement for popular government." At the same time there was a substantial interstate mobilization of forces, at least in the west, to elect progressive candidates in 1910.

Then with the creation of the National Progressive Republican League came the first significant public signs of unity. A local progressive republican league was organized in the state of Washington in the fall of 1909. The elections of 1910 stimulated an interest in organizing on a national scale. By December of that year La Follette, working closely with Bristow, Bourne, and Amos Pinchot, Gifford's brother, was perfecting plans. The National League would organize state leagues and provide literature and speakers in support of progressive state legislation. The emphasis would be upon "popular government" and the specific goals would be the direct election of senators, direct primaries, "the direct election of delegates to national conventions with opportunity for the voter to express his choice for President and Vice President," the initiative, referendum and recall, and a comprehensive corrupt practices act. Officially the National League came into existence at La Follette's home in Washington on January 21, 1911. Within a comparatively few weeks local leagues were formed in numerous western states, and most of the leading progressives had joined.

Within an equally short time, however, it became evident that even this progressive movement was not as unified as at first had seemed to be the case. The expressed aims of the league soon gave way to the more practical aim of preventing Taft's nomination in 1912. The progressives agreed that his nomination should be prevented, but they did not agree as to who should replace him. Those individuals who had fought their way to positions of local and perhaps national leadership against the entrenched opposition of local political machines were proud of their independence. In most instances, they had won these victories by building up strong political organizations. They were critical of backsliding, and in some instances compromise was considered sinful. The "progressives" by definition were otherwise-minded, and it is not surprising that to get agreement upon national leadership was difficult. During Roosevelt's term of office, he had built up an enthusiastic popular following; yet because of his frank willingness to compromise, he had lost the respect of some of those with whose goals he probably was in agreement.

Realistically, only two possible candidates, Roosevelt and La Follette, had the national following to challenge Taft. Probably the leading progressives in theory preferred La Follette to Roosevelt on the grounds that Roosevelt had compromised too much. Yet since those progressive leaders were practical politicians, they would choose Roosevelt because they respected his enormous popular following.

Thus was laid the basis for one of the bitterest feuds of the era. Although hindsight shows that Roosevelt was clearly not out of the running, he insisted that he was not a candidate, and he probably was not consciously trying to deceive anyone. A high point in friendly relationships with La Follette came with an enthusiastic article about Wisconsin in the *Outlook* in May 1911. During the same period, moreover, he seems to have been attempting to restore friendly relations with Taft. Yet there were too many differences. Taft favored the solution of disputes between nations by arbitration treaties. Roosevelt opposed them. He continued to be suspicious of Taft's conservation policies, and he considered the president's antitrust campaign almost a personal slap against him.

In the last analysis, it may have been Taft's antitrust campaign that ensured a third party in 1912. Taft had had the temerity to bring suit against both the U.S. Steel and International Harvester corporations with which Roosevelt had had friendly relations, and in the process Taft implicitly criticized some of Roosevelt's relations with George Perkins and J.P. Morgan. Not only did Taft's actions, therefore, alienate influential business elements, but it infuriated Roosevelt who reiterated his views on good and bad corporations, insisted that wholesale attacks on all combinations were "bound to fail," and defended his own policies. From these differences emerged several obvious facts—business leaders, who were turning away from Taft, would not support the trust-busting La Follette, but might well support Roosevelt.

The New Nationalism and the Roosevelt Coalition

In the meantime, Roosevelt had been given an intellectual boost for a return to politics in the publication of an unusually influential book, *The Promise of American Life* (1909) by Herbert Croly. Croly's father,

once editor in chief of the *New York Daily Graphic*, had early indoc-
trinated him with an American modification of August Comte's Positivism,
a "religion of humanity" which sought to rid society of the superstitions
in traditional orthodox religion and substitute a belief in human reason
and the creativity of modern science. Young Croly dabbled with a Harvard
education, studied with Royce, Santayana, and especially William James,
and emerged as a pragmatist. After leaving Harvard, he led the cultured
life, but became depressed at the problem of the artist in a democratic
society, increasingly characterized by industrialization and materialistic
individualism. Croly hardly represents the "status revolt" in the sense
hypothesized by Richard Hofstadter, but he does represent those men of
culture who had lost status in American society of the late nineteenth
century.

Faced with what he considered a disintegration of American society,
Croly saw the promise of American life in a "new nationalism." Instead
of finding the solution in Jeffersonian liberty and equality and in destroying the trusts and the political machines, however, he turned to planning
and nationalism. Croly pointed out that two of Jefferson's principles
might cancel each other since unbridled liberty could easily lead to the
loss of equality. What Croly proposed, as Arthur Link has suggested, was
to make a virtue of the strong national government of Jefferson's rival,
Hamilton, as a means to achieve desirable Jeffersonian goals.

Croly favored a strong foreign policy. Like Mahan and Roosevelt he
argued that national interests made isolationism impossible. A proper
exercise of national power, he believed, could preserve international peace,
while in the rivalries of the twentieth-century world, a weak nation might
go "down with a crash." His formula for a strong nation was greater
centralization at home. Croly would strengthen the federal government at
the expense of the states in economic matters. He would repeal the
Sherman Act, encourage industrial consolidation, but control these giants
by a system of national incorporation and either strict supervision or
actual expropriation. Considering the accumulation of large fortunes to
be contrary to the spirit of a democratic community, Croly advocated a
high federal inheritance tax. Acceptance of bigness in business, in Croly's
view, also required bigness in labor. Unions, he thought, were "the most
effective machinery for the economic and social amelioration of the
laboring class," and thus he favored federal protection of the workers'
rights to organize, even to the point of contracts that required the employment of union workers only. "The creation of a strong, centralized
government, the promotion of labor unions, the restraint and eventual
nationalization of big business," as Charles Forcey put it, "such was the
three-pronged program of reconstructive legislation that Croly advocated
for progressives." This "reconstructive policy," he insisted, was not
socialistic but nationalistic.

Croly believed that the new nationalism could be put into effect by
a democratic elite, strong leadership, and the Republican party. To pro-

vide this leadership, Croly turned to Theodore Roosevelt, called on him to return to the political wars and put the new nationalism into effect. Roosevelt was delighted with the book, no doubt in part because its views so closely paralleled his. He, too, had long advocated a strong foreign policy; he had shown an ardent distaste for Jefferson in his earliest historical writings; as early as 1902, he had said that "the man who advocates destroying the trusts by measures which would paralyze the industries of the country is at least a quack and at worst an enemy to the Republic"; his constitutional theory implemented time and time again while president had aimed at the de-emphasis of the states, the strengthening of the federal government, and the necessity for presidential leadership. On the other hand, Roosevelt never went so far as Croly in advocating the protection of the right of labor to organize, and the kind of regulatory commission favored by Roosevelt was quite different from either the rather general supervision or the outright expropriation envisaged by Croly.

Roosevelt frankly borrowed the term "new nationalism" as he began to put on the record a personal platform that went further in advocating the development of national power than any other serious contender for the presidency had ever gone. As early as August and September 1910, he began to turn politics upside down by a whirlwind speaking tour through the Midwest. As the *Chicago Tribune* put it, "The greatest living moral force is passing over the Western States in the form of a dynamic Ego—a militant I, an omni-supervisory I, an omni-percipient I, a castigatory, admonitory, prophetic, decapitatory I." In an address at Osawatomie in Kansas on August 31, Roosevelt showed how far he had moved away from the McKinley platform of 1900 by putting together a program much of which would be incorporated in the progressive platform of 1912.

The intricacies of Roosevelt's maneuvers during the next two years are perhaps interesting from a personal point of view, but less important from the point of view of the forces at work leading to the development of national power. Once he had lost confidence in Taft and had concluded that La Follette could not be elected, it was a foregone conclusion that he would throw his own hat into the ring. With that decision, he had to form a coalition that would provide a reasonable hope of victory, and the elements in the coalition were available. They included successful professional politicians such as the Republican Governors Cummins of Iowa and Johnson of California, financial resources from men of wealth such as Frank Munsey, an important publisher, and George Perkins, social reformers such as Jane Addams, and advocates of a strong foreign policy.

One of the most controversial members of the coalition was George Perkins who had parted company with J. P. Morgan in 1910. Perkins was known to hold the views that unrestricted competition was wasteful, that industrial combinations made possible greater efficiency and production, that unequivocal enforcement of the Sherman Act threatened

industrial progress, and that what was really needed was industrial cooperation supervised by a powerful agency of the federal government.

Perkins had been happy with relationships between business and government during the Roosevelt administrations. U.S. Steel and International
Harvester, in both of which Perkins had had a considerable role as a
Morgan associate, welcomed investigations by the Bureau of Corporations,
and Roosevelt, satisfied that these were "good" trusts, launched no suits
against them. However the climate changed under Taft. The Bureau of
Corporations became more critical, a congressional committee opened
an investigation of the steel industry, and Taft's Department of Justice
filed suits against U.S. Steel in 1911 and International Harvester in 1912.
Nothing more was needed to undermine Perkins' confidence in the
Republican party headed by Taft.

The support of people such as Perkins, necessary though it was to
provide campaign finances and logical though it was in view of Roosevelt's
long-expressed views, upset many of his progressive supporters. They
found it difficult to accept a former partner of J. P. Morgan. Yet Roosevelt more than compensated for his business connections by bringing into
his camp reinforcements whose progressive credentials were impeccable.
These were the social workers who for years had been campaigning on the
local level for urban reforms of various kinds. The primary energies of
these social workers had previously been channeled through such organizations as the National Conference of Charities and Correction, the National
United Labor Committee, and the National Trade Union League. In 1909,
when Jane Addams was its president, the National Conference of Charities
and Correction (in 1917 the name was changed to the National Conference
of Social Work) sponsored a committee, chaired first by Paul Kellogg,
editor of the *Survey,* to determine "certain minimum requirements of well
being" for industrial workers. In June 1912 the committee presented its
report, "Social Standards for Industry." The report called for an "eight-
hour day in continuous twenty-four hour industries, a six-day week for
all, the abolition of tenement manufacture, the improvement of housing
conditions, the prohibition of child labor under sixteen . . ., the careful
regulation of employment for women, [and] . . . a federal system of
accident, old age, and unemployment insurance."

A number of these social workers, convinced that their reform crusades
must intensify pressures at the national level, decided to bring this "minimum platform" to the attention of the national political parties. Kellogg
and several others presented it to the Republican Platform Committee
without success. Roosevelt, however, indicated an interest, and in July
he gave them positive assurances that he would adopt their program.

Roosevelt's endorsement introduced another ingredient to his coalition.
Until 1912, he had been noticeably cool to women's suffrage. In 1908,
he had informed leaders of the movement that although he personally
favored women's suffrage, he was not convinced that it was an important
reform or that women favored it. He told them that he believed that a

woman's function as homemaker was far more important than anything any man could do; but that if he could be persuaded that women wished the right to vote, he would support it. His immediate advice to them had been—"Get another State."

By 1912, the situation had changed. The popular view, as expressed by Roosevelt in 1908, that "the indispensable field, for the usefulness of woman is as the mother of the family," was becomingly less widely held. Urban living and increasing employment of women in office and factory were producing a veritable revolution in relationships between the sexes.

Nor could Roosevelt have failed to be impressed with how well the ladies had followed his advice. The suffragists had acquired two other states in dramatic campaigns in Washington and California, while their effective work in the settlement houses and their qualities of leadership in reform organizations appealed to his political sense. In any case, he endorsed in the Progressive platform an unequivocal statement supporting equal suffrage and urged the inclusion of women in the campaign. He may not have satisfied all social workers on the depth of his convictions, but he satisfied Jane Addams that he was "one of the few men in our public life who has responded to the social appeal."

Another essential ingredient in the program of the new nationalism was that of national security. Roosevelt was committed to the need for national power. He never forgot his ludicrous experiences at the outbreak of the Spanish-American War when he discovered how far down the nation's defenses were. As president one of his principal goals had been to build up the army and the navy. At times his glorification of virility and war took on an emotional coloration which some have laid to his own personal battles against weakness and ill-health in his youth, but basically he argued rationally for a nation's ability to defend itself in a world of aggressive nations; he warned about the decline of world powers, and as William Harbaugh has put it, preached "the moral obligations of advanced peoples to support the onward march of civilization." He linked national security with conservation as being most important in the survival of a nation. Thus when the Progressive party went on record as favoring the settlement of international disputes by peaceful means and by limiting naval forces by international agreement, Roosevelt insisted on including in the platform a pledge to build two battleships a year—until an international agreement were in effect.

From Republican to Progressive

Roosevelt's decision to run was based upon the assumption that "the people" favored his candidacy even though Taft controlled the machinery of the Republican party. Roosevelt's only hope, therefore, was to call upon the people through the direct primary, a device designed by political reformers to overcome the influence of entrenched political machines.

Thirteen states held presidential primaries. From these primaries, 36 delegates for La Follette were elected, 48 for Taft, and 278 for Roosevelt. The great majority of the 1,078 delegates, however, were selected in state conventions, and Taft won almost all of these, although Roosevelt's managers contested 254 seats. If he were to win 70 of these cases, he would receive the nomination. The National Committee, consisting of appointees of the president, awarded 235 of the contested delegates to Taft. Thus the Taft men organized the convention, and on June 22, 1912, Taft was nominated on the first ballot. Probably Roosevelt should have received about 25 more of the contested delegates, a number sufficient to have prevented Taft's nomination on the first ballot, and perhaps such a delay would have given some of the wavering Taft and La Follette delegates an excuse to bolt to Roosevelt and thus make possible his nomination. Charging that at least 72 delegates had been illegally seated, the Roosevelt delegates withdrew, and heard their leader dramatically cry "Thou Shall Not Steal!"

The Republican convention, as Mr. Dooley described it, had been "a combination iv th' Chicago fire, Saint Bartholomew's massacre, the battle iv th' Boyne, th' life of Jesse James, an' the night iv th' big wind." The Progressives assembled in convention on August 5, and mixed practical politics with a moving religious crusade. They sang *Onward Christian Soldiers,* the *Doxology,* and the *Battle Hymn of the Republic.* Roosevelt who had, at the Republican Convention, summoned his followers with "we stand at Armageddon and we battle for the Lord," accepted the nomination of the Progressive party with his "Confession of Faith."

The new party's platform included virtually all the reforms advocated by twentieth-century progressives. It called for a "self-controlled democracy" expressing its will through representatives of the people, and supported direct primaries for state and national offices, nationwide preferential primaries for presidential candidates, the direct election of senators, woman suffrage, and the initiative, referendum, and recall; the platform proposed a limitation on the use of injunctions in labor disputes, standards of safety and health in industry, the prohibition of child labor, wage and hour limitations for women, social insurance against sickness, unemployment, and age, and improvement of conditions on the farms. Recognizing that the concentration of business might be necessary, it proposed a strong national agency to regulate interstate corporations; it urged action by Congress to extend foreign commerce; the platform outlined a sweeping program for the conservation of natural resources; it advocated a system of national highways and the improvement of the internal waterways; it called for a tariff commission as a means of promoting a scientific revision of the tariff, and it expressed support for a graduated inheritance tax and the ratification of the income tax amendment.

Prior to the convention, Amos Pinchot had warned Roosevelt that many progressives doubted his progressivism, and certainly as a Republican professional he was not above political opportunism. Yet there seems no good reason for him to have spelled out such a program, almost a model for twentieth-century progressivism, item by item unless he believed in them. From the beginning of his presidency he had consistently argued for the development of national power in both foreign and domestic policy. Now with equal consistency Roosevelt was arguing that human rights must be considered superior to property rights, that special privilege could prove a threat to humane government, and that all three branches of the government must be made more responsive to the will of the people. The progressive platform could have done little else than to incorporate Roosevelt's views, for seldom has there been a political convention that has reflected so much the personality of a single individual.

Yet the story of the Progressive convention illustrates the paradox of early twentieth-century progressivism. It was partly the fact that Roosevelt's campaign attracted some of the old Republican pros such as Dan Hanna of Ohio and William Flinn of Pennsylvania who were at odds with Taft leaders in their own states. Part of the paradox included the role of wealthy advocates of the "new competition" such as George Perkins, whose financial support was considered necessary if the party were to function successfully. Even more it was the confusion in the party on the role of the black delegates from the South. At least three states sent two delegations to the convention, one of them in each case "lily white," and the credentials committee was faced with a crisis in conscience.

The question was whether the Progressives should offer the voters of the New South an alternative to the Democratic party. To most white southerners, that alternative had not existed because they would not vote Republican, a party associated with the scalawags, carpetbaggers, and blacks of Reconstruction. To provide the alternative, therefore, the Progressive party would have to endorse "a lily white" policy and exclude blacks. Thus in spite of the protests of the intellectual descendants of the abolitionists, the Credentials Committee by a vote of seventeen to sixteen seated the all-white delegations.

And Roosevelt upheld the Credentials Committee. Arguing that the impotence of the Republican party in the South had resulted from its association with black people, he warned against trying to build the Progressive party in the same way. Insisting that his own record showed him a champion of the rights of blacks, he argued that for the time being the best interests of the black would be met by relying on "the best white men" in the South.

Roosevelt's decision was not out of character. He consistently had argued that every individual should be judged according to his ability rather than because of his race or religion. With equal consistency, he had uttered views that were in accord with those of the white supremacist. He admitted that some blacks were able, but in general he had not endorsed enfranchisement or equal rights for them. He had made several black appointments in the South, had publicized his friendship with Booker T. Washington, but there is little evidence of any significant interest in black rights after 1903. Civil rights for minorities simply was not necessarily a progressive reform. Within two weeks of the convention, Booker T. Washington rather sadly announced that he would vote for Taft.

The Democrats and Woodrow Wilson

By the time the Progressive convention met in August, Roosevelt had become quite fatalistic about the presidential race. The outcome of the Democratic national convention in June had been a great blow to him. His hopes for victory had been based upon the Democrats nominating a dignified conservative such as Underwood of Alabama or Harmon of Ohio, who would have repelled the progressives, or William Jennings Bryan, who would have repelled everyone else. Instead they had nominated Woodrow Wilson, a fifty-five-year-old college president and governor of New Jersey. Roosevelt confidently expected to get more votes than Taft, but Wilson posed a different problem. As Roosevelt put it, "There is of course a chance that my movement may gain strength enough to enable me to beat Wilson, but I think this very improbable."

Woodrow Wilson was the first professional scholar to run for the presidency. At the same time, he was perhaps the only presidential candidate whose religious convictions and internal gyroscope had convinced him at an early age that he was destined for political leadership. The most powerful influence in stimulating these convictions in Wilson's early youth was his father, a scholarly Presbyterian minister, kindly as a parent but at the same time demanding as an intellectual disciplinarian. From both parents, he absorbed the beliefs and practices of his church. He assumed a fundamental moral order, governed by a sovereign God who watched over his people. Although he probably did not accept predestination in the literal sense, he undoubtedly believed that individuals who trusted in God and assumed their responsibilities were destined for leadership.

A political career was in the forefront of his mind as he moved through one year at Davidson College, four years at Princeton, and another at the University of Virginia Law School. He studied the careers and activities of great political leaders, particularly those of England. He was fascinated by the careers of Gladstone and Burke, in part because he had concluded that oratory was the key to effective statesmanship. He was far from an academic recluse: he sang in the glee club as well as in barber shop quartets; and he participated as actively in athletics as his five-foot-ten frame and 150-pound weight would permit. His favorite extracurricular activities were constructing constitutions for student organizations and participating in political debates, either formal or informal. He delighted in female companionship. During his courtship, his devotion to the lovely Ellen

Axson almost overwhelmed him. His passion for her clearly revealed in daily letters continued unreservedly after their marriage.

After graduating from Princeton, he entered the University of Virginia Law School, dropped out after a year because of ill-health, studied law on his own for more than a year, and then in 1882 set up practice in Atlanta. Although he probably was as successful as many other beginning lawyers, he soon decided that that profession was not for him, and in 1883 he applied for admission to the graduate school of Johns Hopkins where he planned to prepare himself for teaching history, political science, or English literature. He had now convinced himself that he could, as he put it, "accomplish the most useful results by entering a profession which is entirely in keeping with my most pronounced tastes." Yet he retained a "chief interest in politics," and "in history as it furnishes object-lessons for the present."

He taught at Bryn Mawr, and Wesleyan in Connecticut, and in 1890 received an appointment at the College of New Jersey which became Princeton University in 1896. By that time, he had published six books and innumerable articles and was one of the most famous college professors in the United States. It was impossible for him to accept all the invitations he received for speaking engagements. Students packed his classes, stood by the windows to hear him when there were no more seats, and frequently broke into spontaneous cheers. He was "so persuasive," wrote one of them, "that he could often make his hearers believe that black was white."

Few were surprised in 1902 that Wilson was chosen president of Princeton. He was an alumnus, the University's most distinguished faculty member, and perhaps the nation's leading authority on public administration, political theory, and constitutional law. His presidency was a distinguished one. He strengthened the faculty, raised academic standards, developed a new curriculum and introduced the preceptorial system of instruction. Then he met two shattering setbacks. He wanted to abolish Princeton's famous eating clubs, and he was determined to coordinate closely the newly organized graduate school with the other elements of the University. In battling for these, he split the faculty, alienated many of the alumni, upset the student body, and lost the confidence of a majority of the Board of Trustees.

Fortuitously for all concerned, the New Jersey Democratic organization was looking for a respectable candidate for governor to lead their party out of fifteen years in the political wilderness. Colonel Harvey, editor of *Harper's Weekly,* had spotted Wilson several years before as a likely candidate and now urged him on James Smith, Jr., one of the principal managers of the New Jersey Democrats. On June 26, 1910, the party leaders asked Wilson to run, and he responded favorably. What kind of politician would the academic make when he came down from his ivory tower?

The answer to this question is important because it relates to the problem of interpreting Woodrow Wilson. An analysis of Wilson's character at any given time might well lead to the conclusion that he was an uncompromising idealist who constantly looked at the world through moralistically colored glasses. However a careful study of his career, at least until 1919, shows that he was not necessarily uncompromising, that his views were modified by conditions, and that although he had certain ideals for which he fought, he at times took highly realistic means of achieving them.

The principal characteristic of Wilson's political philosophy in the years before he became president of Princeton was his devotion to British political and economic ideas. He was profoundly attracted, for example, to Walter Bagehot's *The English Constitution.* Bagehot was exceedingly critical of the "presidential system" of government as it existed in the United States, where, as he saw it, issues were inadequately debated and the executive was quite separate from the legislative branches of government. Wilson considered Bagehot's criticism borne out by the way in which the American government operated, and contrasted it unfavorably with the British system. At the same time he praised the free trade teachings of the Manchester school and the oratory and political leadership of Gladstone.

A high point of Wilson's early political thought came with his first book, *Congressional Government,* written in 1884 during his second year at Johns Hopkins. In writing this work, Wilson was attempting to explain the "Machinery of power" of the federal government. He did not think that the theory of balance or separation of powers was working. The center of power, he believed, lay in Congress, particularly in the standing committees of Congress. He was concerned at the growing dominance of the national government over the states, and yet he recognized that many questions demanded "uniformity of treatment and power of administration" which could "not be realized by the separate, unconcerted action of the States."

At Johns Hopkins, Wilson's economic liberalism underwent significant revision. He enrolled in a tough seminar led by Herbert Baxter Adams and including on its roll Richard T. Ely, J. Franklin Jameson, and Davis R. Dewey. Although Adams is perhaps best noted for bringing the standards of German scholarship to the American university, this seminar took for granted that a function of the scholar was to promote reform. The concept of reform, it is true, was a moderate one, simply urging the educated to promote good citizenship and to take the lead in fighting political corruption, urban poverty, and illiteracy. Richard Ely would have gone farther. He had only recently returned from Germany where he had been converted to the historical school of economics. He went so far as to advocate municipal ownership of utilities. Wilson took a course with Ely at Hopkins, and considered him his "preceptor in political economy." Wilson was also impressed with the writings of John Bates Clark. Although perhaps the most conservative of the historical school, Clark denounced the extreme individualism of Spencer and Sumner, argued that combinations had "vitiated" individual competition, and called for competition regulated by law and by "moral force."

During the 1890s while Wilson was distinguishing himself at Princeton, he was no ivory tower professor. The demands of his profession required him to study the issues of the day which included contemporary socialism, Populism, and labor uprisings. Then while delivering a series of lectures at Johns Hopkins in 1896, he became involved in a campaign for the reform of the municipal government of Baltimore. Although his writings do not reflect particular concern for the human suffering of the time, he obviously realized that "change" and "reform" were necessary. In 1893 he indicated that he had changed his intellectual mentor from Bagehot to Burke—the Burke who was horrified by the excesses of the French revolution but who favored change. At the turn of the century, Wilson grappled with the problem of overseas expansion. In theory he opposed it; in practice, as other nations fought for dependencies, he could see no alternative from either a strategic or moral point of view except to join in. He was impressed by the effect which the involvement in world affairs had upon presidential leadership. Providentially, Wilson thought, Roosevelt became President and demonstrated what a strong man could do in taking the Constitution as he found it and reviving presidential powers. He is "the political leader of the nation, or has it in his choice to be," Wilson declared in 1907. "His office is anything he has the sagacity and force to make it."

Even with his recognition of the scope of the presidential office and his belief in executive authority, in 1908 he opposed any significant extension of the power of the national government. Although he considered the history of that growth one of "noble, dramatic, even epic, majesty," he feared the extension of the authority of the interstate commerce clause. If the power to regulate commerce, he said, were stretched to regulate "labor in mills and factories," that power could be used "to embrace every particular of the industrial organization and action of the country."

Wilson was not unsympathetic to the growth of business. Perhaps reflecting his mentor, Edmund Burke, he was inclined to believe that anything which grew naturally was right. By 1910, at least, Wilson was saying that corporate development was natural and "indispensable to modern business enterprise." He was equally convinced that, with the end of the continental frontier, expansion into world markets was necessary. Economic expansion, he believed, should be promoted aggressively because it could bring with it Christianity, democracy, and international understanding.

Up to a point Wilson was quite willing to use the federal government as a positive instrument in both encouraging and regulating the nation's economic life. Yet by the end of the first decade of the century, there was little in Wilson's public utterances or record that would alienate the American conservative or the rank and file of American business. By that time, he was consciously competing for leadership in the Democratic party, and it was likely that his ambition, as well as his convictions, led him to say to a friend in 1907, "Would that we could do something, at once, dignified and effective to knock Mr. Bryan, once for all, into a cocked hat."

Although it is understandable why conservative Democrats adopted Wilson, it is equally clear that Wilson was groping for solutions to the problems of which he was increasingly becoming aware.

The political situation in New Jersey was made to order for the emergence of a hero. It had been predominantly a Democratic state until 1894. Then scandals rocked Democratic administrations, and the Republicans took over. Throughout the first decade of the century, however, a reform element known as the New Idea group battled for regulation of the business interests. Most progressives were Republicans, such as George L. Record, but some were Democrats, such as Mark Sullivan and Joe Tumulty who normally were fighting the Democratic political bosses, such as James Smith, Jr. in Newark and young Frank Hague in Jersey City. By 1900 these bosses, sometimes rivals, were ready to combine their forces with the sole purpose of throwing out the Republicans, but in order to have a chance for success, they must find an attractive candidate for governor. Who could be better for a boss-controlled state than a highly respectable, young, articulate, famous, politically innocent college professor, straight from his ivory tower?

The bosses were probably not aware of the turmoil that had been intellectually disturbing Wilson for the previous decade. They were also quite unaware of the fact that although Wilson came from a university he did not live in an ivory tower and that he was willing to combine his moral goal with practical politics. Moreover he not only saw that progressivism was good politics, he had also come to support many of its goals at least on the local level. Thus in accepting the nomination for governor and in carrying on his campaign, he defied the bosses and won the support of the progressives.

The extent of Wilson's conversion to progressivism is reflected in the accomplishments of his administration. He announced in his inaugural address that the state must have a worker's compensation law, effective state regulation of corporations, election reform including direct primaries, and corrupt practices legislation. These measures were passed. In addition he supported the campaign sponsored by progressives in the legislature for "school reforms, storage and food inspection laws, and laws that required stringent factory inspection and regulated the hours and the kind of labor of women and children."

Although he had to have support in order to put this program on the books, his leadership was primarily responsible. He took seriously his own formulae so often repeated during the previous thirty years: He used his eloquence to bring the issues clearly before the people of the state; he used all kinds of persuasion with the Democratic legislators, persuading them individually, upsetting tradition by appearing in the party caucus, actually threatening them with political perdition; he cajoled many Republican legislators into supporting a good share of his program; he used the veto, particularly in the second session of the legislature, from 1911 to 1912. This second session, however, was unproductive in comparison with its predecessor and brought out some of his less attractive qualities. At the same time, he was diverted from his state responsibilities as his heart became more and more set upon being the next president of the United States.

By the end of the first session of the New Jersey legislature Wilson had clearly established himself as a progressive. At least he was enough of a progressive to persuade Bryan, perhaps somewhat reluctantly, to swing his support to the New Jersey governor at the Democratic convention in 1912, and although Bryan's choice was a minor factor in the preconvention campaign, it does symbolize the fact that the Democrats, at a critical point in their history, had chosen the high road of progressivism in making their choice of presidential candidates.

The Election of 1912

An American voter interested in ideology had an unusual choice in 1912. At the one extreme was Taft who took an increasingly conservative position in the face of Roosevelt's attacks, but who, in the process, became tired and depressed. "I think I might as well give up so far as being a candidate is concerned," he told his wife in late July. "There are so many people in the country who don't like me."

At the other edge of the ideological spectrum from Taft, the socialists offered the American voter another choice. That party's platform declared that "the capitalist system has outgrown its historical function, and has become utterly incapable of meeting the problems now confronting society"; it described society as being "divided into warring groups and classes, based upon material interests"; it proposed that "since all social necessities today are socially produced, the means of their production and distribution shall be socially owned and democratically controlled." Although the socialist party itself was divided into warring groups, in Eugene Debs it offered to the electorate a candidate who had succeeded in keeping himself sufficiently above intraparty quarrels that he could win the presidential nomination in four successive campaigns. On the one hand, he placated the radicals by denouncing capitalism as an institution that could not be reformed; on the other, he appeased the "slowcialists" by condemning violence and calling for change through education.

The election of 1912 was a significant turning point in American socialism. Labor parties and social democratic parties were making great progress abroad. As local victories occurred in the United States and as party membership increased, the question was asked, Why will it not happen here? Even though membership of the party was only slightly over 100,000, these were paid members, and at the convention of 1912, delegations appeared from every state except South Carolina. Moreover, in the previous election, socialists had won elections in a dozen or so cities and towns including Milwaukee and Syracuse and had sent nineteen members to state legislatures and Victor Berger to Congress from his district in Wisconsin.

Yet the socialist party needed both complete unity of effort and a unique program to attract the American voter, and it had neither. The party was divided over how to capitalize on the growing strength of organized labor, whether to countenance sabotage and violence as techniques to destroy capitalism, or whether to accept immediate reforms as steps toward socialism rather than to emphasize the Marxist theory of the class struggle. Although the radical faction, "the impossibilists," which included Bill Haywood, William E. Walling, and Louis Boudin, won an occasional victory, the "bourgeois reformers" or "slowcialists," including Morris Hillquit, John Spargo, and Victor Berger, kept control of the party machinery. Thus after initially denouncing the capitalist system, the party platform called for conservation of natural resources, wage, hour, child labor, and inspection legislation, women's suffrage, and the initiative, referendum, and recall. Then when the delegates at the national convention adopted a resolution which effectively drove the IWW's from the party, even some of the IWW's rejoiced: "Cut out the bickering with politicians," urged the IWW paper *Solidarity,* "and get busy with the slaves who . . . are insisting more strongly upon the industrial organization of their class."

If the election of 1912 was a watershed for American socialism, it was also a time of soul-searching for the nonsocialist liberal: how to decide between Roosevelt and Wilson. Roosevelt stood firmly on his platform and on the principles of the New Nationalism. He insisted that the development of bigness in business was a natural development but that it should be regulated by an agency of the federal government strong enough to regulate. As the campaign progressed, moreover, he became increasingly specific in his support of wage and hour legislation, workmen's compensation, and the regulation of "conditions of work in factories, the conditions of life in tenement-houses, the conditions of life and work in construction camps."

Wilson's mind was less made up than Roosevelt's. Indeed the campaign was another important landmark in the education of Woodrow Wilson. Wilson was obviously groping with the problem of bigness. As early as 1907, he made it clear that he accepted large corporations as an essential ingredient in modern industry. He confirmed this conviction when he accepted the Democratic nomination in 1912, and added "Big business is not dangerous because it is big, but because its bigness is an unwholesome inflation created by privileges and exemptions which it ought not to enjoy." Big business might obtain discriminatory privileges and powers by "absolutely unrestricted competition," he argued. Thus the little people no longer had a chance to establish themselves. What Wilson called for, therefore, were laws which would "give the little man a start." "There will be no greater burden in our generation," he concluded, "than to organize the forces of liberty in our time, in order to make conquest of a new freedom for America."

In that unobtrusive fashion was coined the term *New Freedom,* which was to identify Wilson's domestic program throughout his presidency and to distinguish it from that of Theodore Roosevelt. Clearly he was calling for a Democratic victory to free the national government from the influences which destroyed the freedom which Wilson proposed to restore. Clearly also he called for a revision of the tariff to restore foreign competition, a revision of the banking system to eliminate discriminatory practice and to make credit available on a more equitable basis, and a revision of the antitrust laws to prevent the destruction of competition. In short, "a basic aim of the New Freedom . . . was to achieve free enterprise; not, however, by the application of laissez-faire principles but by the use of federal powers to eliminate economic maladjustments so that the economy might run freely."

That much was clear. What Wilson did not make clear, however, was the extent to which he supported the social reforms endorsed by Roosevelt progressives. Roosevelt attacked Wilson for endorsing outdated "laissez-faire doctrine of the English political economists three-quarters of a century ago," and it is true that Wilson referred disparagingly to paternalistic powers of centralization. Actually Wilson's position was much more complex than Roosevelt made it out to be. Wilson was opposing a government dominated by business. In his acceptance speech he said, "No law that safeguards their life [that of the working people], that makes their hours of labor rational and tolerable, that gives them freedom to act in their own interest, and that protects them where they cannot protect themselves, can properly be regarded as class legislation or as anything but as a measure taken in the interest of the whole people." In September, he trumpeted the need for a government which would be "more concerned about human rights than about property rights," called for conservation of human resources as well as natural resources, and said that "the strength of America is proportionate to the health, the buoyancy, the elasticity, the hope, the energy of the American people." On September 27, he argued that it was not worth debating the "humanitarian schemes" described in the Progressive platform until it was certain that the party in control of the government could "do those things to the people without debauching them." He acknowledged that he opposed "a benevolent government" but claimed that he wanted a "just government." Such government, he asserted, "is based upon the right of men to breathe pure air, to live; upon the right of women to bear children and not be overburdened so that disease and breakdown will come upon them; upon the right of children to thrive and grow up and be strong; upon all those fundamental things which appeal, indeed to our hearts, but which our minds conceive to be part of the fundamental justice of life."

As the campaign developed, Democratic optimism increased, and Wilson's victory was not unexpected. He received more than 6 million votes, Roosevelt more than 4 million, Taft almost 3.5 million, and Debs not quite 1 million. Although Wilson won overwhelmingly in the electoral college (435 votes to 88 for Roosevelt and 8 for Taft), he was a minority president, and he actually received 200,000 votes fewer than Bryan in 1908. In spite of the excitement of the election, the total vote was only 150,000 larger than in 1908. Indeed, total voter participation was declining from the high percentages of the nineteenth century. The election, moreover, did not necessarily indicate an overwhelmingly "progressive" sentiment in the nation. The votes for Debs probably were largely ideological, but the bounce and enthusiasm of Roosevelt undoubtedly attracted votes that had little if any reference to his platform, and the Democrats regularly had polled more than six million votes since 1896, of which almost three million came from the southern states. In all three of his campaigns Bryan had polled larger votes than did Wilson in 1912. Wilson carried 1,973 out of the total of 2,971 counties, but had a majority in only 1,246, whereas Bryan in 1896 had a majority in 1500. Wilson's vote was larger than the largest Bryan vote only in New England and the Pacific section. The importance of Roosevelt's candidacy is reflected by the fact that "in the greatest number of counties (1,382) no party had a majority."

Of equal importance to the presidential vote was that the Democrats carried both houses of Congress for the first time since 1894. Only twice since the Civil War had both houses of Congress been Democratic, from 1879 to 1881 and from 1893 to 1895. Superficially Wilson would seem to have had safe support in Congress since the Democrats had 50 senators to 44 Republicans and 291 representatives to only 127 Republicans, the largest margin in the House enjoyed by either party since 1893. The House, to be sure, had gone Democratic in 1910 for the first time since 1892, by a margin of 228 to 162.* Indeed, elections from 1908 through 1912

*In 1912, eighteen states returned only Democratic congressmen. These were all southern states except Colorado, Delaware, Maryland, Indiana, which had been predominantly Republican until 1909, New Hampshire and Connecticut which hitherto had usually returned only Republicans. The states of Kentucky, Missouri, Tennessee, and Virginia, normally Democratic remained Democratic with some Republican representation. Important shifts to the Democratic columns took place in Illinois, which had not had a Democratic delegation in the twentieth century, Kansas which normally was strongly Republican, New Jersey and Ohio which had Democratic delegations for the first time in the twentieth century in 1910, and New York which usually went Republican. Of twenty-six states with Democratic congressional delegations, all went Democratic in the presidential election except Illinois and Kansas, which voted for Roosevelt. Seventeen states sent predominantly Republican delegations to the House. Of these, Montana, Idaho, saw an undermining of Republican strength. The southern states remained Democratic throughout and the Pacific states Republican. But New England, the Middle Atlantic states, and the East-North Central states showed a definite shift, enough, indeed, to make the House Democratic in 1911; by 1913, with the Republican split, all sections except the Pacific states and the West-North Central states had stronger Democratic representation than Republican, and in the latter section representation was almost equal.

In any case, Thomas Woodrow Wilson, the first Democratic president since Grover Cleveland and the first southern-born president since Andrew Johnson, would soon apply skills developed in the ivory towers of academia and the jungle of New Jersey politics to much more complex problems on the national and international scene.

Bibliography

Pages 136–138

For Taft, see Henry Pringle, *Life and Times of William Howard Taft; A Biography,* 2 vols. (1939); Paolo E. Coletta, *The Presidency of William Howard Taft* (1973); Stanley D. Solvick, "William Howard Taft and Cannonism," *Wisconsin Magazine of History,* 48 (Autumn 1964), 48–58, and "The Conservative as Progressive: William Howard Taft and the Politics of the Square Deal," *Northwest Ohio Quarterly,* 39 (Summer 1967), 38–48.

Pages 138–139

For the income tax amendment, see also John Buenker, "Urban Liberalism and the Federal Income Tax Amendment," *Pennsylvania History,* 36 (April 1969), 192–215; Laurence J. Holt, *Congressional Insurgents and the Party System, 1909–1916* (1967).

Page 139

For Taft's foreign policy, see P. Edward Haley, *Revolution and Intervention: The Diplomacy of Taft and Wilson with Mexico, 1910–1917* (1970); Walter V. and Marie Scholes, *The Foreign Policies of the Taft Administration* (1970); Robert F. Smith, "Cuba: Laboratory for Dollar Diplomacy, 1898–1917," *Historian,* 28 (August 1966), 586–609.

Oregon, South Dakota, North Dakota, Utah, Vermont, Washington, Oregon, Nevada, and Wyoming were entirely Republican, and California, Maine, Pennsylvania, although remaining Republican as they had traditionally been, made substantial Democratic gains. Of these Republican states, California, Pennsylvania, Maine, Vermont, Iowa, Michigan, Minnesota, North Dakota, and South Dakota, went for Roosevelt in the presidential election; Massachusetts and Wisconsin for the first time chose Democratic presidential electors, and Utah cast its vote for Taft.

Pages 139–140

For the tariff, the Pinchot-Ballinger episode, and the rules hassle, see also David W. Detzer, "Businessmen, Reformers, and Tariff Revision: The Payne-Aldrich Tariff of 1909," *Historian*, 35 (February 1973), 196–204; Thomas R. Ross, *Jonathan Prentiss Dolliver; A Study in Political Integrity and Independence* (1958); George Mowry, *Theodore Roosevelt and the Progressive Movement* (1946); Martin L. Fausold, *Gifford Pinchot, Bull Moose Progressive* (1961); James L. Penick, Jr., *Progressive Politics and Conservation; the Ballinger-Pinchot Affair* (1968). John D. Baker questions whether the rules' changes should be considered a progressive reform. See "The Character of the Congressional Revolution of 1910," *Journal of American History*, 60 (December 1973), 679–691.

Page 140

The press quotations on Roosevelt's return are from the *Literary Digest*, 39 (October 2, 1909), 510–512; (November 20, 1909), 890; 40 (June 18, 1910), 1211; the quotation of June 18, 1910, is from Henry Pringle, *Theodore Roosevelt, A Biography* (1931), p. 534.

Pages 140–142

For the breakdown of the Republican party, see Kenneth W. Hechler, *Insurgency; Personalities and Policies of the Taft Era* (1940); and especially Mowry, *Theodore Roosevelt and the Progressive Movement* and Belle and Fola La Follette, *La Follette*, I.

Page 142

For Taft's antitrust campaign, see also James Weinstein, *The Corporate Ideal in the Liberal State, 1900–1918* (1968) and especially James C. German, Jr., "The Taft Administration and the Sherman Anti-Trust Act," *Mid-America*, 54 (July 1972), 172–186.

Pages 142–144

My interpretation of Herbert Croly's contribution is borrowed from Charles Forcey, *The Crossroads of Liberalism; Croly, Weyl, Lippmann, and the Progressive Era, 1900–1925* (1961). See also Arthur S. Link, *Woodrow Wilson and the Progressive Era, 1910–1917* (1954), pp. 18–20. David W. Noble, "Herbert Croly and American Progressive Thought," *Western Political Quarterly*, 7 (December 1954), 537–553; Byron Dexter, "Herbert Croly and *The Promise of American Life*," *Political Science Quarterly*, 70 (June 1955), 197–218.

Page 144

On the early development of "the new nationalism," the *Chicago Tribune* quotation is from the *Literary Digest*, 41 (September 10, 1910), 367; H. M. Hooker, ed., Amos Pinchot, *History of the Progressive Party, 1912–1916* (1958).

Pages 144-145

For the business support of Roosevelt, see Kolko, *Triumph of Conservatism;* Weinstein, *Corporate Ideal;* Garraty, *Right Hand Man;* Wiebe, *Businessmen and Reform;* Amos Pinchot; and particularly George Mowry, *Theodore Roosevelt and the Progressive Movement.*

Pages 145-146

For the social workers, Allen Davis, *Spearheads for Reform; the Social Settlements and the Progressive Movement, 1890-1914* (1967); see Walter I. Trattner, "Theodore Roosevelt, Social Workers, and the Election of 1912; a Note," *Mid-America,* 50 (January 1968), 64-70. On woman suffrage, see Roosevelt to Harriet Taylor Upton, November 10, 1908, Morison, ed., *Roosevelt Letters,* VI, 1340; Carrie C. Catt and Nettie R. Shuler, *Woman Suffrage and Politics; The Inner Story of the Suffrage Movement* (1923), p. 227; Roosevelt to Jane Addams, two undated telegrams and notes, Morison, ed., *Roosevelt Letters,* VII, 594-595.

Pages 146-149

For the story of the conventions, see Mowry, *Theodore Roosevelt and the Progressive Movement;* Arthur S. Link, *Woodrow Wilson and the Progressive Era, 1910-1917* (1954); Harbaugh, *Theodore Roosevelt;* Belle and Fola La Follette, *La Follette,* I; Pringle, *Taft,* II; Fausold, *Pinchot.* For the racial question, see Seth M. Schiener, "President Theodore Roosevelt and the Negro, 1901-1908," *Journal of Negro History,* 47 (July 1962), 169-182. For a defense of his position, see Roosevelt to Julian Harris, August 1, 1912, Morison, ed., *Roosevelt Letters,* VII, 584-590.

Page 149

For Roosevelt's comments on the outcome of the Democratic convention, see Roosevelt to Horace Plunkett, August 3, 1912, and to Arthur H. Lee, August 14, 1912, Morison, ed., *Roosevelt Letters,* VII, 591-594 and 597-598.

Pages 149-153

For Woodrow Wilson's early career, see Henry W. Bragdon, *Woodrow Wilson: The Academic Years* (1967) and George C. Osborn, *Woodrow Wilson; The Early Years* (1968). But please sample the magnificently edited volumes of his published papers. Arthur S. Link, et al., eds., *The Papers of Woodrow Wilson* (1966-?). Sixteen volumes had been published by 1973, covering the period from 1856 to 1907. See also Link, *Wilson: The Road to the White House* (1947); William Diamond, *The Economic Thought of Woodrow Wilson* (1943); Joseph Dorfman, *The Economic Mind in American Civilization, 1865-1918,* vol. III (1949), pp. 193-194; on the importance of Burke, see Link, ed., *The Papers of Woodrow Wilson,* VIII (1970), 313-318; Arthur S. Link, "Woodrow Wilson: The Philosophy, Methods, and Impact of Leadership," in Arthur P.

Dudden, ed., *Woodrow Wilson and the World of Today* (1957); for Wilson's attitude toward business, see Martin J. Sklar, "Woodrow Wilson and the Political Economy of Modern Liberalism," *Studies on the Left,* I, no. 3 (1960), 17–47, and N. Gordon Levin, *Woodrow Wilson and World Politics; America's Response to War and Revolution* (1968).

Pages 153–158
For New Jersey politics and Wilson's nomination, see Ransom E. Noble, Jr., *New Jersey Progressivism Before Wilson* (1946); Link, *Wilson: Road to the White House;* John M. Blum, *Joe Tumulty and the Wilson Era* (1951). On Taft in the election, see Mowry, *Theodore Roosevelt and the Progressive Movement;* and Pringle, *Taft,* II; the Taft quotation is on p. 817. On the socialists in the election, see H. Wayne Morgan, "Eugene Debs and the Socialist Campaign of 1912," *Mid-America,* 39 (October 1957), 210–226. For Roosevelt's speech, see Hermann Hagedorn, *The Works Of Theodore Roosevelt* XVII (1926), 306–314. For the influence of Louis Brandeis on Wilson's campaign, see Norman Hapgood's preface to Louis D. Brandeis, *Other People's Money and How the Bankers Use It* (1933), p. xliv. See especially *A Crossroads of Freedom: The 1912 Campaign Speeches of Woodrow Wilson,* ingeniously edited by John Wells Davidson (1956), especially pp. 27, 206, 325, 4, 9–10, 30–31, 190, 294–295. For the analysis of the vote, see Robinson, *The Presidential Vote,* pp. 14–17.

6

Progressivism and Interventionism, 1913-1917

The New Administration

Emotions had run high during the campaign, and Wilson's inaugural address was an impressive call for unity. Reflecting the inadequacy of Taft's presidency, even the strongly Republican *New York Tribune* praised the inaugural and commented, "The nation is hungry for leadership like that." Those who were concerned about the scope of Wilson's progressivism may have been encouraged. He did more than spell out specific wrongs that he wanted righted in international trade, in the banking and currency system, in the industrial system, and in agriculture. He also criticized the defenders of laissez faire: "Our thought has been," he said, " 'Let every man look out for himself . . . ' while we reared giant machinery which made it impossible that any but those who stood at the levers of control should have a chance to look out for themselves." "We have not studied," he added, "the means by which government may be put at the service of humanity, in safeguarding the health of the Nation, the health of its men and its women and its children, as well as their rights in the struggle for existence. . . . There can be no equality of opportunity, the first essential of justice in the body politic, if men and women and children be not shielded in their lives . . . from the consequences of great industrial and social processes which they cannot alter. . . . Sanitary laws, pure food laws, and laws determining conditions of labor which individuals are powerless to determine for themselves are intimate parts of the very business of justice and legal efficiency."

Shortly before his inauguration, Wilson had said that "it would be the irony of fate if my administration had to deal chiefly with foreign affairs."

He did not refer to foreign affairs in his inaugural; nor did his cabinet choices suggest concern about the nation's relations with other powers. William Jennings Bryan, the secretary of state, was no authority on foreign affairs, while Josephus Daniels, a small-town southern newspaper editor, and Lindley Garrison, a judge of the Chancery Court in New Jersey, were no better equipped for the positions of secretary of the navy and secretary of war, respectively. In spite of increasing responsibilities abroad, professionalism in the diplomatic corps initially declined after Wilson took office. The Balkan wars and the rebellion in China undoubtedly seemed quite distant, even though "young Turks" in the State Department were demanding more economic participation in the affairs of China in order to make the Open Door a reality. Moreover the barbarities of the Mexican revolution were close at hand, and American troops were stationed along the border, while the near completion of the Panama Canal provided a reminder that the United States had a significant stake in the Caribbean.

Bryan had early developed plans to promote international peace. He supported proposals for bilateral arbitration treaties and agreed with Wilson that the end toward which mankind was moving was "an orderly and righteous international society." Both men favored policies that would encourage foreign trade and investment as a means of building a stable world order. Yet both men lacked an understanding of the power relationships that characterized international relations on the eve of the First World War.

Wilson was probably even less prepared to cope with the problems of defense than with those of foreign relations. He hated militarism and distrusted the military professional. He apparently had little interest in strategy and seemed to follow the principle that the less he had to do with the army and the navy the better. He undoubtedly soon found out that the actual strength of the army was just under eighty thousand, of which number about fifty-eight thousand were in the United States, and that much of that army was now alerted because of increasing disturbances on the Mexican border. Mexico had been in a turmoil at least since the revolution against Madero erupted, and a border patrol was charged with keeping back "crowds of curious citizen sightseers" and preventing "the use of American territory by the contending parties."

If Wilson overlooked foreign policy and the armed forces before his inauguration, he had given a great deal of thought to the problem of administering the presidency. His academic research, in fact, had provided the knowledge and his public and private career the experience in executive leadership and administration. Even more than Theodore Roosevelt, Wilson contributed to the development of presidential power. He was aware of the constitutional provisions which authorized the president to "give to the Congress information of the State of the Union, and recommend to their consideration such measures as he shall judge necessary and expedient." Through this authorization, Wilson envisaged the possibility of moving toward the parliamentary democracy which had been for so long his ideal form of government. He envisaged the American Constitution in a way comparable to the British Constitution as one which had not developed according to a conscious plan, but as having been shaped by "customs, practice, impact of dominant personalities, and social and political forces." He made use of his messages, his power of the veto, and his authority to convene Congress. He framed legislation; he talked directly to congressmen in the president's room in the capitol; and he electrified the Congress by adopting the practice, which Jefferson had abandoned, of addressing both houses in person on important legislative matters. In so doing he used those oratorical skills which he had nurtured over the years. As his students would cheer him at the end of an inspiring lecture, so would the congressmen, brought to their feet in spite of themselves. He appealed to the public through the press to build up support, to explain the opposition of certain interests, or to undermine Republican opposition.

The purpose of presidential leadership is primarily to enact a legislative program and Wilson was willing to go to the ultimate length of a parliamentary leader, resignation, if he did not have the legislative support to put his program across. When Wilson came into office, it was not known how effective his congressional leadership would be. There were Democrats making sounds about overthrowing the party machinery. Part of the undercurrent of revolt was against seniority, part of it was against southern domination of committees, and part of it was a revolt against "conservatism." Wilson gave little aid to those who wished to upset the status quo, and the revolt simply did not come off. Seniority prevailed in the choice of committee heads, and the South emerged in control of the machinery. Of twenty-three important committees in the House, southerners chaired twenty, and in the Senate, of twenty-four important committees southerners chaired eighteen.

The South's domination of the committees, however, did not necessarily forecast the nature of the legislative program. Southerners had dominated the committee chairmanships in the previous House of Representatives and had taken the lead in supporting such measures as those establishing a children's bureau, outlawing the use of the injunction in labor disputes, and providing for the direct election of senators. Now, with the presidency in Democratic hands, they had a chance to make a record that could quite properly be labeled a Democratic record, and Wilson, the prime minister, was prepared to provide the leadership.

Pressure Groups

Wilson soon learned, however, that executive leadership meant much more than preparing a seemingly ideal legislative program and then persuading the Congress to approve it. As power became more centralized, the national government found itself increasingly a target of numerous pressure groups, each apparently convinced of the rectitude of its position. Among the most active of these were women's suffrage organizations. Nine states had granted women's suffrage by 1913, and nine more would vote on the issue before 1916. With such victories behind them, the National Council of Women Voters and the National American Woman Suffrage Association were now confidently campaigning for a federal law. In December 1913, some fifty-five suffragists, led by Dr. Anna Howard Shaw, president of the National American Woman Suffrage Association, confronted President Wilson in the White House. Wilson, however, artfully dodged the issue, saying that he was "not at liberty to urge upon Congress, in messages, policies which have not had the organic consideration of those for whom I am spokesman."

Wilson was equally unenthusiastic about a much more popular local issue, that of prohibition. By 1913, nine states had prohibition laws, and restrictions throughout the nation had "expelled" the saloon "from two-thirds of the geographical area and one-half of the population of the country." Even though these arid areas contained only three cities of more than 100,000 population and a foreign-born population of little more than 1 percent of the total, prohibitionists were now aiming at a federal law. In October 1913, the Woman's Christian Temperance Union of America held its fortieth convention and endorsed national prohibition. A month later the Antisaloon League of America, by now perhaps the most effective pressure group in the United States, boasting a million dollars contributed during the year, held its twentieth annual meeting in Columbus, Ohio. The antisaloon leaguers too endorsed "National Constitutional Prohibition" and sent representatives on the day following the convention to a meeting of the Council of One Hundred, representing all the temperance forces of the country. The year's events came to a climax in December when Senator Morris Sheppard of Texas and Representative Richmond Hobson of Alabama, and of Spanish-American War fame, introduced a constitutional amendment that would authorize national prohibition. Some 2,000 delegates of the Antisaloon League and perhaps 1,000 from the WCTU celebrated this event on the Capitol steps.

Farm organizations too were ready to take on the new administration and gain legislation that they considered had been promised to them. For years such organizations as the Grange, the Southern Cotton Growers Association, and the Farmers Union had been advocating lower tariffs, enforcement of the antitrust laws, a federal income tax, a parcel post and rural free delivery system, and banking and credit facilities more responsive to the farmers' needs. In the twentieth century, support for the farmer became better organized and more highly centralized. Seaman Knapp had discovered the value of demonstration farms and county agents in aiding agriculture shortly after the turn of the century. Within the decade Knapp gained support for his experiment in the Department of

Agriculture, the General Education Board, and the agricultural colleges. Knapp found that local businessmen were frequently concerned about the economic health of the farmers, and he succeeded in persuading numerous big and little businesses including leading railroads, the American Bankers Association, the American Steel and Wire Company, and Wells Fargo to support farm legislation. Representatives of "nearly all the leading transportation companies and large numbers of financial institutions and manufacturing concerns" had combined in the National Soil Fertility League, an organization designed to urge federal support for vocational education in agriculture and industry.

A campaign also intensified to improve credit facilities for the farmer. It is impossible to state specifically what farmers were charged in interest for first mortgage loans. Although some states had set 6 percent as a maximum rate, there were ways of avoiding such ceilings by making special charges for the use of money, and examples have been cited of charges of 200 percent to black farmers. Moreover, rates varied widely from state to state—or even within states. In 1915, one estimate placed the variation as 5 to 12 percent with an average of 8½ percent. By 1913 Congress had established a federal commission to study European credit institutions for farmers. The commission discovered that with only two or three important exceptions (Norway, Sweden, and Greece) all European countries had some sort of "rural cooperative credit," and that credit was more readily available and interest rates generally lower than in the United States. The commission thus recommended federal and state support for cooperative credit and land banks.

In the meantime, the Department of Agriculture had been quietly extending its activities so that by 1913 probably no federal agency had greater power over a segment of the economy. For the previous sixteen years, James Wilson had served as secretary and had seen the department grow from a payroll of fewer than 3,000 persons to one of almost 14,000 and from a budget of slightly more than $3 million to one of about $25 million. Accepted as a department which should improve the lot of the farmer through education and research, it was increasingly playing the role of a police officer as Congress put the enforcement of various regulatory laws in its hands. It was responsible, for example, for the administration of the Pure Food and Drug Act and the Meat Inspection Act, as well as for preventing cruelty to animals in interstate commerce, regulating the sale of insecticides and fungicides, and protecting the resources and watersheds of the national forests.

Except for the fact that President Wilson was a southerner, there was perhaps no good reason for assuming that he would be sympathetic to the needs of the farmers. Bryan's appointment to the State Department meant that at least the farmers would have a friend in court, it is true, and the new secretary of agriculture, David Houston, was interested in agricultural economics and was a former president of an agricultural college. From the point of view of those who endorsed substantial credit facilities for the farmer, however, Houston's position was conservative. Although he saw the need for rural credit facilities, he saw no need as he put it, "for unique legislation . . . which shall aim to give the farmer credit on easier terms than other members of society secure." Clearly with a strong minority in House and Senate, including A. S. Lever of South Carolina, chairman of the House Committee on Agriculture, favoring more elaborate intervention of the federal government, tension would develop here.

Another important pressure group at the time of Wilson's inauguration, and one that was becoming increasingly interested in political action, was that of organized labor. Total trades union membership in 1913 came to about 2.7 million, of which approximately 2 million were in the AFL. Like Woodrow Wilson himself, Samuel Gompers, the president of the AFL, had rather reluctantly turned toward the federal government to seek protection for the laborer and had concluded in 1908 that the Democratic party was best equipped to provide that protection. Through a legislative committee, the AFL kept a careful record of how congressmen voted on legislation of interest to labor and increasingly concentrated on electing friends of labor to Congress. In 1910, for example, fifteen labor union members were elected. Although their principal efforts were to protect the right to organize and to strike, they also endorsed various eight-hour bills on federal projects, the establishment of the Children's Bureau, workers' compensation for federal workers, a federal Bureau of Health, and bills to protect sailors and to restrict immigration. Another indication of the pressures building up was the organization in 1913 of the American Committee on Social Insurance designed to study not only compensation for accidents but also insurance against "vicissitudes which menace the workers" such as sickness, old age, and unemployment.

As with so many other issues, Wilson's labor policies could not be made in a vacuum. He obviously had outgrown his antilabor views of the 1880s and 1890s, and he pleased the trades unionists by appointing William Wilson as secretary of labor. "Our Billy," as the United Mine Workers called him, had been secretary-treasurer of that union when elected to Congress from Pennsylvania in 1906, and he later "fathered the measure that created the position which he was the first to fill." President Wilson came into office at a time when conditions did not make the development of a labor policy easy. The cost of living had been steadily climbing since the 1890s, and laborers were complaining that their food budget was out of sight. In New York in February 1913, fifteen selected eggs cost 25 cents, a loin of pork 12.5 cents, Armour Shield brand ham 16.5 cents, bacon 18 cents, and coffee 25 cents a pound.

Perhaps reflecting the increased cost of living, strikes were growing not merely in numbers involved but in violence. In Paterson, New Jersey, for example, the silk workers launched a strike over issues that involved wages, hours, working conditions, and especially the kind of machinery that should be employed. These issues were made even more complex by the early intervention of the Industrial Workers of the World which for some years had been engaged in vigorous battle not only with employers over working conditions but also with the AFL for control of the labor movement. As "Big Bill" Haywood put it, "The IWW wants to wipe out the power of Sam Gompers, John Mitchell, Jim Lynch, and John Golden, who banquet with the capitalist class at night and talk to working men in the daytime." So Haywood, Carlo Tresca, who made "fiery appeals" to his "fellow-Italians," and Elizabeth Gurley Flynn took the lead at Paterson and painted a rosy picture of industrial society when the workers had taken over. When John Golden, President of the United Textile Workers, AFL, arrived on the scene, the workers would have none of him, some accusing him of being a tool of the mill owners. Even a commentator obviously concerned about the impact of the syndicalist philosophy of the IWW was warning that an increasing number of industrial communities made up, as at Paterson, largely of low-paid workers of foreign extraction might accept revolutionary leadership unless other leadership were provided in their search for economic justice.

To those who considered unions a threat, the mysteries of syndicalism were probably no more threatening than the actual violence that characterized labor relations in the coal fields. Disorder there was epidemic, but a particularly serious dispute, largely over union recognition, broke out in Kanawha County, West Virginia, in April 1912. Fights between miners and mine guards led to two proclamations of martial law and the calling out of the National Guard. One pitched battle took sixteen lives and led to the personal intervention of Governor Hatfield of West Virginia. In July 1913 he brought the strike to an end with terms essentially favorable to the union. Later an even more bloody strike broke out in the coal fields of southern Colorado. In this case, the employees requested the newly organized Department of Labor to mediate, but the employers refused the department's good offices.

Concern about the plight of the laborer was not limited to the labor department or the ranks of labor itself. An increasing number of persons who had been active in various social justice movements in the early years of the century became convinced that the public did not have enough information about conditions in industry. Most of these individuals were members of such organizations as the American Committee on Social Insurance, the Women's Trade Union League, the National Consumers' League, the National Child Labor Committee, or the National Conference of Charities and Corrections. In December 1911, Jane Addams, Lillian Wald, Florence Kelley, Rabbi Stephen Wise, and John Haynes Holmes among others, met in the offices of the *Survey*, a periodical that reflected the attitudes of numerous reform groups, and began the agitation for the appointment of a federal commission to investigate the general condition of labor in the principal industries of the United States. The campaign was successful, and the commission was authorized in the closing days of the Taft administration, appointed by Woodrow Wilson, and for two years held extensive hearings. Although the commission was divided on many of its recommendations, it convincingly documented the maldistribution of wealth, the uncertainties of employment, the inequities of the law, and the denial of the right of labor to organize. The final staff report recommended state and federal legislation for such relatively conventional matters as wages, hours, working conditions, and the right to organize, as well as for the establishment of a federal system of health insurance and nationalized telephone and telegraph systems.

While the Industrial Commission was investigating the conditions that led to these unconventional recommendations, Congress could contemplate other reports, already in hand, on the concentration of business and banking. Since 1910, the National Citizens' League for the Promotion of a Sound Banking System had been rousing businessmen for the need of better banking facilities. A year later, a subcommittee of the Committee on Banking and Currency under the chairmanship of Arsene Pujo of Louisiana began investigating accusations that a sinister conspiracy existed to control credit. Coming on top of earlier investigations, the Pujo committee provided a wealth of information about the centralization of financial power and the failure of either local or federal government to cope with it. Even George Baker, head of the First National Bank of New York, had testified that the concentration of credit had "gone about far enough."

The report of the committee raised the question of what federal responsibilities were when confronting economic power blocs potentially more powerful than government itself. Although the majority of the committee, the six Democrats, did not find that an organized trust in money and credit existed, it did point to the "rapidly growing concentration of the control of money and credit in the hands of these few men." It showed how, through interlocking directorates, certain individuals and their companies influenced insurance companies, railroads, and industries. It pointed the finger at J. P. Morgan and Company; Higginson and Company; Kidder, Peabody and Company; and Kuhn, Loeb and Company. Even the principal minority of three Republicans saw "a dangerous concentration of credit in New York City and to some extent in Boston and Chicago," and J. P. Morgan and Company, while insisting that a "money trust" was an impossibility, agreed that the banking system was "clumsy and outworn."

The publicity given to the concentration of banking and credit facilities reinforced the popular attitude concerning the concentration of industry which had existed since the last decade of the nineteenth century. In spite of the Bureau of Corporations, the activities of Roosevelt's Department of Justice, and the even more effective trustbusting activities of Taft, neither conditions nor popular attitudes toward monopolies had probably changed much by the time Wilson took office. Indeed, decisions of the Supreme Court in the Standard Oil and American Tobacco Company cases in 1911 raised the question whether the federal government needed additional powers to cope with the industrial giants. The Supreme Court, it is true, had ordered the dissolution of these behemoths, but it had based those decisions not on the grounds that these corporations were in restraint of trade but that their restraints of trade were "unreasonable." Such a "rule of reason" called for some definitions as to what constituted unreasonable practices. The Senate Committee on Interstate Commerce assumed the task of determining what changes in the antitrust law were then needed, at the same time that a House committee launched an investigation of the U.S. Steel Corporation. The Senate committee reported on the eve of Wilson's inauguration and found the need for legislation to facilitate enforcement of the antitrust laws, and, even more importantly, recommended the establishment of a federal trade commission to provide better administration and enforcement of these laws.

In view of the various investigations which seemed to be throwing a bad light on the activities of business and industrial corporations, it is not surprising that business leaders not only became rather defensive but mobilized to promote their own interests at home and abroad. Among the most significant, in the light of increasing American interests abroad and Wilson's long-time support of foreign trade, were a large number of organizations designed to promote overseas trade and investment. The American Asiatic Association and the Pan-American Society were pushing their geographical interests. The American Manufacturers Export Association was formed in 1910 and the United States Chamber of Commerce two years later. In 1914, all of these organizations as well as officers of the nation's leading industries created the National Foreign Trade Council. Encouraged by Wilson's secretary of commerce, William C. Redfield, this powerful organization was designed to bring business and government together in support of a vigorous foreign trade policy.

Pressures from various directions would also compel Wilson to seek solutions to some of the conservation problems inherited from the administrations of Roosevelt and Taft. The issue of conservation became increasingly complex as the nation's industries and cities demanded vast quantities of natural resources. Wilson soon found that regardless of his convictions on conservation, federal policy could not be made in a vacuum. From a constitutional point of view, it was clear that the federal government had control over the federal public domain. By withdrawing public lands from private use, or from exploitation, as the conservationists would have it, he was performing a legitimate federal function. Yet not until 1937 would Congress and the courts accept federal power to promote conservation practices on privately owned land.

Wilson soon found, moreover, that all wisdom was not on the side of the conservationists. The question was how to guard natural resources on the one hand and to develop a wise and efficient program for use of those resources on the other. From a political point of view the question was a crusty one, because the conservationists favoring federal regulation were well organized and particularly popular in the East, while interests in oil, timber, cattle, and hydroelectric power were politically powerful in the West. The battle was joined in 1913 at the fifth annual session of the National Conservation Congress. In one corner were the Nationalists led by Gifford Pinchot who believed that "the people of a state, Esau-like, are too prone to sell their birthright for a mess of pottage." In the other corner, Senator John Bankhead of Alabama led those who opposed "dictation from Washington" and complained that conservation policy tied up "resources in red tape so that nobody can get any benefit from them." The Arkansas delegation felt so strongly on the issue that it introduced a resolution to abolish the forest reserve and "contended that the waterways of their state belonged to the state." The Pinchot forces carried a resolution supporting "the principle of Federal control of water power," but it was resented so bitterly that the Arkansas delegation withdrew, and those of Montana, Washington, and Oregon indicated that their states might not be represented again.

The two issues in conservation that perhaps best illustrate the way in which developments of the twentieth century led to the expansion of federal power were those involving oil and hydroelectric power. Production of hydroelectric power had increased from approximately two billion kilowatt hours in 1902 to more than seven billion in 1912. Thus the potentialities of electric power for industrialization and comfort had already been recognized, and the industry expected a glorious future. Yet existing legislation and administrative practices limited the expansion of hydroelectric power facilities. The General Dam Act of 1906 was the chief culprit since it required congressional approval for hydroelectric projects on navigable rivers, and conservation influences were sufficiently strong in Congress to prevent the approval of any projects unless the public interest was clearly protected; moreover neither the Department of the Interior nor the Department of Agriculture was about to hand over to private interests unrestricted permits to exploit sites in the public domain or national forests. Private power companies had managed to gobble up practically all the accessible sites not controlled by the federal government, and that government now loomed as the barrier to further expansion. Thus the battle was joined between the power lobby with western and southern supporters on the one side and on the other the conservationists supported by Wilson and his secretary of the interior, Franklin P. Lane, for control of the federal sites.*

In this battle, Wilson and Lane retained the confidence of the con-

---

*Neither side could budge the other until the closing months of Wilson's presidency—when in 1920, the Water Power Act was passed which established the Federal Power Commission and empowered it to issue licenses for the construction of dams on navigable rivers or on the public lands, and to control rates of the power produced at these dams.

servationists. The same happy condition did not exist, however, with regard to the issue of oil reserves. The usefulness of oil in industry had become obvious. By 1913, the prognosis was that nearly all marine boilers would be "oil fired since advantages of more 'uniform steaming,' 'greater steaming radius,' and a smaller crew gave oil a significant advantage over coal." Yet the resources in oil were an uncertain quantity. One estimate in 1916 put the U.S. oil supply at 5,763 million barrels, a reserve which it was thought "would last at the present rate of production 22 years, or perhaps if the supply could be protected, for 50 to 75 years." Given the increasing dependence of the navy on oil, the federal government became concerned about the reserves. Taft had withdrawn approximately 3 million acres of oil lands from the public domain and established Elk Hills and Buena Vista Hills in California as naval reserves. In 1915, Wilson added the Teapot Dome reserve in Wyoming to this list.

Probably no knowledgeable person at this time denied the need to modernize the laws controlling mineral lands. Unfortunately, however, these were private claims, and a real hassle developed between the navy department and conservationists on the one hand and private interests on the other. Year after year the debate continued. The administration itself was divided, particularly as western states created political dangers for the party toward the end of the war. Western Democrats such as Pittman of Nevada, Walsh of Montana, and Ashurst of Arizona found support from Secretary of the Interior Lane. Increasingly the opposite track was being taken by the two Wisconsin senators, La Follette and Lenroct, supported by the National Conservation Association and its indefatigable secretary Harry Slattery and most famous member Gifford Pinchot. To them, Daniels and Attorney General Gregory within the administration were on the right course. The ten-year controversy possibly came to a temporary conclusion with a series of actions—which have appropriately been called the Compromise of 1920.*

It would have been difficult for Wilson, when he assumed the presidency

---

*The most important element in the compromise was the passage of the mineral leasing law in February. This law applied to "deposits of coal, phosphate, sodium, oil, oil shale, or gas, and lands containing such deposits owned by the United States, including those in the national forests, but excluding lands acquired under the act known as the Appalachian Forest Act, approved March 1, 1911 . . ., and those in national parks, and in lands withdrawn for military uses or purposes, . . . shall be subject to disposition in the form and manner provided by this act." The act then provided for the leasing of sections of this land for prospecting and mining, but with provisions for royalties to the federal government and careful restrictions upon the procedures by which the leases were made. Then in June of the same year, Daniels won a major victory when the Naval Appropriations Act directed the secretary of the navy "to take possession of all properties within the Naval petroleum reserves as are or may become subject to the control and use by the United States for naval purposes," and upon which no claims which resulted from the Mineral Leasing Act were pending. The secretary was then authorized "to conserve, develop, use, and operate the same in his discretion, directly or by contract, lease, or otherwise."

in 1913, to have foreseen the bitterness that would develop over the disposition of the mineral reserves, but as a devoted automobile driver, he undoubtedly shared the concern as to where adequate fuel supplies were coming from. Indeed, few developments were creating more excitement than the development of the automobile industry. By 1913, total registration had grown from a few thousand in 1900 to more than 1 million automobiles; annual production of pleasure cars reached 325,000 in 1913 with an average price of $975. Only six years before the average had been about $2,140. Truck production too was beginning to become significant with about 51,500 trucks produced in 1913, more than double the number produced in 1912. Concern about fuel for these vehicles reflected the belief that oil and gasoline supplies were limited. The wholesale price had increased from 10¢ to 16¢ a gallon, and the assertion was seriously made that denatured alcohol was "bound to be the ultimate fuel" since its supply was inexhaustible. Equally important for the usefulness of the automobile would be the availability of spare parts, and the Standards Committee of the Society of Automotive Engineers was sparing no effort in pushing for standardization in steels, alloys, tires, bearings, brake connections, washers, lights, and all the innumerable items necessary to make the automobile go.

Clearly the automobile industry was becoming a significant factor in the national economy, but the road system of the United States built for wagons and generally maintained through local efforts was simply not keeping up. Individuals, automobile clubs, and interested industries begged for the funds necessary to build more and better roads. State expenditures did increase—from about $2 million in 1903 to about $43 million in 1912. Understandably, Administration policy, to begin with, was cautious. Although Congress had recently authorized the appropriation of $500,000 to improve rural roads, Secretary of Agriculture Houston made clear that as a principle he favored the expenditures of $2 by the state for every $1 by the federal government.

A problem which would prove periodically embarrassing to President Wilson was that of black people. The racial issue continued to be a paradox of American progressivism. In the southern states, the emotionalism of populism and the disfranchising campaigns had not had a chance to die down. Between 1900 and 1906 states and cities in the South had passed Jim Crow streetcar laws which had resulted in boycotts by black people in about every southern city. In 1910 in Baltimore, the City Council approved an ordinance providing for residential segregation of the races, and numerous cities in North Carolina, Virginia, Georgia, and Kentucky followed suit. There were, moreover, forty-five recorded lynchings during the first ten months of 1913. The Democratic party in the South, even its members who might be described as progressive when it came to economic issues such as railroad and business regulations, boasted of its acceptance of white supremacy. Southern Republicans convinced by the twentieth century that associating with blacks could only hurt them

politically, purged the blacks and boasted that their party was "lily white."
Roosevelt had tried to ride both horses on this issue but his Machiavellian
move at the Progressive convention in 1912 probably destroyed whatever
support he had had among the black leadership. Taft had already lost
the confidence of the blacks because of his unwillingness to appoint
them in the South.

Wilson was an uncertain quantity. He was a southerner; his wife was
from Georgia; Princeton, while he was its president, had not admitted
blacks; some of his closest political associates were southerners. Wilson
himself refused to commit himself unequivocally on the racial issue. In
July 1912, when the president of the Washington branch of the NAACP,
J. Nelson Waldron, claimed that Wilson had made a statement promising
equality of treatment, Wilson denied it. Very much alarmed, Oswald
Villard, an enthusiastic supporter of Wilson, urged Wilson to provide a
"quotable" statement. Finally, less than a month before the election
Wilson assured another black leader, Bishop Alexander Walters, a member
of the Board of the NAACP and President of the National Colored
Democratic League, that he favored "not mere grudging justice, but
justice executed with liberality and cordial good feeling." On the basis of
this statement and hope, Wilson received substantial political support from
the black leadership.

Shortly after the election, the Board of Directors of the NAACP suggested that Villard and DuBois propose to Wilson the appointment of a
national race commission to improve race relations. The commission
would make "a nonpartisan, scientific study of the status of the Negro
in the life of the nation, with particular reference to his economic situation." Villard presented the plan to Wilson in May 1913 and was delighted
at Wilson's reaction. The political atmosphere soon changed, however,
as Wilson's southern associates had their influence. Postmaster General
Burleson pointed out that it was "unpleasant" for white men to work
with blacks in railway mail cars "where it is almost impossible to have
different drinking vessels and towels." He claimed that he had discussed
the problem "with Bishop Walters and other prominent Negroes," and
that most of them thought that the segregation of white and black
employees in all departments of the government "would be a great thing
to do." In discussing appointments, Wilson indicated that he had promised
only "justice" to blacks, that he did not want to reduce the number of
positions which they now held, but that his main concern was to prevent
friction. He also warned that the Senate would not confirm a black for
the position of Registrar of the Treasury—even though a black already
held that position. Gradually segregation practices were established in the
Post Office, the Treasury Department, and various other offices. A number of blacks were removed from their offices; and only one significant
black reappointment was made, that of Judge Robert H. Terrell to the
Municipal Court of the District of Columbia.

Unquestionably Wilson found himself torn among his own ideas of justice, his background, and political realities which included the black vote on the one hand and southern influence in Congress on the other. He refused to appoint the commission in August, assuring Villard that he wished to do justice to the blacks, but that he had had no idea of the "complexity and difficulty" of the problem of race relations. He found himself "absolutely blocked" not only by southerners but by senators "from various parts of the country." Although he assured Villard that he hoped "to handle the matter with the greatest possible patience and tact," he considered segregation advantageous for the blacks, and therefore favored it.

Black organizations, alerted to the hostility in Congress, maintained a careful watch on congressional activities. The NAACP promptly publicized antiblack legislation. Numerous Jim Crow streetcar bills and anti-inter-marriage bills for the District of Columbia, a bill to prohibit black non-commissioned officers in the army and navy, to exclude black immigrants, and to have the Supreme Court consider the "validity" of the fourteenth and fifteenth Amendments did not get far.

In spite of their efforts the status of black people suffered during the Wilson administrations, but the president's stand on the position of the black is hardly a fair measure of his progressivism. To members of the NAACP, it might have been, but to few others in the campaign for social justice was the lot of the black a particularly significant issue. Moreover the Wilson administration did not introduce segregation. It had existed in the nineteenth century; it continued to exist under Theodore Roosevelt; it probably became worse under Taft; it continued to expand under Harding and Coolidge and was not improved under Hoover.

The Wilson torn between practical considerations and principle symbolizes the position of any president seeking to advance a legislative program. During the four years 1913 to 1917, pressures were intense for tariff, banking, and antitrust reform, for legislation that would help the farmer and protect labor, give women the right to vote, and limit the beverages that a citizen could drink. In the meantime, small wars in the Balkans had spread to include all major powers except the United States, and chaos south of the border had led to a veritable war with Mexico. Simultaneously crises in foreign policy compelled a reassessment as to whether the military forces were capable in force and in doctrine in meeting possible challenges of the twentieth century. To complicate matters even further, the president, a devoted father and husband, was made desperately lonely—he lost his two daughters by marriage and saw his beloved wife gradually waste away until she died in August 1914, within a few days after the explosion in Europe which shook the world.

Yet Wilson in that first year in the White House gave every indication that he was in control of the situation. He kept a meticulous office schedule. He prescribed himself a daily golf game for exercise and fresh air. He attended plays "good, bad, and indifferent," and if nothing better offered—vaudeville. In less than a year one observer concluded, the president was no longer considered an academic. "His capacities and his abilities measure up to the office he holds. He is, indeed, chief magistrate to the uttermost fringe of his authority. Everybody at Washington knows it."

When Wilson took office, he appeared confident that he could put a program through which combined much-needed reforms with hardheaded calculations concerning the interests of the United States. The clamor for tariff and banking reform and improvement of the antitrust laws had accounted for a substantial amount of Wilson's popular support, and Wilson proposed to fight for these reforms. At the same time, Wilson believed, perhaps with equal conviction, that America's mission in the world was commercial supremacy, and he saw tariff reform, a central banking system, a merchant marine, and an appropriately regulated corporate structure as essential means of carrying out that mission.

The Legislative Program: The New Freedom

The effectiveness of his administration is illustrated by the way in which he put through his program. The first item on the agenda was tariff reform, and by a typical demonstration of leadership working through two southerners, Oscar Underwood of Alabama in the House and Furnifold M. Simmons of North Carolina in the Senate, he succeeded in gaining the first significant reform of the tariff since 1846. Even though superficially the tariff issue seemed to be a simple one—reformers favored a lower tariff and "interests" favored protection—it never had been a simple one, and in 1913 it was as complex as ever. A lobby investigation brought out rather clearly that of the largest combinations, such as those in steel and sewing machines, only those in domestic sugar lobbied in favor of the tariff. The principal supporters of the tariff were actually the smaller manufacturers, frequently those represented by the National Association of Manufacturers, who needed the tariff to keep them in business in spite of competition with larger enterprises.

Even more important than the tariff itself was a rider attached to the tariff bill providing for an income tax. Cordell Hull, a forty-two-year-old congressman from Tennessee, had been a student of taxation for some twenty years and, after having been elected to the House in 1906, had been in the midst of the congressional battles that led to the ratification of the income tax amendment. Understandably Underwood assigned him the responsibility of writing the new law and guiding it through the Congress.

The measure when first introduced called for a normal tax of 1 percent upon an individual's net income of more than $4,000 and for a small surtax on larger incomes. The tax was attacked from all sides; some, arguing that an income tax should be used only as a wartime emergency, considered it "an act of bad faith on the part of the Democratic party." Others claimed that the purpose was not revenue, but "taxation of the few for the benefit of the many." Apparently more persuasive, however, were those who argued that the measure was class legislation and undemocratic because of the $4,000 exemption. The *San Francisco Chronicle* pointed out that in England the exemption was $750 and in Prussia only $225. In any case the Senate committee changed the exemption figures to $3,000 and $4,000 for a married couple. The basic normal tax remained at 1 percent with additional surtaxes of 1 percent levied at increments above $20,000, making possible a total tax of 7 percent above $500,000.

The importance of the income tax both as to the principles involved and as to its practical effect can hardly be exaggerated. In principle, it established ability to pay as basic to a tax system; it accepted the role of the federal government as a kind of supervisor of incomes. From a practical point of view, it meant reducing the importance of customs revenues in the national fiscal system, providing an almost unlimited source of revenue, and encouraging the collecting of information about the national income which simply had not been available before. To the critic it meant "inquisitorial interference with the citizen everywhere."

For the Treasury Department, the income tax required considerable reorganization. The official estimate was that 425,000 individuals would be subject to the tax. The bill had been passed in early October, and somehow the regulations had to be prepared for the collection of the tax from "the source" by November 1—just one month after the approval of the bill. The immediate practical effects of the income tax were not sensational. The total number of returns (357,598) and the revenue collected ($28.3 millions) were substantially lower than expected. But the flexibility of the law was demonstrated when the European war interfered with imports; customs revenues fell substantially; government expenditures began to skyrocket; and the income tax schedules were quickly adjusted to quadruple the revenue from that item.

The second item on Wilson's legislative agenda was the reform of the banking and currency system. Yet because of the inseparability of banking and currency and the "economy," it was an issue of extreme sensitivity. For those who worshipped at the throne of laissez faire any subordination of the banking system to government control smacked of heresy. In 1913, that system was truly complex. There were between 27,000 and 28,000 banks in the United States with total assets of approximately $26 billion. Of these between 7,000 and 8,000 were national banks, authorized by the National Banking Act of 1863 with total assets of approximately $11 billion. The 20,000 nonnational banks were essentially state commercial banks. Although the Comptroller of the Currency presumably supervised all national banks, his control was minimal, and the inability of the federal government to mobilize resources in time of economic crisis was illustrated in 1907 when J. P. Morgan "bulldozed his reluctant New York rivals into temporary and extra-legal cooperation."

Complaints about the banking and currency systems had built up during the Populist revolt, and were only somewhat muted in the more prosperous years of the early twentieth century. One very glaring weakness was the inability of the system to provide a currency that would work. The Gold Standard Act of 1900 had preserved the gold standard, to be sure, and it had authorized national banks to issue bank notes to the full value (rather than only a fraction of the value) of the government bonds which they held. But government bonds provided a currency which, though safe, did not expand or contract with the needs of the economy, and thus reformers were raising the cry for greater flexibility. Moreover westerners and southerners were convinced that a money trust existed, that interlocking directorates made it possible for directors of railroads and industries to sit on the boards of banks, that these interests were concentrated in the Northeast, and that they were responsive first to the demands of the Northeast.

The Democratic platform called for banking reforms, and after Wilson's election, negotiations began which were to be subject to pressures so varied, numerous, and changing that they can hardly be identified. Bankers themselves were far from united—size, location, political rivalries, sectional interests, agrarian or industrial needs, suspicion of Wall Street, and personal philosophies and associations, all played their part. Under the circumstances presidential leadership was vital, and given the differences that existed among Wilson's own supporters, the passage of the Federal Reserve Bill was even more impressive than had been the Underwood-Simmons tariff. Wilson was convinced that any bill must reduce the concentration of the "money power" in Wall Street and must recognize the role of government in making "fundamental financial decisions."

In steering his way through the intricacies of these negotiations, Wilson turned to Louis Brandeis whose advice he was increasingly soliciting. Brandeis, who had little if any confidence in the large private banking houses, recommended a currency exclusively controlled by the government and questioned the reliability of "a Board composed wholly or in part of bankers." Wilson was convinced on the essentials of the bill. On June 23, ten days after communicating with Brandeis, he again outlined the measure to a joint session of Congress, and for the next six months used a combination of toughness and conciliation in meeting the opposition, but above all keeping the pressure on until the bill was passed.

Although the bill did not go so far as some of the progressives and agrarian interests wished in undermining private control and making available easy credit, it provided effective national control of the banking and currency system for the first time. It set up a Federal Reserve Board to consist of the secretary of the treasury, the comptroller of the currency, and five additional members appointed by the president with sweeping supervisory powers over the Federal Reserve banks; it divided the country into eight to twelve Federal Reserve Districts with a Federal Reserve bank in each district; each Federal Reserve Bank was to have the power to issue federal reserve bank notes upon the deposit of government bonds and federal reserve notes on the basis of short-term commercial paper and the power to buy and sell government securities and commercial paper on the open market; it required all national banks to belong to the system and permitted other banks to belong.

Wilson looked upon the year's contributions of his administration not only as reform at home but as a coherent policy for developing foreign trade. His secretary of commerce had strengthened the Bureau of Foreign and Domestic Commerce and encouraged trade associations; the tariff was designed partly on the principle that if we were to sell abroad, we must buy foreign products at home; the Federal Reserve Act made possible American branch banking abroad and encouraged foreign investment; and both Bryan and Wilson assured American traders that there was nothing in which they were "more interested than the fullest development of the trade of this country and its righteous conquest of foreign markets."

With the passage of the Federal Reserve Act, a substantial number of Wilson's advisers thought that enough had been accomplished for the time being, and that it was time for a breather. In fact, the economy was acting unfavorably, and Republicans blamed the Wilson administration. "Men today, both in factories and financial institutions," postulated Representative Mann, Republican floor leader in the house, "are nearly scared to death." On the other hand Senator F. M. Simmons, colegislative author of the tariff law, accused "a little coterie of moneyed men who control big finances in this country" of an attempt to discredit the administration.

In spite of threatening business conditions, however, some argued that certain needs had to be met: the agrarians demanding long-term rural credits not provided in the Federal Reserve Act; the National Child Labor Committee at least partially victorious in forty-seven states now ready for a federal law; the suffragists demanding women's suffrage; the anti-saloon leaguers demanding prohibition; organized labor demanding laws to protect sailors, to restrict immigration, to provide federal aid for industrial education, to provide greater federal protection against accidents, and to limit the use of the injunction in labor disputes.

However, the demand that was probably closest to the heart of Wilson—and that came from no single interest—was the demand to make the antitrust laws more effective. Against all the advice to give business a breather, Bryan urged Wilson to carry out his campaign promises on that point, and, probably more importantly, Brandeis, warning that progressives were questioning Wilson's courage, advised that "the fearless course" was "the wise one."

In the campaign of 1912, Wilson had pursued no issue more vigorously than antitrust reform, and to him antitrust reform meant not necessarily destroying large corporations but outlawing evil practices and protecting competition. Although such a program apparently persuaded a substantial portion of the electorate, it worried many business leaders including a rapidly growing number who were endorsing what was coming to be called the "New Competition." The principal goals of the New Competition were stability and cooperation, quality and service rather than price cutting and ruthless competition, goals which Roosevelt had enthusiastically embraced while working with George Perkins and Elbert Gary of U.S. Steel.

Superficially the philosophy of the New Freedom would not appear compatible with the New Competition. Even after the election of 1912 Wilson went so far as to threaten those who would limit competition with a "gibbet as high as Haman's." He hoped to develop an antitrust policy which would maintain competition and be in the public interest. If possible, it would spell out unfair practices; in any case it would be based upon law and precedent rather than individual whim.

Wilson allowed the members of Congress only a brief Christmas holiday in December 1913 before confronting them anew with a demand for legislation to regulate trusts. Although he gave assurances that "antagonism between business and government" was over, he went on to demand outlawing interlocking directorates, penalties for individuals guilty of malpractices, and "a federal commission to provide businessmen with the 'advice, the definite guidance, and information' which they need, but not having power to 'make terms with monopoly or . . . assume control of business.'"

The president delivered this message at a time when he was becoming an increasingly harried man. Not only were economic signs still pointing to a depression but relations with Japan were reaching a critical point over the rights of Japanese citizens in the United States; negotiations with Nicaragua about an alternative canal route were having political repercussions in the United States; a complicated debate was developing with Congress and within Great Britain over tolls to be charged American vessels using the Panama Canal; the Mexican Civil War was continually raising new and unexpected problems; Mrs. Wilson could not seem to recover from a debilitating illness; and the European war always was ominously in the background.

Under the circumstances, Wilson spoke softly and solicitously to business and tossed the responsibility of framing legislation to his congressional leaders. After much tugging and pulling and compromising on all sides, a measure authorizing a Federal Trade Commission was approved on September 26, 1914. It represented a sweeping extension of national power. The act very simply stated that "unfair methods of competition in commerce are hereby declared unlawful." Then it went on to authorize the five commissioners to determine what constituted unfair competition. The commission could hold hearings, investigate the activities of corporations engaged in commerce (save for those subject to the Interstate Commerce Commission), require regular or special reports from these corporations, investigate alleged violations of the antitrust acts, make rules for carrying out the provisions of the act, and summon witnesses and documentary evidence. These powers were enforceable in the federal circuit and district courts and were subject to fine or imprisonment or both.

Given the broad framework provided by the Trade Commission Act, the Clayton Antitrust Act approved three weeks later (October 15, 1914) was somewhat anticlimactic. It did, however, specifically outlaw interlocking directorates—one of the principal bogeys of the critics of the money trust—as well as specify other practices as illegal. Perhaps most controversial, historically, were the labor clauses. The Democratic platform had promised labor exemptions from the antitrust laws, and Wilson's campaign seemed to support this position. The bill as finally passed stated that labor is not "a commodity or article of commerce," and that neither labor nor agricultural organizations should be considered "illegal combinations." Injunctions were not to be granted in a labor dispute "unless necessary to prevent irreparable injury to property," and injunctions to prevent persons from persuading others "by peaceful means" to strike were banned.

These provisions met with a mixed reception. The NAM described them as "class legislation," "vicious and unAmerican." The *Wall Street Journal* complained that Congress had "handed the labor leader a license to commit crime." Gompers, on the other hand, praised the Act as "Labor's Magna Carta," while Secretary of Labor Wilson called it "the greatest step that has been taken by labor and for labor within the past two generations."

These views were exaggerated. President Wilson insisted that the Clayton Act should not "exempt" labor organizations from the antitrust laws or from prosecution for illegal activities but should establish the legality of unions. The framers of the law had phrased each concession carefully. Only "peaceful" or "lawful" actions were protected, phrases which the courts would interpret.

Under almost any circumstances the question of the role of the federal government in labor disputes has been controversial, but during the negotiations over the labor provisions of the antitrust laws tension was particularly high since two particularly unpleasant examples of labor-management relations were then running a bloody course in Michigan and Colorado. At Ludlow in Colorado at least nineteen were killed including two women and eleven children when a tent colony of coal strikers was set on fire. In both cases, the federal government attempted an intervention. In both cases, the strike failed, but in Colorado only the intervention of federal troops brought the carnage to an end. Under the circumstances, with public opinion divided and the majority of congressmen hostile, the declaration in the Clayton Act defending unions and the right to strike and endorsing a limitation in the use of the injunction justified labor's claim to victory.

The Clayton Antitrust Act, the Federal Trade Commission Act, the Simmons-Underwood Tariff, and the Federal Reserve Act had one important goal in common: They all were designed to strengthen the posture of the United States in its competition for foreign markets. An important section of the Trade Commission Act, actually written by George Rublee, a member of the special committee on trade commission legislation of the U.S. Chamber of Commerce, provided for the investigation of world trade by the commission, and the Clayton Act made possible certain kinds of price discriminations in foreign trade which were prohibited within the United States.

The passage of the Clayton Antitrust Act signaled the end of the first phase of Wilson's domestic program. Other items had appeared on the legislative docket, but Wilson was not pushing them for various reasons, not the least of which was the unsettling effect of the war in Europe.

The Rights of a Neutral

Although an analysis of the American mind is a dangerous undertaking, it seems safe to assume that few Americans in the spring of 1914 expected the outbreak of a major European war—let alone the involvement of the United States in it. Unhistorical though the view might have been, the assumption that peace rather than war was a normal condition was probably generally accepted. Even the belligerent Theodore Roosevelt had provided the stimulus for the Second Hague Peace Conference which had met in 1907.

Indeed, the ideal of the peaceful settlement of international disputes was receiving much attention in the first decade of the century. The two Hague Conferences, it is true, had met with only token success. However, the first conference in 1899, attended by delegates from twenty-six nations, had framed an arbitration convention as well as declarations against the use of certain kinds of weapons, such as asphyxiating gas, and provided for a Permanent Court of Arbitration. Attempts were also made to define neutral rights and neutral duties on land and sea. Arbitration provisions held out great hopes to the peace-seekers, and actually more than 130 arbitration treaties, designed to require submitting disputes to an impartial commission, were signed between 1899 and 1910.

In the United States some sixty-three peace organizations existed in 1914. Such organizations as the American Peace Society and the American Society for the Judicial Settlement of International Disputes were supplemented by the activities of schools, churches, and universities. The Federal Council of Churches of Christ in America included a department of peace. In 1912, the Fifth International Congress of the Chambers of Commerce came out for judicial settlement of international disputes. Labor unions opposed militarism. Philanthropists used their wealth in support of peace. Edward Ginn, a wealthy textbook publisher from Boston, endowed the World Peace Foundation in 1910 with one million dollars. In December 1910, Andrew Carnegie established the Carnegie Endowment for International Peace with an initial grant of ten million dollars. Supported by such funding and the genuine urge to make the world better, peace congresses both in the United States and Europe became regular events.

How widespread actually was the belief that pacifist organizations, churches, labor unions, Chambers of Commerce could really keep the peace? On July 31, 1914, some fifty representatives of peace organizations from all over the world including England, France, and Germany meeting in Brussels saw the collapse of their hopes. They called on the belligerent governments to check mobilization. They turned to Wilson as the executive of the most uninvolved power and urged him to propose mediation, but his advisers were divided, and he himself was distraught as he watched Mrs. Wilson slowly dying. He composed an offer of mediation at his wife's bedside on August 4, but on that day the Germans poured into Belgium.

Although Wilson had received strong warnings from his adviser, Colonel Edward House, who had gone abroad in May, that the situation in Europe was inflammatory he was in no condition to take any decisive action. Yet he was sensitive to his role as commander in chief and the possible impact of the war on the United States. At first surprisingly ignorant of the intricacies of European politics, he devoted much time to study. He soon recognized the complexity of the origins of the war and concluded that although an Allied victory would serve the interest of the United States, a deadlock and a peace of reconciliation would be preferable. Although he became increasingly concerned about the results of the war if it should continue, he was equally concerned about the possibility of the nation's becoming involved. To him, moreover, the practical and moral arguments for neutrality were convincing.

For almost three years, while attempting to guide to passage a complicated domestic program and win victory for the Democrats at the polls, he was finding his administration more and more involved in foreign policy. He found the country divided—by interests, by sections, by ethnic groups. His personal advisers were as far apart as Secretary of State William J. Bryan, who was essentially a pacifist, and Under Secretary of State Robert Lansing, who talked in terms of the balance of power and feared a German victory. He was subjected to advice from individuals and pressure groups on all sides. Both the Central and Allied powers were flooding the United States with propaganda, true, exaggerated, and false.

Wilson's concern from the beginning was to protect the interests of the United States. And these interests were complex. They were principally economic. They included the highly profitable loans of American bankers such as J. P. Morgan and Company who saw to it that the millions of dollars worth of Allied loans which Morgan floated were almost fully secured regardless of the outcome of the war. More importantly, these interests involved a skyrocketing trade in farm products such as wheat, oats, horses, and mules, and basic industrial products such as pig iron and barbed wire. Upon this trade depended the well-being of millions of farmers and wage earners—even more influential politically, no doubt, than the businessmen, who were divided any number of ways on their attitude toward war and peace.

The interests of the United States changed substantially in those three years as American prestige became involved in the controversy. Wilson soon found that foreign policy could not be made in a vacuum, that other nations were carrying out policies in accord with their interests, and that the political parties, the newspapers, the legislatures, and governments of other countries might help shape American foreign policy. It was in the interests of Great Britain to use her superior navy to clamp down a blockade against the Central Powers. It was in the interests of Germany to clamp down a blockade against Britain by using the comparatively new weapon—the submarine. Wilson believed not only that under principles of international law the United States had a right to trade but that the economic stability of the country depended upon trade. Thus even though he may have wished to develop an independent policy, he was forced to respond to what other nations did.

Both the Allied blockade and German submarine warfare posed a threat to vital American trade. Partly by clever timing and partly by coincidence Britain's blockade was made more palatable to the United States by Germany's submarine policy. Wilson was willing to wait until the end of the war to gain compensation for property damage; he claimed that there was no adequate compensation for loss of life. Hence early in 1915 he informed the German government that he would hold that government to strict accountability for loss of American lives or ships. He pointedly did not challenge "the right of the Imperial authorities to invoke the law of reprisal in undertaking a ruthless campaign against *enemy* merchant shipping." Wilson was no fool. He knew that if American ships sailed into belligerent waters, and if Americans traveled on passenger vessels of belligerents, they were in danger. Yet these were rights, and, in his view a great nation could not afford to abandon them. The shocking sinking of the *Lusitania,* the later sinking of the *Arabic* and the *Sussex* demonstrated the problem. Wilson's diplomacy was skillful in negotiating agreements, but he knew that the only sure way of avoiding a crisis would be to end the war—so on different occasions his trusted emissary, the somewhat enigmatic Colonel House, was dispatched to Europe to attempt to bring the war to an end.

In spite of Wilson's increasing skill as a negotiator, he apparently did not consider the possibility that his negotiations would have more weight if his military power were greater. Throughout complex negotiations of 1914 and 1915, for which no precedent existed in American experience, comparatively little attention was focused on the nation's armed forces. Indeed, when in 1915 the House of Representatives debated the Army Appropriations Bill for the fiscal year 1916, Representative James Hay of Virginia, the economically minded chairman of the House Committee on Military Affairs, announced that the United States was then "safer from attack than she ever had been in her history because of the involvement of potential aggressors in the fighting in Europe." To put funds into an expansion of the regular army, Hay argued, would be at the expense of improved harbors, public buildings, and roads. Others ridiculed the argument that any nations had the resources to accumulate the number of transports necessary to bring to American shores an invasion force large enough to conquer the country. Even if any nation were able, Representative S. F. Prouty of Iowa argued, with the army numbering 80,000 and the National Guard 120,000 and 1 million men ready to spring to arms, no invading force would "dare to leave the protections of their ships and undertake to go inland."

Preparedness

There was no clear-cut party line on preparedness. The Democrats were divided. The most consistent opposition probably came from rural, southern representatives. The strongest support for preparedness came from Republicans such as Senator Henry Cabot Lodge and his son-in-law Augustus Gardner. The Republican insurgents, such as La Follette and Norris, on the other hand, became increasingly critical of administration policy on the ground that it was leading toward war. Their main hope was to warn Americans to stay out of the war zone. On the question of preparedness, however, the insurgents were less united than on the issue of neutral trade and intervention and in the voting were almost equally divided; even Robert La Follette voted for naval expansion in 1916.

Actually the army had been undergoing significant changes since the Root reforms of 1903, but it was questionable whether it was adequately prepared even for defensive operations against a powerful aggressor. During the last years of the Taft administration Henry F. Stimson had served as secretary of war and Leonard Wood, Theodore Roosevelt's friend and one-time superior officer, as chief of staff. Wood, like Roosevelt, believed that the geographical and economic position of the United States required a development of American international power, and thus he was determined to strengthen the army to a point that it could defeat any potential enemy.

The main obstacles in the way of centralized planning and a greater coordination in operations were still the chiefs of the bureaus and their congressional allies. Stimson and Wood, therefore, were determined to renew the drive for reform begun ten years ago by Roosevelt and Root. In a vigorous confrontation, Stimson went farther along the road toward concentrating the planning function within the General Staff, and even forced the resignation of Major General Fred C. Ainsworth, the adjutant general and symbol of the old guard. Moreover, following the advice of a bright young captain of the staff, John M. Palmer, Stimson endorsed the concept of building units ready to fight immediately rather than the historic principle of considering the U.S. Army a skeleton in time of peace expansible by volunteers in time of war. Thus Wood began to organize the army into tactical divisions. In addition, Stimson, concerned about the lack of a federally controlled reserve force, persuaded Congress to make some preliminary efforts to establish a reserve.

In the meantime, several technological developments were promising revolutionary changes in military tactics. By 1912, the possible usefulness of the airplane in war had captured the imagination of a few officers in the signal corps. The army officially was slow to evince an interest. In spite of efforts on the part of the Wright brothers, shortly after they had made their first flight in 1903, to inform the army of what an airplane could do, the ordnance department had remained skeptical. Not until 1907, after the Wrights had begun to negotiate with European governments, did the U.S. Army sign its first contract. By 1912, Brigadier General George P. Scriven, chief of the Signal Corps, considered aviation for an army a "vital necessity," yet expressed uncertainty as to its function. Scriven, personally, preferred dirigibles for offensive warfare because they could carry more guns and explosives than an airplane, but considered the latter indispensable for reconnaissance and fire control for the artillery.

Congress was slow to appropriate funds for the new weapon. By 1912, the United States had spent only $255,000 in aeronautics "since the inception of the art," and appropriated only $125,000 for 1913, a year in which France appropriated $7,400,000 and Mexico $400,000 for the same purpose. Secretary of War Garrison justified such economy by arguing that the United States could take advantage of experiments "being carried on in other countries at great expense." In 1914, Congress seemed more interested, approved setting up an aviation section in the Signal Corps and appropriated $250,000 for purchasing and operating aircraft. By 1915, American production had reached about 100 planes a month, but General Scriven considered no American-built motors "entirely reliable."

The navy was fully as conservative about experimenting with air power as the army. As early as 1898, Assistant Secretary Theodore Roosevelt had expressed interest in a model plane, designed by Samuel P. Langley, and envisaged the use of airplanes in war. Observers from the navy as well as the army watched the Wright brothers make an exhibition flight at

Fort Myer in 1908. In 1910, Captain Washington Irving Chambers, a young naval officer, became interested in aviation and devoted a great deal of time to calculating how airplanes could be carried on ships for scouting purposes, how airplanes could be hoisted on and off the water from a ship, how a launching platform could be mounted on a ship, and how a catapult could be designed which would facilitate such a launching. The first plane took off from the deck of a ship in 1910 and in 1912 a successful catapult launching took place.

The navy was thus somewhat ahead of the army in experimenting with airplanes, but it was still slow in building up its flying strength. In 1914, there were nine airplanes in the naval service, and four of these had proved their worth as scouts particularly in locating submarine mines in the Vera Cruz operation. Recognizing that the use of aircraft in warfare was in its infancy, Secretary of the Navy Josephus Daniels appointed a board of officers to advise him as to how the navy could best use the new weapon. As a result an abandoned navy yard at Pensacola was converted to an aeronautical station which began to experiment with material and flying techniques. In 1915, Congress authorized the sum of $1 million for the development of naval aeronautics. Unfortunately so great was the demand from the Allied governments for aircraft (some 288 were exported in the first year of the war) that American manufacturers had little interest in developing types desired by the navy.

Another development that seemed to promise revolutionary changes in battle tactics was that of radio. By the end of the first decade of the twentieth century, wireless telegraphy had proven itself. It had been used successfully in the Russo-Japanese War, and the U.S. Signal Corps installed radio stations at all its principal posts in the United States and the Philippine Islands. At the same time technicians were experimenting with radio pack sets for use in the field. By 1914, they had developed one with a range of twenty-five miles and expected soon to have one with ten times that range. They had also developed a radio transmitter to be used on airplanes—but it was more of a problem to devise a receiver that could be heard over the clatter made by the planes' engines.

The United States was probably in the forefront of the development of naval radio. In 1913, the navy operated about fifty shore stations in the United States and its possessions, and some two hundred ships, virtually all of the seagoing navy, had radio installations. It also operated a powerful station at the Naval Observatory at Arlington, Virginia, where time signals were set out at regular intervals to enable ships at sea "to determine their exact chronometer correction," as well as to provide jewelers and others interested with the exact time. Other naval stations were providing storm warnings and weather forecasts and were experimenting with providing data that would enable a ship to determine its exact location.

The wireless obviously posed an unusual problem of regulation. By

1912, a thousand or more amateurs were filling the air with their dots and dashes and seriously interfering with governmental and commercial communication. In August, Congress responded to a demand for some sort of control by the establishment of wavelengths and by requiring licensing of all private stations by the Department of Commerce. The coming of the war further complicated the problem. By 1914, the beginning of an international radio network existed. Germany, for example, had two wireless stations in the United States, one at Sayesville on Long Island which communicated with a station near Berlin and another at Tuckerton in New Jersey with a corresponding station near Hanover in Germany. Great Britain also installed a station in the vicinity of New Brunswick, New Jersey, designed to reach a station in Wales. In the meantime, in collaboration with the American Telephone and Telegraph Company and Western Electric, the navy was experimenting with long-distance wireless telephone communication. On September 29, 1915, the first conversation was carried across the continent, from Arlington, Virginia, to Mare Island, California, and before the end of the year it was possible to transact routine business by wireless telephone.

Given this situation, it was obviously possible for all kinds of communications to be sent from the United States to belligerent countries, and Wilson was confronted with the novel question of whether he should attempt to regulate them. After considerable deliberation, he issued on August 5, 1914, an executive order prohibiting any radio station within American jurisdiction from sending or receiving any "unneutral message." The Secretary of the Navy, as Wilson's agent, ordered all belligerent ships to seal their wireless apparatus while within the jurisdiction of the United States. After considerable negotiating among the United States, Britain, and Germany, however, limited radio communication was allowed to continue to satisfy Germany, who argued that their station at Sayesville was the only direct means of communication with the United States, since Britain had cut the German cables.

The principal significance of the airplane and radio, however, lay in the future. For the present, the question was how ready were the army land forces and the surface navy. When Josephus Daniels became secretary of the navy, he almost turned it upside down. A convinced "small *d* democrat" with a Bryanesque suspicion of both war makers and businessmen, he decided "to make the Navy a great university, with college extensions afloat and ashore" and to give "less thought to the guns than to the men behind the guns." Although considering the navy "the right arm of American defense," Daniels hoped that pressures for peace together with the skyrocketing expenditures for construction would persuade the naval powers to agree upon a vacation in naval construction.

In the meantime he struck at the military-industrial-congressional complex. His progressive background revolted at the ways by which industry, particularly the armor plate companies and the oil companies, were profiting from navy contracts. He pointed out, for example, that armor plate companies were selling armor plate to foreign countries at a price substantially less than that charged to their own government, and that as the navy began to substitute oil burners in its ships for coal, the price of oil had doubled between 1911 and 1913. The only answer, he was convinced, was for the government to manufacture its own armor plate and for the navy to become a producer and refiner of oil. Moreover Daniels cited examples of padded contracts and identical bids to the nearest penny, which, since the companies involved were prohibited from collusion by law, must have been arrived at by mental telepathy. He was determined to prevent war preparations from resulting in private enrichment, and the Naval Appropriations Act of 1914 reflected that determination. Although there were loopholes, it essentially required the navy to purchase its vessels, munitions, in fact all its supplies and equipment from government plants unless private industry could clearly supply them more economically. Thanks to Daniels various navy yards were converted from mere repair facilities to real shipyards for new construction, and when bids for new battleships exceeded authorized costs, he announced that they would be constructed in the navy yards. Such radical views at first created consternation in Congress and among the industrialists, some of whom cried "socialism," but Wilson was willing to leave this problem to Daniels and his young assistant secretary, Franklin D. Roosevelt. As a result a somewhat different complex developed, sparked by Daniels in alliance with populistically inclined southerners such as Claude Swanson of Virginia and Ben Tillman of South Carolina on the Senate Committee on Naval Affairs. In a kind of regional alliance, they led the way to building up federally owned industry based in Norfolk and Charleston.

Although Daniels seemed confident of the readiness of the navy, both the Navy General Board and the Army General Staff were alarmed at the readiness of the forces for which they were responsible. In July 1914, Admiral George Dewey, then chairman of the Navy General Board, pointed out that in 1903 the General Board had proposed building up to a battleship strength of forty-eight by 1919 and that this program was so much in arrears that instead of forty-seven battleships either with the fleet, under construction, or authorized, actually the total was thirty with the fleet, four under construction, and three authorized. Although both destroyers and submarines were also needed, Dewey insisted that "the backbone of any Navy that can command the sea consists of the strongest sea-going, sea-keeping ships of its day, or, of its battleships."

A new army chief of staff was equally dissatisfied with the readiness of the army. Upon General Leonard Wood's retirement as chief of staff in April, 1914, Major General W. W. Wotherspoon, chief of the Mobile Army Division, assumed that position. The regular army consisted of approximately 90,000 in personnel, with perhaps 125,000 in the National

Guard. There was some uncertainty as to whether small arms and ammunition were sufficient for an emergency. There was no uncertainty at all, among the military at least, that the army was seriously lacking in artillery and artillery ammunition. The horrifying effectiveness, and expense, of artillery on the western front had shocked military planners everywhere. European experience, moreover, had demonstrated the effectiveness of motor transport. The American army in 1914 had approximately eleven thousand horses and mules for draft purposes in the United States and Hawaii, but only seventy-five trucks on hand and fifteen more on order for 1915. Wotherspoon, surveying this situation shortly after assuming his new post, described his forces as being understrength, inadequately equipped, and poorly trained, and proposed building up a mobile force of 500,000 regulars and reserves backed up by 300,000 in the organized militia.

Wotherspoon's recommendation led to a vigorous debate sparked by increasing activity of pressure groups campaigning for preparedness. The National Security League, whose numbers included Theodore Roosevelt, Henry Cabot Lodge, and Henry F. Stimson, the Army League, the National Defense League, and most effective of all the ten-year-old Navy League, were arguing that the new war proved that hopes for permanent peace were illusory, and that the only hope for peace was to be ready to fight.

In December 1914, Wilson would not consider an extensive preparedness program. His foreign policy was a policy of peace, and he refused to prepare for war in order to preserve peace. He denied that the government had neglected the nation's defenses. He refused to consider asking young men to spend "the best years of their lives making soldiers of themselves." Security, Wilson insisted, should rest not upon a standing army or a reserve army "but upon a citizenry trained and accustomed to arms." The National Guard, yes; a strong navy adequate for defense, yes; but to advocate more would not be consistent with his determination to preserve the peace, and he was determined not to alter his attitude "because some amongst us are nervous and excited."

In spite of Wilson's attitude, events in 1915 forced a change in American military policy. In Mexico, the situation did seem somewhat more tranquil as a Pan-American conference was working out arrangements for a recognition of Carranja, the newest victor, but elsewhere marines had occupied Haiti, and in May 1915 a German submarine sank the *Lusitania*. During the heated diplomatic exchanges resulting from the *Lusitania* and later the *Arabic* crises, the German negotiators undoubtedly wondered how the United States would fight, if war should come. The situation was further complicated by the fact that the American presidential election was only one year away. If the Republicans could heal their wounds of 1912, they would once more be the majority party and would pose a serious threat to Wilson's re-election if they could find a strong candidate and a popular issue. The Navy League was determined to make preparedness that issue, and set out to organize committees in each state, particularly in the Midwest where preparedness had been most opposed. It organized a junior Navy League and a Women's Section and stirred up patriotic emotions by holding preparedness rallies in all the major cities.

In July 1915 Wilson responded to the growing agitation by requesting new national defense programs from the War and Navy Departments. This request launched a debate that became acrimonious, as Republicans and Democrats, preparedness advocates and pacifists, Nationalists and States' Rights advocates fought for control of military policy. One of the most bitter controversies that developed concerned the future of the state-supported National Guard. Key people in the War Department and in the regular army insisted that the National Guard would prove unreliable in any crisis. Such public pronouncements brought a kind of undeclared war between the National Guard Association and the advocates of a greater degree of national power. So great was the National Guard's influence among congressmen, however, that even the most ardent advocates of national power recognized the impossibility of reducing the power of the Guard. One solution to the problem which Wilson endorsed in November 1915 was to continue to accept the National Guard, to strengthen the regular army, and at the same time to create a national reserve force known as the Continental Army.

Wilson's annual message to Congress in December 1915 called for preparedness for a possible defensive war. He would strengthen the army, the navy, and the merchant marine; rather emotionally he warned of forces of "passion, disloyalty and anarchy" plotting and spying in the United States, and requested laws "by which we may be purged of their corrupt distempers." Military preparedness, Wilson proclaimed, was closely related to domestic policy and depended in the last analysis upon the people and the "organization and freedom and vitality of our economic life." Thus he urged economic mobilization through "the right instrumentalities" and with particular attention to the railroads and the merchant marine.

This message provoked even more heated debate. In the House, the majority leader, the influential Claude Kitchen of North Carolina, openly fought the president, complained about the machinations of munitions makers, and called for economy. States' rightists preferred the National Guard to the Continental Army and questioned anything that increased national power. Elihu Root saw the move to strengthen the merchant marine as leading to state socialism. Big army advocates, strong in the Senate, thought that the administration scheme was inadequate. Garrison and his associates in the War Department, insensitive to political realities, fought without finesse for the Continental Army. Bryan, who had resigned as secretary of state because of his concern that American policy following the *Lusitania* crisis would lead to war, was now rallying huge crowds against the preparedness program. Just at this point, much to the horror of some of his political advisers, it became known that Wilson had fallen in love with Mrs. Edith Galt, a lovely widow and close friend of Wilson's cousin and housekeeper, Miss Helen Woodrow Bones. In spite of dire warnings about the political effect of a wedding within fifteen months of the death of the first Mrs. Wilson, Mrs. Galt and Wilson were married on December 18, 1915. They honeymooned for two weeks.

By the time he returned, so confused was the public about preparedness that Wilson's advisers were urging him to reassert his leadership. Confident of his oratory, he took the preparedness issue to the country in an intensive speaking tour from January 27 to February 3. Perhaps a million people heard him and were moved by his eloquence, but all shades of opinion remained. Yet in spite of confusing public and private pressures, events would not wait for public agreement on a course of action.

The submarine issue had not died down. Lansing, Bryan's successor in the State Department, was engaged in delicate negotiations with the Germans, and Colonel House on December 28, 1915, started off on another trip to Europe to explore the possibilities of American mediation of the war. In January 1916, too, the Mexican imbroglio was moving to another crisis. Pancho Villa and his irregulars seemed to murder people, including Americans, with very little compunction, and in March they swept across the border into New Mexico and killed nineteen more Americans. Wilson then unhappily dispatched an American force of twelve thousand under the command of Brigadier General John J. Pershing across the border to capture Villa. This expedition provided a serious test of transportation and communication facilities as well as of the training of the troops, and undoubtedly spurred on the debates on preparedness measures.

In spite of these ominous conditions and the restored vigor of Wilson's leadership, Congress refused to accept without modification the administration's program. Hay informed Wilson in February 1916 that the Continental Army was dead, and then pushed a compromise. Negotiations between the House and Senate marked with suggestions and concessions on the part of Wilson led at last to a new bill. By August 1916, three important preparedness statutes, the National Defense Act and the Army and Navy Appropriation Acts had been passed.

Although a compromise, the National Defense Act of June 3, 1916, represented one of the most sweeping extensions of national power in American history. It established the Army of the United States, which was to consist of the Regular Army, the Volunteer Army, the Reserve Force, and the National Guard. It doubled the size of the regular army to more than 200,000. More importantly, it launched the ROTC program and provided that land-grant colleges as well as other state and private institutions could establish a curriculum leading to a reserve officer's commission. The militia was divided, as in 1903, between the unorganized, consisting of every able-bodied man between the ages of eighteen and twenty-one, and the National Guard. Federal funds would provide the arms and equipment for the National Guard; the equipment and the discipline for the Regular Army and National Guard were to be the same; and the president was authorized to draft members of the National Guard "into the military service of the United States." The president and secretary of war were also given sweeping emergency powers over the economy. The secretary was instructed to make a list of privately owned plants capable of manufacturing arms and ammunition and to prepare plans for transferring these plants to the most appropriate war service; the president was authorized to appoint "a Board on mobilization of Industries essential for military preparedness," to investigate the most efficient means of the production of nitrates and other products for munitions" either by water power or other method, to designate dam sites on either navigable or nonnavigable rivers, and harness the river water for water power and the improvement of navigation. Although the primary purpose was the production of munitions at such points as Muscle Shoals in Alabama, the way was thus cleared for the Tennessee Valley Authority seventeen years later.

On August 29, 1916, Congress approved both the Military and Naval Appropriations Acts, and showed how far from traditional laissez faire it had been persuaded to go. The Army Appropriations Act, for example, actually authorized a Council of National Defense of cabinet members advised by technical experts to coordinate "industries and resources for the national security and welfare." Even more sensational, it empowered the president to "assume control of any system or systems of transportation" and to make whatever use of it he might see fit to meet a wartime emergency. The Naval Appropriations Act authorized the construction of plants to manufacture projectiles and manufacture armor plate for naval vessels, and at least partly satisfied those naval officers who had for years been campaigning for a long-range ship-building program. In spite of strenuous resistance led by Claude Kitchen in the House, the final bill included a 3-year-program involving 157 new units with 4 battleships to be authorized the first year. The total cost was to be almost $600 million, twice the amount approved for the previous year.

The Politics of Shipping

Closely associated with the other preparedness legislation was a bill to provide merchant shipping for American trade. Wilson, convinced of the vital importance of foreign trade, was horrified at the deterioration of the American merchant marine. He could point out that in 1860 American vessels had carried 66.5 percent in value of the nation's foreign trade, but that between 1880 and 1915 the percentage had fluctuated between 9.3 and 14.3. In 1914 only nine American merchant ships were on active service in trans-Atlantic or trans-Pacific trade. The outbreak of war brought a crisis to the American economy. For a time, foreign commerce virtually ceased; ship owners kept their ships in the harbors until they could see what the dangers of maritime trade might be; German and Austrian ships totaling about six million tons were promptly interned; and a good portion of Britain's huge merchant fleet, about half the world's total, was diverted to the service of the British army and navy.

The shipping crisis was reflected in a sensational increase in ocean freight rates. Between January 1914 and December 1915, rates between the United States and European ports increased between 500 and 1000 percent. Agricultural regions were particularly hard hit, as overseas demand normally determined farm prices. In 1914, crops were generally bountiful, and the maritime crisis came at harvest time. Cotton and grain producing areas feared ruin and the call went up for Congress to take steps to see that crops reached their markets. Wilson specifically urged congressional leaders to provide the ships to "carry our commerce to all ports of the world."

Among the most perceptive members of the Wilson administration was Secretary of the Treasury William G. McAdoo. Even before the war, he dreamed of how American commerce might expand. He sensed immediately the impact of the war on international exchange and summoned a series of conferences to seek remedies. One of these consisting of government officials, congressmen, and businessmen and bankers from all over the country met in Washington on August 14, 1914. The background was one of crisis: how could American products be moved in time of war in order to keep the economy sound; at the same time how might American commerce profit from this crisis. As William Stone, chairman of the Senate Committee on Foreign Relations, put it, "A most opportunistic time has arisen for the United States . . . to enlarge the commercial intercourse with the Republics of the South." Increasingly a mood developed between the representatives of business and government that reflected a belief that both parties would profit from cooperation. This mood led promptly to the passage on September 2 of a War Risk Insurance Act by which the Treasury Department would provide insurance that private companies were refusing to write for the merchant marine because of the menace of the submarine.

This was government enterprise with a vengeance, but an even more important question was whether business and government would provide ships to carry the products. McAdoo undoubtedly saw the crisis as an opportunity to develop a merchant marine, which private operators had failed to do, and Wilson was equally interested in seeing the expansion of trade. The first move took place with comparatively little congressional opposition. On August 18, 1914, Wilson approved an enactment that "repealed a requirement that foreign-built ships be less than five years old if they were to be transferred to American registry." Some hoped that German and Austrian ship owners might now sell out to the United

States, but, although many American owners of ships traveling under foreign registry now transferred to the American flag, German and Austrian owners did not. Even though the diplomatic language became rather murky on this point, England and France took a dim view of enemy vessels traveling under the American flag, and few ship owners wished to take a chance on what Allied hostility might mean.

In the meantime, McAdoo proposed the creation of a federally owned merchant fleet, and the president, although knowing full well that "reactionaries" would oppose such a bill, decided in mid-August 1914 to fight for it. The bill authorized the creation of a government corporation that would purchase and operate ships in foreign trade. A shipping board, to consist of the secretaries of commerce and the treasury and the postmaster general, would supervise the operations of the corporation.

This measure soon became embroiled in the politics of American shipping, a subject which had been fascinating the House Committee on Merchant Marine and the Fisheries since 1910. This committee had discovered that ships engaged in the foreign trade of the United States operated almost without exception under cooperative agreements worked out by the various steamship lines. These agreements provided for the fixing of rates, apportionment of traffic, and the pooling of at least some earnings. It was obvious that any comprehensive control of American shipping would have to take into account the existence of these agreements. In general the steamship lines favored their continuation, while the shippers, although not opposing them in principle, complained of excessive rates and discrimination. The House committee came to the conclusion that orderly control of the industry was essential, and proposed that the Interstate Commerce Commission provide the necessary regulation. It was only a step from that recommendation to the proposal of the president to create a supervisory shipping board and to provide for a corporation to purchase ships. As Wilson saw it, the need was to correct abuses, to provide the ships to develop trade at reasonable rates, particularly with the Americas, and to withdraw when the trade had become "sufficiently profitable to attract . . . private capital."

This unprecedented proposal inspired a bitter debate involving questions of international policy, fear of socialism, and party loyalty. McAdoo put his convictions on the line, hitting at those bound by the "mere dogma. . . . that the government must never go into private business." That argument, he asserted, "is always urged against any progressive step of this character. . . . I am not afraid of the Government going into business where private capital refuses, and where the business in which the Government is to engage is for the benefit of *all* the people of the country." Wilson called his opponents ignorant and misguided, but he could not even persuade all Democrats to support him. In one critical vote, the House refused to accept a Senate amendment that would "perpetuate government ownership of shipping indefinitely." This move alienated progressive senators. Then the Republican establishment organized by Senator

Gallinger of New Hampshire produced a filibuster. Senator Smoot spoke for more than eleven hours and then dropped "into a litter of worn out words"; on February 9, 1915, senators slept on cots in cloakroom and corridors and continued in session for fifty-five hours and eleven minutes—the longest congressional session then on record. It served its purpose; the bill was abandoned for the session.

The fight continued for more than a year, but Wilson finally won a substantial victory in 1916. The administration bill, with some compromises worked out by Secretary of the Treasury McAdoo and Secretary of Commerce Redfield, established a shipping board and gave the board authority to regulate commerce on the seas and Great Lakes; it "impowered the Board to spend a maximum sum of $50,000,000 in acquiring ships which should be leased or sold to private capitalists," or if such private capital were not available "should be operated" under a corporation in which the government was a majority stockholder.

Opponents of the measure soon made themselves heard. Although McAdoo had called on Bernard N. Baker, long-time president of the Atlantic Transport lines, for help in drafting the bill, most shipowners opposed it, and "a swarm of lobbyists" raising "the specter of government ownership" attempted to convert wavering congressmen. The Republican members of the House Committee on the Merchant Marine, sensing a good political issue, echoed these criticisms. The bill, however, picked up support. Even some who agreed in principle with the Republicans endorsed the need for a government agency to deal with the "famine in shipping." The *Washington Post*, for example, defended it as a temporary condition, possibly necessary until private investors were willing to take over the shipbuilding facilities. Looking further ahead, John H. Fahey, recently a president of the United States Chamber of Commerce, bemoaned opportunities in South American trade's being lost because of a lack of shipping. "The need for the shipping bill," he concluded, "is to be found also in the fact that all of the export trade of the United States is pouring through a funnel not nearly large enough to accommodate it. There must be more ships if the congestion is to be relieved and if a real merchant marine is to be built upon the present exceptional opportunities.

Hearings and debates resulted in several significant modifications. One change ruled out the purchase of ships owned by belligerents, thus preventing McAdoo's rather questionable plan to acquire German vessels; and another required that any corporation formed by the board to operate ships should be dissolved five years after the end of the war, and that all the ships were to be "sold, leased, or chartered" to private citizens. The House passed the amended measure in May 1916 by a partisan vote of 211 to 161; only 9 Republicans supported this version, and only 2 Democrats opposed. The Senate vote in August showed 38 Democrats in favor and 21 Republicans opposed. Rarely had the Democratic caucus worked so well. Thus was created one of the most controversial, important, and potentially most powerful of the war agencies.

The passage of the preparedness measures had once more indicated the paradox of American progressivism. The strengthening of the armed forces represented a substantial strengthening of national power, but went against the principles of the progressives who endorsed the settlement of disputes without resort to war and who in many cases accepted as valid the contention that preparedness was the handmaiden of selfish business interests. At the same time, the authorization of the Council of National Defense and especially of the shipping board established precedents acceptable to such progressives as Norris, La Follette, and Cummins. Yet they joined conservative Republicans such as Lodge and Root to oppose the shipping bill. Cummins, for example, criticized the government corporation because private interests as well as government officialdom would be represented; he was particularly irked at the provision that would end government operation after the end of the war. On balance, it seems probable that the preparedness legislation, while strengthening the federal government, alienated more progressive reformers than it attracted.

The Legislative Program: The New Nationalism

During the same period, however, the Wilson administration was making an impressive record in domestic legislation. In March 1915, Wilson had approved an act to protect the rights of sailors on the high seas and another to require safety inspection for railway locomotives. In 1916, he nominated Brandeis to the Supreme Court—a nomination that horrified conservatives and delighted progressives; then he went on to approve the Adamson Act, which relieved a difficult situation on the railways by providing for an eight-hour day, the Federal Highway Act, a workers' compensation act for federal employees, an act to subsidize vocational education, a rural credits act, and a child labor law.

Perhaps, in view of Wilson's southern constituency, the record of his administration in legislating for the farmer was understandable. Although many southern congressmen opposed federal social justice legislation, they were responsive to the difficulties of the farmer, and were becoming accustomed to what the Department of Agriculture could do for them. The western farmer, traditionally Republican in orientation, was less certain to support any Wilsonian proposals. In elections prior to 1912, an overwhelming number of counties in the western states normally went Republican. In 1912, however, a large number went Democratic or progressive, and contributed substantially to Wilson's victory, but their future votes would depend upon how the administration responded to the farmers' interests. Such organizations as the American Rural Credits Association, for example, were making it clear that rural credits legislation would have a wholesome effect upon the western voter.

Prior to 1916, Wilson had taken a contradictory position on aid to the farmer. In his annual message to Congress in 1913, he had indicated that farmers should expect "no special privilege such as extending to them the credit of the government itself." Yet he added that the farmer had special problems because of his dependence upon nature and because of his need for credit based upon a different kind of security customarily recognized by banks. In accord with Secretary of Agriculture Houston, he hesitated to endorse "government credit," on the ground that lending money to farmers out of the Treasury would be class legislation.

After 1914, the American farmer had to face the problem of war as well as the traditional problems of climate and disease. Staple crops saw record yields in 1914, but meat production and dairy farming did not meet the demands of the population. The able staff of the Department of Agriculture made special efforts to combat diseases. In 1915, an unusually serious outbreak of foot-and-mouth disease threatened the livestock industry in the United States. The Bureau of Animal Husbandry, in cooperation with state agencies, located infected areas, quarantined and slaughtered livestock, compensated owners, and divided the costs evenly between the federal government and the states. Other diseases such as hog cholera and tuberculosis were attacked, and Congress made a special appropriation in 1915 of $1,250,000 to provide protection against diseases that might pose a threat to the livestock industry.

One of the problems most urgently faced involved cotton, a product which was then more influenced by foreign disturbances than any other farm product since about 65 percent of the total cotton crop was exported. After the outbreak of war, southern cotton growers became greatly alarmed as the cotton price received by farmers fell from 12.4 cents to 6.3 cents per pound between August and November 1914. The situation became so critical that a high-pressure campaign developed throughout the country to "buy a bale of cotton" at $50 a bale and hold it until the market became normal. Doctors, lawyers, teachers, and even Wilson responded.

The root of the problem was that the British were determined to suppress the cotton trade to central Europe. By early 1915, they were stopping ships carrying cotton and threatening to put it on the list of absolute contraband. Southern cotton growers went into a panic, and the State Department protested. Lord Grey, determined to prevent relations with the United States from deteriorating to the point of no return, arranged an unofficial agreement by which Britain agreed to purchase enough cotton to keep the price between 8 cents and 10 cents a pound. At the same time Secretary of the Treasury McAdoo, Federal Reserve officials, and Wilson himself took the unprecedented step of assuring the South that federal funds would be available to enable farmers to hold their crops if need be.

In the meantime Congress passed an impressive list of statutes that benefited the farmer: In 1914, the Smith-Lever Act provided federal funds to match state funds to support agricultural extension work; a

Grain Standards Act, the Warehouse Act, which authorized the Department of Agriculture to license bonded warehouses to store specified
products upon which negotiable warehouse receipts could be issued,
the Federal Highway Act, and Federal Farm Loan Act made 1916 a
banner year.

The Highway Act had greater implications for the future than appeared
at the time. It provided for federal funds to match state funds in constructing rural post roads and roads within national forests. It had originally been introduced in 1914 and had stirred up considerable controversy
among those who saw it as another abridgment of states' rights. Pressure
mounted, however, as automobiles poured out of the factories. Local
automobile clubs, the American Automobile Association, the dealers,
the engineers, and the contractors bombarded Congress with requests to
improve the roads. The House Committee on Roads was created in 1913,
and its head introduced the first measure calling for an appropriation of
$25 million. In 1916, Congress yielded to the pressure and accepted the
principle of dollar-for-dollar matching by the states; on such a basis,
limited federal aid would be granted with the understanding that each
state "accept control as a condition precedent to Federal Aid."

Equally significant was the passage of the Federal Farm Loan Act. This
measure was controversial over the question not of whether special credit
for farmers was necessary, but of whether it should be provided by the
federal government. Southern and western agrarians demanded action,
and Wilson tossed the problem to Congress where it fell to a joint committee on rural credits headed by Representative A. F. Lever of South
Carolina and Senator Henry F. Hollis of New Hampshire. This committee
worked out an ingenious bill providing for a Federal Farm Loan Board
charged with organizing at least twelve Federal Land Banks. These banks
could provide long-range credit by a complicated system whereby the
federal government would guarantee the availability of funds if sufficient
funds were not provided by the sale of Land Bank Bonds. The bill was
enough of a compromise to satisfy many who had opposed federal funding, including Wilson. Although described by the *New York Sun* as "rural
credits run mad," it passed both houses with only token opposition.

Perhaps the most momentous enactment of 1916 in domestic legislation
was the Keating-Owen Child Labor Law. A campaign for improving the
lot of children had begun long before the beginning of the twentieth
century, and some twenty-eight states had put restrictions on the employment of children in manufacturing, and an additional state prohibited
child labor in mining. These laws, however, were inadequately enforced,
and states such as Alabama, North Carolina, South Carolina, and Georgia,
where thousands of children worked in textile mills, had no laws at all.

With the twentieth century, a more intense campaign against child
labor began. Jacob Riis in *The Children of the Poor* (1892) showed how
children fared in New York—a state which had a child labor law. John

Spargo in *The Bitter Cry of the Children* (1906) showed how interests in textiles, glass, coal, canneries, and needlework opposed restrictions. Florence Kelley, the general secretary of the National Consumers' League after 1899, fought for legislation to see that goods were manufactured under decent conditions, and then joined with Lillian Wald in New York to set up a state child labor committee. This committee's agitation resulted in an investigation of conditions in the state and the passage of an effective state law in 1903. Other local groups were organized, but the question was obviously more than a local one, and, in 1904, Florence Kelley, Lillian Wald, Jane Addams, and Edgar Gardner Murphy who had pushed for legislation in Alabama organized the National Child Labor Committee with a distinguished membership—and a determination to eliminate child labor.

The issue became popular and attracted the attention of politicians. Theodore Roosevelt vainly attempted to persuade Congress to sponsor an investigation of child labor conditions in 1904. Then Albert Beveridge became interested. Horrified about conditions in which children labored, and probably sensing the political popularity of the child labor issue, he called for national legislation to remedy what he saw as a "clumsy, ineffectual tangle of state statutes." To those who argued that only the states could constitutionally regulate manufacturing within the states, he pointed to the principle of the Meat Inspection Act which he had sponsored. If the federal government could prevent bad meat from being shipped in interstate commerce, why could it not ban goods manufactured by child labor?

For the next two years, Beveridge vainly fought for a national law. However opposition was too great. The AFL leadership was divided and refused to back the bill. President Roosevelt likewise refused support—although he did endorse investigation by the Bureau of Labor and a model bill for the District of Columbia. Most discouraging of all, the National Child Labor Committee was divided. Edgar Gardner Murphy, whose dedication to the cause of child labor was unquestioned, resigned from the committee when the committee endorsed the principle of a federal law. "Shall we . . . turn over the police functions of the States wholly to the federal power?" he asked. The supporters of the measure counterattacked. Alexander McKelway, the committee's southern organizer, argued that without the federal law it might take a quarter of a century to set the proper standard in the southern states.

In the meantime, the National Child Labor Committee intensified its work on the local level. It worked in the south and joined with other groups attempting to standardize state laws. All the states were by this time sending commissioners to an annual conference designed to promote uniformity in state lawmaking. They produced model statutes on such questions as divorce and family desertion. In 1911, the National Child Labor Committee produced "a uniform Child Labor Law." This model called for a "minimum age of fourteen in manufacturing and sixteen in mining, a maximum workday of eight hours, a prohibition of night work between 7 P.M. and 6 A.M., and documentary proof of age." No state had met these requirements in 1904 and only nine by 1914. Reformers had succeeded in improving conditions in which children worked, but one child in every six still worked, the same ratio as in 1900.

By 1914, disillusionment about local action led to increasing support for federal legislation. The National Child Labor Committee now appeared to be united, and it received reinforcements from the AFL, the Federal Council of Churches, and the American Medical Association. In the campaign of 1912, the Progressive platform had come out for a prohibition on child labor, but the Democratic platform had not mentioned it. Now Congress was controlled by hostile southerners, and Wilson's New Freedom theoretically opposed class legislation. However, Owen R. Lovejoy, secretary of the National Child Labor Committee, prepared a bill based upon the interstate commerce clause and persuaded A. Mitchell Palmer, a Pennsylvania congressman, to introduce it in January 1914. The bill, in spite of strong southern opposition including threats of a filibuster from James Byrnes of South Carolina, passed the House by a vote of 233 to 43 in February, 1915. Although Wilson in his inaugural address in 1913 strongly supported legislation to aid women and children, it soon became obvious that he had equally strong reservations as to the constitutionality of a measure such as the one Palmer had introduced. He refused to throw his support to the measure, and thus the bill died.

Social justice advocates, however, were persistent. The House again passed the bill on February 2, 1916, over opposition largely from southern congressmen: from Representative Doughton of North Carolina who insisted that the owners "have a humane interest in the welfare of those who work in their mills"; from James Byrnes who expressed himself in favor of child labor legislation but only by the states—and indeed his state of South Carolina passed a bill putting a fourteen-year lower limit for child workers. On the vote, in the House, forty-five of the forty-six nays came from the South.

At first it appeared that the bill would die in the Senate. The National Association of Manufacturers pointed to the dire consequences of accepting the principle of federal regulation based upon the interstate commerce clause—other legislation, came the warning, would promptly be passed "prohibiting the shipment in interstate commerce of any commodity produced in whole or in part by the labor of men or women who work more than eight hours, receive less than a minimum wage, or have not certain educational qualifications." These arguments, combined with the resistance of southern senators, bottled the measure up.

In the meantime, however, the national party conventions occurred. The Republican party meeting first called for "vocational education, the enactment and rigid enforcement of a Federal Child Labor Law, the enactment and rigid enforcement of a generous and comprehensive workers' compensation law covering all government employees." The Democratic platform rivaled the Republican, advocating a living wage for government employees, an eight-hour day, safety regulations, accident compensation, and special protection for women. Additional safety regulations were urged and "the speedy enactment of an effective Child Labor Law."

The Democratic platform has been called by Arthur Link "one of the most important documents in the history of American democracy." Link points to its "unabashed espousal of internationalism abroad and bold nationalistic progressivism at home." Wilson himself had worked over parts of it and approved all of it, and thus he was easily convinced that those measures, endorsed by the platform, but still not passed, such as the Federal Farm Loan Act, the Federal Highway Act, the Federal Child Labor Act, the Federal Workmen's Compensation Act, and the Vocational Education Act, should have priority.

Congress had dallied the longest over the Child Labor Act, and McKelway and others did not hesitate to warn Wilson of the political repercussions of further delay. Hughes, wrote McKelway, "has already agreed to swallow the social justice programme whole." Wilson immediately went to the Capitol on July 18 and instructed the Democratic Steering Committee to put both the Child Labor Act and the Workmen's Compensation Act through.

Wilson's request resulted in a renewed debate in the Senate. A strong southern bloc opposed, with Senator Overman, a kindly person from North Carolina, justifying child labor as a means of keeping children out of mischief. Several other senators, such as Senator Works of California, praised the humanitarian aims of the bill, but opposed it on constitutional grounds. The final vote saw twelve negative votes—all southerners except the two Pennsylvania senators, Penrose and Oliver. The basis for support or opposition to the bill, however, is not clear. Robinson of Arkansas took the lead in supporting the bill. Underwood of Alabama, Vardaman of Mississippi, Martin and Swanson of Virginia, Ramsdell of Louisiana, and both Texas senators voted aye. There was substantial support in the southern press for it, and some of those who voted against it claimed unconstitutionality as their reason. Tillman, although expressing shock at the "quibbling and selfishness of cotton-mill owners," feared the precedent and voted nay.

Repercussions were immediate. Some reflected the dire forebodings of the National Association of Manufacturers, but more frequently, from Wilson's point of view, the results must have been favorable. As the *American Federationist* put it, "Nothing that the President of the United States has done has met with such general approval as his laying aside the critical affairs of state to go to the Capitol to make personal protest against the program which omitted the Keating Owen bill from the list of legislation to be enacted at this session of Congress." Moreover the

Literary Digest polling 457 labor leaders in 31 states found that 332 thought that their members favored Wilson, 47 the Socialist Candidate, and 43 Hughes. In fact the leadership that Wilson provided to Congress in the summer before election has rarely been surpassed. Both houses had approved the Rural Credits Bill by June 26, the Road Bill by June 29, the Child Labor Bill by August 18, and the Workmen's Compensation Act by September 1.

The record of Wilson's first administration shows that he had moved far from the rather limited goals of the New Freedom. On September 2, 1916, in accepting his renomination, he boasted that "we have in four years come very near to carrying out the platform of the Progressive Party as well as our own," thus admitting that the label of the New Freedom should not be applied to such legislation as the Seamen's Act, Rural Credits, the Adamson Act, and the Federal Child Labor Law.

One explanation for the new direction of Wilson's program is that he consciously shifted his position in order to attract the progressive and independent voters necessary to win the presidential election in 1916. Those who endorse this explanation argue that in the first part of his administration he had opposed immigration restriction, the Federal Seamen's Act, long-term federal rural credits, and a federal child labor law and had supported racial segregation in the Civil Service; that after 1914, with the passage of the Simmons-Underwood Tariff, the Federal Reserve Act, the Clayton Antitrust Act, and the Federal Trades Commission Act, he ceased to push for more legislation; but that when Democratic political weaknesses became apparent and the presidential election approached, Wilson appeared to do an about-face and pushed dramatically for bill after bill that would attract the support of the progressive voter.

Although the evidence for this hypothesis is substantial, political expediency alone is too simple an explanation for the complex activities of the Wilson administration.

Political realities might well have merely stimulated changes in Wilson's attitudes, which were already in the process of change. Wilson's economic and social philosophy changed periodically before he became president. He was "eminently educable." His speeches in the campaign of 1912 and his inaugural address indicated that more changes were on the way and that he no longer considered social justice legislation either discriminatory or unconstitutional.

Moreover, no president formulates a program and then in a kind of vacuum carries it out according to schedule. Any program is the function of numerous factors: the executive, his advisers, congressional leadership, the rank and file of Congress, pressure groups, public opinion, economic and social conditions, and acts of God. Indeed almost as important as the attitudes and effectiveness of the executive are those of the congressional leadership and committee leaders. In Wilson's case, he had to deal with an almost solid block of southern congressmen, most of whom were suspicious of any increase in national power, but who would follow him on New Freedom legislation where precedents existed and about which there was little question of constitutionality. Thus the tariff, the bank, and antitrust bills could be pushed through with dispatch. The more controversial bills logically would take longer; at the same time the worsening business situation, the increasing complexity of foreign policy—the Mexican and European crises—and the illness and death of his beloved wife would have compelled a pause in domestic reform by mid-1914 regardless of the attitudes of either the president or the congressional leaders.

In the midst of conflicting pressures, it would have been difficult to determine what a "progressive position" was on any series of issues and even more difficult to find anyone in public office who consistently took the progressive positions on all the issues. Wilson's position on any given point does not necessarily indicate the extent of his progressivism. The issue of the treatment of black people, for example, could hardly be considered an issue that identified a progressive unless all southerners who were white supremacists, all Californians and others who were anti-oriental, and a whole catalogue of reformers who favored immigration restriction on the grounds of Anglo-Saxon supremacy may never be considered progressive.

The question of immigration seriously beclouds the issue of progressivism. Labor unions and many urban reformers favored immigration restriction as a means of maintaining American standards against low-paid foreign workers and of protecting urban living conditions against additional slum dwellers. Wilson did not accept these arguments and stood on the traditional and humanitarian, though perhaps not progressive, position of regarding the United States as a haven for the political refugee and those seeking economic opportunity.

Another measure that gained the support of progressive reformers was the La Follette seamen's bill. In trying to find a position on this bill, Wilson found himself in a cruel dilemma. He had little sympathy for the position of the ship owners who argued that "passage of the seamen's bill would indicate 'abject servility' to the interests of one class 'unprecedented in American history.'" He learned about the "brutal treatment and unbearable living conditions" of the sailors. He was concerned, however, about the fact that certain provisions of the bill would abrogate some twenty treaties which provided for the arrest of deserters from foreign vessels and would also undermine the work of an international conference on safety at sea soon to be held in London. Moreover, in spite of the humanitarian concerns that underlay the agitation for the measure, Andrew Furuseth, the dedicated crusader who had campaigned some thirty years for federal action, frankly admitted that his bill was based upon the principle of white supremacy. It included a provision that 75 percent of the crew must understand the orders of their officers. As Furuseth put it "It will mean safety to our part of the human race, national safety, and racial safety as well." Specifically it was designed to "curtail the tendency 'to substitute oriental crews for the sturdy sailors once the pride of the Occident.'"

Wilson negotiated to work out the international wrinkles and at the same time satisfy Furuseth. He favored the kind of protection which the seamen's bill provided the seamen, but he was equally concerned with the international safety convention and the relations with other powers. He finally agreed to sign the measure in March 1915, even though he thus was required to accept a significant reservation to the International Convention.

Wilson faced almost as difficult a decision in taking a position on the Federal Child Labor Act. He had not supported the bill prior to 1916, and he clearly had doubts about its constitutionality. Many others had similar doubts, but sentiment appeared overwhelmingly in favor of its passage. The political value to the Democrats of its passage was clear, and Wilson shifted. The bill passed, but the Supreme Court in 1918 justified Wilson's initial position when it declared the Child Labor Law unconstitutional in *Hammer* v. *Dagenhart* on the grounds that the "purpose" of that federal law was not to regulate commerce, clearly a constitutional function, but to outlaw child labor, which was not.

Wilson's position shifted on a number of these measures: on child labor legislation, on rural credits legislation, and even subtly on the tariff when in 1916 he came out in support of a tariff commission. This new stand horrified tariff reformers such as Kitchen and Underwood who feared that a tariff commission might propose a protective tariff. These were significant shifts, but who can tell whether Wilson changed his views for political reasons or as a result of the process of education through argument and changed conditions?

The Election of 1916

Regardless of Wilson's motives in throwing his support to a program that essentially accepted the platform of the Progressive party of 1912, it is unlikely that he could have won in 1916 had he not done so. The Republicans were still the majority party; they had lost in 1912 only because of their party's split; and the professionals in both factions were working to restore unity. In this instance Roosevelt cooperated, and they shrewdly nominated Charles Evans Hughes, with impressive credentials as a progressive governor of New York State and as a highly respected associate justice of the Supreme Court. Moreover the platform accepted Roosevelt's national progressivism: protection of American rights at home and abroad, strict neutrality, "complete national defense," tariff protection, strict regulation of corporations, rural credits, subsidies for merchant shipping, federal control of both interstate and intrastate transportation, vocational education, a federal child labor law, worker's compensation "within the commerce power of Congress" as well as an accident compensation law for federal employees, development of natural resources without waste, and women's suffrage approved by the states.

It is quite possible that had Hughes been elected, his program would have been as satisfactory to the progressives as was Wilson's. At the same time the concepts of the presidential office of the two men were quite different. Hughes sounded much like Taft when, in a statement a week or so before the election, he described the role of the president as being that of an executive and an administrator, but not of a policy maker or a political leader.

The Democratic campaign, almost from the beginning, was built upon two cornerstones of progressivism and peace. These cornerstones were firmly based. Wilson compromised on only one important progressive issue, that of women's suffrage. He refused to endorse the women's suffrage amendment, but he assured the National American Woman Suffrage Convention in September that he considered women's suffrage inevitable and that he had come to fight on their side. "We feel the tide," he said, "we rejoice in the strength of it; and we shall not quarrel in the long run as to the method of it." Although the more ardent suffragists, the Congressional Union, preferred Hughes and the National American Woman Suffrage Association reaffirmed a nonpartisan position, Mrs. Carrie Chapman Catt, president of the Association assured Wilson that "you touched our hearts and won our fealty."

In short his progressivism seemed almost complete. He took the offensive on the eight-hour day—an issue that the Republicans had considered a chink in his armor because of the way that he had allegedly succumbed to labor's threats of national disruption. "The judgment of society," he said, "the vote of every Legislature in America that has voted upon it is a verdict in favor of the eight-hour day." The business of government," he went on, "is to see that no other organization is as strong as itself; to see that no body or group of men, no matter what their private interest is, may come into competition with the authority of society." He praised the Progressive party because "it had the real red blood of human sympathy in its veins." He claimed that he was also a progressive who favored as much speed in prompting reform as those who spelled the term with a capital *P*. He talked about a new organization of society and the need for sufficient authority to require employers to "establish proper working conditions."

The cornerstone of peace was upon an almost equally firm base in the campaign. Although there may be differences of opinion as to whether the policies of the Wilson administration were best calculated to preserve American neutrality, there can be no question that Wilson intended to keep the United States out of the war. His successful negotiations of the *Lusitania,* the *Arabic,* and the *Sussex* crises showed his interest in negotiation rather than action. From the time of Colonel House's first trip to

Europe in 1914, Wilson's principal strategy had been to promote mediation and a negotiated settlement of the war. By 1916, his thoughts were turning to peacekeeping machinery, and on May 27 he spoke before the League to Enforce Peace, an organization founded in 1915 to persuade the United States to join some sort of postwar league of nations. Here, in one of his most important speeches, he declared American isolationism at an end and called for a "universal association of the nations" to protect foreign commerce and prevent wars.

The Democratic convention and the campaign brought clear indications that the sentiment for peace was pervasive. One of the most effective slogans of the campaign, "He kept us out of the War," rather unexpectedly grew out of the enthusiastic, almost emotional applause that greeted any recital of Wilson's efforts to preserve peace. Although Wilson himself did not state that he would keep the nation out of war, the Democratic campaign carried that implication. Indeed when the belligerent Roosevelt went on the campaign trail for Hughes, Hughes found it difficult to combat the implication that his election would harm the chance of remaining at peace. "Let the issue not be misunderstood," trumpeted a Democratic campaign pamphlet, "a vote for Hughes is a potential vote for war."

The election on November 7 turned out to be a cliffhanger. The result was not certain until late at night on November 9. Wilson received 9,127,695 votes, the largest popular vote ever received by a president, and approximately 600,000 more than Hughes. The total vote was 18,527,863—3,500,000 more than in 1912. The electoral vote, 277 for Wilson and 254 for Hughes, was the closest since 1876. Although Wilson carried California, a state which had never gone Democratic in a presidential election, and 18 others that were normally not considered Democratic states, the most notable feature of the election was that Wilson's sectional strength outside of the South came from the states west of the Mississippi. Wilson carried 2,031 counties, Hughes only 976—a record low for the Republicans. Wilson carried 200 counties never before Democratic, with the biggest gains in California, Kansas, Minnesota, Nebraska, and Ohio. At the same time, Wilson's plurality in most of these counties was slight, and there was no clear indication that the Democrats were now in a safe majority. The principal city-counties, for example (Los Angeles, San Francisco, Chicago, Baltimore, Boston, Detroit, St. Louis, New York, Cleveland, Philadelphia, and Milwaukee) had been strongly Republican in the presidential elections of the twentieth century except for Baltimore, which went Democratic in 1904 and 1912, New York, which went Republican only in 1908, and Milwaukee, which went Democratic in 1912. If Middlesex and Suffolk counties are both counted, Boston had been consistently Republican except in 1912. In 1916, San Francisco went Democratic by 15,000 votes, Baltimore by 12,000 votes, the two Boston counties by 7,000 votes, New York by 28,000 votes, Cleveland by 20,000 votes, and Milwaukee by 7,000 votes.

Hughes carried New England, the Middle Atlantic states, and the East

North Central States (Indiana, Illinois, Michigan, and Wisconsin), but the Democrats carried Ohio and the Republican margin was substantially cut in Wisconsin.

An analysis of this vote shows that there is no simple explanation of Wilson's victory. He started out with a strong, essential cushion of votes in the solid South (114 electoral votes) which probably was not significantly influenced by issues. The same might also be true of the border states of Kentucky (13), Oklahoma (10), and Tennessee (12), (35 electoral). Local factors undoubtedly persuaded many voters. The famous case is that of California where Hughes and his advisers were unable to steer an acceptable course between rival wings of the Republican party. In Utah, the voters may have been punishing a local Republican machine; in Wyoming the unprecedented prosperity of the wool growers and in Kansas that of the wheat farmers probably helped the party in power.

Although the women's suffrage amendment had not yet been ratified, ten states had already given women the franchise, and electioneering among the women was vigorous. Although the most radical of the suffragists organized a women's party for Hughes, the peace issue countered their argument, and particularly in Idaho, Washington, Kansas, and Montana women seemed to have preferred Wilson. At the same time, Montana elected Miss Jeanette Rankin, a Republican, as the first woman member of either branch of Congress.

Certainly the various issues that added up to progressivism helped Wilson. On August 3, a conference was held at Indianapolis by a substantial group of Progressives, some from the national committee of the Progressive party. This conference addressed "the Progressives of the Country," criticizing the national committee for having endorsed Hughes in June, and a majority of those who had written the Progressive platform in 1912 published an appeal for Wilson's election shortly before the ballots were cast. Lincoln Steffens, Frederick Howe, A. S. McKelway, Jane Addams, John Dewey, Amos Pinchot, and many others of the leading social justice leaders worked for Wilson. Independent farm leadership, including those in the Non-Partisan League, had swung to Wilson. Even Herbert Croly and Walter Lippmann—once avid supporters of Theodore Roosevelt endorsed Wilson in the *New Republic.* To Croly, the question related to the development of national power. "The New Freedom has been discarded. . . . ," he wrote in October, "The party program no longer seeks localistic individualism. It foreshadows rather a continuing process of purposive national reorganization determined in method by the realities of the task but dedicated to the ultimate enhancement of individual and associated life within and without the American commonwealth."

In a careful analysis of the reports of its correspondents, the *New York Times* said flatly that "two classes of voters, and two only accomplished the result . . . the Progressives and the women." The radical activities of the women's party for Hughes actually alienated voters, as did a train sponsored and financed by wealthy women in the East which campaigned through the West. These factors, the *Times* concluded, and particularly Wilson's record for the past four years, more than counterbalanced any tendency of the hyphen vote to go for Hughes. A *New York Times* analyst concluded on November 19 that the hyphen vote could be buried as a myth. "It was repudiated," the *Times* concluded, "as an insult to [the hyphen voters] themselves."

The Progressive vote and the peace vote obviously were related. Roosevelt's belligerent position was not typical of the rank and file progressive, and it would be virtually impossible to separate the two issues in certain areas. William Jennings Bryan, for example, campaigned vigorously for Wilson throughout the West. He covered nineteen states in eight weeks, making four or five speeches a day, stressing, according to the *Literary Digest,* two points: "that the government should not be turned over to the reactionaries who were repudiated by the progressive element of their own party in 1912, and that the President should not be rebuked for keeping the country out of war with Mexico and Europe."

The Decision for War

Although the outcome of the presidential election may have been the topic of most continuous interest to the American people in the summer and fall of 1916, questions of foreign policy were always in the background, sometimes in the foreground, of the election and actually closing in on Wilson. Although the Sussex Pledge had resulted in a relaxation of tension with Germany, it had been the result of a virtual ultimatum, and hence it implied that were the Germans to return to unrestricted submarine warfare, the United States would break off diplomatic relations. Wilson thus was sitting on a powder keg. He was concerned at the growing involvement of American creditors with Allied debtors and supported a warning against unsecured loans. He realized that Germany might at any time launch a submarine campaign that would kill Americans and sink their ships. Thus he sought through diplomacy to bring the war to an end in order to secure the nation's interests and called for a "just peace" protected by a "community of power" with American principles applied to the world.

The belligerents took these negotiations seriously only when they were in accord with their own interests. The Allies were intensifying the blockade and arming their merchant ships against the submarine. They were opposed to any peace conference that might result in terms unfavorable to them. In Germany, there was almost continuous debate over the use of the submarine. Those involved in the debate knew that the use of unrestricted submarine warfare, the sinking of all types of ships (belligerent or neutral, warships, merchant ships, or liners) without warning would bring the United States into the war. The question was whether the

United States could bring sufficient military power into the war soon enough to make any difference in the outcome.

By January 1917, the doubters in Germany were overwhelmed. The admiralty staff and the principal military leaders, supported by strong political pressures and news media called for unlimited submarine warfare, and on January 9, 1917, the emperor decreed "that unlimited submarine warfare begin with all possible vigor."

The decision was made public on January 31. From then until April 4, Wilson prayerfully contemplated alternatives. He consulted widely. He even considered "withdrawal and surrender." To some extent he did withdraw, for in breaking off diplomatic relations on February 3, 1917, he threatened no further action unless American ships and American lives were destroyed "in contravention of law." He described even that action in a way that seemed to mean a resort to armed neutrality rather than actual belligerency.

To the Allies and to the interventionists in the United States, the president's action seemed indecisive. A president's time, however, is never his own, and while he grappled with the horrifying alternative of leading his country into war, he was forced to deal with other problems in the life of a presidential administration. He meticulously carried out the social responsibilities of his office and watched the legislative process. He vetoed an immigration bill calling for a literacy test, only to see it passed over his veto on February 5. He approved a vocational education bill on February 23 and a revenue measure that included an excess profits tax a few weeks later. Most complicated of all was the Mexican imbroglio which had been continually boiling over since mid-1914. In the intervening period, Wilson had supported the revolution, had prevented European intervention, and had refused to be goaded by either the Mexicans or American jingoes into a full-scale war. His launching of the punitive expedition against Pancho Villa in 1916, however, had roused Mexican hostility in spite of Wilson's good intentions, and Carranza, who might have been aided by the destruction of Villa, refused to accept what seemed to be a high-handed invasion of Mexican sovereignty by the United States. By defeating Villa and standing on his principles, Carranza convinced Wilson of the desirability of withdrawing the expedition early in January 1917 and restoring normal diplomatic relations in March.

In the meantime, a series of events during February and March formed a web from which Wilson could see no escape except by war. The threat of submarine attack so frightened shippers that few ships were leaving American ports—trade was almost paralyzed. Emotions that were roused over the submarine campaign became further inflamed by German diplomatic bungling. The British secret service intercepted a telegram of January 19 from the German foreign minister, Zimmermann, to the German minister in Mexico which discussed the possibility of an alliance between Germany and Mexico and the return of former Mexican territories (such as Texas and California) to Mexico in the event of war between Germany and the United States. On February 24 the British secret service delicately sent the telegram to Wilson, who authorized its publication four days later. Within a few days the confusion of events was further confounded by reports early in March of a revolution in Russia which overthrew the Czar and substituted what many Americans piously hoped would be a democratic regime—and thus one much more acceptable as a possible ally. Wilson, still toying with the idea of an armed neutrality, pressed for congressional authority to arm American merchant ships, but about a dozen senators, led by Robert La Follette prevented the measure from coming to a vote, thus earning Wilson's hostility and the designation of "a little group of willful men." The session of Congress adjourned, whereupon Wilson armed the ships by executive order. Then came the *casus belli:* on March 18, word was received of the sinking of three American ships, two without warning. Again Wilson consulted his cabinet—it unanimously recommended a declaration of war. At the time, he gave them no indication of his decision, but the ensuing events spoke for themselves.

Nothing so well illustrates the power of a central government over its citizens than the power of waging war. Nothing so well illustrates the powerful role of the president of the United States than his power to lead the nation into war. The president faced numerous conditions of unprecedented complexity. Principles like freedom of the seas, the horror of submarine warfare, and distaste for militarism were involved. At issue were not simply narrow economic interests like the profits of munitions makers and money lenders but the inherent right to trade, the threat to the hemisphere from a hostile power, and the need to maintain national prestige in a competitive world. As Arthur Link contends, there was a "conviction that American belligerency now offered the surest hope for early peace and the construction of the international community."

As in his domestic policy, Wilson was an idealist who looked at foreign policy through realistic eyes. Possibly, as Patrick Devlin has put it, the president "had been given a sudden revelation of the tragedy at the fount of all human endeavor—which is that it is bad to fight but that only by fighting can the good be reached." More probably, all things considered, Wilson finally saw no alternative to war. He made the decision but other individuals and groups of varying nationalities and attitudes helped him along the way.

Bibliography

This chapter depended heavily upon the magisterial works of Arthur S. Link. His stamp is on both the domestic and diplomatic history of the period. Particularly important are *Wilson: The New Freedom* (1956);

Wilson: The Struggle for Neutrality (1960); *Wilson: Confusions and Crisis* (1964); and *Wilson: Campaigns for Progressivism and Peace* (1965). I have also made extensive use of the annual reports of the secretaries of war, navy, treasury, labor, and agriculture and the *American Year Book* for the appropriate years.

Pages 162–163

For the quotation from the *New York Tribune,* see *Literary Digest,* March 15, 1913, p. 556. For his inaugural address, see Henry Steel Commager, ed., *Documents of American History,* 2 vols. (1968), II, 82–84.

Page 163

For the civil service and foreign policy, see also Paul P. Van Riper, *History of the United States Civil Service* (1958).

Page 163

For the strength of the army, the *Annual Report of the Secretary of War* does not always agree with *Historical Statistics.* See also Russell F. Weigley, *History of the United States Army* (1967).

Page 164

Wilson was perhaps the leading academic authority on "administration" in the United States. Sample vols. V, VI, VII of Link, et al., eds., *The Papers of Woodrow Wilson* (1968, 1969), for example, V, 482–484. The quotations in the text are from Henry A. Turner, "Woodrow Wilson: Exponent of Executive Leadership," *Western Political Quarterly,* 4 (March 1951), 97–115. Edward S. Corwin, "Woodrow Wilson and the Presidency," *Virginia Law Review,* 42 (October 1956), 761–783; Arthur W. MacMahon, "Woodrow Wilson as Legislative Leader and Administrator," *American Political Science Review,* 50 (September 1956), 641–675.

Page 164

On Wilson and the press, see John M. Blum, *Joe Tumulty and the Wilson Era* (1951); on the seniority question, see the *Washington Post,* March 16, 1914; Link, *The New Freedom;* also Anne Firor Scott, "A Progressive Wind from the South, 1906–1913," *Journal of Southern History,* 29 (February 1963), 53–70.

Pages 164–165

On woman suffrage, see *Literary Digest,* 47 (December 20, 1913), 1209; *American Year Book,* 1913, p. 70; Eleanor Flexner, *Century of Struggle: The Woman's Rights Movement in the United States* (1959).

Pages 165–167

For prohibition, *American Year Book,* 1913, p. 470. For farm organizations and agriculture, Theodore Saloutos, *Farmer Movements in the South, 1865–1933* (1960), pp. 212–214; Grant McConnell, *The Decline of Agrarian Democracy* (1953); *American Year Book,* 1913, p. 481;

Myron T. Herrick and R. Ingals, *Rural Credits, Land and Coöperative* (1914); James B. Morman, *The Principles of Rural Credit as Applied in Europe and as Suggested for America* (1919); *Report of the Secretary of Agriculture,* 1912, 1913.

Pages 167-169

For the legislative committee of the AFL, see *American Federationist,* 19 (November 1912), 889-894; Report of the President of the AFL, November 11, 1912, in *ibid.* (December 1912), 1000-1007; on "Our Billy," see *Literary Digest,* 46 (March 20, 1913), 693; food prices were taken from the *New York Herald;* for the strikes see *Literary Digest,* 46 (May 10, 1913), 1043-1044, and (February 22, 1913), 385-386; Secretary Wilson's quotation is from the *Report of the Secretary of Labor,* 1913, pp. 21-22, 63-67; for social workers and labor, see Allen Davis, "The Campaign for the Industrial Relations Commission, 1911-1913," *Mid-America,* 45 (October 1963), 211-228; *Final Report of the Commission on Industrial Relations* (1916), vol. I, pp. 13-269. For the IWW, see Melvin Dubofsky and Philip Foner cited in Chapter 3.

Pages 169-170

On the money trust, see Vincent P. Carosso, "The Wall Street Money Trust from Pujo through Medina," *Business History Review,* 47 (Winter 1973) 421-437; see also *Report of Committee pursuant to House Resolutions 429 and 504 to Investigate the Concentration of Control of Money and Credit,* 62nd Cong., 3d sess., Rpt. No. 1593, Washington, 1913 (Pujo Committee); National Monetary Commission, Sen. Doc. 243, 62nd Cong., 2d sess., Washington, 1912. George Baker quotation from *Literary Digest,* 46 (January 25, 1913), 163-164; the Morgan quotation is from *American Year Book,* 1913, p. 6. For foreign trade associations, see Martin Sklar, "Woodrow Wilson and the Political Economy of Modern Liberalism," *Studies on the Left,* 1 (1960), 29-30.

Pages 170-173

On conservation, see Thomas LeDuc, "The Historiography of Conservation," *Forest History,* 9 (October 1965), 23-28; for the Fifth National Conservation Congress, see *Literary Digest,* 47 (December 6, 1913), 1103-1104; J. Leonard Bates, *The Origins of Teapot Dome: Progressives, Parties, and Petroleum, 1909-1921* (1963).

Pages 173-175

On black people and the Wilson administration, see *Literary Digest,* 47 (November 1, 1913), 801; Charles F. Kellogg, *NAACP, A History of the National Association for the Advancement of Colored People* (1967); Henry Blumenthal, "Woodrow Wilson and the Race Question," *Journal of Negro History,* 48 (January 1963), 1-21; Wilson to Villard, August 21, 1913, Wilson Papers, Library of Congress; Herbert J. Doherty, Jr., "Alexander J. McKelway: Preacher to Progressive," *Journal of Southern History,*

24 (May 1958), 177–190; Nancy J. Weiss, "The Negro and the New Freedom: Fighting Wilsonian Segregation," *Political Science Quarterly,* 84 (March 1969), 61–79; Link, *The New Freedom.* See especially August Meier and Elliott Rudwick, "The Rise of Segregation in the Federal Bureaucracy, 1900–1930," *Phylon,* 28 (Summer 1967), 178–184.

Pages 175–177

The quotation on Wilson the chief magistrate is from *Harpers Weekly,* 58 (January 10, 1914), 25–26; for the New Freedom and foreign commerce, see Sklar, "Woodrow Wilson and the Political Economy of Modern Liberalism"; on the tariff, see A. K. Steigerwalt, "The NAM and the Congressional Investigations of 1913 . . .," *Business History Review,* 34 (Autumn 1960), 335–344; Frank Burdick, "Woodrow Wilson and the Underwood Tariff," *Mid-America,* 50 (October 1968), 272–290; and for Cordell Hull and the income tax, *Memoirs of Cordell Hull* (1948) I, 45–71; for comments on the income tax, see *Literary Digest,* 46 (April 19, 1913), 877; (February 15, 1913), 326.

Pages 177–179

On the federal reserve system, see Frederic L. Paxson, *American Democracy and the World War,* Vol. I, (1936) 85–91; Benjamin H. Beckhart, *Federal Reserve System* (1972); and especially Link, *The New Freedom;* but contrast Gabriel Kolko, *The Triumph of Conservatism. A Re-interpretation of American History, 1900–1916* (1963).

Pages 179–182

On the Clayton Antitrust Act, see Melvin I. Urofsky, *Big Steel and the Wilson Administration; A Study in Business-Government Relations* (1969); for the relationship between banking and foreign trade, see Sklar, "Woodrow Wilson and the Political Economy of Modern Liberalism"; for the Mann and Simmons quotations, see *Literary Digest,* 47 (December 27, 1913), 1257–1258. Compare Link, *The New Freedom,* and Kolko, *Triumph of Conservatism,* for different treatments. On the labor question, Robert K. Murray, "Public Opinion, Labor, and the Clayton Act," *Historian,* 21 (May 1959), 255–270; and Billie Barnes Jensen, "Woodrow Wilson's Intervention in the Coal Strike of 1914," *Labor History,* 15 (Winter 1974) 63–77. See also Graham Adams, Jr., *Age of Industrial Violence, 1910–1915; The Activities and Findings of the United States Commission on Industrial Relations* (1966).

Pages 182–183

On the peace movement a comprehensive study is C. Roland Marchand, *The American Peace Movement and Social Reform, 1898–1918* (1973) and an important monograph is Calvin D. Davis, *The United States and the First Hague Peace Conference* (1962); see also Merle E. Curti, *Peace or War: The American Struggle, 1636–1936* (1936); Peter Brock, *Pacifism in the United States from the Colonial Era to the First World War* (1968);

Peter J. Filene, "The World Peace Foundation and Progressivism: 1910–1918," *New England Quarterly,* 36 (December 1963), 478–501.

Pages 183–184

Significant historiographical articles on U.S. entry into World War I are Richard W. Leopold, "The Problem of American Intervention, 1917, An Historical Retrospect," *World Politics,* 2 (April 1950), 405–425; and Daniel M. Smith, "National Interest and American Intervention, 1917, An Historiographical Appraisal," *Journal of American History,* 52 (June 1965), 5–24. Arthur Link's volumes provide a superb coverage. An excellent one-volume treatment is Ernest R. May, *The World War and American Isolation, 1914–1917* (1959). Brief interpretations are Daniel M. Smith, *The Great Departure; The United States and World War I, 1914–1920* (1965), and Ross Gregory, *The Origins of American Intervention in the First World War* (1971). See also A. Anne Trotter, "The Development of the Merchants of Death Theory of Intervention," unpub. doctoral diss., Duke University, 1966; Harold C. Syrett, "The Business Press and American Neutrality, 1914–1917," *Mississippi Valley Historical Review,* 32 (September 1945), 215–230; and Paul Birdsall, "Neutrality and Economic Pressures, 1914–1917," *Science and Society,* 3 (Spring 1939), 217–228.

Page 184

On neutral rights, in addition to the Link and May volumes, see Karl E. Birnbaum, *Peace Moves and U-Boat Warfare; A Study of Imperial Germany's Policy Towards the United States, April 18, 1916–January 9, 1917* (1958); Marion C. Siney, *The Allied Blockade of Germany, 1914–1917* (1957).

Page 185

On preparedness, see *Congressional Record,* 63d Cong. 3d sess., Jan. 21, 1915, pp. 2066–2069 for Gardner and Hay. See also George C. Herring, Jr., "James Hay and the Preparedness Controversy, 1915–1916," *Journal of Southern History,* 30 (November 1964), 383–404; Laurence J. Holt, *Congressional Insurgents and the Party System, 1909–1916* (1967); Howard W. Allen, "Republican Reformers and Foreign Policy, 1913–1917," *Mid-America,* 44 (October 1962), 222–229.

Page 186

On Stimson's policy, see Henry L. Stimson and McGeorge Bundy, *On Active Service in Peace and War* (1948); Mabel E. Deutrich, *Struggle for Supremacy: The Career of Fred C. Ainsworth* (1962).

Pages 186–187

For the Wright brother's curious relations with Ordnance, see Fred C. Kelly, ed., *Miracle at Kitty Hawk: The Letters of Wilbur and Orville Wright* (1951). See also Archibald D. Turnbull and Clifford L. Lord, *History of United States Naval Aviation* (1949).

Pages 187–189

For naval policy, I have relied principally on the Annual Reports of the secretaries; Link, *The New Freedom;* Joseph L. Morrison, *Josephus Daniels; the Small-d Democrat* (1966); Melvin I. Urofsky, "Josephus Daniels and the Armor Trust," *North Carolina Historical Review,* 45 (Summer 1968), 237–263; and Frank Freidel, *Franklin D. Roosevelt: The Apprenticeship.* For the point on federal industry in the South, I am indebted to Henry C. Ferrell, Jr., "Regional Rivalries and Congress in the Creation of the Military-Industrial Complex: the Navy Yards at Norfolk and Charleston, 1913–1920," unpub. paper presented at the annual meeting of the Southern Historical Association, November 18, 1971.

Pages 189–193

For various preparedness organizations, see Paxson I, 200–202 and Armin Rappaport, *The Navy League of the United States* (1962); and Weigley, *History of the United States Army.* For the national guard, see William H. Riker, *Soldiers of the States; The Role of the National Guard in American Democracy* (1957); Daniel R. Beaver, *Newton D. Baker and the American War Effort, 1917–1919* (1966). The *Literary Digest* carried out a state-by-state poll of newspaper editors on preparedness, see 52 (March 11, 1916), 617 et seq.

Pages 193–197

On shipping, see Jeffrey J. Safford, "The United States Merchant Marine and American Commercial Expansion, 1860–1920," unpub. doctoral diss., Rutgers University, 1968. See also William G. McAdoo, *Crowded Years, The Reminiscences of William G. McAdoo* (1931). For shipping statistics, see Committee on Commerce, July 17, 1916, *Senate Report,* No. 689, 64th Cong., 1st sess., pp. 23–24. See also the House Committee on Merchant Marine and the Fisheries, *House Report,* May 9, 1916, No. 659, 64th Cong., 1st sess.; minority views of the House Committee on Merchant Marine and Fisheries, *House Report,* No. 659, pt. 2, 64th Cong., 1st sess.; for *Washington Post* and Fahey quotations, see *Literary Digest,* 52 (May 27, 1916), 1522–1523; Select Committee on U.S. Shipping Board Operations, March 2, 1921, *House Report,* No. 1399, 66th Cong., 3d sess.

Pages 197–199

For a brief summary of Wilson's legislative program in 1915 and 1916, see Arthur S. Link, *Woodrow Wilson and the Progressive Era, 1910–1917* (1954); see also Richard Abrams, "Woodrow Wilson and the Southern Congressmen, 1913–1916," *Journal of Southern History,* 22 (November 1956), 417–437; for the counties supporting Wilson, see Robinson, *The Presidential Vote, 1896–1932,* p. 58. On Wilson's farm program, see David F. Houston, *Eight Years with Wilson's Cabinet, 1913–1920; With a Personal Estimate of the President* (1926). For the "buy a bale" program, see *Literary Digest,* 49 (October 10, 1914), 669, and for attitudes toward the Road Act, see *ibid.,* 48 (February 29, 1914), 415–417; and toward the Rural Credits Act, *ibid.,* 52 (May 20, 1916), 1442.

Pages 199–203

On the Child Labor Law, see Jeremy A. Felt, *Hostages of Fortune: Child Labor Reform in New York State* (1965); Stephen B. Wood, *Constitutional Politics in the Progressive Era; Child Labor and the Law* (1968); John Braeman, "Albert J. Beveridge and the First National Child Labor Bill," *Indiana Magazine of History,* 60 (March 1964), 1–36; Stanley Coben, *A. Mitchell Palmer: Politician* (1963); Doughton and Byrnes quotations are from *Literary Digest,* 52 (March 4, 1916), 553; NAM quotation from Link, *Campaigns for Progressivism and Peace,* p. 57; Link also comments on the conventions and platforms, *ibid.,* pp. 57–59. For comments on the vote, see *Literary Digest,* 53 (September 2, 1916), 547–548; *American Federationist* quotation is in Link, *Campaigns for Progressivism and Peace; Literary Digest* poll in 53 (October 7, 1916), 871–873; see also Walter I. Trattner, *Crusade for the Children: A History of the National Child Labor Committee and Child Labor Reform in America* (1970); Roger W. Walker, "The AFL and Child-Labor Legislation: An Exercise in Frustration," *Labor History,* 11 (Summer 1970), 323–340.

Pages 203–205

Arthur Link advances the hypothesis of the transformation of the New Freedom to New Nationalism most clearly in *Woodrow Wilson and the Progressive Era* and in "The South and the New Freedom: An Interpretation," *American Scholar,* 20 (Summer 1951), 314–324. My comments on this thesis can be found in more detail in "Woodrow Wilson and His Interpreters, 1947–1957," *Mississippi Valley Historical Review,* 44 (September 1957), 212–220. See also John Wells Davidson, *A Crossroads of Freedom, The 1912 Campaign Speeches* (1956), pp. 3–11. On the Seamen's Act, see Jerold S. Auerbach, "Progressives at Sea: The La Follette Act of 1915," *Labor History,* 2 (Fall 1961), 344–360; Hyman Weintraub, *Andrew Furuseth; Emancipator of the Seamen* (1959).

Pages 205–209

For the election of 1916, see Mowry, *Theodore Roosevelt and the Progressive Movement;* and Blum, *Joe Tumulty;* Edward Cuddy, "Irish-Americans and the 1916 Election: An Episode in Immigrant Adjustment," *American Quarterly,* 21 (Summer 1969), 228–243; and Dexter Perkins, *Charles Evans Hughes and American Democratic Statesmanship* (1956). The Wilson quotation about women's suffrage comes from Shaw, *The Messages and Papers of Woodrow Wilson,* 1 (1924), 326; Mrs. Catt's quotation is from Link, *Campaigns for Progressivism and Peace,* pp. 96–97; other

Wilson quotations during the campaign are from Link, *ibid.,* pp. 104, 119, and 26. The analysis of the vote is based on Robinson, *Presidential Vote, 1896–1932,* principally Table IX. For Hiram Johnson's role in the campaign, see Spencer C. Olin, Jr., *California's Prodigal Sons: Hiram Johnson and the Progressives, 1911–1917* (1968); Michael P. Rogin and John L. Shover, *Political Change in California; Critical Elections and Social Movements, 1890–1966* (1970). See also analysis in the *Literary Digest,* 53 (November 18, 1916), 1312–1316. On the woman suffrage issue, see *ibid.; American Year Book,* 1916, p. 451; Flexner, *Century of Struggle.* The Croly quotation is in Link, *Campaigns for Progressivism and Peace,* p. 130. For the *New York Times* analyses, see November 12, 1916; and "The Hyphen Vote was Practically a Myth," *New York Times Magazine,* November 19, 1916, pp. 3–4. The *Literary Digest* disagrees somewhat with the *Times,* 53 (November 25, 1916), 1394; on William Jennings Bryan, see *ibid.* (November 18, 1916), 1312.

Pages 209–211

On the building of tensions leading to war, see especially Link, Birnbaum, and May. The Link quotation is from Link, *Wilson,* Vol. V, 414. The Devlin quotation is from Arthur Walworth's perceptive review of Patrick Devlin, *Too Proud to Fight: Woodrow Wilson's Neutrality* (1975) in *Yale Review* (Spring 1975), 448. See also Warren I. Cohen, *The American Revisionists: The Lessons of Intervention in World War I* (1967); John Milton Cooper, Jr., *The Vanity of Power; American Isolationism and the First World War, 1914–1917* (1969).

7

The First World War

Preliminary Organization

The entry of the United States into the war on April 7, 1917, led to the most sweeping extension of national power experienced by the country up to that time. The soul-searching—even agony of conscience—on the part of Wilson indicated his concern over the impact that the war would have upon the United States. He knew that war meant hardship, suffering, and death. He also sensed that a twentieth-century war would require economic and social mobilization that could touch every man, woman, and child, and would inevitably affect their traditional liberties.

Although Wilson's war message met with enthusiastic acclaim, dissent was still significant. Six senators and fifty representatives voted against the war resolution, and in states as far apart as Wisconsin and North Carolina antiwar sentiments were strong. Progressives and socialists were divided. La Follette, for example, took an essentially pacifist position while Norris blamed our entry into the war upon forces with a lust for profits. Associates of Theodore Roosevelt such as Amos Pinchot, Albert Cummins, Frederick Howe, Jane Addams, and even the one-time imperialist, Albert Beveridge, opposed America's entry. They feared that war would set back reform by restoring the prestige and power of the elements in business that progressivism had been striving to control. On the other hand, Ray Stannard Baker, Ida Tarbell, Brand Whitlock, Harold Ickes, Fiorella La Guardia, and others favored intervention.

Some progressives saw the war as an opportunity to achieve positive domestic goals. These progressives included those associated with the *New Republic* such as Walter Lippmann, Herbert Croly, and John Dewey, and also socialists such as Morris Hillquit, John Spargo, and Harry W. Laidler. Croly and Lippmann were much more nationalistic than the socialists, but all saw the war as making possible a stronger, more highly centralized state and a collective economy dedicated to the welfare of all the people. Lippmann and Croly went so far as to claim that "men of intelligence" had led the United States into the war, and that they should now take the lead in using the war as an opportunity to destroy "the typical evils of the sprawling half-educated competitive capitalism." Indeed, shortly after the declaration of war, a group of progressives, including Hiram Johnson, Harold Ickes, Miles Poindexter, and William Allen White, urged the administration to support universal military service; "universal industrial service of both men and property"; the encouragement of farm production by guaranteeing favorable prices; price control of rent, food, fuel, and other necessities; federal and state guarantees of the rights of labor; government support of commercial enterprises; a more steeply graduated income tax; and conservation of grain for food purposes.

The experiences of the European countries provided evidence of how the requirements of modern war brought about change even in countries that had been living for years in the shadow of war. Military insecurity since 1870 had resulted in the adopting of universal military training in many European countries. Britain was a notable exception. Russia, Germany, and France could each call upon a reservoir of nearly five million trained soldiers. Perhaps on the assumption that any war would be a short one, however, none of the belligerents had sensed how extensive a mobilization would be necessary to wage a long war. Offices with varying powers were created to meet specific problems in shipping, in internal transportation, in fuel, and in mobilizing manpower.

Few Americans envisaged the scope of what their country's commitment to victory was to be, but they soon learned what their new allies expected of them. No sooner had Congress declared war than Britain and France dispatched to the United States distinguished war missions, headed by Lord Balfour and Marshal Joffre. They quickly made clear their countries' need of money, supplies, and especially large numbers of troops. Now the warnings of the advocates of preparedness were coming home to roost. Even the General Staff had not considered the requirements for dispatching a large expeditionary force overseas. Still more embarrassing was the government's lack of information about how to convert the economy to the war effort.

Fortunately a beginning had been made. In 1910, President Taft had called for a Council of National Defense to coordinate the agencies of government concerned with national defense, and in December of that year, Representative Richmond Hobson, a hero of the Spanish-American War, had introduced a measure authorizing such an institution. Fellow congressmen refused to take the proposal seriously, and although Hobson introduced it several times, various parliamentary maneuvers kept it from being considered. In 1912, however, the Democratic platform endorsed it, and shortly thereafter the Navy League began to focus attention on it. By 1915, it was no longer taken as a joke. Senator

Cummins warned that such a council would "do more to turn the public over to the control of the military arm of the Government than the creation of large armies or the construction of large navies."

In the meantime, in various unique ways Secretary of the Navy Josephus Daniels was seeking to prepare the navy for modern war. In 1915, he invited the leading engineering associations in the country to choose two of its members to sit on a Naval Consulting Board that would be chaired by Thomas A. Edison. The purpose, as Daniels put it, was to make use of the "best brains and knowledge of the country" in preparing the nation "for any duty." Specifically the board was to "make an inventory of manufacturing plants of the country that were capable of making munitions." The board gave this responsibility to a Committee on Industrial Preparedness, chaired by a dynamo, Howard E. Coffin, vice president of the Hudson Motor Company and president of the Society of Automobile Engineers. Coffin organized state subcommittees, which by September 1916 had collected data from more than twenty thousand "manufacturing plants." These efforts received only moderate cooperation from industry, but the need for an inventory was at least demonstrated when the army in 1916, scrambling to equip itself for the Mexican invasion, inquired of the committee "where they could buy some machine guns right away."

In the meantime several other organizations such as the National Advisory Committee on Aeronautics, the National Research Council, and the National Committee of Physicians for Medical Preparedness, were organized to support the preparedness program. By 1916, behind the congressional scene elaborate discussions were taking place inspired by Secretary of War Garrison and, later, Secretary Baker, Secretary of the Treasury McAdoo, Leonard Wood, Elihu Root, Dr. Hollis Godfrey, president of the Drexel Institute, and Dr. Harry E. Crampton, distinguished chemist in the Institute of Industrial Research. As a result, both the National Defense Act and the Army Appropriation Acts of 1916 provided for a Council of National Defense. The council was to consist of the Secretaries of War, Navy, Interior, Agriculture, Commerce, and Labor. It could then appoint an advisory commission of up to seven members who were to be specialists in some aspect of the economy. The council was to advise the president on how to coordinate rail, motor, and water transportation and how to mobilize resources for defense purposes.

Obviously the scope of the council's activities called for the appointment of a representative advisory commission of unusual ability. After much discussion the president in October 1916 appointed Daniel Willard, president of the Baltimore and Ohio Railroad; Bernard Baruch, a financier; Howard E. Coffin; Julius Rosenwald, president of Sears, Roebuck; Hollis Godfrey; Samuel Gompers, president of the American Federation of Labor; and Dr. Franklin Martin, secretary-general of the American College of Surgeons.

The initial meetings of the council were exploratory. No precedent existed for their activities, and their instructions were vague. In the Civil War, even though Union expenditures had jumped from $63 million in 1860 to more than $1 billion in 1865, little thought was given toward regulating the economy. Lincoln did exercise arbitrary powers of imprisonment and censorship and actually took over the telegraphs, but to satisfy the needs of military supply, the army and navy went into the market and purchased what they wanted.

In 1916, it became clear that such haphazard buying could bring disaster. Allied demand was adding new purchasing power to the economy, some $5 billion in little more than two years. J. P. Morgan & Company, tapped as purchasing agents for France and Great Britain, was soliciting orders the like of which American industry had never before received. Wholesale prices increased more than 70 percent between 1914 and 1917: New York market reports in March 1917 showed that in two months the price of potatoes had risen 100 percent, onions 366 percent, and beans 300 percent. Women in New York and Brooklyn upset pushcarts of food peddlers, poured kerosene on stock, and marched on City Hall shouting "feed our children." And the commissioners undoubtedly envisaged struggles for scarce raw materials and labor as demand mounted.

As a war atmosphere began to infect the nation, even before war was declared, the advisory commission found itself at the center of an unprecedented whirlpool of activity. Its members were simply overwhelmed by pressures, suggestions, and complaints. They groped for procedures and elected as head first Hollis Godfrey and then Daniel Willard. They divided themselves up into seven committees each with a function. They set Walter Gifford, a thirty-one-year-old statistician from the American Telephone and Telegraph Company, to preparing reports on the state of industrial preparedness, and he and his staff became the center of a rapidly growing bureaucracy whose function was to put hundreds of businessmen and industrialists in touch with the appropriate government agency. They attempted to keep some kind of control over the sometimes enthusiastic, but perhaps ill-advised preparedness efforts of the several states by setting up state Councils of National Defense designed to encourage but at the same time to keep the forty-eight separate efforts from going their separate ways.

Fighting Men

In early February 1917, long before the Allied War Missions urgently requested aid, the advisory commission had asked the General Staff to estimate the materiel needs for an army of one million men! The commission discovered that the much overworked General Staff had not prepared "even hypothetical plans" for equipping an army of any size. The staff itself could hardly be blamed for such neglect since Wilson had angrily discouraged any planning for a war with Germany lest it complicate the delicate negotiations in the prewar period. Secretary of War Baker, once a convinced pacifist, was also partly responsible for this lack of planning since he was chairman of the Council of National Defense; yet he too was concerned that a meeting of the council to discuss preparedness might unduly alarm the country. All evidence showed how weak the American army actually was: the publicly admitted size, the abortive attempts at maneuvers in 1911, and the inadequacy of the mobilization to meet the Mexican crises. It is little wonder that the German decision makers concluded in January 1917 that there was little risk in renewing unrestricted submarine warfare.

Although the National Defense Act had provided a solid base for developing a new military policy, this development had not gone far by January 1917. In spite of a vigorous recruiting campaign, the strength of the army was substantially below the authorized number of approximately 145,000. Even more unfortunate was the state of military planning. The staff planners (there were only 19 of them) were overworked and in 1916 were concentrating on the Mexican crisis. By December 1916, however, the planners had concluded that a wartime army should be raised by conscription, and by mid-February, they had prepared a plan for raising an army of 4 million, although they estimated that it would be more than two years before American manpower could reach the western front.

The break in diplomatic relations with Germany in February was the signal for the Chief of Staff to recommend a conscription law. Even Wilson now saw that drastic actions would have to be taken in order to have sufficient military force should war come, and both he and the pacifist, Secretary of War Baker, came to the conclusion that conscription might be necessary. His mind made up, Wilson instructed Baker to prepare a plan for conscription on February 4, and the president had one in his hand within a day. Baker himself was now ready to push for mobilization and called a meeting of the Council of National Defense on March 24. The commission in turn recommended raising an army of "at least a million men," and thus Wilson had firm support when in his war message, on April 2, he urged increasing the army through "universal liability to service."

By mid-April, both the House and Senate Committees on Military Affairs introduced bills in accord with Wilson's wishes, and one of the bitterest debates of all time was on. Conscription was, according to critics, "unnecessary, undemocratic, conducive to militarism, and in violation of the constitutional provision of involuntary servitude." Some southern opposition stemmed from the fear of a male black population trained in the use of firearms, while Samuel Gompers feared that it might lead to conscripting labor. Throughout the debate, Wilson paid numerous visits to Capitol Hill and personally appealed to uncommitted congressmen. The press appeared to be overwhelmingly favorable, but congressional mail seemed to be divided. Undoubtedly the arguments for efficiency and need for a sure system of securing manpower were important, but much was made of the need to stand in symbolic unity behind the president.

The bill churned through three conference reports. Several of the Democratic leaders in the House, including Champ Clark, the Speaker, Claude Kitchin, the majority leader, and H. Stanley Dent of Alabama, head of the House Committee on Military Affairs, opposed it. A majority of Dent's committee presented a report recommending a volunteer force of local units. Thus the administration plan was incorporated in the minority report presented, ironically, by Congressman Julius Kahn, a German-born Californian and Republican, endorsed by the Progressive party. In eloquently supporting the administration's measure, Kahn traced in detail what he considered the historical failure of the volunteer system. Those who praised the traditional British system of volunteers, Kahn said, failed to tell how pressure through "derisive colored posters," white feathers, yellow ribbons, anonymous letters, and social ostracism had been used to secure volunteers. Even then after two years, Kahn pointed out, "England was compelled for her own protection to adopt a system of universal obligation to service." In the preliminary voting, the House leadership fought for limiting amendments, but they were beaten back by a bipartisan coalition from all sections of the country, and with overwhelming support from the Northeast and Southwest. When the final vote on the measure was taken, much of the initial opposition disappeared. The count showed 397 yeas, 24 nays, and 10 not voting. Twelve Republicans, ten Democrats, one socialist, and one prohibitionist voted against the bill. None of the negative votes came from New England and only one, a socialist, from the Middle Atlantic states; seven came from the South (Alabama, Florida, South Carolina, Mississippi, and Kentucky), four from California, four from Ohio, two from Colorado, and one each from Minnesota and Michigan. When the chips were down, the Democratic leadership could not vote against the bill, although Champ Clark, Claude Kitchin, and Stanley Dent figuratively held their noses as they voted aye.

The Senate debate was equally vigorous, but here both the Democratic and Republican leadership supported the bill. Senator George Chamberlain of Oregon, leader of the Senate Committee on Military Affairs, in introducing the measure denounced the volunteer system as "undemocratic, unreliable, extravagant, inefficient, and, above all, unsafe" and insisted that universal military service was based upon the fundamental responsibility of a freeman to the state. Initial opposition came from those who feared delay in putting the selective service law into effect and thought that a volunteer system would be a more effective means of prosecuting the war, but the die-hards were those who opposed conscription in principle. Of these, Robert La Follette, the most vitriolic opponent, warned that the bill would give one man or his agents the power "to enter at will every home in our country, at any hour of the day or night . . . and violently lay hold of 1,000,000 of our finest . . . boys . . . , and against their will . . . deport them across the seas . . . and require them . . . to wound and kill other young boys . . . toward whom they felt no hostility and have no cause to feel any." The original bill passed the Senate on April 28 by a vote of 81 to 8 with 7 not voting.

The president formally approved the act "to increase temporarily the Military Establishment of the United States," sometimes called the selective draft, on May 18, 1917. Those responsible for formulating the measure had been sensitive to history and to the weaknesses of the conscription acts passed during the Civil War. They emphasized the temporary nature of the act; they attempted to deemphasize the role of the military in implementing the act; and they involved as much as possible neighborhood boards in determining who would serve. The act first authorized the president to bring existing regular army units up to full strength, to draft into the federal service any members of the National Guard, to raise by a draft two additional forces of five hundred thousand men each whose officers would be drawn from the regular army, the officers reserve, or the National Guard, and to raise by "voluntary enlistment" (clearly at the president's volition) a force not to exceed four infantry divisions. This last was an amendment forced into one of the conference reports by Theodore Roosevelt's friends.

The selection was to be made from a pool of young men between the ages of twenty-one and thirty who were to register at such time as chosen by the president. Quotas for states were to be chosen on the basis of population. Selection of those who were to serve was to be made by local boards of civilians chosen by the president for each county or for each unit of approximately thirty thousand persons. The decisions of these local boards could be appealed to district boards. No bounties were to be paid to encourage enlistment, nor could any person "liable for military service" be permitted to secure a substitute, as had been possible in the Civil War. The act made provisions for conscientious objection on religious grounds or on the grounds of a pacifist creed of an "organization at present organized." The act also exempted from the draft men "physically and morally deficient" and for other specific causes. Finally, the secretary of war was instructed to prevent the operation of bawdy houses near military camps, and, although the president was authorized to make regulations concerning the sale of alcoholic beverages in or near military posts, "no person, corporation, partnership, or association" was permitted to "sell, supply, or have in his or its possession any intoxicating or spirituous liquors" at a post then in official military use.

The measure was ingenious, but visions of draft riots and wholesale evasion led to preparation not only for registration but for a considerable campaign of education. Before the end of May, three weeks before the act had been approved, the Judge Advocate General, Enoch Crowder, wrote confidentially to the state governors explaining the bills, and Major Hugh Johnson, an aide to Crowder and sixteen years later to be the unconventional chief of the New Deal's National Recovery Administration, took local sheriffs and mayors into his confidence and mailed them registration forms pleading for secrecy until the selective service measure actually had passed. As soon as the bill had passed, every effort was made to prepare the nation psychologically for registration. The president took the lead. He chose June 5 as registration day, called for the nation's support for a process that was "in no sense a conscription," but, rather, a "selection from a nation which has volunteered in mass." Tension, nevertheless, was high. Resistance groups sprang up all over the country; in New York on June 4, for example, a huge crowd in Hunt's Palace in the Bronx heard the draft described as the "entering wedge of military despotism."

The miracle did happen. On June 5, 1917, approximately ten million between the ages of twenty and thirty went to their voting precincts and registered. "It staggers the imagination," editorialized the *Chicago Herald.* "A nation, the freest of all democracies . . . calls by law to the most rigid of all employments one tenth of her population." In a little more than a month even more tension was generated when the lottery was held in Washington that determined the order of selection of each draftee. Each registered person within each district was given a number from one to the largest number registered in the district. Duplicate numbers were placed in a large glass bowl and a blindfolded Newton D. Baker drew out the first number—number 258. This number identified the individual to be selected first by each local board.

Although the procedure was widely applauded, the law brought some hostile reaction in all parts of the country. The Industrial Workers of the World never let up in its opposition. Criticisms of favoritism soon reached Baker: that local boards were being politically packed or that the rich were exempted and the poor selected. Such rumors led to changes, a quick order from Baker, for example, that each draft board should include a labor representative. More fundamentally, the act was "violently assailed" on constitutional grounds. For some of the constitutional critics, Daniel Webster, who in 1812 had argued eloquently against compulsory military service, served as a model. "Where is it written in the constitution," Webster had said, "that you may take children from their parents and parents from their children and compel them to fight the battles of any war?" Others argued that a soldier enjoyed "a common-law right . . . not to be sent out of the country," that the act deprived persons of equal protection of the laws, and that it imposed slavery or involuntary servitude.

On January 7, 1918, the Supreme Court in a unanimous decision upheld the law. It based its argument largely on the grant to Congress of the powers to raise and support armies, to declare war, and to make laws necessary and proper for executing granted powers. It denied the complaints of the plaintiffs and concluded that "contributing to the defense of the rights and honor of the nation" was a citizen's "supreme and noble duty."

While the debates over selective service were delaying the passage of the act, the army could not wait. It sent its recruiters out into the states and called on state councils of defense for help. The councils used their local influence to secure speakers, induce moving picture theaters to display posters, and see that recruiting leaflets received wide distribution. Although an increasing number of volunteers were added to the rolls, by the end of the war it could be said that for the first time American fighting forces were made up largely of conscripted men rather than volunteers. In approximately a year and a half more than twenty-four million registered, six million were given physical examinations, three million were inducted, and two million served overseas.

Financing the War

As the nation moved toward war in the early weeks of 1917, few prophets foresaw the decisive contribution to the war effort that would be made by the two million troops that would fight on the western front. Many Americans at first assumed that their contribution would be primarily financial and economic, and indeed an important long-term effect of the war was the conversion of the United States from a debtor to a creditor nation. This change was the result of its possession of needed resources combined with its relationship to the war itself: as a neutral it became the storehouse for the Allies; as a belligerent it not only continued to supply the Allies but had to supply its own armed forces and maintain the war economy. This unprecedented combination of circumstances required a revolutionary development in federal financing. The Federal Reserve System had fortunately been established in November 1914. However, the war in Europe, three months old at the time, had drastically upset normal industrial, commercial, and financial relationships, and the Federal Reserve System in adapting itself to an abnormal situation became a different sort of institution from what it otherwise would have been. In theory the Federal Reserve System was to be independent of the executive and Congress, with the secretary of the treasury as *ex officio* head of the Federal Reserve Board (and with William G. McAdoo, vigorous and independent minded, as the secretary). However, in jurisdictional disputes the independence of the board was more apparent than real.

Prior to American entry into the war, McAdoo demonstrated energetic leadership. He worked with bankers and the stock exchanges to bring order into international policy and made use of extraordinary powers to issue emergency currency to ease stringency at home. In the meantime, Congress made no significant change in the tax structure after introducing the token income tax in 1913. Expenditures for preparedness, however, required quick action and in November 1916, Congress doubled the normal income tax rate, to 2 percent, increased the maximum surtax from 6 to 13 percent, and added both a tax of 12.5 percent on the net profits of munitions manufacturers and a graduated estates tax. Even these new taxes proved to be inadequate and another emergency measure was passed in March 1917. Included in this measure, moreover, was a significant innovation, an authorization to the Treasury to borrow $300 million by selling short-term certificates in anticipation of taxes.

America's entry into the war created a financial explosion. The country faced a bewildering situation: overseas allies with financial resources approaching exhaustion, a war to be fought whose unprecedented costs in lives and munitions had already been demonstrated by action on the western front, increasingly sophisticated and expensive weaponry on land and air, and a need for ships caused in part by sinkings and in part by the demand for American products overseas. Clearly these and other factors not yet foreseen would call for expenditures, the like of which the United States had never experienced before.

The Treasury thus faced certain responsibilities. It had to convince the people that sacrifices were necessary and that funds normally used for consumer spending had to be channeled to the war effort. Without a Budget Bureau or Council of Economic Advisers, moreover, it had to estimate how much the annual cost of the war would be, and it had to determine how to raise the funds for waging the war—what proportion should be raised through taxation and what proportion through borrowing.

Unfortunately the European belligerents had not found helpful precedents when they declared war in 1914. The experiences of recent wars seemed to indicate that wars "would produce no abnormal effects upon the monetary situation." The fact that the outbreak of war shook financial markets and prevented governments from raising funds in traditional ways came as a surprise.

McAdoo studied the Civil War experience, but he was not impressed with the way the Treasury had financed that war. He would not consider the issuing of greenbacks; he thought that more emphasis should have been placed on taxation in the Civil War; he opposed restricted bond issues as well as the kind of commission selling that had been entrusted to Jay Cooke in 1863. At the same time, he favored the kind of organizational drive for the selling of bonds that Cooke eventually set up.

With the declaration of war, McAdoo was forced to make quick decisions. He first estimated that he would have to raise $3.5 billion to provide for 1 million men in the armed forces and an additional $3 billion for loans to the Allies. He decided that about 50 percent of this amount should be raised by taxes, and that the other 50 percent should be raised through a broadly based borrowing campaign at a low interest rate. All of these points were controversial. Early estimates of the costs of the war were low. By December 1917 McAdoo changed the estimate to more than $11.5 billion for war purposes with more than $6 billion as loans to allies. The increased figure persuaded McAdoo that no more than one-third of total costs need be raised by taxation. Theories clashed on this point. Some economists urged high taxes as a means of withdrawing consumer purchasing power and thus relieving inflationary pressures. Others warned that war taxes "lessen social output," and would hamper war production. Tension developed between the Treasury and the Federal Reserve Board in part because McAdoo seemed determined to restrict the independence of the board and partly because the Federal Reserve Board considered the Treasury's means of financing the war inflationary.

Equally controversial was the question of the kind of bond-selling campaign that should take place. McAdoo was determined that the campaign give thousands of American citizens a sense of participation in the war effort by buying bonds. He would keep the interest rates lower than on the open market, thus saving the American people millions of dollars in future taxes and at the same time encouraging depositors to keep their already accumulated savings in savings banks where they were drawing higher interest rates. In spite of warnings that a huge loan at low interest rates was bound to fail, McAdoo went ahead and planned a publicity campaign that would attract consumer purchasing power to the war effort.

On April 7, 1917, McAdoo called congressional leaders to meet with him to discuss fiscal policy. This was to be a bipartisan effort, and although the delegation was led by Senator F. M. Simmons, Democratic chairman of the Finance Committee, it included his two ranking Republican colleagues on that committee, Reed Smoot of Utah and Henry Cabot Lodge of Massachusetts. From the House came Cordell Hull of Tennessee, John N. Garner of Texas, and H. T. Rainey of Illinois, Democrats, and J. W. Fordney, Republican of Michigan of the House Committee on Ways and Means and Swager Sherley, Democrat of the Committee on Appropriations. The results of the conference made the headlines. The administration was requesting legislation which would authorize borrowing $5 billion, three-fifths of which would be loaned to the Allies and the remainder used to finance American efforts.

Claude Kitchin, head of the Committee on Ways and Means, had not attended the conference because he was then in North Carolina. Since Kitchin had voted against the war resolution, some assumed that he would not support the administration's war program and that Cordell Hull would present it to the House. On April 13, 1917, however, Kitchin introduced the first measure for the emergency financing of the war. It provided for an issue of $5 billion in bonds and an issue of $2 billion in one-year certificates of indebtedness; both issues were to bear an interest rate of not more than 3.5 percent. Few wartime measures met with such unanimous support; the entire Ways and Means Committee supported it; the House considered only minor changes in the bill. For, as Representative Fordney, the highly respected ranking Republican on the committee, was applauded for stating, "It is an unusual situation to find in this House Democrats and Republicans in the same bed," especially, when hitherto "no authorization for raising such an immense sum of money has ever been presented in any legislative body in the world before." The bill passed in a record vote without dissent and with 390 members voting aye.

To the action of the House, the Senate added strong support. In presenting the bill on April 17, the Finance Committee's head, the diminutive F. M. Simmons from North Carolina, urged its immediate passage. The decision to wage war has already been made, Simmons said, now show the Allied mission which will arrive in Washington tomorrow that we mean it. We should be able to say to them: "To aid you and to prepare and equip ourselves to efficiently do our part in the great struggle we have just passed, by a unanimous vote of both Houses of Congress, the greatest budget that has ever been enacted by the legislature of any nation of the world," a budget larger than your first, second, and perhaps your third war budget put together, "a sum so stupendous that it staggers the imagination and mind of man."

No senator expressed himself as willing to vote against the measure. Some, however, were concerned with the terms of the bill. Borah and Norris, for example, were concerned lest provisions in the bill permit businessmen to profit unduly. Penrose of Pennsylvania replied to such arguments that if favorable provisions were not provided, the financial community would refuse to invest. Senator Stone of Missouri criticized the extent to which the measure would burden future generations and argued that the authorized $5 billion should be in short-term certificates of indebtedness and thus repayable immediately by taxes. Senator Cummins warned against loaning money to the Allies. Give them the $3 billion as our present contribution to the war effort, he urged; these countries when they emerge from the war will be bankrupt, and our laons will "create an embarrassment from which the men of those times will find it difficult to escape." The key vote in the Senate was on an amendment that would have put greater restrictions upon the secretary of the treasury as to how the bonds should be issued and when they should terminate. The Republicans voted solidly in favor of the amendment, but it was defeated by a vote of thirty-seven to forty-two. Immediately thereafter, still on April 17, Simmons called for the final vote and it passed the Senate by a vote of eighty to zero.

The fiscal program that now ensued was a mixed bag. In order to obtain needed funds immediately, McAdoo made use of his new authority to issue short-term certificates by selling $868 million worth of 3 percent certificates to commercial banks in April, May, and June. These were to be paid back through the returns from the much more highly publicized long-term bond drive that was launched in May.

This drive was definitely McAdoo's project. He defied most of his advisers who said that no more than $500 million or at the most $1 billion could be borrowed at 3.5 percent. McAdoo set the goal of $2 billion, called it the First Liberty Loan, and then organized to make it go. Each of the twelve federal reserve banks served as a central agency, and set up Liberty Loan committees in every city and town. McAdoo personally traveled the country east of the Rockies speaking in twenty-three cities, explaining the bond issue, and calling on the patriotism of every citizen. The reaction was sensational. Advertising agencies offered services free; newspapers opened their advertising columns; department stores offered to solicit; express companies offered their money order departments; patriotic societies and civic organizations all fell into line. Street-corner lecturers and "four-minute men" in theaters urged their hearers to be patriotic and buy. However, with patriotic emotionalism out of the way, the banks would perform the most important and sustained function.

The First Liberty Loan seemed to meet with overwhelming success. Between May 14 and June 15 more than 4 million people contributed more than $3 billion. Some 99 percent of the contributions were in the $50 to $10,000 category, indicating that McAdoo's campaign to reach the "people" throughout the country had been successful. However, 40 percent of the loan was used to pay back the short-term certificates sold in April; some $500 million per month was credited for the needs of Allied governments; and by September the entire proceeds of the First Loan were exhausted—so more short-term notes had to be sold.

In the meantime, Congress was debating the extent to which the costs of the war should be paid by taxes. Claude Kitchin, for the House Committee on Ways and Means, introduced the War Revenue Measure to the House on May 10, 1917. His aim was to raise $1.8 billion through taxation. This amount together with an additional $1.5 billion, estimated as postal receipts, would about equal the sum to be raised through the first bond campaign for domestic purposes. In general, the position of the committee was that it was "sound economic policy for the present generation to bear a fair and equitable portion of the burden of financing the war." The measure then called essentially for doubling the normal income tax and corporation tax rates to 4 percent, raising the surtax rates to a maximum of 33 percent, doubling the excess profits tax rate to 16 percent, and increasing other excise taxes substantially.

Partisanship remained at a minimum during the extended debate on this measure, but the House of Representatives, in spite of pleas for haste from Kitchin, refused to be rushed. Particularly controversial were the

questions of postage rates for newspapers and magazines and the extent
to which funds should be raised by taxation. Representative C. W.
Ramsyer (Republican) of Iowa called for conscripting dollars as well as
men and argued that placing the burden of the war on future generations
was "unmanly and cowardly." The Democratic leadership held firm,
however, and the bill passed by a vote of 329 to 76.

If the House Committee on Ways and Means could be accused of undue
haste in presenting a complicated revenue measure to Congress, no one
could have accused the Senate of such superficiality. The Finance Committee took more than eight weeks to consider the bill. Such careful
consideration was typical of the chairman of the Finance Committee, F. M.
Simmons. Simmons' committee held a full week of formal hearings and
informal conferences with representatives of the business community
while Simmons himself was working on details with experts from the
Treasury, the Bureau of Internal Revenue, and the Tariff Commission.

In introducing the measure to the Senate, on August 11, 1917, Simmons stressed its precedent-shaking nature. He reminded the Senate that
before the war federal expenditures ran well under a billion dollars
annually, and that revenue was drawn largely from tariffs and from excise
taxes on liquor and tobacco. Now, Simmons pointed out, Congress was
faced with wartime expenditures of at least $10 billion. What was needed,
he said, was a "scientific" tax structure, strong and flexible enough not
only to meet the needs of the war but to provide a model for the postwar
period. He proposed to broaden the tax base, yet not to impose taxes
that would discourage enterprise. Of the expected annual expenditure of
$10 billion he proposed to raise $3,330,000 through taxes. Approximately
$2 billion of this amount was to be raised from the present bill, and of
that sum approximately $1.5 billion would be raised by taxes on incomes,
war profits, and alcoholic beverages; and the remainder from other types
of consumption and excise taxes. On this distribution, the Finance Committee could not agree. Even though Simmons himself believed that a substantial proportion of the revenues should be drawn from "phenomenally
high" war profits, he also argued that "practically everybody" should
contribute to some extent. La Follette, however, argued that a higher
percentage of total expenditures should be paid for by taxes rather than
from a bond issue and that all of the amount to be raised by taxation
should be raised from incomes, war profits, liquors, and tobacco.

The issue was joined when La Follette introduced an amendment which
would have substantially increased the graduated income tax rates. On
incomes, over $25,000, for example, rates would have been doubled
(26 percent) and the highest rates would have been 62 percent as opposed
to 50 percent recommended by the committee. Simmons bitterly attacked
La Follette's amendment, virtually accusing those who favored such tax
rates as being insidiously attempting to turn the present generation
against the war and insisting that rates arrived at by the committee were

as near scientific as possible and certainly did not result from any desire to "distribute improperly the burdens and the expense of war." He argued that the committee's rates were more equitable than La Follette's. The senator from Wisconsin ridiculed Simmons' arguments that those who favored a greater emphasis on taxation were guilty of disloyalty and that the committee's rate schedules were more equitable. "Lift the load from those who must furnish the great body of the soldiery that will be sent to slaughter," he urged, "and place it upon those who are able to bear it, the owners of surplus incomes and those making profits from war."

Although La Follette received strong support, the committee's position held. The amendment was defeated on August 23 by a vote of twenty-one to fifty-eight, with "progressive" Republicans (Borah, Gronna, Johnson of California, Kenyon, Townsend, McNary, Norris, and Poindexter) and a few Democrats (Gore, Hardwick, Hollis, McKellar, Owen, Reed, Kirby, Trammell, and Vardaman) supporting La Follette.

Simmons' position during this controversy, and indeed the position of the Senate's leadership, was complicated by uncertainty as to how much revenue was actually needed. The Treasury was itself getting unreliable data from the spending agencies, particularly the War Department, and thus changed its estimates by a few billion dollars several times. As the *Nation* put it, "Nobody can agree within several thousand million dollars on what our probable national disbursements will be" nor "arrive at the same result as the alleged treasury computation."

One of the new estimates reached Simmons at the time that Borah and Johnson were fighting for increased rates on war profits and made him reconsider his bill. The bill passed by the House had included a tax on prewar excess profits. Claude Kitchin supported this tax on the grounds that companies which had made large profits in the years before the United States became involved in the war would pay little or nothing under a "war" profits tax. Whether Simmons was convinced by the strength of Kitchin's argument, the persuasiveness of La Follette and Johnson, or the needs of the Treasury matter little. Simmons held firm on the war profits tax, but added an excess profits tax to it. The bill finally passed by a vote of sixty-nine to four. Even Johnson and Vardaman voted aye, but La Follette, Borah, Norris, and Gronna held out to the end. The bill went to conference and was not finally approved by both houses until October 1917. La Follette bitterly attacked the conference report, asserting that the only sound financial principle was to pay for war while it was being fought, that the tax upon surplus incomes and war profits was "grossly and wrongfully insufficient," and that the bond issues authorized were "wickedly excessive." As the *Cleveland Press* put it, the law reached five million Americans who had not been taxed directly before: "You cannot buy any article that has been freighted by rail or water, you cannot ride on a train, send a telegram, visit a theater or ball park, buy a bottle of patent medicine, a baseball bat or any other kind of sporting goods, a tube of toothpaste or any other toilet article, own an auto, a motor cycle, or a motor boat, draw a time draft, buy a bond or share of stock, or send in a proxy for an election, without paying tribute to Uncle Sam."

Before the tax bill had been passed, the funds from the First Liberty Loan were exhausted, and the Treasury was forced to resort to more short-term notes. This cycle was continued through four Liberty Loans and a victory loan, and in general the same organization and campaign techniques were followed in the last loans as in the first: the Treasury at the top, the twelve Federal Reserve Banks as fiscal agents, liberty loan committees in the communities, and high-pressure publicity agents in collaboration with bankers, businessmen, the news media, and various professional societies. Increasingly, emphasis was placed upon savings in order to buy bonds, and in September 1917, the Treasury determined to make a conscious effort to combat the idea of business as usual by calling for thrift, and offering war savings certificates and thrift stamps for sale, convertible into bonds, for as low as 25 cents. Although the sale of these certificates moved slowly at first, an effective organization developed. Some 150,000 war savings societies were organized with more than 31 million members pledged to economize and to buy stamps, before the end of 1918 they had actually purchased $900 million worth.

Although each liberty loan drive was publicized as a huge success, McAdoo did not leave it entirely to patriotism to determine the result. In the first place, the interest rate of 3.5 percent could not be maintained, and after the first drive the rate was increased to 4 percent, then to 4.25 percent, and the victory loan to 4.75 percent. In addition, favorable tax arrangements were provided to encourage purchase. McAdoo was particularly alarmed at the tendency of the prices of bonds to go down after a drive. He feared that such a decline would frighten patriots for further bond drives, so he obtained authority in the Third Liberty Loan for the Treasury to purchase 5 percent of each issue. To carry out this authority, the Treasury sold certificates of indebtedness, put the proceeds into a kind of sinking fund, which was then used to buy bonds from time to time on the New York Stock Exchange. Between April 1918 and February 1919, some $347 million of bonds were so bought, a daily sale varying from $15,000 to $25 million.

War Finance Corporation

The tremendous expansion of governmental expenditures required expansion not only of industries clearly related to the war effort but of other industries as well. Public utilities from streetcar companies to power plants, for example, had to extend their facilities to meet new demands; and at the same time private industries were not averse to expanding in order to take advantage of the boom.

In spite of the prosperous conditions brought on by the war, American industry was not always able to find the capital necessary to expand. In part, this condition resulted from the government's effective efforts to sell its own securities, and thus to guide funds normally available for private investment into government purchases. Wartime conditions too created a climate of uncertainty hostile to private investment. Savings banks were threatened by patrons withdrawing their deposits to put into the more profitable liberty bonds. Public utilities were particularly hard hit because their rates were fixed to the point that they could not easily meet increased costs of labor and material.

Secretary of the Treasury McAdoo was concerned lest there be a complete collapse of the financial system. The banks were already straining to meet the country's requirements, and would have found it even more difficult were it not for the fortuitous existence of the Federal Reserve System. The assets of the federal reserve banks, created only in November 1914, amounted to more than $3 billion, three times the assets of one year before. Even so, by late 1917, further federal action seemed necessary. Bankers, businessmen, and other government officers urged McAdoo to exert some control over new enterprises and new securities. McAdoo at first attempted to investigate personally when questions were referred to him. Finding the job too time consuming, however, he created a "Capital Issues Committee" of the Federal Reserve Board chaired by Paul Warburg and instructed to determine whether new security issues would aid or detract from the war effort. At the same time, McAdoo urged bankers and businessmen to confer with the new committee before considering expansion requiring new capital.

By mid-January 1918, the committee was functioning, and although without coercive power, its efforts brought results. Stock exchanges, the Investment Bankers Association, various chambers of commerce, and other business associations cooperated in blackballing stock issues which the committee had not approved. Publicity given to the committee's activities led to voluntary retrenchment. States and municipalities took the hint, and public building construction almost came to a halt for the duration.

Still, business and government were finding it difficult to coordinate their activities. The Capital Issues Committee felt the need of some power of coercion to get at the unpatriotic citizen "who has seen fit to pursue unhampered his own course regardless of the interests of his country." Moreover the question of how to provide financial support for legitimate expansion had not been answered. To meet these needs, McAdoo drafted a measure which would establish a government corporation, to be known as the War Finance Corporation, to provide the financial support for essential industry and to establish a Capital Issues Committee with the investigatory and coercive powers which the present committee of the Federal Reserve Board lacked.

This bill was at once recognized as a precedent-shaking measure. Claude

Kitchin, chairman of the House Committee on Ways and Means to which
the bill was sent, described it as "so radical, so unprecedented, and . . .
economically so revolutionary, that the mind of the most radical would
hesitate to endorse it at first blush." He was, however, willing to consider
it as a war measure, and so it was maneuvered to his committee rather
than to the Committee on Banking and Currency where opposition was
so obvious that it might have held the bill indefinitely. A similar maneuver
took place in the Senate where the bill was channeled to the Committee
on Finance chaired by Simmons, a good friend of McAdoo, rather than
to the Banking and Currency Committee where the position of Robert
Owen, of Oklahoma, the chairman, was far less certain.

Simmons introduced the measure into the Senate in February 1918,
with the general blessing of the Finance Committee even though its
members shuddered at its unprecedented character. One of the most
controversial parts of the bill as presented involved the Capital Issues
Committee. In its original form the measure authorized the committee
to license the sale of securities, and provided that any one selling securities without such a license was subject to a $5,000 fine or a one-year
prison term. Senator after senator denounced this provision. The rebel
Democrat James Reed of Missouri called it so "monstrous" that it would
not even have been introduced in the German Reichstag. Senator Owen,
a Democrat and a particularly knowledgeable senator on matters of
banking, pointed out that although France and Britain had a similar
watchdog committee, its coercive powers were purely voluntary. Senator
Brandegee of Connecticut, a Republican, distrusted the entire regulatory
feature, arguing that it would stifle the initiative of legitimate business.
Simmons at first refused to accept these objections. He would not acknowl-
edge that voluntary controls were sufficient to restrict unnecessary capital
expenditures and to conserve investment capital for war purposes. He
admitted that Britain appeared to have a voluntary system of controls,
but he showed how restrictions there left almost no industry engaged in
any kind of activity not associated with the war effort. In fact, he concluded, the British system was not voluntary because the sweeping powers
of the Statute of the Realm Act provided whatever coercive powers
necessary.

Sentiment continued to build up, however, against the licensing and
coercive features of the bill. On March 4, Owen and Henry F. Hollis, a
New Hampshire Democrat, neither of whom got along particularly well
with Simmons, threatened a filibuster. At this point both informally and
formally a group of senators worked on an amendment that would give
the committee the power to investigate and publicize but with only
moral pressures to control. Simmons, always open to compromise in
order to get a respectable bill, acceded to the amendment.

He was the more willing to compromise on the regulatory features
because he was convinced that the provision for the War Finance Corporation was much more important. Although numerous senators apparently

feared the implication of such an institution, few questioned the need
for it. Senator Asle J. Gronna of North Dakota inquired how his fellow
senators could support the War Finance Corporation when they had
denounced subsidies and loans for agriculture on the ground that they
were socialistic schemes. The War Finance Corporation, he said, is a
government bank, authorized "to issue bonds to the extent of eight
times the amount of capital stock so called." Such an institution, he
insisted "is communistic," it is "socialistic," and "would make Carl Marx
[*sic*] and other great socialists turn in their grave." Yet Gronna supported
the final bill when it came to a vote on March 7 as did seventy-three other
senators; only three opposed. The House did not consider the bill until
the Senate had passed it and then essentially accepted the Senate's bill,
with only two representatives voting nay.

The bill provided for a War Finance Corporation to be incorporated
in the District of Columbia. The corporation would have directors consisting of the secretary of the treasury and four additional persons and
capital stock of $500 million subscribed by the United States. It would
be authorized to make loans to banks and to individuals or corporations
"in exceptional cases" conducting a business in the United States "necessary or contributory" to the war effort. The corporation could make
loans up to a total of $4 billion. The president would also appoint "a
Capital Issues Committee" of seven members, at least three of whom
were to be members of the Federal Reserve Board. This committee was
given the power to determine whether the issuance of most new securities
was in the national interest.

By the end of May 1918, the War Finance Corporation was in business.
McAdoo was ex officio chairman of the board, and W. P. G. Harding,
governor of the Federal Reserve Board, was managing director; thus
close ties between the Treasury and the Federal Reserve System were
established. The corporation found many industries, principally public
utility companies waiting at the door, pleading for funds, but it established
a policy of helping these companies directly only in extreme emergencies
and with adequate security. Instead aid was given to banks which in turn
would supply credit to those who needed it. As a matter of fact, little
actual funding for industry and utilities was provided. The very existence
of the corporation provided a sense of security that funds would be
available if needed. In the case of public utilities, for example, almost $41
million was advanced by November 30, 1918, of which almost $12
million had already been repaid. Rather unexpectedly, the corporation
found a need for its support in food-producing industries. In the government's food conservation program, a considerable emphasis upon the
expansion of the canning industry was encouraged. This expansion took
place mainly in small towns where credit was not available. The cattle
industry was in desperate straits because of droughts in some areas and
had overworked banks and cattle loan companies. The corporation
established loan agencies in both Dallas and Kansas City in order to make

direct loans to cattle raisers and protect the future meat supply. The corporation advanced slightly more than $71 million before November 30, of which more than half had been repaid.

The Capital Issues Committee, like the War Finance Corporation, found that its very existence reduced the pressures for capital expansion. Both local subcommittees and the committee itself were able to persuade individuals and corporations to postpone plans. Moreover, appeals to investment bankers, local government officials, and the business public in general led to the development of organized support through such organizations as the Investment Bankers Association of America for a policy of investment restraint. Actually, the committee passed upon 2,289 applications totaling approximately $2.6 million worth of securities. It approved approximately $2 million worth.

The Pen Is Mightier than the Sword

A pervasive question that haunted the campaigns to provide both personnel and funds to wage the war at home and abroad was whether a nation of such divers peoples would accept the kind of national power necessary to make an effective contribution to the war effort. When the war broke out in Europe, Wilson seemed unconcerned about internal dissent. When he endorsed a preparedness program in 1915, however, he became almost emotional about those who were pouring "the poison of disloyalty into the very arteries of our national life," and he urged legislation to crush out "such creatures of passion, disloyalty, and anarchy."

Both politics and security probably played a part in Wilson's changed views. Wilson's secretary, Joe Tumulty, with his fingers on the pulse of northeastern votes, sensed an issue for the campaign of 1916; and at various times, the military expressed concern about their inability to impose censorship over publications that might endanger the national security. The army General Staff in 1915, for example, urged Congress to authorize the president to censor telegraph, cable, wireless, and the mail wherever necessary. In December 1915, Wilson's cabinet agreed that legislation was necessary and instructed the attorney general, Thomas Gregory, to draft it.

Gregory was personally sensitive to the possibility of the abridgment of civil liberties in wartime. He recognized the difficulty of drawing a line between properly protecting the nation's security and improperly abridging civil liberties. He decided, however, to take executive action as soon as he learned that Germany had renewed unlimited submarine warfare, and on February 2, 1917, he instructed United States attorneys to prosecute any persons who might "attempt to engage in activities detrimental to the United States." Suspicion boiled around the eight million aliens in the country whom even in peacetime some patriots considered potential subversives. The question became so sensitive that on February 15, the Advisory Commission of the Council of National Defense reminded the council of "our national doctrines of tolerance and personal liberty," and urged that "all Americans . . . meet these millions of foreign born with unchanged manner and with unprejudiced mind." As soon as the United States actually entered the war, however, moderation seemed to be suspect, and intolerance and superpatriotism became the norm.

The immediate question was what kind of controls should be imposed over the release of information. Wilson turned to his close friend, Secretary of the Navy Daniels, former editor of the *Raleigh News and Observer,* for guidance, and then on April 14, 1917, announced the creation of the Committee on Public Information (CPI) with George Creel, a lively and liberal journalist, as head, and Baker, Daniels, and Lansing as members of the committee. The committee promptly assumed the position that mobilization of the mind was as important as mobilization of manpower and industry. "The *war-will,* the will-to-win, of a democracy," Creel asserted, "depends upon the degree to which each one of all the people of that democracy can concentrate and consecrate body and soul and spirit in the supreme effort of service and sacrifice."

Creel made Guy Stanton Ford, head of the Department of History and dean of the Graduate School at the University of Minnesota, responsible for what Creel called "the world's greatest adventure in advertising." Ford in turn called on scholars from colleges and universities to write "Loyalty Leaflets" and to prepare pamphlets for a Red, White, and Blue Series and a War Information Series. Although Ford instructed his authors to write "so carefully" that they would not be ashamed of their product twenty years later, the underlying principle was undoubtedly that "the pen was mightier than the sword," and canons of scholarship were not always observed. The topics of the pamphlets included "reasons for entering the war, . . . the nature of our free institutions, our war aims, . . . the purposes of the imperial German Government, and full exposure of the enemy's misrepresentations, aggressions, and barbarities."

The scope of the activities of the CPI was unprecedented. It printed dozens of pamphlets in millions of copies, organized seventy-five thousand speakers as "four-minute men" to speak on all sorts of occasions, supplied "selected" articles for the foreign language press; planned exhibits for state fairs; solicited free advertising space in periodicals and newspapers and on billboards; mobilized artists, novelists, and historians; furnished special information to the rural press, labor press, and religious press; and prepared feature films for the relatively new medium of the motion picture as well as more traditional photographs and stereoptican slides. It made use of cable, wireless, and mail service in aiming "a true picture of the American democracy" at Allied and neutral powers. Through the neutral press the word reached the central powers, and "mortar-guns, loaded with 'paper bullets,' and airplanes, carrying pamphlet matter, bombarded the German front."

Creel, perhaps more than any other federal administrator, depended upon the local councils of defense for his organization. State councils prepared posters, organized public meetings, distributed pamphlets, and made speeches available. Arthur E. Bestor, president of the Chatauqua Institute and chief of the speakers division of the CPI, worked out a system of state and local conferences in conjunction with the councils. The Indiana council for example, imported Sousa's band for the occasion late in 1917, "and everything went off with a whoop and a holler" in spite of an "inconveniently timed blizzard."

Creel denied accusations that he was a censor. He insisted that he would not use war measures "to limit the peace-time freedom of individuals or professions," but would ask the press to agree not to print information relating to troop and ship movements and other matters of military significance. Such voluntary restrictions combined with the censorship imposed in actual military areas and the unity inspired by the positive program of releasing information, Creel considered a sufficient protection of the national interest.

Wilson, however, was of a different mind. He favored legislation that would punish disloyalty. In his message requesting a declaration of war, he had assured German-Americans of fair treatment, but promised "stern repression" to those guilty of disloyalty. Laws on the statute books to prevent conspiracies during the Civil War were revived, but these laws had not been aimed against individuals unless treason were involved, and the legal definition of treason did not include utterances. Senator George Chamberlain from Oregon, head of the Senate Committee on Military Affairs, had a relatively simple solution to this problem: He would convert the whole country into a military zone and define espionage as anything "endangering the success of the military forces." Such an arrangement would not only provide punishment for the dangerous utterance but would make all citizens subject to court martial.

Although Wilson opposed this proposal, he did favor the repression of actions or utterances that might jeopardize the war effort. Thus his Department of Justice provided Congress with proposals which were to lead to the statute known as the Espionage Act. This enactment contained one section that provided for press censorship. Even though that section contained a proviso guaranteeing the right to criticize the government, the *New York Times* editorialized almost daily against it. "Let the attempt to suppress freedom of speech, in whatever guise it appears, be defeated unanimously," it trumpeted, "while we are warring to make democracy safe in the world, let us keep it safe in the United States."

A great deal of parliamentary maneuvering took place over this section. The Republicans fought it and defeated it in the House. In the Senate, Lodge and other Old Guard senators complained about the power the measure would give to the president, and Borah, supported by both independent Republicans such as La Follette and Norris and Independent Democrats such as Watson and Vardaman denounced it as abridging the First Amendment. A key vote on an amendment giving the Postmaster General sweeping powers of censorship over the mails saw anti-Wilson Republicans like Lodge combine against the amendment with Democratic and Republican independents like Norris, La Follette, and Vardaman. They could rally only twenty-nine votes, however, and the amendment passed.

The Espionage Act granted extreme powers to the federal government. Its provisions to prevent espionage included controls over shipping, exports, and arms shipments. At the same time, Wilson probably got the censorship powers that he wanted. One section, for example, author-ized a penalty of a $10,000 fine or a prison term of not more than twenty years—or both—for those who in wartime should "willfully make or convey false reports or false statements with intent to interfere with the operation or success of the military or naval forces of the United States or to promote the success of its enemies," or "cause or attempt to cause insubordination, disloyalty, mutiny, or refusal of duty in the military or naval forces of the United States, or shall willfully obstruct the recruiting or enlistment service of the United States." In addition it barred from the mails any sort of writing or picture in violation of any of the provisions of this act or "containing any matter advocating or urging treason, insurrection, or forcible resistance to any law of the United States."

Enforcement was the key to how the sweeping extension of federal power would be used, and the key to enforcement was the attorney general of the United States. The plight of Attorney General Gregory illustrates the dilemma of a public official forced to choose among difficult alternatives in making decisions. Essentially a humane man, sensitive to his responsibilities in protecting civil liberties, Gregory was even more sensitive to threats against the security of the nation. Approving of the Espionage Act on the ground that he now could deal with "dis-turbing malcontents," he established a special War Emergency Division in his department, and increased fivefold the number of special agents in the Division of Investigation between 1916 and 1918. Even then he considered his investigating forces short-handed, so he encouraged the organization of local committees "for the purpose of being on the lookout for disloyal or enemy activities." The most important of these private groups was the American Protective League, whose membership included leaders in communities throughout the United States. Although both Secretary of the Treasury McAdoo and President Wilson were disturbed by the implications of such a private force, Gregory refused to repudiate it. By 1918, the organization had some 250,000 members, and Gregory proudly announced that "it is safe to say that never in its history has this country been so thoroughly policed."

Local authorities and individuals enthusiastically joined the campaign to enforce loyalty. Organizations such as the Boy Spies of America and the Knights of Liberty supplemented the activities of the American Protective League. The Council of National Defense at first encouraged local councils to report "cases of disloyalty and seditious utterances" to the Department of Justice. States and municipalities outdid the federal government in passing restrictive laws and promoting uniformity. Textbooks were carefully scrutinized for pro-German leanings, and in some communities teachers who tried to be objective found themselves denounced as being unpatriotic. Colleges and universities were not immune from hysteria. Faculty members at Minnesota, Illinois, Nebraska, Michigan, and other state universities were dismissed. At Columbia, Henry W. L. Dana, a member of the English department, and James M. Cattell of the psychology department were dropped for pacifist utterances. Charles A. Beard, John Dewey, and James Harvey Robinson vigorously criticized the university's infringement on academic freedom, and Beard resigned in protest, accusing the trustees of using war hysteria to rid the university of articulate liberals.

Superpatriotism became so emotional that some federal officials sought to restrain it. The Council of National Defense became concerned about the antiseditious activities of some of the state councils and attempted to emphasize education rather than intimidation. The Bureau of Education, led by P. P. Claxton, fought to encourage the maintenance of educational standards. George Creel condemned the persecution of immigrants. Ford, Creel, and Claxton were particularly active in condemning the banning of the teaching of German and of the singing of German songs. Such moderating counsel, however, had a limited effect when people such as Elihu Root upon his return from a mission to Russia could say that "there were men walking our city streets who ought to be taken out at sunrise and shot for treason."

Among those caught up in the fever of war were those who opposed the war so strongly that they refused to serve. The Selective Service Act did take into account religious objection to war, and in June 1917 the president ordered local draft boards to classify conscientious objectors on this basis for noncombatant service. In the patriotic atmosphere of wartime, organizations such as the Anti–Yellow Dog League soon sprang up to make life uncomfortable for potential objectors, but those actually classified as conscientious objectors were remanded to the military arm. Most military personnel did not waste sympathy upon the objectors and usually tried to persuade them to change their minds. They were successful in the cases of approximately sixteen thousand of some twenty thousand draftees who had been granted exemption from combatant service. How many of these made this change freely is impossible to determine. Some of them were well treated, others were hazed and brutally beaten. Within a year, they were made subject to court martial if their sincerity was questioned, and a board of inquiry was established to determine sincerity. Five hundred forty objectors were court martialed, only one of whom was acquitted. Seventeen were given death sentences and 142 life imprisonment, but all the death sentences were commuted.

The American Union against Militarism, an organization that developed in 1916 out of antipreparedness activism, took the lead in advocating humane treatment of the objectors. Immediately after passage of the Selective Service Act, Roger Baldwin, a wealthy social worker who had recently joined the union, organized the Bureau for Conscientious Objectors as a special subagency, and in October 1917 the bureau became an independent organization with the name of the National Civil Liberties Bureau. Baldwin, Norman Thomas, Oswald Villard, and others were indefatigable in ferreting out information about the treatment of objectors and in urging Secretary of War Baker to require more equitable procedures. Baker was sympathetic. He supported a policy of segregating the objectors and giving them noncombatant tasks to perform. Then in December 1917, he broadened the definition of a conscientious objector to include all who had "personal scruples against war," and gained Wilson's support for this definition. Hardship and brutality continued, but even Norman Thomas agreed that by the end of the war official policy toward objectors was reasonable.

In view of the attitudes toward aliens, conscientious objectors, and others with unconventional views during the war years, it is not surprising that the war saw an intensification of racial strife and discrimination at a time when all citizens were being asked to give their all toward winning the war. Black people had participated in every war fought by the United States, and thousands of them had served in the regular army and navy. In 1917, some ten thousand black troops of the regular army were serving in 4 all-black regiments which had fought with distinction in the Spanish-American War, in the Philippines, and on the Mexican border. An additional 10,000 were called as National Guardsmen. Under the Selective Service Act some 24,000,000 registered between June 1917 and September 1918; of this total, 2,290,527 (or about 9.63 percent) were blacks. In the same period, 367,710 blacks and 2,442,586 whites were drafted.

The official policy of the War Department was to frown on racial discrimination. Secretary Baker, a moderate on the racial question, did not propose to change the nation's social institutions, but he did appoint Emmett Scott, long-time secretary of Booker T. Washington, as a special assistant on black affairs. Scott spent a great deal of time traveling from camp to camp attempting to resolve issues leading to racial tension. Baker also listened to protests of those who objected to enrolling black soldiers only in noncombat units. Although the great majority continued to serve in stevedore and labor battalions, at least one combat division was created. Regardless of official policy, the treatment of blacks usually depended upon local commanders and local conditions, and official statements at times only obscured discrimination and inhumane treatment.

The NAACP frequently publicized examples of discrimination by draft boards, brutality by military police, segregation of black troops on railroads, and lack of proper facilities.

The fact that blacks were serving with the military forces overseas in no way made their lot easier in civilian life. The emotionalism of the superpatriot converged on the black as much as on the suspected alien. Lynchings continued to occur. In 1915, at least forty-two blacks were lynched; in 1916 the number was forty-eight; in 1917, thirty-eight; and in 1918, fifty-eight. Others were undoubtedly killed, abused, or tortured without being officially recorded. German propagandists attempted to undermine the support of various groups in the United States for the war effort, and not the least of their aims was to create disaffection among the blacks. One story was apparently circulated that if Germany should win the war "a certain section of the United States would be set aside where the Negroes could rule themselves." Little stimulus was required to persuade the more venturesome black to try to escape such an environment, and the opportunity came with the wartime demand for workers.

The demand for workers seemed unlimited, but the usual pool of un-skilled workers, the newly arrived immigrants, had almost completely dried up. Wages for unskilled black workers, which before the war had been about 19 cents an hour, almost doubled. At the same time in the South black tenants were barely able to scrape out an existence; farm laborers generally received from 50 to 75 cents a day—women and children less than that. Workers in southern saw mills and cotton mills received from $1.25 to $1.90 a day. Employers sent agents to the South to advertise the social and economic opportunities that a move north would bring. At first the U.S. Employment Service, concerned about the personnel needs of war industry, gave its blessing to such advertising. In the South, too, there was some feeling that the migration would channel off the independent, unruly blacks from areas where a surplus of labor existed.

Such optimism did not last. It soon became clear that reliable farm workers, mechanics, even professionals were joining the exodus. Black workers poured into New York, New Jersey, Pennsylvania, Ohio, Indiana, Illinois, and Michigan while more than five hundred thousand blacks migrated from southern states between 1910 and 1920. Many of these blacks it appears, were at first quite satisfied. On the other hand, costs were higher than in southern communities. Labor agents were frequently unscrupulous and lured workers from one northern industry to another. Housing and living conditions in labor camps were frequently depressing. The result was that the labor force was unstable and labor turnover high. The experience of an employment agent at the Carnegie Steel plant at Youngstown, Ohio, was apparently not unique "in having to keep hiring five men all the while to have every two jobs filled."

It may be that given these unstable conditions, racial friction was not excessive. However, the blacks who migrated soon found that, with few exceptions, they were destined only for unskilled work. Skilled mechanics, carpenters, bricklayers, and professional people had difficulty in finding a place for themselves. Even the unskilled black was not always welcome, in spite of the need. An editorial in the *Chicago Tribune* probably indicated more than it intended about northern attitudes: "We taunt the South with race prejudice when it burns a 'bad nigger' . . . but just see how we Northerners detest even 'good niggers.' . . . Our observation goes to show that the Negro is happiest when the white race asserts its superiority, provided that sympathy and understanding accompany the assertion."

Race riots or near riots occurred in numerous cities—in New York, Pennsylvania, Ohio, and New Jersey, but undoubtedly the most serious occurred in East St. Louis in July 1917 where police and soldiers made little effort to prevent beatings, shootings, and the destruction of more than three hundred homes of blacks. At least eight whites and thirty-eight blacks were killed.

The administration's position on the riots and the racial tension was ambivalent. Wilson expressed his distaste for the violence, denounced the deterioration in race relations, but refused to take any federal action. Baker, intellectually more sympathetic to black people and practically concerned about the effect of racial discord upon the war effort, appointed Walter Lippmann and Felix Frankfurter to work with him on the black problem. They in turn called on such friends of the black as George Foster Peabody, New York philanthropist, and Oswald Garrison Villard for advice and conferred with black intellectuals such as Robert R. Moton, principal of Tuskegee Institute, John Hope, president of Morehouse College, and Bishop George W. Clinton of the American Methodist Zion church.

Other efforts were made to assure black people that the government was interested in them. In May 1918, the Committee on Public Information, following a suggestion of Scott, organized a Committee of One Hundred consisting of black leaders in various occupations to work with the state councils of defense. In the spring of 1918, Secretary of Labor Wilson, concerned about the effect of racial tension on the efficiency of the labor force, concluded that he needed an adviser in the field of black affairs. He created a Division of Negro Economics in his department and appointed as its director Dr. George E. Haynes, professor of Economics and Sociology at Fisk University. Secretary Wilson and Haynes, in an attempt to promote cooperation among white and black leaders in states and communities, then appointed state supervisors of black economics to work with state representatives of the United States Employment Service and to conduct publicity campaigns to encourage good relations between the races. Governors in most of the states, state councils of defense, and private benevolent, religious, and educational associations supported the new division, and Secretary Wilson found that early in 1919 some two hundred twenty-five local committees existed, and he set out to organize a conference of welfare agencies to discuss problems of black life.

In the meantime, the NAACP launched a campaign to promote federal action in lynching cases. In 1918 John R. Shellady, the association's secretary asked members to write and telegraph the president urging him to make a statement condemning lynching. Wilson had privately denounced the bloodshed in East St. Louis in 1917 but had indicated that he was too busy to become formally involved in that tragedy. Attorney General Gregory had been equally unwilling to become officially involved, asserting that the federal government did not have jurisdiction because lynching was unrelated to the war effort. Gregory finally did recommend an educational campaign against lynching, and late in July 1918, President Wilson publicly denounced the deterioration in race relations. Secretary of War Baker, however, was increasingly concerned about the effect of black resentment upon the war effort, and, dissatisfied with the administration's image, he suggested to Wilson that he urge "the governor of some state in which a lynching had quite recently taken place" to use the state's power to "search out and prosecute the offenders." Wilson refused to take any positive action, but he did publicly rebuke those who participated in lynchings as betrayers of democracy.

Although President Wilson and the Attorney General did little to protect black people in their civil rights during the war years, the president was willing to take stronger action against those who were speaking or acting in a way that might threaten the nation's security. He considered that even the Espionage Act had not given the government sufficient power to deal with disloyal utterances. To be sure, part of the problem was that individuals and groups were taking the law into their own hands and were punishing members of the Socialist party, the IWW's, the International Bible Students' Association, the Nonpartisan League, almost any one who was antiestablishment, and state law rarely hindered, even sometimes abetted, the repression. Attorney General Gregory argued that the Espionage Act did not cover "disloyal utterances," which were, he believed, angering local communities and leading to violence and irritation at the lack of federal law. Thus he concluded that a federal law properly enforced would remove the cause of violence. Substantial support existed for stronger laws, and many congressmen agreed. As Henry Cabot Lodge noted, if laws are not adequate, lynch law will result.

Actually the federal government was already imposing greater restrictions over speech and press than ever before. The Navy Department had controlled the wireless stations since 1914 and the submarine cable since April 1917, and the army had assumed control of the telephone and telegraph lines on the same date. Then in May the Department of Justice began prosecuting cases under the Espionage Act and used that act with particular delight against the IWW. In October 1917, the hand of the government was strengthened by the passage of the Trading-with-the-Enemy Act. This act was long and complicated, much of it dealt with legitimate questions of trade, even protecting certain kinds of trading with the enemy, but it was primarily concerned with developing an increasingly effective blockage of the central powers. It also authorized the president to censor "communications by mail, cable, radio, or other means of transmission" between the United States and a foreign country during the war. It prohibited the circulation of matter declared unmailable in the Espionage Act and prohibited the printing in any foreign language of anything which related to the government of the United States or of any belligerent government unless a complete translation of the items were filed with the postmaster at the place of publication.

On October 12, 1917, less than a week after the passage of the Trading-with-the-Enemy Act, Wilson established a Board of Censorship consisting of the head of the Committee on Public Information and of representatives of the postmaster general, of the secretaries of war and navy, and of the War Trade Board. The Post Office department obtained a predominant influence on the board in part because the postal representative, Robert L. Maddox; a "cool and adroit" career person, was appointed head of the board, and because the funds for its activities, more than $2 billion, came from postal appropriations. Officially the policy of the postal authorities was to use great care in issuing licenses to foreign-language newspapers in order "to guard against German propaganda and the circulation of disloyal and seditious utterances" without interfering with "the free expression of opinion not directed against the national welfare." However, Postmaster General Albert Burleson interpreted his powers broadly and he excluded from the mails anything that he wished to exclude. Although he was particularly hard on the socialist press, his net was a wide one. For example, he said that "papers may not say that the Government is controlled by Wall Street or munitions manufacturers, or any other special interests . . . we will not tolerate campaigns against conscription, enlistments, sale of securities (Liberty Bonds) or revenue collections. We will not permit the publication of anything hampering the war's prosecutions or attacking improperly our allies."

Wilson was concerned about the extent of the censorship powers and attempted to be a moderating influence by cautioning Gregory and Burleson to use discretion. Burleson, however, threatened resignation if this authority to censor was undermined. Wilson had confidence in Burleson and needed him politically. Moreover, while liberal in his views on civil liberties in peace time, the president repeatedly indicated his lack of sympathy for "utterances" which might in any way obstruct the war effort.

In the meantime, Congress was taking action. Early in 1918 a bill prohibiting disloyal utterances passed the House with only one negative vote, that of Representative London, a socialist from New York, but with

134 representatives listed as not voting. In the Senate, 48 senators of whom 10 were Republicans voted for the bill; while 26 senators, of whom 3 were Democrats, opposed. As in the espionage bill, the nays included conservatives, such as Harding and Lodge, opposed to presidential power, and independents such as Norris arguing that individuals should have the right to criticize the president; that decisions should be made by courts rather than the postmaster general prior to an offense; and that the rights of freedom of speech and of the press were being abridged.

Technically the measure as approved on May 16, 1918, known as the Sedition Act, was an amendment to the Espionage Act, and completely replaced a section of that act. It contained not only prohibitions against conveying false reports and obstructing recruitment of the military forces, but added:

> Whoever, when the United States is at war, shall willfully utter, print, write, or publish any disloyal, profane, scurrilous, or abusive language about the form of government of the United States, or the Constitution of the United States, or the military or naval forces of the United States, or the flag of the United States, or the uniform of the Army and Navy of the United States . . . or advocate any curtailment of production in this country of any thing or things . . . necessary . . . to the prosecution of the war . . . with intent . . . to cripple or hinder the United States in the prosecution of the war . . . shall be punished by a fine of not more than $10,000 or imprisonment for not more than twenty years or both.

The Sedition Act, with the exception of an act of October 1918 authorizing the deportation of any anarchist alien, completed the security measures of the First World War. Supported by public opinion and a president not willing to draw fine lines of distinction, the Postal Department and the Department of Justice enforced the laws with a will. Between 1918 and 1921, the years in which the Espionage and Sedition Acts were enforced, the Justice Department prosecuted 2,168 cases, the great majority of them in 1918 and 1919. Of these, 1,055 brought convictions.

Food Will Win the War

While minority groups, dissident individuals, some public figures, and intellectuals were either criticizing or feeling the effects of governmental restrictions on speech and press, every person in the United States was undoubtedly becoming aware that the war had affected the availability and the cost of food. Average food prices had been steadily rising, it is true, since 1896, but between 1915 and 1917 they rose perhaps six times as rapidly as in previous years. This increase resulted from a simultaneous increase of European demand and a decrease in American supply. In

Europe, millions of workers moved from farms to the armies. Armies also needed horses and mules for transportation and for meat to feed their soldiers. Farms deprived of workers, horsepower, and manure for fertilizer could not meet the demand for their products. At the same time, the Central powers had separated Britain, France, and Belgium from the granaries of Russia, Bulgaria, and Rumania. Allied agents then turned to the United States for supplies to meet normal demand and to compensate for the products lost from submarine sinkings. Thus the food exports from the United States increased more than 250 percent between the immediate prewar years and 1918. At the same time farm production in the United States declined in 1916, and bad weather was jeopardizing the wheat crop for 1917.

With the entrance of the United States into the war, the problem became a strategic problem of supporting the Allied and the American military effort. Complications increased. Thousands of American farmers moved either into the services or into more highly paying industry. City youth from school and office ate much more in the services than formerly, and the army supply and food services, inexperienced and rapidly expanding, did not know how to economize. Thus home demand increased while Allied needs were multiplying. Not only were available supplies inadequate, but food speculators expected them to be even shorter, and played the market so that prices moved strangely.

One of the committees of the Council of National Defense, that on supplies headed by Julius Rosenwald, was charged with considering the problem of food. Somehow existing supplies had to be conserved; production had to be increased; and price and general economic stability had to be secured by controlling speculation and profiteering. The question was whether the people of the United States would approve the unprecedented controls that such a program would require.

Long before the American declaration of war, the Council of National Defense decided that some sort of "Committee on food supply and prices" was necessary. By this time, a young American mining engineer, Herbert C. Hoover, had made a worldwide reputation as director of war relief in Belgium, and the council invited him to discuss "the mobilization, distribution, and conservation of food supplies in Europe" at a joint meeting of the council and the Advisory Commission on February 15, 1917. Hoover's presentation was so effective that the commission immediately recommended to the council that he be asked to "contribute his services" to the war effort.

Hoover, forty-two years old in 1917, had been orphaned at the age of eight and had worked himself up to be a distinguished mining engineer. Although his main base of operations was California, he had a home in London and was there when war broke out in August 1914. He organized an American committee to get stranded Americans home, and his efficiency and reputation led to his being asked to organize Belgian relief.

Hoover arrived in the United States on May 3, 1917, and on the following day accepted an appointment as food administrator. Wilson trying to avoid anything that smacked of dictatorship had favored a commission rather than a director, but Hoover opposed this approach. He argued that divided responsibility in Europe had failed and that "his authority must cover every phase of food administration, from the soil to the stomach." At the same time, he opposed the government's replacing private agencies in distributing food, as had been the case, he pointed out, in Europe. He emphasized that volunteers would be used in important positions, that conservation practices would be carried out voluntarily, and he called for cooperation from other agencies both private and public along with the mobilization of "the spirit of self-denial and self-sacrifice."

Hoover's demand for centralization raised the question of his relationship to the Department of Agriculture. Hoover clearly did not want to be under any existing department, and Wilson feared the reaction of Secretary of Agriculture Houston to giving Hoover the kind of independence he wanted. Houston, even before the United States entered the war, had set the complicated machinery of the department at work to increase production. The county agents, the agricultural colleges, farmers associations, agricultural journals, were all used to inform the farmers of the crisis. In southern states special efforts were made to persuade both black and white farmers to support the war effort. As war approached, Houston called on the nation's farm leadership—state commissions of agriculture, editors of farm journals, presidents of land-grant colleges, the National Grange—for advice. Thus shortly after the United States entered the war Houston was ready to recommend an emergency agricultural policy to the House Committee on Agriculture.

The recommendations became the basis for two bills—one of which was designed to support the Department of Agriculture in its traditional responsibilities; the other was designed to give statutory support for the activities of a powerful food administration. The first bill appropriated more than $11 million for the eradication of animal and plant diseases, the conservation of farm products, the making of seeds available at reasonable prices, the surveying of available food supplies, the extending of information services, and the enlarging of services dealing with the farm labor problem. Although this bill promoted some controversy, the controversy was mild in comparison with that provoked by the "food control bill" designed to bring about presidential control of the "manufacture, procurement, storage, distribution, sale, marketing, pledging, financing, and consumption of necessaries." Representative Lever, head of the House Committee on Agriculture in introducing the bill, warned that the need was so urgent that "screams and squalls about conferring autocratic powers upon the president" would only temporarily delay "the day of wrath."

Although there were some "screams and squalls" in the House over creating a dictatorship, far greater opposition came in the Senate. Here even the chairman of the Committee on Agriculture, Senator Thomas P. Gore of Oklahoma, refused to support the bill, insisting that it was unconstitutionally putting "the control of all the nations food supply in the hands of one man." Other opposition came from western and southern senators who did not want regulation unless it applied to industry as well as agriculture; from a bipartisan bloc of fifty-three senators led by Republican Senator John W. Weeks of Massachusetts who added a bipartisan, congressional, supervisory committee on the conduct of the war to the basic act; and from Senator Reed of Missouri who, expressing the common knowledge that Hoover would be the food "dictator," complained that he was more British than American and had not voted in the United States for twenty years. Reed succeeded in substituting a requirement for a commission of three to administer the act rather than a single individual.

Both the food enactments then were fought over in conference. By this time, Hoover had convinced Wilson that divided authority would not work, and Wilson told a friend "if I can help it 'there ain't going to be no Food Control Board,'" and he wielded his influence in favor of one-person control. Even more opposed to the congressional supervisory committee, he argued that such a committee would inevitably assume administrative powers and he threatened to veto the bill if such a provision were included.

The act established as a principle that national security demanded an adequate supply and efficient distribution of food, fertilizer, fuel, and the tools and machinery necessary for the production of food and fuel. It, therefore, gave the president virtually complete control over production, conservation, and distribution of these "necessaries." The amendments for the three-member commission and the congressional supervisory committee were dropped, but one which prohibited, with only slight exception, the manufacture or importation of distilled spirits and limited the manufacture of wines and beers was retained. Perhaps it was "the most drastic and far-reaching piece of legislature ever enacted by the American Congress" as the *New York American* described it; others agreed that it was the "largest step toward state socialism ever taken by the national government." The House passed the final conference report overwhelmingly with 360 voting aye and no negative votes. The Senate likewise overwhelmingly endorsed the measure by a vote of 66 to 7.

Both the agricultural bills were approved on August 10—after the "Hundred Days' War," as the *New York World* put it. In the meantime, Houston and Hoover busied themselves in doing what they could without legislation. Houston mobilized the land-grant colleges and the Cooperative Extension Service with its federal specialists, county and home demonstration agents, and farm bureaus. Hundreds of new local organizations to aid the county agents were set up, many of them by the state councils of defense; home gardening was stimulated; techniques for canning, drying, salting, and storing of perishables were explained; the women were enlisted in a campaign against waste; special campaigns were initiated against pests and diseases; and complicated procedures to increase production of staple crops, meat, and dairy products were inaugurated.

Although the Food Administration technically did not exist until the passage of the Lever Act, Hoover had appointed state food administrators responsible to him and launched his voluntary conservation program in June, two months before the passage of the act. Characteristically, he analyzed the question of conservation carefully, and explained what "waste" meant in terms of time, efficiency, and product. He enlisted the press, advertising agencies, motion picture theaters, educational institutions, public eating places, retail stores, and libraries to publicize ways by which conservation could be effected. He estimated that milling companies, dealers, railroads, and streetcars contributed the equivalent of close to $20 million by advertising conservation practices. The Food Administration circulated pledge cards to housewives, the signers of which would receive window cards indicating that the resident had agreed to follow the direction of the administration. A well-publicized effort established "meatless Tuesdays," "wheatless Mondays and Wednesdays," and "sugarless" days, and, according to official calculations, saved more than 250 million pounds of wheat, 300 million pounds of meat, and 56 million pounds of sugar—or rations for 8 million soldiers for a month.

Hoover established a complicated organization, largely of volunteers. Typical of Hoover's system, it combined centralization with local responsibility. Special local committees on product or function brought personal responsibilities home to virtually every citizen. More than 750,000 fulltime and part-time volunteers worked with some 3,000 paid employees. A novel experiment of the administration was the establishment of two government corporations, the United States Grain Corporation and the Sugar Equalization Board. With the authority of the Lever Act, the Grain Corporation was armed with a fund of $150 million to purchase and sell food; it also had the power to give licenses for the sale of food or to deny licenses to uncooperative dealers. So it allotted grain to millers, arranged prices and charges with grain elevators, adjusted freight rates, calculated the most efficient utilization of transportation and storage facilities, made agreements with dealers on prices and profits, and established margins between costs and prices. Equally complicated but efficient procedures were developed by the Sugar Equalization Board.

Hoover decided against establishing a rigid system of rationing or price control. Although other nations had introduced rationing, Hoover concluded that the size and complexity of the United States would make any such system unworkable. Moreover he was opposed to the "bureaucratic expense" that would be involved. Rationing would require "a vast administrative organization," he warned; it would cost more than $10 million and every householder would be overwhelmed with tickets and coupons.

Price control was another matter. Hoover insisted that his agency did not "fix" prices. Though he might oppose fixing prices, he used his strategic position to influence them and he steered a fine course between a price that would stimulate production and one that would not crucify the consumer. The facts were that Allied governments representing some 120 million people channeled their purchasing through the Food Administration; in addition, purchases for the American military services, constituting additional millions of people, were channeled through the Food Administration. This near "monopoly of buying" came close to dominating the market and determining the price. In order to protect both consumer and producer, Hoover recognized that price regulation was necessary in a manner "never contemplated in economic history or theory, and" as he put it, "it is time that economic thinkers denuded [sic] themselves of their procrustean formulas of supply and demand."

Given the extreme powers granted to the new agency it would have been surprising had not resentment developed. McAdoo on several occasions blew up when Hoover publicly criticized the Railroad Administration. Many farmers did not trust either Houston or Hoover. Farmers generally had been delighted with Houston's predecessor "Tama Jim" Wilson, who had been secretary for the previous sixteen years. Houston, on the other hand, was primarily an economist, and his short presidency of Texas Agricultural and Mechanical College did not make him "rural minded." Hoover was even more suspect. The Wallaces, Henry C. and young Henry A., editors of *Wallace's Farmer,* a widely approved farm journal, had never heard of him in the early years of the war and could not understand how his services as a mining engineer qualified him for food administration.

Although criticism of Hoover was muted during the early months of the war, unrest built up in the Midwest and almost blew the lid off in 1918. Some midwestern farmers may never have forgiven Hoover for the way in which his agency manipulated the price of hogs and wheat. Young Henry Wallace, one of the administration's consultants, for example, while admitting that the Food Administration had done its job efficiently, charged Hoover with juggling figures and treating a promise as a "scrap of paper." Wheat farmers were particularly incensed because they did not think that Hoover had put a high enough floor under wheat prices. They were making a profit, but they saw the price of cotton skyrocketing—from 6 cents a pound in 1914 to 36 in April 1918, and cotton had been specifically excluded from controls by a southern-dominated Congress and a sympathetic president. To the wheat farmer, such a variation of treatment was pure and simple sectional discrimination. And the midwestern Republican supported by the midwestern farmer called for the defeat of those Democrats responsible for food administration control in the election of 1918.

Politics aside and from the point of view of wartime mobilization the

Food Administration must be rated a success. Food production was stimulated, waste was curtailed, prices were stabilized. In the last analysis Hoover's administration cost the taxpayer nothing. Congressional and presidential appropriations for the Food Administration amounted to less than $8 million; the $155 million provided as capital for the Grain Corporation and the Sugar Equalization Fund was not touched, and the profits of those corporations came to more than $60 million. As Hoover put it, "the [Food] Administration cost the government over $50,000,000 less than nothing." Yet Hoover is something of an enigma as to motives and goals; he seemed more interested in stimulating production than in protecting the consumer; and his policies resulted in huge profits by the food industries.

Fuel

Although Hoover may have thought that food might win the war, his colleague, H. A. Garfield, the fuel administrator, made a good case for his product. "Without fuel," he said, "neither food nor clothing nor shelter can be provided in adequate quantities. Without fuel, furnaces would be idle and transportation by sea and land virtually cease." In some respects the food and fuel problems were similar. The war made unprecedented demands for both fuel and food, and, as in the case of food, war conditions led to a decline in coal production in many countries. In France and Russia, German troops overran coal-producing areas early in the war. In these and other countries the mine workers marched off to the armies. Moreover, eccentricities of transportation in all countries interfered with the coal supply: lack of coal cars, difficulties in determining priorities, submarine sinkings, and complexities of ocean transport all led to shortages, confusion, and high rates.

All countries took steps to meet the coal crises. Wherever possible inland waterways replaced railways; consumers were urged to store coal in the summer; wages and working conditions were improved to keep miners on the job; maximum prices were established; and efforts were made to use prewar voluntary associations of coal operators to provide coordination. In Germany and France, the coal cartel had for years been a characteristic feature of the economy. In Britain, in a period of high prosperity just before the war, Lord Rhondda had organized a powerful combination of coal properties, domestic selling agencies, and export machinery. In the United States, numerous state and local associations had developed between 1914 and 1917, and in 1917 at least three national combinations materialized, the National Coal Operators' Association, the National Jobbers' Association, and the National Retail Coal Dealers' Association.

In the United States, before the war, the coal industry and in particular bituminous coal, had been in "a deplorable condition." Labor relationships were unstable, cutthroat competition prevailed, mining methods were

wasteful. Prices at the mines had hovered not much above $1.00 per ton—
a condition which pleased the consumer, but kept profits negligible.
Then in 1916, prices started to rise so sensationally that Congress instructed the Federal Trades Commission to investigate both the anthracite
and bituminous coal industries. In making its investigation the commission
received "intelligent and willing cooperation" from the anthracite industry,
largely concentrated in Pennsylvania, and conditions in anthracite might
have stabilized had it not been for the "evil conditions" in the bituminous
industry and in transportation. The FTC could supervise the highly
concentrated anthracite industry, but such supervision did little good
"so long as bituminous runs wild," and the commission threw up its
hands at regulating that complex and diffuse industry. Actually the mines
could have produced the coal, but speculators and inefficient transportation produced chaos. Prices continued to skyrocket from the nearly-a-
dollar figure to three, four, sometimes five dollars a ton. The FTC found
that all fears were justified—"the coal industry is paralyzing the industries
of the country," and "the coal industry itself is paralyzed by the failure
of transportation." The only way out, the commission concluded, was
to entrust the production and distribution of coal and coke to a government agency and to operate all transportation agencies as a unit under
the direction of the president.

Conditions had become even more chaotic by the time the commission's
report was issued on June 20, 1917. Government officials urged the coal
operators to do something voluntarily, warning that if they did not,
drastic action from outside would be necessary. Talk of price-fixing and
state socialism was commonplace. One cooperative effort on the part of
some three hundred fifty operators to bring the price down to $3.00 a ton
had some effect, but did not satisfy the critics. In Illinois, Samuel Insull,
president of the Commonwealth Edison Utility Company and also head
of the state Council of National Defense, threatened to seize the mines
and fix prices. Concerned that the issue might get out of hand, the
president stepped in forcefully and in August fixed the price of coal by
executive order varying from $1.65 in Alabama to $3.50 in Washington.

In the meantime Congress had moved in on the problem, and was
increasingly focusing its attention on the Lever Act, which had from the
beginning included fuel with food as one of the necessaries. The debates
in the House and Senate largely concentrated on the provisions which
related to the question of food, but there were those, particularly from
the mining areas, who protested vigorously against the features of the
bill which related to coal. Representative Edward E. Robbins of Pennsylvania, who himself had some interests in coal mining, complained that
the law would take the coal industry of the United States "away from its
rightful owners and put [it] . . . under the food dictator." He insisted
that coal pricing was more complicated than the critics made it out to
be, that coal prices had risen about 100 percent rather than 200 or 300

percent as was frequently stated, and that the coal industry had made no profit from 1900 to 1915. He blamed the skyrocketing prices not on the coal industry but on the failure of the railroads to distribute their freight cars properly.

Although the Lever Act did not nationalize coal, it went about as far as the critics of the coal companies wished in establishing government regulation. It gave the president war powers to fix the price of coal and coke, to regulate production, distribution, and storage either for foreign or domestic commerce, and, in case of an uncooperative operator or dealer, to "requisition" and "operate" the plant or business. The Federal Trades Commission was to determine reasonable prices.

The Lever Act was approved on August 10, 1917. On August 23, Wilson announced the establishment of the United States Fuel Administration and the appointment of H. A. Garfield, son of the late President Garfield and himself president-on-leave from Williams College, as director. Garfield, a one-time teacher of Latin and Roman history, a practicing lawyer and former professor of law and politics, was already serving with Hoover on the Food Administration, but on September 1, he assumed the position of fuel administrator. Having been associated with Hoover, it is not surprising that he was influenced by Hoover's methods. Volunteers and local responsibility were emphasized. Indeed, one of the first actions was to launch a campaign in consultation with state councils of defense to find men of ability who would be willing to serve without compensation as fuel administrators for each state in cooperation with numerous volunteer county or local committees.

The immediate concern of the Fuel Administration was to publicize methods of conserving coal. Industries found that they could make phenomenal savings by more efficient operation. Within a few months, for example, the brewers had agreed to new work days that would save over 700,000 tons of coal, and the boxboard manufacturers were running their plants only 5 days a week, thus saving some 1,000,000 tons of coal during the year and some 30,000 railroad cars. Electric signs and outdoor lighting were restricted to two nights a week; Pullman and passenger cars were kept at temperatures of 68°. Studies were made to discover how excess water power could be used, power systems better integrated, and wood substituted for coal and oil. With these efforts, according to the Bureau of Conservation, more than 32,000,000 tons of coal were saved between October 1917 and February 1919.

Although these savings were substantial, even greater efforts were needed to increase production. Promptly upon taking office, Garfield appealed to labor and management leaders to lay aside differences and get on with producing coal. At the time that the Fuel Administration was established, a conference of operators and labor leaders was preparing an agreement that included a substantial increase in wages. Good labor relations were obviously essential for continuous mining of coal, and by

1918 Garfield saw a need for a special bureau devoted to labor relations. This agency, headed by John P. White, formerly president of the United Mine Workers, and Rembrandt Peale, a Pennsylvania coal operator, worked closely with the officers of the United Mine Workers—Frank J. Hayes, president, John L. Lewis, vice president, and William Green, secretary and treasurer—and negotiated principles that provided a workable framework during the war years. Disputes developed, but operators agreed not to discharge workers for union membership and strikes were allowed after the Fuel Administration had reviewed the issues.

Although the most important factor in production was stability in labor-management relations, other factors contributed importantly. One of the most sensitive questions was to settle how local draft boards would treat miners. Although the provost marshal feared setting precedents, he was persuaded to defer "essential" mineworkers and to arrange special furloughs for drafted mineworkers not sent overseas. In addition, the Fuel Administration worked closely with the railroads and various government agencies in establishing priorities for shipment and returning railroad cars. Perhaps of most importance, 28 production districts were established in which committees of management and labor, consisting of some thirty thousand persons, were set up to maintain production. These devices worked—between June and November 1918, over 30 million more tons of coal were mined than during a comparable period of the previous year.

Perhaps the most controversial responsibility of the Fuel Administration was to fix reasonable prices on coal. Garfield was quite sensitive to the attitude that prices were sacred and governed only by supply, demand, and competition. At the same time, he believed that since government had permitted the development of gigantic concentrations, it had the responsibility of regulating them. When he took over the administration, he had to answer innumerable complaints that the price set by Wilson in August was too low, but he kept the operators producing by promising them that their complaints would be studied, and reimbursement provided if justified. Actually revisions in prices were few, and Garfield estimated that on the 806 million tons of bituminous coal produced between the imposition of price control in August 1917 and the lifting of controls in February 1919, there was an average saving of 38.8 cents a ton to the consumer or a total of $312,728,000.

The Fuel Administration made its most drastic decision in January 1918 when it appeared that the coal crisis might explode. The winter was unusually severe. War orders suddenly became overwhelming; industrialists, particulary the steel industry, naturally demanded the prompt delivery of their raw materials including coal; docks and terminals were jammed; transportation was at a standstill—480 ships (containing food, fuel, and munitions) were lying in the harbors waiting to have their bunkers filled with coal. The entire war effort was breaking down. After conferring with rail leaders and with Baker, Daniels, and the president, Garfield took action. Without prior warning, on January 16, 1918, he ordered all factories east of the Mississippi River (where 85 percent of the country's steam plants were) to cease operations for five days beginning on January 18. Furthermore he requested that offices, factories, and most stores should drastically limit fuel consumption every Monday for ten weeks— the much advertised "fuelless Mondays."

This order met with frantic criticism. But it served its purpose: "bunker coal went forward; the ships in harbor were released," and finally shipments of steel products essential for war manufacture came back to normal levels.

The Fuel Administration had to cope not only with the problems of coal but with those of petroleum products, the demand for which had been increasing in a geometrical ratio since the beginning of the century. Automobiles were now consuming millions of gallons of gasoline. The airplane industry was getting off the ground; and the world's navies were increasingly using oil. By the time the United States entered the war, all United States submarines and destroyers used oil, and the new giant dreadnaughts were being built for oil. American oil production, which in 1900 was approximately 63.6 million gallons had risen to 335.3 million by 1917.

In spite of the increasing demand, the prices of petroleum products had not increased sensationally, largely because of the exploitation of new fields in Oklahoma. However war fever hit the industry shortly after the United States entered the war, and prices went up about 50 percent in 1917. By 1918, in "dollars and cents" oil products were equal in value to coal products in the United States.

Even more than in the case of coal, efforts to regulate the oil industry were inspired by the ideals of the "New Competition." During the early months of 1917 a committee of leading oil industrialists, a kind of "Chamber-of-Commerce Committee," was appointed to cooperate with Bernard Baruch as head of the Raw Materials Committee of the Council of National Defense. Although the Lever Act included oil as one of the "necessaries" to be controlled, it did not authorize price fixing. By 1918, however, Garfield became alarmed at the confusion in the industry, and established a special oil division of his administration with Mark J. Requa, a mining engineer and another Hoover volunteer, as director.

Requa was convinced that the oil industry, being well-organized and rather highly centralized, would be able to govern itself with only moderate direction. Pleas, however, did not keep the price down, and in the early spring of 1918, Requa warned the industry that prices simply had to be held in check. Numerous conferences took place within the industry culminating in a meeting on August 6, 1918, of the National Petroleum War Service Committee, a committee of the Council of National Defense. The committee at this meeting drafted the plan which arranged for local subcommittees to work with the national committee in keeping "an uninterrupted flow of crude oil in existing channels" and in stabilizing prices. Taken in conjunction with the government's ability to fix prices on oil sold to foreign governments and to the services, prices were effectively controlled.

In spite of the voluntary characteristics of the oil program, at least fifteen bureaus were set up within the oil division to "observe" almost every phase of the petroleum industry. The Bureau of Conservation, for example, sent inspectors to advise manufacturers on how to promote economical practices and eliminate waste; domestic users were told how to conserve natural gas; cities and towns were requested not to burn street lights twenty-four hours a day. In spite of these efforts, domestic consumption increased, and warnings came from abroad that a continuous supply of oil was necessary else the war would be lost. Thus on August 27, 1918, the oil division issued a public appeal for people living east of the Mississippi to cease using automobiles, motor boats, and motorcycles on Sunday until further notice.

Although such limitations upon the use of petroleum products seemed drastic, Requa was determined that the policy of his division would be based upon "mutual confidence and cooperation." Perhaps even more than for coal, "voluntary control" was the watchword. Even though the voluntary system had some weaknesses, the net results were favorable. The National Petroleum War Service Committee, staffed by operators under the supervision of the oil division, saw to it that the nation's oil was pooled and then distributed "regardless of ownership"; on the Pacific coast at least, a subcommittee of the War Service Committee took complete control of pipe lines and tankers; and in spite of increasing demands, in natural growth and inspired by the war, prices were kept down.

Transportation

A recurring theme in mobilizing the economy was the weakness of the internal transportation system. Coal operators usually claimed that they could produce the coal; oil refiners claimed that they could refine the oil; steel manufacturers claimed that they could manufacture the steel. The weakness in the system, they all insisted at one time or another, was not in production but in distribution. Prior to the railroads, inland transportation depended upon wagons and the waterways. During the First World War, the inland waterways were comparatively unimportant, and the utility of the twentieth-century wagon, the truck, was only beginning to be recognized. The possible usefulness of the inland waterways had been recognized in the National Defense Act of 1916, but not until the railroads began to break down after the United States entered the war was attention turned to the rivers and canals. In June 1917, the Council of National Defense appointed a Committee of Inland Water Transportation with Major General W. M. Black, chief of the army engineers, as its head, to study the principal inland waterways—including the Mississippi,

Ohio, Tennessee, and Warrior rivers, the Pennsylvania and New York canals, and the Intracoastal Waterway. The committee concluded that with little expenditure, these waterways could be used to relieve rail congestion, and almost $4 million was allotted to build steel barges and steel towboats to transport coal and iron ore on the Mississippi River.

From then until April 1918, there was considerable talk, but little action. Some effort was made to speed up a conversion of the Erie Canal for the use of barges. This canal might have provided an inexpensive route for the transportation of produce from the Great Lakes to the New York port, but it was not completed until 1918. The lack of progress and the desperate need for reliable transportation led to drastic action. On April 11, 1918, the president took over four of the principal Atlantic coastwise shipping lines, authorized McAdoo, who by then had been made director general of railroads, to assume the responsibility for seeing that traffic moved expeditiously either by water or land, and went so far as to commandeer all privately owned floating equipment on the Barge Canal and the Mississippi and Warrior rivers.

Whereas inland waterways kept a touch of the eighteenth century in a twentieth-century war, the truck represented modernization. By the time the United States entered the war, European experience and the experience of American troops in Mexico had demonstrated how useful the motor truck could be. Howard E. Coffin, recently with the Hudson Motor Company and one of the real fathers of industrial preparedness in the United States, made sure that the usefulness of trucks was recognized by both the Council of National Defense and the War Industries Board. In 1916, based upon the Mexican experience, the Quartermaster Corps began to work with the Society of Automotive Engineers and the National Automobile Chamber of Commerce to design a heavy standard truck for a modern army. Designers sacrificed their fees, bonuses, and patents to develop a workable model; the automotive section of the War Industries Board "mobilized all available resources for the Army." The model was in full production by January 1918; and by July some five thousand trucks had been completed.

Prophets were not always in positions where they could make the decisions, and the tough, practical question was whether the automobile industry was sufficiently vital to the war effort to be allocated steel to build enough trucks and automobiles to meet the demand. By July 1918, the issue was clearly drawn and a confrontation between the War Industries Board and the automobile industry occurred.

The board approved truck production, but required the manufacturers to pledge that their production of passenger automobiles and parts would not exceed 25 percent of the production for 1917. Although an immediate reaction of some of the leading automobile manufacturers to this decree was that it was "the beginning of the end," the automobile industry did very well during the war years. In 1917 the industry produced more than

1,700,000 passenger cars and 128,000 trucks; in 1918, 926,000 passenger cars and 227,000 trucks; and approximately 85,000 trucks were apparently delivered to the army by October 1918. At the same time the industry had converted to such an extent that one contemporary authority could write that it "contributed more to the winning of the war than any other peace industry of the country except steel manufacture." Plant after plant produced liberty engines, shells, grenades, gun mounts, lighting plants, recoil mechanisms, spare parts, and numerous other items.

Yet spokesmen for the automotive industry still questioned whether sufficient attention was being devoted to using trucks to break the transportation bottleneck. In March 1918 they offered to break this bottleneck, and urged the Council of National Defense and the local councils to fight local restraints upon "freighting by highway." Although the council tried to impress upon state authorities the need for better road development and maintenance, the industry was not satisfied. In the confrontation between the War Industries Board and the automobile industry in July 1918, Ray Austin Graham, a Detroit truck manufacturer, bluntly told Bernard Baruch, "I don't think you have done half of what you might have done for the highways. Ten thousand trucks, for instance, applied . . . where the needs are very great—could . . . carry one million tons a day."

A significant difference between truck traffic and rail traffic is in the responsibility of building and maintaining the traffic arteries. In the case of railroads, the industry itself puts down the rails. In the case of the trucking industry, government builds the roads. Until 1916, local government had assumed that responsibility, but by the Federal Highway Act of 1916, the federal government assumed a share of the task by furnishing $75 million over a first-year period to be matched by the states. Construction was well under way when the United States entered the war. Then it slowed down as labor and materials were diverted elsewhere. Such construction materials as oils, asphalts, and tars were considered vital to the war effort, and it took some persuasion by Secretary of Agriculture Houston to convince the Fuel Administration that highways were also vital and needed these materials if trucks were to be able to run on them. Houston succeeded in getting a federal agency appointed, the United States Highway Council, to pass on applications for materials during the war, and the council was overwhelmed with applications as month after month traffic increased and wore the roads down. By the end of the war some two thousand "motorized freight companies" were serving shippers.

Yet in comparison with the freight needs of the war effort, the contribution of the trucking industry was minuscule. The entire war effort was clearly dependent upon the effectiveness of the railroads, and when the United States entered the war, the railroads were simply not in a position to meet the country's needs.

By the end of the first decade of the twentieth century, the railroad industry was caught in a maze of conflicting interests. The rates charged effected almost everyone. Savage rate wars in the late nineteenth century had led to the demand for controls by the industries themselves. Although private negotiations between shippers and railroads achieved some stability, continuing conflicts between shippers and roads led to government regulation. States established railroad commissions and Congress passed the Interstate Commerce Act. The Interstate Commerce Commission (ICC) promptly became the focus for various pressure groups seeking support for their positions. The carriers generally favored stability at higher rates and tried to divide the shippers who normally favored lower rates.

Throughout this period, the carriers, claiming that revenues per mile of tonnage carried was declining, were attempting to persuade the ICC and the various state commissions to authorize an increase in rates. The carriers, increasingly irritated at the state commissions as local regulations multiplied, argued that the interstate nature of their business called for federal control only. The ICC was, however, little more responsive than the state commissions. It did authorize a 5 percent increase in 1914, more to stabilize the investors' market than to satisfy the carriers. Even before the outbreak of the war in Europe, the railroads were at the center of a conflict between public and private interests and were financially so shaky that they insisted that they could not provide efficient service without charging higher rates and that bankruptcies, congestion, and shortage of cars were inevitable if revenues did not increase. The operators considered the Adamson Act of 1916, requiring an eight-hour day for railroad workers and thus higher labor costs, the last straw. They accepted regulation in the public service, but argued that regulation should recognize the need for managerial initiative, permit rate increases in order to provide adequate service, and allow combinations in order to improve efficiency.

This argument split the shippers. In urban areas where rail terminals were important, the railroads usually found support in local boards of trade and merchants associations. State regulatory commissions and most shipper organizations outside the large urban areas, however, did not have confidence in railroad management, pointed to the amount of water in railroad stock, and insisted that improved service could take place without increasing rates.

On the eve of war, the Wilson Administration reacted cautiously to the controversy and concluded that the uncertainty as to whether the railroads could cope with the nation's transportation needs in a wartime crisis required a congressional investigation. A joint committee of Congress listened to almost 2,500 pages of testimony in 1916 and 1917 that showed only two things clearly: the complexity of the problem and the lack of agreement as to what should be done about it. Even the railroad representatives, however, were aware that existing transportation facilities were inadequate for a wartime crisis and prophesied that if they did not have greater financial resources, the federal government would have to assume the responsibility for railroad operations.

These hearings were taking place against a backdrop of increasing crisis. By early 1917, although paradoxically war demands had increased profits substantially, traffic on the roads was becoming chaotic. Higher paying war jobs and Selective Service were robbing the railroads of experienced workers, and war orders both from the Allies and from American industry led to transportation demands that simply overwhelmed the system. Shortages of freight cars developed in 1916; no synchronization existed between transatlantic shipping and the railroads; side tracks and even main tracks near eastern ports were clogged with freight cars waiting to be unloaded; harried army and navy supply officers in their concern to get needed equipment slapped priority orders on practically everything, and distinctions between items needed immediately and those of less urgency were soon lost.

At various times during 1916, congressmen involved in the hearings had urged the railroad operators to appoint a committee which would have the courage to get tough with inefficient or uncooperative railroads. Early in 1917, the ICC attempted to provide leadership, but the most effective move resulted from the intervention of the Council of National Defense. On April 7, 1917, the council instructed Daniel Willard to put the freight crisis before the rail executives. Willard, president of the Baltimore and Ohio railroad and chairman of the Committee on Transportation of the Advisory Commission of the Council of National Defense, called some forty-five railroad presidents to Washington and succeeded in persuading them to set up the Railroad's War Board which was charged with developing a continental railway system.

The Railroad's War Board was the final attempt to produce "national transportation efficiency" by private enterprise, and the railroad executives considered the attempt successful. The board did promote more efficient loading, cleared out port facilities, made possible better coal deliveries, and sped up the transportation of troops and construction materials. Indeed, 1917 was a record year for freight and passenger traffic.

Difficulties, however, dogged the private board. Railroads had let their equipment deteriorate; congestion continued; and competing interests refused to stop competing. Some government agencies worked effectively with the board; but the services indiscriminately demanded priorities for their shipments. Differences persisted among the various groups defending their own interests: the railroad workers, the shippers, the state and national commissions, and the railroad executives who insisted that higher rates were necessary.

With the board only partly successful in keeping the railroads running, and a grim winter ahead, pressures mounted for the president to take

over the rail lines. In a brilliant tour de force before the ICC, Clifford
Thorne, counsel for the Shippers National Council, argued that the only
solution to the problem was federal operation of the roads. Henry A.
Garfield, the fuel administrator, Josephus Daniels, secretary of the navy,
William McAdoo, secretary of the treasury, among others within the
administration urged federal control. The Railroad Brotherhood, hoping
for more sympathetic treatment of their wage demands, looked to the
federal government. Perhaps of most importance, the railroad operators
seemed to have no answer to the question of how to finance the rail
operation.

Congress had foreseen the possible need for government operation of
the railroads in wartime and had provided for it in the Army Appropriation Act of 1916. Yet it was still an unprecedented move when, on
December 26, 1917, President Wilson announced that the federal government would "assume control" of all systems of transportation along the
coasts and within the continental limits of the United States. He named
William G. McAdoo as director general, assured the private companies of
fair compensation, and guaranteed the rights of stockholders, bondholders,
and creditors.

Although widespread support greeted Wilson's decision to take over the
railroads, McAdoo and his administration now faced many of the same
conflicts of interests that the private interests had been facing for twenty-
five years. In broad terms, shippers were interested in low rates and hoped
for a continuation of the support that the state and federal regulatory
agencies had provided in the way of rate control; the former operators
still favored high rates and efficiency procedures in order to assure profits
and dividends; labor was interested in higher wages and improved working
conditions; the prewar regulatory agencies wished to retain control over
rates and wished to be consulted by the Railroad Administration; and the
Railroad Administration was interested primarily in seeing that war
material reached its destination as expeditiously as possible.

Although public response seemed to be overwhelmingly favorable to
the taking over of the railroads, complex problems remained. McAdoo's
initial moves went far toward unifying the railroads, but they disturbed
those who were concerned about protecting the consumer and the
shipper. McAdoo in his customary vigorous fashion called for cooperation
and set up an organization designed to keep the freight cars moving. At the
same time. although he continued to seek advice from friends on the ICC
who favored government operations, his inner circle increasingly became
railroad operators—men such as Walker D. Hines, chairman of the board
of the Santa Fe, and A. H. Smith, president of the New York Central.
Moreover, neither legislation nor Wilson's proclamation had spelled out
such details as how much compensation the roads would receive while
under government control, how rates would be determined, and how long
federal operation would continue. These questions were both ideological

and political. Local interests and economic interests were involved and cried loudly for congressional action. After long hearings, the House and Senate Committees on Interstate Commerce introduced a measure to resolve many of these issues; debate began early in February 1918; and the bill was finally approved on March 21.

This statute provided that any carrier under federal control should receive annually as just compensation an amount not to exceed the average, annual operating income for the three years ending June 30, 1917. Additional income would accrue to the federal government; war taxes would be paid out of the carrier's own funds; shortline railroads competing with railroads taken over by the government were also to be taken over; a sum of $500 million was appropriated to pay costs of federal control and to provide necessary terminals and equipment or funds to the carriers for expenses ordered and to support water transportation. The president could initiate rate changes which could not be suspended by the ICC, but which the commission could investigate if requested and present its findings to the president for his final action. The president might at any time return any or all railroads to private operation, but he must do so within twenty-one months following the ratification of the peace treaty.

This measure which accepted the government's responsibility for running the railroads in wartime was, like the authorization for the Shipping Board, a revolutionary step and stimulated a lively debate. On one extreme were those like Senator James Watson of Indiana who bemoaned the taking over of the railroads as a drift toward socialism. On another extreme was Senator Cummins of Iowa who favored Wilson's action but who denounced the provision for compensating the railroads as being "much too generous." As he saw it, the Railroad Administration would do what the railroads should have done in improving their properties—give the railroads millions of dollars in compensation for using the roads and compel the public to pay the bill by charging higher rates. Cummins, like the critics of the "New Competition," saw what amounted to collusion between the government and the railroads.

The clearest statement of the administration's position came from Senator Joe Robinson of Arkansas. Robinson, in effect, refuted both the position that the railroads had met their responsibilities effectively prior to the federal takeover and Cummins' position that too great a compensation was being offered to them. He pointed out that the Fifth Amendment guaranteed that private property would not "be taken for public use without just compensation." Only the courts, he added, could determine just compensation. Yet litigation would be time-consuming and expensive, and, as he put it, "it would be absurd to deny to [the railroads] approximately the amount to which they would be entitled under the law."

Perhaps the bitterest debate developed over the provision that would give the president the right to adjust rates. This roused the fears of those who for years had fought for the right of the ICC and the state commissions to regulate rates. The shippers and those who thought like them in Congress warned that increasing labor costs and the return guaranteed to the roads would lead to pressure for increasing the rates. McAdoo would turn to his new advisers—all railroad men—and rates would be raised. In short, senators such as Cummins were suspicious of what they considered to be an alliance between government and corporate capitalism which, they feared, was taking advantage of the war crisis. To the argument that the president must have authority to prosecute the war, Cummins responded, "The justification is worse than none," and heralds "the end of democracy rather than the beginning of freedom."

The fears of the shippers proved justified. McAdoo, convinced that effective operation depended upon labor harmony, ordered a substantial wage increase to take effect on May 25, 1918. Almost immediately a general rate increase of approximately 25 percent followed. Shippers and state commissioners were aroused by this increase at the same time that they were becoming irritated at the way McAdoo was introducing efficiency procedures that upset established customs. They suspected a conspiracy between the administration and railway management, arguing that a new rate structure was being established which would continue to obtain after the war. Although McAdoo resented such criticism, he promptly created regional and district traffic committees consisting of both operators and shippers to hear complaints about rates, and he and his successor, Walker D. Hines, saw to it that complaints were properly heard.

McAdoo even more vigorously attacked the problem of moving traffic, his principal objective. He attempted to eliminate roundabout and duplicating routes; he centralized purchases, synchronizing them with available cars and the whole system with ships in the harbors; he continued improved loading procedures begun under the Railroads War Board and ruthlessly cut passenger service by eliminating duplicate routes, rearranging transcontinental traffic, and restricting Pullman facilities. In short, before the end of the war, the federal government had assumed unprecedented power to see to it that men and materiel reached their destination.

Bridges of Ships

Unprecedented power to control inland transportation was not enough, however, to see that men and materiel reached the fighting front. They were still separated by three thousand miles of ocean concealing a ruthless enemy in a new kind of ambush. From 1914 to April 1917, the government of the United States attempted to apply its historic principle of freedom of the seas to a twentieth-century war. Britain, the world's greatest sea power, made traditional use of the only weapon in which it had superiority, the surface fleet. It aimed at maintaining control of the seas and strangling its principal enemy, Germany, by blockade. Germany, having discovered the effectiveness of the submarine, planned to starve Britain by destroying the merchant shipping attempting to reach her harbors or the harbors of her allies. Thus not only belligerents but neutrals whose existence depended on trade were involved in the war. From the outbreak of war until April 1917, when the United States entered the war, shipping losses were frightening. Britain and France had lost respectively 3,187,187 and 405,518 tons of merchant shipping. During the same period the United States lost 56,203 tons, Denmark, 114,175 tons, Sweden, 107,534 tons, and Norway, 610,228. The fact that the merchant sailors of the neutral countries continued to go to sea in their fragile freighters against the increasing threat of drowning reflects not only courage but the national stake in world trade.

Although the Allies had more precedents than did Germany to govern their performance in applying the blockade, precedents were of little importance in winning the war. In attaining this goal, precedents might be either observed, modified, or avoided. In order to throttle the German war machine, the Allies observed trade going directly not only to Germany but also to neighboring neutrals. They noted, for example, that in 1913 American merchants had exported products worth $162.1 million to Norway, Sweden, Denmark, and Holland; in 1914 that figure was $187.6 million and in 1915, $330.1 million. In the same period, American exports to the central powers had decreased from $351.1 million to $11.8 million. The conclusion to be drawn from the statistics was clear.

With these figures in mind, the Allies developed a policy of what amounted to rationing the neutrals. The neutrals were to be permitted to receive products essential for their own needs and to trade with the Allies, but they were not to trade with the central powers. The Allies negotiated hundreds of agreements with merchant organizations of the neutral nations to try to put this policy into effect. Such agreements were not easy to enforce, however, because international law did not recognize the right of a belligerent to control trade among neutrals, and because the neutrals that bordered on Germany were dependent upon Germany for iron and steel, coal, cement, drugs, and dyes. Germany took advantage of this situation by negotiating trade agreements with the border neutrals. The agreement with the Netherlands, for example, called for the exchange of such products for Dutch meat and dairy products.

Britain used other methods to control neutral trade. One of these took advantage of the fact that Britain controlled the main sources of coal, "bunker coal," used by the world's merchant shipping. Threatening to deny the use of bunker coal to neutral vessels which refused to conform to Allied trade patterns proved persuasive with those ship owners who wanted to move. For those who, fearful of submarines, preferred to hold their ships in port, the British government first separately and then through a chartering committee, formed in 1916 and representing Britain, France, and Italy, negotiated agreements with the neutral governments for the use of its merchant ships. Where possible these agreements were voluntary, but if the neutral governments demurred, Britain simply commandeered the ships and paid their owners "ample rates of hire." If, in spite of these arrangements, Britain learned through its far-flung intelligence network that a company was carrying out any sort of financial dealing with the central powers, that company was put on a blacklist which would prohibit any Allied company from having any commercial dealings with the blacklisted company.

When the United States entered the war, the American government promptly adopted the trade policy of its new associates. The traditional principles of neutral rights which had been a keystone of American foreign policy for more than a century were conveniently overlooked, and the American government clamped down sweeping trade controls. Congress did its part by passing the Espionage and the Trading-with-the-Enemy acts of June and October 1917. The Espionage Act authorized the president to regulate exports from the United States, and the Trading-with-the-Enemy Act permitted him to regulate imports and enemy trade. With that authority, Wilson appointed a new administrative board, the War Trade Board, in October to carry out some of these objectives.

To lead the War Trade Board, Wilson turned to Vance C. McCormick. A reform-minded mayor of Harrisburg, Pennsylvania, and publisher of two newspapers in that city, McCormick was chairman of the Democratic National Committee that had organized Wilson's reelection campaign in 1916. McCormick's ingenuity now faced the test of regulating trade in order to find cargo space for the United States and its allies and in order to hurt the enemy. In broad outline, the system involved controls by license. Even before McCormick's appointment, in July 1917, Wilson licensed certain exports under the authority of the Espionage Act. In November similar restrictions were imposed on imports. By mid-February 1918, virtually all trade was under licensing controls.

The Wilson Administration recognized immediately that the control of trade was a very complex matter. As in other areas, it chose to work with the businessmen involved in the hope of securing cooperation through persuasion rather than coercion. "Trade advisers" and committees of the trades associations were a part of the organizational structure set up to provide the machinery for the licensing process. Almost immediately, the United States accepted the contention of the Allies that the control of neutral trade was absolutely essential and in July and August 1917 clamped down what amounted to an embargo on exports to the northern neutrals. Britain followed suit and canceled all trade agreements with Holland, Sweden, Norway, and Denmark. The *New York Tribune* put the American position bluntly: "The northern neutrals are . . . in an unfortunate position. But we cannot allow Germany to profit by anything that is being done for their benefit. Germany plunged the world into war. The crime she committed was against all the nations of the world, neutral as well as belligerent, and neutrals must now suffer along with belligerents until that crime is expiated."

In the meantime, a complicated machinery was created to negotiate agreements with the neutrals that it was hoped would make an embargo unnecessary. Coordination was provided by an interallied organization representing Britain, France, Italy, and the United States known as the Allied Blockade Committee, operating in London. Within the neutral countries themselves, local interallied committees kept their antenna up to provide their parent body in London with intelligence about local conditions. The main purpose of this machinery was to negotiate additional commercial agreements which would deprive the central powers of needed products. The neutral countries negotiated these agreements skillfully, and in the case of Holland, postponed the completion of the negotiations until after the war was over.

The case of Holland illustrates the almost excruciating position in which the neutral countries found themselves. Negotiations with the Dutch began late in 1917, presumably to determine what could be exported from the Allied countries to the Netherlands and how Dutch ships, many of which were lying idle in fear of submarines, could be used. Although certain tentative agreements were reached, it soon became obvious that Germany, poised on the Netherland borders, was applying even greater pressure to undermine any agreement with the Allies, and the negotiations were stalemated. At this point, in March 1918, the British and American governments ended the negotiations by requisitioning Dutch shipping in British and American ports in spite of official complaints from the Netherlands that such action was "indefensible" in international law and "unjustifiable when taken against a friendly nation."

A broader dimension of the control of neutral trade was the effort "to control enemy trade and isolate the central powers financially." Here again the War Trade Board followed the precedents of its allies and refined them. The most important device developed here was to identify through the board's intelligence sections merchants all over the world who were maintaining commercial relations with the enemy and to quarantine them. In other words, no Allied merchant was granted a license to trade with them. These were the notorious blacklists, coordinated among the Allied countries and maintained through the information drawn from the board's Bureau of War Trade Intelligence and Bureau of Foreign Agents. By the end of the war, agents of the board were operating in most Latin American and European countries as well as in China, Japan, and Java. They were seeing to it that blacklisted traders were denied the use of American or British coal—and "the voyages were very few and very unimportant in which a ship did not require bunker coal from either a

British or American coaling station." The agents were even watching the sale of newsprint paper and motion picture films in order to control enemy propaganda. Moving picture theaters in Switzerland, for example, were denied American films because they were showing German propaganda films.

The War Trade Board, important though its functions were in undermining the war potential of the central powers, was not responsible for the even more indispensable functions of seeing to it that American troops reached the fighting front, and that both these troops and the Allies received the materiel and supplies necessary for their well-being. The War Trade Board's functions were essentially negative. The positive function of providing shipping for the Allied war effort was the responsibility of the U.S. Shipping Board.

The statute which had established the Shipping Board had become law in September 1916, it will be recalled, as part of Wilson's preparedness program, but also as a means to revive the American merchant marine and to take advantage of the war situation to strengthen American foreign trade. The Shipping Board might regulate commerce on the high seas and the Great Lakes, establish reasonable rates, license vessels and purchase ships which could be leased or sold to private companies, or, "failing such arrangement," be operated by a government corporation. On December 22, 1917, Wilson nominated as board members, William Denman, a progressive Democrat from California and a lawyer experienced in admiralty cases, who was soon chosen head of the board; Bernard N. Baker, a ship owner of Baltimore, also a progressive Democrat; John A. Donald of Baltimore, Democrat and ship owner; John B. White, a lumberman of Kansas City and a progressive Republican; and Theodore Brent of Chicago and New Orleans, a railroader and Republican with "progressive ideas."

As submarine sinkings increased and American merchants became more involved in supplying the Allies, the Shipping Board was confronted with the fact that without many more ships the cause of the Allies was hopeless. The Shipping Act of 1916 had authorized the formation of a government corporation which, if necessary, might acquire or build and operate merchant ships. The war emergency forced the United States to use this option, and thus under provisions of the act, the Emergency Fleet Corporation was organized with Denman as its president and with Major General George W. Goethals, the dynamic builder of the Panama Canal, as its general manager. Goethals was given sweeping power and charged with building a "bridge of ships" to Europe. The United States was in the shipping business.

The story of the Shipping Board provides a fascinating study of the crosscurrents which to a greater or lesser degree influenced all the government agencies of the First World War. Sectionalism was involved—the interests of the Pacific Coast lumber people and shipbuilders; business interests were involved—those involved with lumber as opposed to those involved with steel; private operation as opposed to public operation was involved—whether private shipbuilders should build and private operators operate or whether the Emergency Fleet Corporation should build and the Shipping Board operate; relationships with the allies were involved—whether American shipyards should build ships for the Allies or concentrate on building ships for the Emergency Fleet Corporation, and that question in turn was associated with the interests of American ship owners in capturing overseas markets in the postwar world; personality clashes were involved—the extent to which Denman as president or Goethals as manager should control the construction program.

All these questions led to controversies, but the one that blew the lid off was that between Goethals and Denman. Superficially the issue was over the relative merit of wooden or steel ships. Goethals ridiculed the idea of wooden ships, publicly encouraging the steel people by saying that "birds are still nesting in the trees from which the great wooden fleet was to be made." Actually, Denman and Goethals were not far apart on the issue of whether steel or wooden ships were preferable. They both agreed that steel ships were preferable, but that wooden ships should be built when practicable. The actual point of difference was who was in command of the shipbuilding program. Goethals insisted on the right to make the decisions; when Denman, as president of the corporation refused to give him that right, Goethals would not accept and on July 20, 1917, resigned.

The issues of personality, power, and principle had led to the drawing of battle lines, and the settlement of the dispute was now up to the president. Goethals had hoped that Wilson would back him, but the president obviously feared taking sides so he accepted Goethals' resignation and in order not to make "invidious decisions" requested Denman's resignation also.

In the meantime, Congress was considering a measure to give the Shipping Board special war powers which, almost everyone recognized, were needed if indispensable ships were to be built. These sweeping powers were provided in a precedent-shaking deficiency appropriations bill introduced on April 30, 1917. Introduced into the House by Representative John J. Fitzgerald of New York, chairman of the House Committee on Appropriations, it asked for approximately two and three quarter billions of dollars, "almost ten times as great as any appropriations bill" which had hitherto passed through Congress—"a sum so stupendous" said Representative Frank W. Mondell of Wyoming, "that the mind could hardly grasp it." The Senate began considering the bill approximately two weeks later and promptly noted that the bill provided for not only "deficiencies" but new funds as well as for the expansion of the power of the U.S. Shipping Board. As Senator Underwood, not noted for extravagance, put it, "If this war is to be a success, the first question and the last question to be considered is ships, ships, and more ships."

Although the Republicans were not disposed to make a partisan issue of the bill, they did not hesitate to question various features of it. Senator Smoot raised one of the most significant questions when he argued that authority to commandeer shipping under construction for Britain should not be granted. He insisted that it was poor business to purchase British shipping when that shipping would be used for the interests of the Allies whether flying the British or American flag. Clearly, however, shipping politics was involved in this question too. Denman, Smoot admitted, had desired these ships to be taken over in order to strengthen American foreign commerce in the postwar years, and Senator Kellogg, endorsing this view, looked at the war as an opportunity. German commerce would be destroyed, he pointed out, and other countries would be limited by lack of ships. "I believe that it is of the greatest importance that when this war closes we shall have in our control, and not in the control of Great Britain or any other country, the largest number of ships we can possibly have." Smoot's attempt to restrict Wilson's commandeering power was beaten down by a vote of 49 to 9. The bill went through three conference reports before being passed on June 12 by the House and a day later by the Senate, both by voice votes.

As finally passed, the bill authorized the president to change any contract for the building or purchase of ships, to requisition the output of any plant which produced ships or shipping materials or the plant itself, or to purchase or requisition any ship already constructed or thereafter constructed. The president was to determine the compensation for any action of his with regard to the ships so acquired; he was authorized to delegate these powers to an appropriate agency. As Representative Fitzgerald pointed out, the appropriation authorized was of unprecedented size, more than $3.2 billion. It dealt with the equipping of an army of 1 million men and the support of the navy; it provided for the construction within 18 months of some 3 million tons of cargo ships. Yet "it met with practically no opposition" in either house of Congress.

In spite of the fact that critics had considered the shipping program "paralyzed by differences" between Denman and Goethals, the Shipping Board and the Emergency Fleet Corporation had laid a firm base for the next year's sensational building program. Indeed, the board had placed contracts for 642,800 tons of steel vessels and had prepared the way for an enormous "fabricating" program of 3,000,000 tons; it had organized new shipyards for the construction of wooden vessels and had either let or was negotiating contracts for more than 1,500,000 tons of wooden ships; it was investigating the possibility of the use of concrete ships; it had repaired some 91 ships of German registry and a substantial number of Austrian ships and had put many of them into service. Among the German ships taken over was the liner *Vaterland,* the largest vessel of its kind in the world. Commandeered in July 1917, it was repaired at a cost of

$8,500,000. Renamed the *Leviathan,* it became a hardworking troop ship which would carry some 100,000 American troops to France.

It negotiated a wage agreement for sea personnel; it set up a recruiting service in Boston for merchant sailors; it set up navigation schools on the Atlantic, Pacific, and Gulf coasts which by December were "creating" officers at the rate of about 300 a month. Moreover it provided the initiative for the Deficiency Bill of June 1917. "There can be no question of the diligence and dedication of the incompatible administration of Denman and Goethals."

In spite of the initial successes of the board, Wilson was aware before Goethals' resignation that the time had come for a change of command. The question was who would be able to take over and manage one of the most important, yet controversial, war agencies. In this instance, Wilson made an inspired choice. He turned to one of his early political supporters already in the war service, Edward N. Hurley, a dynamo of energy at the age of fifty-three, and a poor-youth-who-made-good. Beginning as a locomotive attendant fireman and engineer and member of the appropriate railroad organizations, Hurley in 1896 organized the Standard Pneumatic Tool Company, the first company to manufacture the piston air drill. Indeed Hurley claims to have driven "the first rivet in a ship . . . that was ever driven by compressed air on the Clyde in the great British shipyards." In 1902, he retired from business, a millionaire, but in 1908 organized the Hurley Machine Company which developed into a highly prosperous manufacturer of electrical appliances. He became a supporter and friend of Wilson in 1910, served on the Federal Trade Commission, succeeded to the chairmanship and served until February 1917, worked briefly with the Red Cross and the War Trade Board before Wilson persuaded him to leave a relatively obscure position for one that would make headlines immediately.

Like Denman, Hurley had his eyes on a postwar merchant marine. Organize the shipbuilding plants on sound business lines, he urged, and we can become "the leader of commerce" and "the mekka [*sic*] of the ship-building trade of the world," and at the same time perform a service by providing efficient commerce at reasonable rates. These views were firmly in accord with advice which he had given to both business and government before the war which called for efficiency and honesty in business methods, cooperation in the form of trades associations, a benevolent government acting as counselor rather than watchman, a greater emphasis on commercial education, and a vigorous development of foreign trade.

Hurley's dynamic qualities became immediately apparent. After a quick assessment, he concluded that ship construction was not proceeding as expeditiously as it might and decided to take over the shipbuilding industry. On August 3, 1917, within six days after assuming his post, he exercised powers authorized by Wilson on July 11 and commandeered "all power-driven cargo-carrying and passenger vessels above 2,500 tons capacity" that were under construction in 25 yards. Some 431 uncompleted ships were involved, many of them under contract to Norwegian and British owners, totaling more than 3 million deadweight tons.

The result "was as if 431 bombshells" had exploded as the shipyards and ship owners put up "a desperate fight" against the order. The objections had no effect. The commandeering process continued, and on October 12, 1917, the board requisitioned all American steel cargo and passenger vessels of 2,500 tons and over. Other orders requisitioned smaller vessels such as tugs and barges from time to time; but the most important and controversial order was that which took over all vessels of the Netherlands registry within American waters. By this order the United States acquired the use of 87 vessels which were repaired, armed, and remanned with American crews.

Other arrangements for foreign or neutral shipping were made in conjunction with the War Trade Board. Chartering agreements with Norway, Sweden, Denmark, and France, and agreements for chartering, purchasing, and construction of new vessels in Japan added to the total Allied service. The board even signed a contract with a construction company in Shanghai to build four 10,000-ton steel ships.

Although by February 1918 the Shipping Board was managing almost 9 million deadweight tons of shipping, its most novel program, "the fabricated shipyard," had yet to produce its first vessel. Goethals had launched this project shortly after becoming general manager of the Emergency Fleet Corporation, and he had called in Theodore Ferris, "dean of American naval architects," to design not only a wooden ship but a prefabricated steel ship. Ferris' design made old navy hands shudder, but it made possible applying the principle of interchangeable parts to shipbuilding. Hurley took over the project with enthusiasm. "If they can standardize a gun, a motor, an aeroplane, a row of houses, why not standardize ships," he proclaimed, and within two months had approved contracts for three new shipyards, one at Bristol, Pennsylvania, another at Newark Meadows in New Jersey, and a third at Hog Island on the Delaware River near Philadelphia.

Hog Island was the largest project of all. Originally estimated to cost $35 million, the yard with its press and shops actually cost about $65 million and covered 846 acres. Fifty ships could be under construction on the ways at the same time while 28 more could be on the piers being equipped. "We came, we saw, we were amazed," commented the head of a Japanese military mission. It was not an easy yard to build or to maintain. The island itself was swampy, and working conditions were unpleasant. The job was no sooner under way than one of the most severe winters on record hit the East Coast. Labor turnover was disgraceful, by one report averaging more than 100 percent a week and once reaching 700 percent.

In the winter of 1918 labor conditions at best were unstable, and the Philadelphia area was particularly tense since some $2 billion worth of war contracts had been placed there. By the time the building boom reached its peak, almost 35,000 workers were employed.

Given the size of the project, the complexity of the financing, and the pressure for speed rather than economy, it is not surprising that Hog Island became a kind of symbol for the critics of the war effort. Senator Vardaman of Mississippi, who considered American intervention as a device to line the pockets of businessmen and bankers at the expense of the common people, called it a project "conceived in the greed for gain, brought forth in a gush of mock patriotism, and swaddled in the American flag." He quoted approvingly an article in *Pearsons Magazine* entitled "How Uncle Sam Is Swindled: The True Story of Hog Island," which pointed out that the American International Corporation of many years standing had incorporated the American International Shipbuilding Corporation to carry out the Hog Island project; that this new corporation had a capital stock of only $2,000 that was owned without liability by the mother corporation; that it could then enter into contracts, absorb the profits, pay the dividends, and dissolve or go bankrupt without being persecuted for fraud.

Vardaman's diatribes might have been considered so extreme that few would have paid much attention to them were it not for the extravagance in construction and lack of tangible results. The rising storm of criticism was coming to a climax in the fall of 1917 when German offensives were threatening the Allied position and congressional critics were calling for an investigation of the war effort. In November the energetic Hurley, chafing under the criticism, brought about several organizational changes which concentrated the authority for the shipbuilding program in his own hands. Then as the pressure from the Allies for more men and materiel increased, as the Chief of Staff, General March, demanded ships to carry out his responsibilities, as President Wilson instructed him to "go the limit," Hurley brought in Charles M. Schwab to a newly created post of director general in April 1918. Schwab, as founder, president, and chairman of the board of the Bethlehem Steel Corporation, was one of the most highly regarded steel people in the world. Using his genius for "human engineering," Schwab succeeded in bringing the shipbuilding program up to the tempo already achieved by Bethlehem Steel. Schwab aimed at launching 100 ships on July 4, 1918. Approximately 95 ships were actually launched on that day. As the *New York Times* put it, throughout his early career, he was "a sky rocket," and "the Schwabian orbit is still in the ascendant."

The activities of the Shipping Board became increasingly complex as the war progressed and as the concept of "total war" became pervasive. Under such a concept, all shipping even though not carrying goods directly to the battlefield became considered a part of the war effort.

Thus in various ways committees of the Shipping Board began to determine routes and cargoes and "in large measure" to decide rates for virtually all ships leaving American ports.

The synchronization of the infinite number of strands in the world's commercial web did not take place automatically. Conflict was bound to develop among the army which demanded ships and supplies for its own particular purpose, the War Industries Board which looked at the problem of ships and supplies with a somewhat larger vision, and private merchants who might or might not have any vision of the war effort at all. What obviously was needed was some sort of planning body with a bank of statistical information available which could be used to establish priorities. This kind of statistical information did not exist at first.

Probably Judge E. B. Parker, priorities commissioner of the War Industries Board, made the first move to solve this problem by appointing Edwin F. Gay, dean of the Graduate School of Business Administration at Harvard, as his expert adviser on shipping. Gay had already grasped the dimensions of the problem while serving on the Commercial Economy Board of the Council of National Defense (which became the Conservation Division of the War Industries Board in May 1918). Gay's peculiar qualities were brought to the attention of Hurley, who promptly (June 1918) set up a Division of Planning and Statistics of the Shipping Board with Gay as its head. The new bureau was able to provide information and guidance that immeasurably improved the efficiency of the war effort. Cargo capacity, speed, precise location at a given time, the nature and quality of cargo, these and other facts made possible pooling arrangements and the unified direction that went far to supplying the shipping space that was needed.

In the popular mind, and probably in the mind of Congress, however, the success of the shipping rested on the record of the Emergency Fleet Corporation in building ships. Hurley vigorously defended the shipbuilding record of his agency. He pointed out that in 1916 there were 37 steel shipyards in the United States; that by March 1918 the Shipping Board had created 81 new yards and expanded 18 of the old ones. In addition the record showed 101 steel ships requisitioned from private owners in 1917, 221 in 1918, 367 in 1919, and 7 in 1920; 3 steel ships built under contract for the Emergency Fleet Corporation in 1917, 279 in 1918, 732 in 1919, 263 in 1920, and 28 in 1921; 2 wood ships contracted in 1917, 298 in 1918, 273 in 1919, and 16 in 1920; and a total of 18 "composite" and 12 concrete ships; for a grand total of 2,308 ships. Hog Island, the largest shipyard in the world, delivered 122 ships. The original program had called for 3,270 vessels, but with the armistice, cancellations of contracts were made whenever the Shipping Board judged that it could be done legitimately and economically.

The record of the Shipping Board in the construction of ships would appear to have been very good indeed. Shipbuilding increased more than tenfold during the war years. Moreover the ships proved to be efficient and economical. Whether profits were high and whether the shipbuilding program at war rates could have been discontinued earlier is a highly debatable matter—it is clear that only 800 ships of the 2,300 had been launched before the war ended. It is also clear that the minimum fee for the American International Shipbuilding Corporation for a contract to build 180 ships at a cost of $256 million would be almost $9 million. However, as one witness testified in defending the corporation's record at a congressional hearing in December 1918, the program was developed when the Germans were sinking between 700,000 and 900,000 tons a month, and "the whole world . . . was producing less than 200,000 tons a month." Congressmen then were "aghast at the prospect" . . . "we needed ships—anything that would float and propel itself." It was in this atmosphere of crisis that contracts were made with fabricators and subcontractors. These could not simply be canceled without a serious loss. Actually 958 were canceled.

Nevertheless it is also clear that everyone did not agree that the ship-building program should be substantially reduced. Since its inception the board had assumed that one of its long-range responsibilities was to build a "dominant" American merchant marine while at the same time winning the war. The principal officials of the Emergency Fleet Corporation continued to hold this view after the war was over. As one of them pointed out in 1919, "It has cost the nation at least $300,000,000 to teach 300,000 men and 120 new managements how to build ships, and with even temporary financial aid American shippers can be taught to operate profitably even the large fleet which we will have on our hands. At any rate, if we haven't the capacity and initiative to become a large shipping nation, let us at least remain a large ship-building nation now that our tuition has been paid for."

War Industries Board

In spite of valiant attempts to mobilize for the national defense, it is clear that the war effort remained chaotic for almost a year after the United States entered the war. Yet other countries had done little better. In May 1915, the *London Times* complained about "the multiplicity of governments departments, all more or less overwhelmed by the emergency, all clogged by official routine, all unused to business methods and ignorant of manufacturing technicalities, all issuing confused and often contradictory orders, all pressing their requirements without regard to the rest." Not until then, nine months after the outbreak of the war, did Britain really begin to bring some order out of a chaotic situation by placing Lloyd George with authoritarian powers at the head of a newly created ministry of munitions.

In the United States, no agency ever developed such authoritarian powers. The Advisory Commission of the Council of National Defense tried to coordinate economic preparations after October 1916, but governmental agencies were not accustomed to cooperation. The Joint Army Navy Board, almost forgotten, had not solved the problem of service rivalries, and particularly within the army one bureau tried to outdo the other in securing needed supplies. As the months went by, new agencies carved out "independent feudalities," and food, fuel, railroads, shipping, and labor came under separate controls. Although economic mobilization far exceeded what the nation had previously experienced, it had little unity.

Plans for substantial government involvement did not exist simply because the idea of a distant government touching the daily lives of every man was inconceivable. Wilson himself, although not opposed to the "national" consolidation of industry, was sensitive to monopoly as a political issue and critical of the kind of cooperation between industry and government that Roosevelt and Taft had encouraged. Moreover, Newton D. Baker, the secretary of war, did not at first recognize the scope of the war effort and feared powerful federal agencies. Yet, Baker, as chairman of the Council of National Defense, was responsible for providing coordination to the war effort.

The crisis of war forced the council to make decisions without having the information or the power necessary to make them. One basic principle was widely accepted: that the government must rely on private individuals and private interest groups for talent and on private business rather than government plants for munitions and equipment for its military forces. Yet neither the council nor its advisory commission, however, could visualize the intricate relationship between government and industry that was to develop before the end of the war. As Bernard Baruch put it, "it was vaguely foreshadowed" how demands of war would strain the nation's productive capacity and force new relationships between the military forces with a seemingly insatiable demand for supplies and the industries which would have to supply them.

The army proved to be one of the weakest links in the mobilization effort. The centralized purchasing systems of the navy adjusted to the need for wartime priorities, but as late as March 1917 the army had no plans for equipping a substantial force for an overseas expedition. The outcome of the internal battle which had been taking place since 1903 between the bureaus and the General Staff was still in doubt when the war broke out, and each bureau still insisted on purchasing its own supplies. To the army, strategic needs determined supply; since army supply officers questioned whether civilians could understand strategy, they suspected any efforts to control supply. Since both statutes and precedent supported their autonomy in procurement, Baker, secretary of war and strategically placed as chairman of the Council of National Defense, had no intention of undermining that autonomy, and Wilson upheld Baker's position.

At first the only agency in a position to promote coordination was the Advisory Commission of the Council of National Defense. That commission, however, was only advisory, and the service procurement agencies chose when they would cooperate. Groping for solutions, the council in February 1917 created a new board, known as the Munitions Standards Board, designed to advise the War Department in making its purchases, and almost simultaneously urged that industries necessary for the national defense organize themselves and provide representatives to work with the council. The Advisory Commission enthusiastically endorsed this proposal and recommended that each basic industry create industrywide organizations, if they did not already exist, and then choose a small committee to represent each organization. A number of important trades associations, such as the American Iron and Steel Institute, already did exist, and new ones were organized. These associations appointed delegates to serve on "cooperative committees," which, although at first designed to provide information, soon became veritable procurement agencies. Although this development was logical, sometimes these committees seemed to be procuring from themselves, and individual companies without government contacts became incensed when they found themselves left out.

During these early months, Baruch, chairman of the subcommittee on raw materials of the Advisory Commission, emerged as one of the main figures in the entire mobilization process. As a youth, Baruch had gone to Wall Street to make his fortune and had succeeded before the age of thirty. A self-instructed student of the market, he became well acquainted with "great figures of finance and industry." He traveled throughout the United States, "visiting enterprises . . . inspecting . . . talking to men in charge; observing, weighing, comparing." In 1915, he "spent much time thinking about the war" and formulated a plan for economic mobilization. During the next two years, he became acquainted with Wilson and some of Wilson's advisers, including McAdoo and Colonel House. He reluctantly consented to serve on the Advisory Commission of the Council for National Defense, a conception of mobilization which he considered quite inadequate. Once on the commission, however, his reluctance disappeared, although, as he later put it, "it was necessary to proceed gropingly, basing conclusions of the utmost moment on statistics resulting from assumptions on fragmentary and inaccurate information."

Baruch, nonetheless, proceeded vigorously. His style favored the casual, highly individualistic approach, and thus in working with the "cooperative committees," he much preferred to work with powerful leaders in an industry rather than with democratically elected representatives. He worked out arrangements of his own either with committees or individuals representing "the basic industries in the raw materials field," "the producers of aluminum, brass, cement, chemicals—down through the industrial alphabet to steel, wool, and zinc."

He soon demonstrated the utility of his system. Prices of many raw materials, particularly minerals, had been increasing sensationally since the outbreak of war in 1914. Copper, for example, more than doubled in price between 1914 and March 1917. Baruch, realizing that prices might skyrocket with American involvement, persuaded leading copper people, such as Daniel Guggenheim and John D. Ryan, to sell 45 million pounds of copper to the army and navy at 16 2/3 cents a pound. The prevailing market price was then 35 cents. Similar arrangements were made with other large industries controlled by comparatively few producers such as steel, aluminum, lead, and zinc. In March 1917, Baruch arranged for the creation of a committee led by Elbert H. Gary, chairman of the board of the U.S. Steel Corporation, and drawn largely from the American Iron and Steel Institute, the trades association of the industry. This association became the voice of the steel industry in an atmosphere of unprecedented cooperation between that industry and the government. Indeed such relationships became at times so cozy that they led to bitter criticism of the system. Senator James A. Reed of Missouri was particularly vitriolic in questioning Baruch's choice of Arthur V. Davis, president of the Aluminum Company of America, to be head of the Aluminum Coopera-tive Committee. As Reed saw it, Davis would be able to approve aluminum contracts and certify with "solemnity and dignity" that "the price is fair and that the prices contracting are reliable."

The relatively effective organization of sources of supply was not matched by any comparable unity among agencies responsible for pur-chasing. Competition for needed material among various government agencies continued. Attempts to promote coordination by the Munitions Standard Board in March 1917 were futile, and the Advisory Commission became increasingly frustrated; so early in April Wilson appointed a General Munitions Board designed to be a "great cooperative purchasing body." The board worked sixteen-hour days and made some headway under the dedicated leadership of Frank Scott, president of the Warner Swazey Company, but problems multiplied and bureaucracy expanded, until by "June 1917 a jerry-built array of 150 committees was associated helter-skelter with various army bureaus."

By that time, it was obvious again that the system was not working. Some plants accepted orders beyond their capacity to produce. Orders piled up in New York, Pennsylvania, and Ohio to the irritation of business-men in other parts of the country. Other businessmen became even more irritated when it leaked out that some industrialists on the "cooperative committees" were awarding contracts to themselves. Coordination with the military bureaus was sporadic; everything depended upon cooperation, and when that broke down the increased confusion provided evidence for those eager to prove the incompetence of the Wilson Administration.

The growing discontent was reflected in the heated debate over the Lever Act which set up the Food Administration. Bryanite Democrats and independent Republicans, distrusting corporate capitalism, battled with Administration stalwarts who followed Wilson's lead in insisting that only with the cooperation of business could the war needs be met. Opposition senators claimed corruption and extravagance in awarding war contracts, and tacked on the Lever Act a rider which would have established a Joint Committee of Congress on the Conduct of the War. Wilson succeeded in eliminating that provision, but could not prevent the passage of an amendment known as Section 3 which permitted a committee man with a personal interest in a contract to recommend that contract only if the personal interest was disclosed in writing. The bill was passed in August 1917.

In the meantime, concern over mobilization grew among the Administration's friends as well as its critics. Baruch continued to urge a civilian ministry of munitions powerful enough to control both the military and industry and yet able to promote cooperative relations with industry. In May he converted Secretary of the Treasury McAdoo who in turn almost persuaded Wilson. Baker saw that this scheme would deprive him of his control and on June 13, 1917, suggested a plan which would replace the Munitions Board by a War Industries Board with enlarged responsibilities but still subject to the Council of National Defense, which he chaired.

Wilson announced his decision on July 28. Although he modified Baker's recommendations somewhat, the institution created was Baker's and not Baruch's. The president made clear that the War Industries Board was designed to provide the production and coordination needed in the war effort. At the same time, it was equally clear that he had attempted to steer a course between Baker's model which would sustain military autonomy in purchasing and Baruch's which would produce a centralized authority oriented toward business. At the same time he wanted to retain the cooperation of business, and yet mollify to some extent those congressional progressives who wanted to deprive businessmen of their influence in the mobilization process. He appointed as head Frank Scott, who believed like his friend Baker that cooperating with existing military institutions was essential, but also included as members Baruch, Robert S. Lovett, and Robert Brookings, all sympathetic to the business point of view, Hugh Frayne, an active organizer for the AFL, as well as representatives of the army and navy.

Wilson, like Baruch, considered it essential not to lose the support of business leaders. Congress through Section 3 had alarmed numerous businessmen who had been working on the cooperative committees, and many of them were preparing to get out. Public antagonism toward the cooperative committees continued to be so great that early in November 1917, Walter Gifford, the executive director of the Advisory Commission, instructed Baruch to dissolve them. Gifford with the blessing of the Council of National Defense hoped to substitute for the cooperative committees a plan worked out by the Chamber of Commerce in the summer of 1917. This plan was based upon using War Service Committees chosen by the Chamber of Commerce to represent the trades. Although the War Industries Board, and particularly Baruch, preferred to deal with representatives of leading industries, they adjusted to the new arrangements. They created commodity sections, consisting of representatives of the procurement agencies and a businessman, usually paid a "dollar-a-year" but presumably without conflicts of interest. These government agencies were responsible for purchasing a particular commodity and worked with the war service committees of the Chamber of Commerce, each one of which was responsible for obtaining its own product and disciplining its own industry. By mid-December some 125 of these committees had been organized, and the War Committee of the National Chamber of Commerce became a kind of National Executive Committee charged with selecting additional committees. Before the end of the war some 350 of them existed.

In spite of efforts to prevent conflicts of interest, finding knowledgeable men for particular jobs usually resulted in such conflicts. The great majority of the members of the commodity sections, for example, held prominent positions in industries with which their commodity sections would negotiate, and industries undoubtedly liked to have "their representative" in one of these sections. The case of George Peek, twenty years later to be identified with the Agricultural Adjustment Administration of the New Deal, shows how unabashed conflicts of interest could be. Peek was vice president of Deere and Company, of Moline, Illinois. A member of the executive committee of his trade association, the National Implement and Vehicle Association, he was appointed to the War Industries Board in December and became the board's Industrial Representative. In spite of his strategic position in the government, he did not resign from the executive committee of his trade association until March 1918; and his former business did not hesitate to ask him to intercede with government agencies on its behalf. Yet Peek played an almost indispensable role in working out differences about supply problems with a counterpart, Captain Hugh Johnson, who represented the military.

Yet without properly trained civil servants, alternatives to using appointees from business on these committees were not apparent. In any case, the War Industries Board began to grapple with the countless problems of the war effort immediately upon its organization in August 1917. Principles and practices in determining priorities and price fixing were being established; a Conservation Division was working out its program; allied purchasing was being conducted within an Interallied Purchasing Commission; and numerous other procedures and precedents were being established.

On the other hand, the board still had administrative difficulties. Clear lines of authority did not exist, and a struggle for control within the board between civilian and military members exhausted Scott who resigned in September. Scott was succeeded briefly by Robert S. Lovett and then by Daniel Willard, but again the whole war effort seemed on the verge of collapse: shortages, congestion in ports, inadequate berthing facilities, the lack of machine guns, inadequate heating and plumbing facilities in camps, and especially the lack of blankets, heavy clothing, and medical supplies in subzero temperatures infuriated parents and congressmen and exposed the weaknesses of the supply system. These and many other complaints coming at a low point in Allied fortunes roused Congress anew, and war agencies and particularly those responsible for supplying the army came under attack.

Proposals to prevent disaster were not long in coming. Republican leaders, Roosevelt, Lodge, Penrose, and others, wanted to embarrass Wilson and at the very least to get rid of Baker. Some Democratic leaders joined Republican critics. Particularly acerb was Senator George Chamberlain of Oregon, pugnacious chairman of the Military Affairs Committee, who broke with the Administration in a sensational speech on January 19, 1918, before the National Security League and the American Defense Society. Denouncing the War Department's mobilization efforts as blunders and failures, Chamberlain called for heroic measures which would include a Munitions Director and a War Cabinet; then in late January he introduced a bill for a war committee independent of the cabinet and responsible only to the president. Hearings on this bill brought a parade of officials from the Chamber of Commerce and even from the War Industries Board demanding the replacement of Baker, a War Cabinet to direct the war effort, and a Ministry of Munitions separate from the War Department. Criticism of the administration by January 1918 met even more willing hearers than usual because it came at a time when the Fuel Administration had shocked the country by abruptly ordering that virtually all factories east of the Mississippi should be shut down for a week.

However, Baker and Wilson stood firm and launched a counterattack against their critics. The president realized that reorganization was necessary; yet he was determined that Congress should not win control of waging the war, and so he set in motion three important moves to disarm his critics. The first consisted of a moderate reorganization of the army's supply system and the appointment of the tough-minded, efficient Chief of Artillery of the AEF, Peyton C. March, as Chief of Staff. March's appointment in May 1918 had the effect of an "electric shock" on the War Department, and from then on there was little question that there would be unity of command in the army. The other two moves were closely related and involved the introduction of an administration substitute for the Chamberlain bill and the appointment of Bernard Baruch as chairman of the War Industries Board.

The Administration's substitute for the Chamberlain bill authorized the president "to coordinate or consolidate executive bureaus, agencies and offices . . . in the interest of economy and the more efficient concentration of the Government." This measure provoked a bitter debate. In February 1918, Senator Lee S. Overman, a mild-mannered North Carolinian, chairman of the Committee on the Judiciary, agreed to introduce the bill when Senator Martin of Virginia, the Democratic floor leader, refused to do so. Senator Reed Smoot (Republican of Utah) wailed that if the bill should pass, "there would be only one more thing left for Congress to do, and that would be to make the president king." Senator Lawrence Y. Sherman (Republican of Illinois) accused Wilson of choosing as advisers "socialists and economic freaks," "friends of sedition . . . a mysterious bunch of wizards." Wilson, however, refused to back down, and in the final count Reed of Missouri was the only Democrat who voted against the bill. Even Chamberlain fell in line, as did twenty-one Republicans. The final vote was 63 to 13. In the House, the vote was 295 to 2. This sweeping authorization of presidential power was finally authorized on May 20, 1918.

In spite of this victory, the boiling dissatisfaction had shown Wilson that he had to move carefully in order to keep control of the situation. Undoubtedly, the reason for the overwhelming vote for the controversial Overman Act was that on March 4, 1918, he had announced a reorganization of the War Industries Board which had compromised some of the differences between Baker and his critics, yet had put Bernard Baruch, the man who had been advocating tough controls, at the head of it. The core of the compromise was that a civilian board would "assume control of the general direction of the economy" while the army and the navy would remain responsible for procuring their own supplies. This compromise, quite different from that in Britain or France where a civilian board had more complete control, reflected currents of distrust and admiration in the United States toward both business and the military. Although Wilson was determined to retain the cooperation of business leaders, he did not have sufficient confidence in them to put the supply machinery under a ministry of munitions which they might have been able to control. On the other hand, business leaders seemed to be in agreement that a greater degree of benevolent control was necessary, but not in agreement as to whether the War Industries Board should be replaced. Undoubtedly Baruch's appointment upset Baker and those who thought like him. Baruch, however, had strong support from McAdoo and had numerous friends whom he had appointed to strategic positions in the bureaucracy. In any case, Wilson now considered him indispensable, informed him by letter of his appointment on March 4, 1918, and assured him that he "would have the ultimate decision" except in determining prices. Moreover, with the passage of the Overman Act, he was to be shifted to the president's jurisdiction rather than remain under the Council of National Defense. On the other hand, Wilson made clear that Baruch was "to let alone what is being successfully done and interfere as little as possible with the present normal processes of purchase and delivery in the several departments"; that he was to consult with the Food, Fuel, Railway, Shipping, and War Trade Administrations in determining priorities; and that he was to "be governed by the advice"of a special committee in determining prices.

Baruch's appointment, therefore, did not establish one dictatorial, all powerful body such as he had seemed to favor. The board continued to be at the center of a power struggle among government agencies, civil and military, and numerous industries large and small. Baruch, however, made a virtue of this decentralization which was in part necessary because of the impossibility of any other kind of organization, given the complexity of the economy. With his unparalleled knowledge of industry, he appointed able men to important posts—these appointments were among his most important contributions—and then told them to carry out their jobs. As the days went by, relationships became smoother. Within the services the need for cooperation became clearer; within the new civil agencies the atmosphere of the bureaucracy made actions more predictable and thus less irritating. Baruch generally had confidence in industry and at the same time soon identified himself with the board. One of the most thorough students of the board has concluded that Baruch's role "vis-à-vis the W. B. was essentially to legitimize the actions of his subordinates and to represent the W. B. position in the higher councils of government."

Wilson never did give Baruch authority to control prices. Price control had previously been managed in various ways. The National Defense Act of 1916 gave the president and the War Department price-fixing authority and included the Navy Department as one of the functionaries. As war boomed, the question of price loomed increasingly of greater importance. Since the primary goal was to bring about the production necessary to win the war, prices were informally negotiated with this in mind. At the same time, it was obvious that "open market bidding" for limited supplies of products under wartime conditions when survival rather than costs was the determining factor would drive prices up out of sight. Agreement was necessary. And copper and steel, hides and skins, wool, munitions, harness leathers, cotton textiles, sand and gravel, sulphuric and nitric acid, cement, and lumber, and various other items had come under price agreements before March 1918. In addition, the Lever Act had endowed both the Food and Fuel Administrations with power to control prices.

The president was determined that price-fixing authority should remain in his hands and be independent of the business orientation of the War Industries Board. So when he appointed the price-fixing committee late in March, Baruch was put on the board, but Robert S. Brookings, no admirer of Baruch, and perhaps more sensitive to the impact of inflation on people, was made chairman. Other members included representatives of the army, the navy, the AFL, the Fuel Administration, the Tariff Commission, the Federal Trade Commission, and the public.

This high-powered and representative committee still could not "arbitrarily fix prices." It could deal only with some raw materials and even then could only negotiate and then recommend to the president. Even such limited price controls, however, resulted in controversy. Complaints of skyrocketing prices on finished products were not often satisfied by the explanation that profits would be neutralized by excess profits taxes. One of the most sensitive issues developed sectional overtones when no price controls were imposed on cotton, a leading southern product, whereas the Food Administration imposed controls on wheat, equally important in the West. In general, however, and for the short time that limited controls were in effect, they worked reasonably well. Inflationary pressures, however, were threatening, and the War Industries Board was contemplating clamping on sweeping controls when the armistice came.

One of the most necessary functions of the War Industries Board was to establish priorities so that goods needed for the war effort would arrive at their proper destination. In that unhappy period in the fall of 1917, as Grosvenor Clarkson put it, "two-score Government purchasing agencies beat the whirlpool to froth with their bidding and scheming against each other, each obsessed with a mad determination to achieve his own goal." About the only principle that existed when war broke out was that the navy should "have the right of way over the army." This principle, however, was limited in time, and other agencies paid little attention to it. The Lever Act did give the Fuel Administration power to see that fuel reached plants that needed it for the war effort, and Congress had presumably authorized the president to give war materiel preference in transportation, but the problem remained acute. Baruch's solution was relatively simple. He centralized responsibilities in the hands of one of his most trusted associates, Edwin B. Parker, a Texas lawyer, who combined toughness and tact with presidential authority to bring a measure of order to what had appeared to be an impossible situation.

The War Industries Board had another powerful club which it rarely used—the power to commandeer. Although the president might have used his authority as commander in chief to have taken over industrial plants, several enactments beginning with the National Defense Act of 1916 and ending with the Naval Appropriation Act of July 1, 1918, authorized the president to take over virtually any plant which he might consider necessary in order to aid the war effort. This presidential power was assumed by many of his creatures, the war agencies, who abused it, and "in the flush days of rampant commandeering the departments even gayly commandeered each other's goods." Although such unilateral action ignored the total war needs, uncoordinated commandeering continued until September 3, 1918, when Wilson entrusted the commandeering power solely to Baruch.

Although cooperation and persuasion normally characterized the relationships between the War Industries Board and the business community, the abandonment of laissez faire seemed almost un-American to some businessmen. Almost from the date of its establishment, the War Industries Board found itself at sword's point with the automobile industry, led by such colorful individualists as Henry Ford, John Dodge, and "Billy" Durant. The skirmishes reached a high point in 1918 when the British were planning a secret drive to build armored troop and weapons carriers. This program threatened to stretch the American steel industry to more than capacity. Thus the War Industries Board decided to cut back the civilian automobile industry substantially in order to provide more steel for war purposes. The industry's spokesmen were uncooperative, and on one occasion Dodge let it be known that he would not have any "white-haired, white-faced Wall Street speculators telling him how to conduct his business."

At this comment, Baruch recalls that he telephoned McAdoo at the Railroad Administration, and "with the auto people listening said, 'Mac, I want you to take down the names of the following factories, and I want you to stop every wheel going in and going out.'"

"The automobile men looked at me," Baruch added, "astonished and outraged, as I read off the names of Dodge, General Motors, Ford and other plants. This effect was heightened as I put in a call to Secretary of War Baker. 'Mr. Secretary, I would like you to issue an order to commandeer all the steel in the following yards,' I said. Then I called Fuel Administrator Garfield and asked him to seize the manufacturers coal supplies.

"That did it. Billy Durant, head of General Motors, said 'I quit.' The others capitulated soon after."

Baruch's memoirs oversimplify the problem of the automobile industry. On the government side was the complicated interrelationship of the availability of steel, rubber, fuel, and transportation and the need to balance civilian needs and morale against war mobilization. On the automotive side were existing inventories of raw materials, the need to draw the line between the civilian demand for automobiles, tractors, and trucks, and the government's demand for trucks, armored vehicles, airplane motors, and other products necessary for the war effort together with maintaining economically viable communities in states, such as Michigan, Indiana, and Ohio, where the automotive industry played a vital role.

The debate with representatives of the principal automotive organization, the National Automotive Chamber of Commerce, became particularly vigorous between May and August 1918. After much soul-searching, the War Industries Board authorized the industries to acquire additional supplies necessary to liquidate their existing inventories—so long as filling these requirements would not interfere with war production or permit any manufacturer to produce more than 25 percent of the number of passenger automobiles produced during the corresponding period in 1917. The victory for the board was not so complete as Baruch made it out to be.

In considering the plight of industries in wartime, the importance of steel became increasingly obvious. From the early months of the war, when Baruch developed his cooperative arrangements with Judge Gary and his Committee of the American Iron and Steel Institute, one of the principal responsibilities of the wartime agencies was to increase production. Prior to the war only a small amount of steel had been used for military purposes; even when J. Leonard Replogle, "the peppery, youthful president of the American Vanadium Company," joined the War Industries Board in September 1917 he was told that only "17 percent of the total steel production of the country would be required to meet our war program." Within a comparatively few months, however, that figure had jumped to 40 percent and then to 80 percent. By the end of the war substantially more than the nation's entire steel production was requested to satisfy the war needs of the United States and her allies.

The most important series of confrontations between the War Industries Board and steel representatives occurred in September and October 1917. Prices had moved completely out of hand, and even those opposed to price control in principle agreed that something had to be done. On September 21, 1917, Baruch, Replogle, and others from the WIB announced a schedule of prices to 64 hostile representatives of the steel companies. When Judge Gary seemed completely recalcitrant, Baruch showed him a letter from Wilson assuring Baruch that he would not hesitate to commandeer "the United States Steel Corporation or any other business." At that, Gary and Baruch worked out an agreement cutting prices substantially—for example, pig iron dropped from $58.00 to $33.00 per gross ton and steel plates from $11.00 to $3.25. For the remainder of the war, a kind of entente developed which usually worked out differences amicably. Yet Gary could hardly have forgotten that behind the door Baruch, Parker, and Replogle kept a club.

Steel was only one, though the most important, product for which demand outran the supply during the war years. Thus an important function of the War Industries Board was to divert supplies normally going in other directions to wartime needs. Industrial conservation during the war years was largely the brain child of A. W. Shaw, a Chicago publisher and student of "commercial economy." Shaw proved himself to be an ingenious battler against waste and became Baruch's trusted head of the conservation division of the WIB.

He put every imaginable product on a schedule. His economies and diversions became legendary in standardizing "sizes, lengths, widths, thicknesses, weights, gauges," in reducing waste, packing increasing numbers of units per package, and substituting plentiful for scarce materials. By the simple expedient of requiring at least 200 yards of thread rather than 150 yards per spool, approximately 600 carloads of space per year was saved. In the manufacture of corsets, width and thickness of steel were cut from 150 to 21 gauges; the gauges of round wire were reduced in number from 16 to 7; and the Conservation Division had its estimates of how many thousands of carloads such standardization saved.

Shaw's initial plan was to work "cooperatively" with industry. Like Baruch, Shaw believed that voluntarism when it worked strengthened morale and produced better results than compulsion. At times, however, voluntarism did not seem to be quite enough, restrictions of the War Industries Board seemed to pinch the shoe industry, for example, and only after an acrimonious fight did the manufacturers agree to reducing shoe styles and to setting a price on those that remained. The complying shoe stores were rewarded by being able to display an insignia.

More controversial than the function of conservation was that of conversion. Here the question was the relative desirability of converting American industry to war production or of encouraging and supplying the war industry of Britain and France. British and French industry had already undergone a revolutionary conversion when the United States entered the war. In spite of Germany's initial successes in occupying valuable French territory and the substitution of untrained labor in French industry for the skilled workers of the prewar years, munitions production increased. Indeed, Grosvenor Clarkson concluded that if the United States had provided the raw material, French industry could have "supplied our armies indefinitely with guns, projectiles, tanks, and airplanes."

At the beginning of the war, knowledge of ordnance was almost non-existent in most American machine shops. Then the government invested some $7 billion in ordnance production. While American production got off the ground, inter-Allied councils arranged for British and French industry to supply the American armies in exchange for raw materials. The American Expeditionary Force was at first largely dependent upon British and French manufacturers for much of its equipment, except for their rifles, and until September 1918 even the machine guns came largely from the French. By the end of the war the manufacturing of artillery and artillery ammunition had gone into high gear, but it had not started soon enough to supply American units before the armistice. Of the 2,251 pieces of artillery with American units on the firing line, for example, only 130 were of American manufacture, and of the 8,850,000 rounds expended by American artillery, only 208,327 were of American manufacture. American air operations began at the front in March 1918, but not until August were the first American De Havillands flown; by the end of the war about 25 percent of the total of 2,698 planes flown by American squadrons were American built. By March 31, 1919, American producers had completed 797 tanks—but none of these had reached American units which had been using British and French tanks prior to the armistice.

The alternative to the decision of establishing a separate war industry was to integrate our industrial production more closely with the Allies, allow French and British industry to supply American forces, and to concentrate in the United States on providing necessary raw materials while manufacturing only explosives. This arrangement would have saved large expenditures for conversion and construction of new plants and would have released more people for war service. On the other hand, raw materials, being more bulky to transport, would have required more shipping. More importantly, no one knew definitely whether Allied industry would be able to supply American forces; no one could prophesy when the war would end, and "there was always a menacing possibility that France might have been inundated by the Germans, and her industrial potency annihilated." Until little more than a month before the armistice, Marshal Foch still called for massive shipments of American munitions.

No single individual made a single decision to develop American war industry. The practice just grew. Indeed it began before the United States entered the war in response to the frantic efforts of the Allies to assure themselves adequate war materiel; the response led to a substantial expansion of American industry to fulfill contracts, some of which were filled before American entry into the war. Thus some American industrialists were scratching their heads as to what to do with the new buildings and new and converted equipment which might soon be idle. After the United States entered the war, these plants were ready for use. With very little centralized control over either supply or demand, new plants were built and old ones converted, with little thought of anything but the immediate need—or the quick profit. What was necessary was for some one, or some agency, blessed with visions of the future, to decide how many new plants and how much conversion were necessary to win the war and not disrupt the economy in the postwar world.

With the appointment of George Peek as industrial representative of the War Industries Board in December 1917, an important step was taken to see that industry could meet the war needs with the least possible disorganization. After the reorganization of the board, even closer cooperation with industrialists developed, and following a pattern devised by the Ordnance Bureau, the nation was divided into twenty-one zones, each with an industrial committee organized through the local Chambers of Commerce so that information about available production could be speedily communicated to the board. Sometimes new factories had to be built, but frequently existing factories designed for civilian production found ways to make new products. Piano factories, for example, made fuselages and wings of airplanes; pipe organ factories made mosquito netting, and manufacturers of refrigerators turned to hospital tables.

By the end of the war a workable relationship between supply and demand had finally been worked out. Even the traditional army confusion of at least five separate supply bureaus had gradually disappeared. Although army leadership probably still had not accepted the need for close cooperation with civilian agencies, General March had knocked heads together in a series of general orders—which gave the General Staff the kind of coordinating power probably envisaged by Elihu Root in 1903. The War Industries Board by trial and error, by cajoling and at times threatening, had worked out treaties with other government agencies and agreements with industry. It had expanded its controls to nonwar construction and was extending itself into consumer goods. Cooperation was asked and usually given, but the club behind the door was always there.

Labor

"He would be ungrateful indeed who did not recognize that the chief burden of the war was borne by those who risked their lives. But it detracts nothing from their share in the victory to realize that the forces of the world democracies would have been helpless had they not had behind them united peoples and effective industrial forces. Back of the armed men were ships which sped across the ocean with the products of American labor, and railroads which transported those products to the seaboard; behind the railroads in turn were warehouses, workshops, factories, and mines. All these are in the long run but different forms of labor; and had any of this labor faltered we should not now be preparing to enjoy the blessings of peace and liberty."

So wrote Secretary of Labor Wilson in his report describing the events of 1918. Although it is a statement of the obvious, initial planning did not seem to take into account the problem of labor, and as the soldiers marched off to war, as the Food Administration demanded more food, the Fuel Administration more fuel, the Railroad Administration better service, and the Shipping Board more ships, the War Industries Board more production, labor problems, seemingly like all other problems of mobilization, reached unprecedented proportions.

Complaints over wages and living costs were chronic. In the highest paid occupations wage earners were receiving annual incomes of $1,500 to $2,000. Such an income might have made a fair living for a family of moderate size, but most adult male workers earned less than $15 per week, half of them earned less than $10, and few women workers earned as much as $8 a week. The war exacerbated this already unhappy situation. Living costs rose slowly from 1914 through 1916, and then soared. Sirloin steak which in 1911 averaged 27 cents a pound, was 32 in 1917, 39 in 1918, and 42 in 1919; milk at 9 cents a quart in 1915 was 16 in 1919; and bread at 7 cents a pound in 1915 was 10 cents in 1919. Generally food prices advanced 72 percent between 1916 and 1919, while weekly wages of union members increased 42 percent. Average cost of clothing increased some 54 percent, fuel and light 34 percent, and rent 9 percent between 1916 and 1918. In rent, variations were sensational from an increase of 380 percent in Detroit to a decrease of

1 percent in Jacksonville, Florida. An increase in weekly wages, it is true, took place in spite of a decrease in the hours of the work week. The average work week in all manufacturing industries, for example, decreased from sixty hours in 1890 to fifty-five hours in 1916—a 10 percent decline; by 1919 the figure was 52.3—an additional 5 percent in only 3 years. Yet few workers had attained the goal of an eight-hour day and a six-day week.

The larger industries remained hostile to unions, and in 1916 fewer than three million workers were members. From the point of view of the unions, an ominous development took place in November 1916 with the organization of the National Conference Board—a federation of large employers' associations. Although it denied an antiunion bias, its critics seemed to think that it did protest too much. Such employer organizations, moreover, received support from the Supreme Court of Massachusetts which declared unconstitutional that state's law making illegal the use of the injunction in labor disputes, a decision which the United States Supreme Court in 1917 was to uphold in *Hitchman Coal and Coke Company* v. *Mitchell.*

Wartime conditions brought increased confusion to labor management relations. The wage earners for the first time in many years enjoyed an advantage: they were in great demand, and there did not appear to be enough of them. Even before the United States entered the war, the principal source of unskilled labor, new immigration, had begun to dry up. The influx which averaged about 1 million annually from 1903 to 1914 dropped to 327,000 in 1915 and reached a low point of 111,000 in 1918. At the same time army, factory, and field were demanding more and more workers. Military and naval forces increased from fewer than 200,000 in 1916 to almost 3 million in 1918. To house and train these forces, the War Department built 32 cantonments, veritable cities of at least 30,000 people each requiring a water supply, electric utilities, and all the equipment necessary for daily living. These camps were to be completed in ninety days and would require many construction workers, in fact about 700,000 of them. Then several million additional workers to fill new war jobs were needed by the spring of 1918. Federal employees alone jumped from 400,000 in 1916 to 850,000 in 1918. Much of this demand, moreover, was for skilled workers, who could not be found.

Under these circumstances chaos prevailed in the labor market. Government agencies bid against one another. Private employment agencies saw a good thing and made the most of it, moving personnel from one job to another—all for a fee. Employers themselves established employment bureaus which in many cases did not hesitate to raid other firms engaged in the war trade. Labor turnover reached a new high. During the war 100 percent a week was not uncommon, and Secretary Wilson estimated in 1918 that in some cities, labor turnover had reached 3,000 percent annually. Labor soon recognized its power, and strikes for better wages, hours, working conditions, and union rights increased. Work stoppages in 1915 numbered 1,593,000; and in 1917 reached a high of almost 4.5 million.

All elements in the struggle took stock of the situation. Industries hired personnel managers and established departments of employment management, while the government reconsidered the available institutions for coping with labor unrest. Although rather primitive procedures for dealing with labor disputes on interstate railways had existed since 1888, it had not been particularly effective until the closing years of the Roosevelt administration when in virtually every significant railway labor dispute one or the other parties used machinery for mediation established by the Erdman Act of 1898. Weaknesses in the Erdman Act, however, led to a campaign for a new law, and in 1913, extensive conferences involving representatives of labor, management, the Department of Labor, and the National Civic Confederation resulted in the passage of the Newlands Act. The new bill created a board of mediation and conciliation and provided for intervention in controversies when in the public interest. The new board, the United States Board of Mediation and Conciliation, served effectively from July 1913 to September 1916, settling successfully sixty-six out of the seventy-one disputes on railroads which it attempted to adjudicate.

Labor policy reached another landmark with the creation of a separate cabinet post for the Department of Labor in 1913 and the appointment of William B. Wilson to the post. Wilson had come up through the battle-scarred ranks of the United Mine Workers. He had served for six years as a pioneer labor representative in Congress. An "austere but kindly" man, he upheld labor's rights but preferred conciliation to confrontation. When the Department of Labor was established in 1913, Congress appropriated no funds for conciliation, but in the two years, 1916 and 1917, about $75,000 a year was appropriated, and about thirty conciliators handled more than three hundred cases, most of them successfully.

Although conciliation was perhaps the most dramatic function of the Department of Labor, it became increasingly involved in trying to "distribute" workers where needed as the war produced new crises. This responsibility had been a function of the Bureau of Immigration, and since 1907 that bureau had operated an employment office in New York city. Within a year of Secretary Wilson's appointment, he began to work with state and municipal employment bureaus in an effort to bring workers to available jobs. Month after month, demands upon the service increased and from January through November 1918 it received requests from approximately eight million workers, and it referred more than half of them to jobs in war industry. It also dealt with thousands of miners, stevedores, and marine workers, harvesters for the wheat belt, cotton pickers for the Imperial Valley, chard and vineyard workers for New York, and potato diggers for Maine.

In spite of this service, private agencies and individual employers continued to compete for labor. At the same time the sight of "sturdy idlers and loafers" "standing at the street corners and contemplating placidly their own immunity" from the draft infuriated some "right minded" citizens. Although little support was given to conscripting labor as had been done in Germany in December 1916, President Wilson became concerned about the instability of the labor forces. In June 1918, he issued a special proclamation asking employers engaged in war work to recruit only through the Employment Service and urged workers to respond to calls for help in essential industries. At the same time, an amendment to the Selective Service Act approved in May required that those of draft age engaged in nonessential industry either change their jobs to essentials or be drafted. This "work or fight" order led to the summoning of 120,000 more men to the draft boards.

In addition to the Employment Service, Secretary Wilson established the United States Public Service Reserve in June 1917. This agency was a registration agency for patriotic citizens. During the war it proved to be particularly useful in seeking out, through some fifteen thousand enrollment agents, specially trained men for special jobs either civilian or military, whether the demand was for ordnance experts, aviation motor mechanics, or railway men for the Division of Military Railways abroad.

Farm labor posed an unusual problem because large numbers of workers were needed at particular times. Food suppliers and farm leaders became almost emotional as they begged for large-scale exemptions from the draft and demanded the importation of thousands of laborers from Mexico and China—even Californians favored the latter device. The Department of Labor, however, insisted that a sufficient number of domestic workers existed, but did propose using surplus labor from American territories, and the U.S. Employment Service early in 1918 arranged for the employment of more than one hundred thousand from the Virgin Islands to work on the railroads and the farms. The state Councils of Defense were particularly ingenious in supplying farm labor. The Colorado Council, for example, urged businesses to remain closed until 5:00 P.M. at harvest time so that their employees could work on the farms.

Secretary Wilson suspected that the war might be used as an excuse to get more child laborers by relaxing school attendance regulations or other restrictive legislation. In order to maintain some control of the situation, in April 1917 he established the Boy's Working Reserve, under the direction of William E. Hall, an unpaid volunteer. The reserve sought to attract city youths, with a minimum age of sixteen years, who otherwise would not be employed, to farm work. A "farm training camp" at Pennsylvania State College, for example, introduced 1,200 boys to farm activities in a two-week orientation. The state of Pennsylvania provided uniforms and tents and the boys "enjoyed the benefit of military discipline and drill." They then were divided into smaller groups and sent to

"Liberty Camps" where farmers picked them up daily for their services. In 1917 and 1918, approximately 750,000 boys participated.

The experience of other countries and particularly England had demonstrated the importance of rallying women to the support of the war effort. Although Secretary Wilson feared the effect of the employment of women on the labor market after the war, he could not deny that an employment emergency existed and that women were available. What was needed, he thought, was "a clear chart of the location and character of the war industries," of the need for women in these industries, and of the available supply of women workers. In early 1917, however, he did not have the funds to prepare such a study.

At this point, a woman's organization, the League for Women's Service, offered to help. The league grew out of a meeting in Washington in January 1917 of representative Americans, concerned about the possibility of approaching war, under the designation of "the Congress for Constructive Patriotism." At that meeting a group of women, including Mrs. J. Borden Harriman, Dean Gildersleeve of Barnard College, and Mrs. August Belmont, organized the league under the leadership of Miss Maude Wetmore and within a month set up headquarters in New York. Many existing women's organizations agreed to work with the new league, hundreds of women registered and studied practically everything from driving and repairing automobiles to wireless telegraphy and cooking for large numbers. Perhaps of most importance, the women registered their skills, and this information was then made available to the government.

Secretary Wilson promptly accepted the league's offer, and until October 1917 the league acted as a branch of the department. It studied thousands of contracts, determined the suitability of jobs for women, and carried out recruiting campaigns. Although a Women and Girls' Division of the United States Employment Service had existed since 1916, a new Women's Division replaced it in January 1918. In July 1918, Wilson appointed Mary Von Kleeck as director and Mary Anderson as assistant director of a special Women-in-Industry Service. The service was charged with developing standards and policies and working with other branches of the federal government and with state departments of labor.

In the meantime the Council of National Defense, recognizing the need of utilizing women and knowing little about existing organizations, was grappling with the problem of how best to use women in war industry. It finally decided to appoint a committee of "prominent and able women to advise as to how the woman power of the Country could be more effective." On April 21, Dr. Anna Howard Shaw, honorary president of the National American Woman's Suffrage Association, was appointed head of the committee, which included representatives of the National Council of Women Voters, the General Federation of Women's Club, the National League for Women's Service, the National American Woman's Suffrage Association, and the National Society of Colonial Dames.

The women on the committee assumed that they would have considerable authority in determining federal policy in employing women for the war effort, and it promptly sponsored state organizations designed to assume responsibility for all women's organizations involved with war work. In May the National Woman's Committee began negotiating with federal agencies with the intention of learning how women workers could be employed by those agencies and of how needs could be communicated to the state organizations.

The government departments, however, were unwilling to cooperate. Even though there was obviously a need to retain the support of the women's organization and to treat women in war work fairly, it proved impossible to work out an effective organization based upon sex rather than function. Agencies such as the Food Administration and the Fuel Administration appointed their own state and local representatives; departments such as agriculture and labor worked out their own programs; and state councils of defense organized local activities for women with little coordination with the National Woman's Committee. The contribution of women to winning the war was formidable, but the role of the National Woman's Committee was secondary. The distinguished women of the committee recognized that their contributions were far less than their aspirations, but conscientiously maintained the facade of a workable organization knowing that if they should resign, they might well provoke disruption among the numerous women's organizations which they represented.

One of the most important achievements of the National Woman's Committee was in waging the "Children's Year Campaign" for the Children's Bureau of the Department of Labor. In this campaign Julia Lathrop of the Children's Bureau worked with Dr. Jessica B. Peixotto borrowed from the University of California to be executive chairperson of the Child Welfare Department of the National Woman's Committee. These two able women, defying the allegation that the welfare of babies was unessential to the war effort, organized a campaign to improve maternity care, assure enforcement of child labor laws, and provide adequate recreation for youths. They pointed to the example of Britain where during the first year of the war infant mortality skyrocketed without government attention but was brought under control by government action thereafter.

The National Woman's Committee informed the state divisions of the campaign on January 31, 1918, and in February suggested a plan of organization. The plan called for child welfare committees organized in state, county, and local units. The first goal of the campaign in 1918 was to cut down by one-third the projected death rate of children under six. According to statistics, 300,000 children of that age were expected to die in that year. The method was to weigh and measure the children, to make every effort to discover ailments, to report them to parents, and to attempt to see that the children received care. Some 7 million record cards were printed, and doctors and nurses gave their services. By January 1919 about 1.5 million records were in; some 16,811 communities had programs, and approximately 50 percent of the children were weighed and measured. The defects publicized by this campaign woke up many communities. It led to setting up new state divisions of child hygiene in 6 states, appointing new state superintendents of nurses in 5 states, adding 151 public health nurses in 24 states, and establishing new health centers and milk stations.

Just as Secretary of Labor Wilson was concerned about the effect of the employment of women upon the labor market after the war, the leaders of the trades unions were concerned about the effect of the war on labor's standards. By 1916, President Wilson's attitude toward organized labor had shifted radically from his earlier antiunion attitude. Thus he provided a seat for labor on the Advisory Commission for the Council of National Defense, and, following Secretary Wilson's recommendation, appointed Samuel Gompers to it. To appoint the president of the American Federation of Labor to a federal agency was a precedent in itself. To put him on the same board with Daniel Willard who had represented the railroad operators in the strikes of 1916 was considered dangerous. Gompers, courteous and eloquent, promptly put everyone at ease. Several days after their first meeting, Daniel Willard mused, "If anyone had told me that my personal antagonism toward Samuel Gompers would change within one week to ardent admiration and real affection, I would have pronounced that individual a fit candidate for an insane asylum."

Gompers, one-time pacifist, had been converted to the war effort, and by 1917 was "seething with revolt against the . . . Kaiser's ruthlessness." He was determined to marshal the forces of labor behind the war effort, and at the same time protect their interests, so long as they were laborers loyal to the AFL. An important conference, representative of the trades union movement, except for the IWW, was held on March 1, 1917, and resulted in a pledge to support the war effort if war with Germany should be declared. The pledge, nonetheless, insisted upon labor's right to organize and did not abandon its right to strike, but expressed the hope that disputes would be negotiated. Gompers was determined that the war would not be used as an excuse to lower hard-earned standards of labor. Such a threat was real. Several state legislatures, for example, authorized suspending labor laws under certain circumstances, and Congress authorized the president to suspend the eight-hour law on public contracts so long as time and a half were paid for overtime.

A good many consumer and labor groups viewed with rising concern such nibbling at labor standards. On March 23, 1917, the American Association for Labor Legislation, a professional organization whose president was Professor Irving Fisher of Yale, issued a call for the protection of workers during the war years. Maintain the existing standards, the Association insisted, of hours, child labor, woman's work, safety, one day of rest in seven, time and a half for overtime, wage standards in accord with living costs, and compensation for occupational diseases. Other groups such as the National Child Labor Committee and the National Consumers' League were equally solicitous.

Samuel Gompers saw to it that the question of labor standards was kept before the Council of National Defense. On the day war was declared he pushed through a resolution appealing to employers and employees not to use the emergency to force changes and urging state authorities to maintain existing standards. By September 1917, he had organized the American Alliance for Labor and Democracy with the obvious aim of combatting socialism and pacificism in the labor movement, even to the point of encouraging repression, while at the same time, hopefully, winning new gains for labor from the Wilson administration. Wilson supported Gompers' efforts. In November 1917 he spoke at the annual convention of the AFL, the first president to make this gesture, and brought the attending delegates to their feet with his assurance that "while we are fighting for freedom, we must see, among other things that labor is free." To support this pledge union members were appointed to numerous committees designed to help resolve some of the problems of the war effort, and a Labor Adjustment Commission of the Council of National Defense attempted to maintain jurisdiction over the hours of labor as required by federal eight-hour laws.

Except for the Labor Adjustment Commission, these committees had little power beyond that of investigation. Disputes increased in number, and serious threats to the war effort resulted. Many of these were worked out within existing agencies, and in some instances special agencies to resolve specific problems came into existence. The first of these was the establishment in June of the Cantonment Adjustment Commission to guarantee union standards in cantonment construction and to provide a representative three-person commission to settle controversies by agreement binding on all parties. Such arrangements, however, were only piecemeal solutions.

As early as April 1917 Gompers recommended to the Council of National Defense the creation of a centralized administration to cope with labor disputes, but the recommendation had become bogged down in controversy. In September 1917, however, the idea received a significant boost when the National Industrial Conference representing some 18,000 manufacturers, urged the appointment of a board similar to the one Gompers had recommended. The manufacturers pledged that they would not take advantage of the war to change conditions and agreed to abide by the decisions of the board. At the same time, several labor disputes inspired by the IWW in the Arizona copper mines, in the California oil fields, in the telephone system on the West Coast, and in the lumber industry were getting out of hand. Consequently on September 18, President Wilson appointed a special mediation commission with Secretary Wilson, as chairman, and Felix Frankfurter, an able young Harvard Law School graduate, as secretary not only to mediate in these and other specific disputes but to report on the causes of labor unrest.

The commission worked out solutions to the disputes and reported in January 1918. It concluded that the war had intensified old problems. It pointed to the need to eliminate profiteering and to accept the eight-hour day as a principle only to be broken in case of emergency. It emphasized that "some form of collective [rather than individual] relationship between management and men" was indispensable. It especially urged "continuous administrative machinery" to resolve differences before they should come to the surface and "a single-headed administration" to provide unity during the war. In the meantime the council had been discussing labor policy with representatives of the War and Navy Departments and other interested organizations, and on January 3, 1918, had recommended action to President Wilson. The president then requested Secretary Wilson to present a plan. Wilson in turn appointed a representative advisory committee consisting of seven members chaired by John Lind, former governor of Minnesota.

This committee took its responsibilities very seriously indeed. It recognized the need for machinery that would be representative and unprejudiced. It proposed the appointment of a war labor conference board of twelve persons, five representing the AFL and five representing the Industrial Conference Board. Each group in turn would select a public representative. This board would formulate a labor program. As Lind put it, this conference might prove to be "one of the most significant developments in the history of America's participation in the war." The public representatives chosen were Frank P. Walsh, outspoken advocate of labor reform and former head of the Industrial Relations Commission, and ex-President William Howard Taft. Late in March 1918, the board agreed unanimously on its report, the principal recommendation of which was for a national war labor board to serve for the duration of the war. This board would settle disputes, which affected the war effort, by mediation or conciliation, but might determine a settlement if voluntary agreement were impossible. It would not assume jurisdiction in areas where labor-management machinery already existed.

Not content with establishing machinery, the conference board outlined what amounted to a magna carta of labor: both employers and employees were to be guaranteed the right to organize and bargain collectively; employers were not to discharge workers for union activity, although unions were not to coerce workers to join up; health and safety regulations were to be observed; women were to enjoy equal pay for equal work; the eight-hour day was looked on as a norm; although local conditions would help determine labor standards, the right to a living wage sufficient to "insure the subsistence of the worker and his family in health and reasonable comfort" was proclaimed.

That there could be unanimous agreement in such a document was remarkable. That Taft, whose antilabor prejudices were well known, would agree was particularly noteworthy. Actually Taft bucked at the living wage, but Walsh, whom Taft came to respect, and W. Tilt Lauch, the secretary of the board, convinced him. Indeed Taft found himself in "curiously agreeable relations with the labor men." Some of the employers on the board were horrified at the "living wage" provisions and Taft agreed to "read the riot act" to them.

Secretary Wilson promptly recommended to the president that members of the conference board be appointed to the new National War Labor Board. Moreover since neither labor nor industry representatives could agree happily on a single head, Walsh and Taft were proposed as cochairmen with the understanding that they would preside alternately. The president announced the appointment of the board on April 8, 1918.

In the meantime, Secretary Wilson had become concerned by the labor problems faced by the increasing number of government agencies. Recognizing that each agency would attempt to solve its own problem in its own way, he created on May 13, 1918, a War Labor Policies Board chaired by Felix Frankfurter and consisting of representatives of government agencies engaged in the war effort. This board developed policies designed to control labor mobility, to provide uniform labor standards for men and women on government contracts, to regularize industrial exemptions from selective service, to stabilize wages, to prevent profiteering, and to make a survey of industrial plants which might be used in the war effort. The board continued its activities until March 1919.

The National War Labor Board was a precedent-making institution. It had no funds appropriated directly to it nor did it have congressional authorization. It did not have original jurisdiction over many important wartime areas. Yet it developed a prestige which justified its being thought of as an industrial supreme court. Its prestige was partly based upon public respect for its members and partly on the skill and efficiency with which its duties were performed. Public opinion soon proved a mighty force of support. However, its effectiveness was also a function of the fact that behind the board's facade was the presidential office and the president as commander in chief.

The board apparently did not foresee the burden of cases which would be placed upon it and hoped to hear all cases itself. However, in the 16 months of its existence 1,251 cases came before it, and it was impossible for one board to deal fairly with all of them. Thus the board divided itself into sections of one labor and one industrial representative to hear each case; decisions of each section were submitted to the board for final approval or, if a section did not agree, the case went to the board for decision. Soon, however, the burden upon sections became too great, and increasingly the Department of Examination, consisting of some 30 experienced examiners, carried out the hearings—serving complaints, summoning witnesses, performing investigations, analyzing and digesting evidence for the use of the board. Some 66 percent of the hearings were carried out by the examiners. The evidence was then submitted to the board for its final decision.

The board thus worked out its procedure as it went along. The board itself did not act as a "conciliatory agency." The local investigators and examiners served in that capacity, and at least 116 cases were settled voluntarily before reaching the board. However, the board did serve as a court to decide cases. If it concluded that jurisdiction should lie within another agency, the cases were appropriately referred. Three hundred and fifteen cases fell into this category. If, following a complaint, both parties agreed to abide by the board's decision, the issue was quite clear— and a state of almost compulsory arbitration existed. One hundred ninety- nine cases fell into this category. In cases where one party refused to accept arbitration, a decision need be only by majority and constituted little more than a recommendation. In fact, however, the standing of the board was so great and the support from other government agencies so assured that few cases resulted in serious controversy. About half the cases before the board involved disputes over wages; next in order of priority was the question of hours; followed by the problem of discrim- ination against workers for union affiliation; and then a whole range of miscellaneous issues such as working conditions and the rights of women.

The questions of "a living wage" and union recognition probably were the most sensitive ones. Actually the board never arrived at a clear-cut decision as to what constituted a living wage but simply made its decision in specific cases usually depending upon local conditions—not, however, upon the employer's ability to pay. In these cases, Taft's position became significant. Originally suspicious of complaints about low wages, he personally conducted hearings involving southern textile mills, munitions factories, and scrubwomen employed by the General Electric Company. In each case, he supported the plea for higher wages—"How can people live on such wages?" he queried, before recommending the tripling of wages in certain southern textile mills.

In only three significant cases was there clear-cut defiance of the decisions of the board. One of these involved the Western Union Company in which the company had fired some 450 employees for union activity. They complained to the board; the board investigated; the president of the company, although willing to arbitrate the question of wages and hours, was not willing to rehire the discharged men unless a majority of his workers indicated a willingness to join the union. Taft concluded that such a position "denied to the minority of some 10,000 workers the right to join" a union. In the course of the board's consideration of this case, it became clear that it would not enforce a yellow-dog contract by which a worker would agree not to join a union as a condition of employment. Western Union refused to accept the decision of the board which called for reinstatement of the workers if they would agree not to strike. Whereupon President Wilson promptly urged the company to agree; and when the company refused, Congress authorized taking over the telephones and telegraph lines for the duration of the war.

The president took equally vigorous action with respect to the Smith and Wesson Company of Springfield, Massachusetts. As the President put it, that company "refused to accept the mediation of the . . . board and . . . flaunted its rules of decision approved by presidential proclamation." He, therefore, promptly authorized the War Department to commandeer the plant. In the third case, several thousand machinists engaged in war work at Bridgeport, Connecticut, refused to abide by the decision of the arbitrator provided by the National War Labor Board. Wilson denounced the strike against the award of the board as "a breach of faith . . . disloyalty and dishonor." He informed the workers that if they did not return to work, they would be barred for a period of one year from employment in any war industry in the community in which the strike had occurred. "During that time," he went on, "the United States Employment Service will decline to obtain employment for you in any war industry elsewhere in the United States, as well as under . . . all other Government agencies, and the draft boards will be instructed to reject any claim of exemption based on your alleged usefulness on war production."

The board proved to be a hardworking, indispensable agency. Its influence far transcended the more than 1,200 cases which were submitted to it, and the "138 recorded instances" in which the board averted strikes. Frequently a decision served as an example which was accepted by other comparable companies, and other adjustment boards used decisions of the board as models. The work of the board continued for several months after the war's end, but its influence declined "partly from lack of interest." On August 12, 1919, it held its last meeting.

Unfortunately there was an underside to labor relations during the war which did not reflect the sweet reasonableness of the National War Labor Board. The wartime atmosphere stimulated opposition to radicalism; radicalism could easily be identified with subversion; and certain employers, particularly in the western mines, timberlands, and even in the wheat fields were not above making use of the crisis to break the Industrial Workers of the World. Indeed this was a goal which attracted numerous allies among local and state officials, local federal attorneys, even AFL affiliates. Ironically, suffering from local repression, the IWW's led by Big Bill Haywood turned to the federal government for aid: as Melvin Dubofsky put it, to "the Capitalist laws they condemned, the public officials they ridiculed, and the President they despised."

Instead of help, the IWW's met with further repression. Although employer prejudices no doubt had their influences, the main aim of federal action was to prevent all actions obstructive to the war effort. Thus federal troops were assigned to protect utilities, railroads, mines, western farms, and forests. The Wobblies' own words, carefully selected, were used against them, and the Justice Department undoubtedly was determined to wipe them out. Even the Labor Department, although convinced that lumberers and miners had legitimate grievances, favored eliminating the Wobblies and substituting AFL affiliates. Felix Frankfurter, as secretary of a commission appointed to deal with labor unrest in the West there performed brilliantly, worked out solutions, but solutions which undermined the IWW's. The workers, no doubt, were confused. On the one hand they were being repressed by local officials and federal soldiers and arrested by federal officials, while on the other they were being assured by the Labor Department's representatives and the National War Labor Board that their rights would be protected. Such ambivalence boded ill for Gomper's hopes of maintaining labor's gains after the war.

Bibliography

This chapter makes only passing reference to the actual fighting fronts. For those interested in that aspect of the war, see Edward M. Coffman, *The War to End All Wars: The American Military Experience in World War I* (1968); Harvey Arthur DeWeerd, *President Wilson Fights His War: World War I and the American Intervention* (1968); and S. L. A. Marshall, *The American Heritage History of World War I* (1964). An important effort to weave togather the overseas activities with those at home is Frederick L. Paxson, *American Democracy and the World War:* vol. II, *America at War, 1917–1918* (1939). The following general works are used extensively throughout the chapter: Grosvenor B. Clarkson, *Industrial America in the World War, Strategy Behind the Line, 1917–1918* (1923); Marvin A. Kriedberg and Norton G. Henry, *History of Military Mobilization in the United States Army, 1775–1945* (1955); Seward W. Livermore, *Politics Is Adjourned: Woodrow Wilson and the War Congress, 1916–1918* (1966); George Soule, *Prosperity Decade: From War to Depression, 1917–1929* (1947); H. J. Tobin and Percy W. Bidwell, *Mobilizing Civilian America* (1940); Russell F. Weigley, *History of the United States Army* (1967); William F. Willoughby, *Government Organization in Wartime and After, A Survey of the Federal Civil Agencies Created For the Prosecution of the War* (1919).

The following government documents were likewise used extensively throughout this chapter:

The Annual Reports of the Secretary of War and of the Secretary of the Navy. These documents include reports and statistical tables from the various subdivisions of the army and the navy.

Minutes of the War Industries Board, August 1, 1917–December 19, 1918. 74th Cong., 1st sess. (1935), Senate Committee prints Nos. 4 and 5.

Minutes of the Council of National Defense, 74th Cong., 2d sess. (1936), Senate Committee print No. 7.

Minutes of the Advisory Commission of the Council of National Defense and Minutes of the Munitions Standards Board, 74th Cong., 2d sess. (1936), Senate Committee print No. 8.

Minutes of the General Munitions Board from April 4 to August 9, 1917, 74th Cong., 2d sess. (1936), Senate Committee Print No. 6.

Final Report of the Chairman of the War Industries Board . . . February, 1919 (1935), 74th Cong., 1st sess., Senate Committee print No. 3.

Digest of the Proceedings of the Council of National Defense . . . Senate Document 193, 73d Cong., 2d sess.

Frederick Lewis Allen, "The Council of National Defense Systems," May 9, 1919, unpublished manuscript in the National Archives, a microfilm used through the kindness of Dr. William Breen.

Page 219
On the point of Wilson's concern about war, see Jerold S. Auerbach, "Woodrow Wilson's 'Prediction' to Frank Cobb: Words Historians Should Doubt Ever Got Spoken," *Journal of American History,* 54 (December 1967), 608–617, and the discussion between Auerbach and Arthur S. Link in *ibid.,* 55 (June 1968), 231–238. For the vote on war, see Link, *Wilson: Campaigns for Progressivism and Peace* (1965), p. 429. For dissenting views see Alex M. Arnett, *Claude Kitchin and the Wilson War Policies* (1937).

Pages 219–220
On reformers and the war, see Allen F. Davis, "Welfare, Reform, and World War I," *American Quarterly,* 19 (Fall 1967), 516–533; Walter I. Trattner, "Progressivism and World War I, a Re-appraisal," *Mid-America,* 44 (July 1962), 131–145; Charles Hirschfeld, "Nationalist Progressivism and World War I," *ibid.,* 45 (July 1963), 139–156.

Page 220
For the internal mobilization of European countries, see Frank P. Chambers, *The War Behind the War, 1914–1918; A History of the Political and Civilian Fronts* (1939).

Pages 220-221

For early interest in a Council of National Defense, see *House Report,* No. 2078, 61st Cong., 3d sess.; and particularly Robert D. Cuff's ground-breaking *The War Industries Board: Business-Government Relations During World War I* (1973). For the Navy League, see Armin Rappaport, *The Navy League of the United States* (1962); for Secretary Daniels' interest in mobilization, see *Report of the Secretary of the Navy,* 1915. For Coffin and the Committee on Industrial Preparedness and the organization of the Council of National Defense, see William J. Breen, "The Council of National Defense: Industrial and Social Mobilization in the United States, 1916–1920," unpub. doctoral diss. (Duke University, 1968); Theodore A. Thelander, "Josephus Daniels and the Publicity Campaign for Naval and Industrial Preparedness Before World War I," *North Carolina Historical Review,* 43 (Summer 1966), 316–332.

Pages 221-222

On the early military planning, see also Daniel R. Beaver, *Newton D. Baker and the American War Effort, 1917–1919* (1966), pp. 23–24; John M. Palmer, *America in Arms: The Experience of the United States with Military Organization* (1941), pp. 135–154. The inadequacy of the planning staff is brought out in Frederick M. Palmer, *Newton D. Baker, America at War,* 2 vols. (1931), and Edward M. Coffman, *The Hilt of the Sword; The Career of Peyton C. March* (1966), an excellent biography.

Pages 222-226

For Selective Service, see David A. Lockmiller, *Enoch M. Crowder: Soldier, Lawyer, Statesman* (1955); Beaver, *Newton D. Baker,* pp. 26–30; Link, *Wilson: Campaigns for Progressivism and Peace,* p. 424. For comments on the idea of conscription, see *Literary Digest,* 54 (April 21, 1917), 1147–1148. For minority views, see *House Report,* No. 17, pt. 2, 65th Cong., 1st sess. For Kahn's comments, see *Congressional Record,* 65th Cong., 1st sess. (April 27, 1917), pp. 1368–1376. The conference report passed the Senate on March 17 with 65 ayes, 8 nays, and 23 not voting. *Congressional Record,* 65th Cong., 1st sess., pp. 2457, 1500. The La Follette quotation was taken from Lockmiller, *Crowder,* p. 158. For the preparations for the passage of the act, see Lockmiller, *Crowder,* pp. 157–165; Palmer, *Baker,* I, 212–213. For reactions to registration, see *Literary Digest,* 54 (May 26, 1917), 1580, and (June 16, 1917), 1830; Beaver, *Baker,* pp. 33–37; and especially Robert W. Dubay, "The Opposition to Selective Service, 1916–1918," *Southern Quarterly,* 7 (April 1969), 301–322.

Pages 226-227

The selective Draft Law Cases are 245 U.S. *Reports* 366–390. For the Webster quotation, see Louis Smith, *American Democracy and Military*

Power; A Study of Civil Control of the Military Power in the United States (1951), 289.

Pages 227–238

For general works that relate to financing the war, and general fiscal and monetary policy during this period, see especially Elmus R. Wicker, *Federal Reserve Monetary Policy, 1917–1933* (1966), chap. I, and Paul Studenski and Herman E. Krooss, *Financial History of the United States,* 2d ed. (1963), chap. 23. Cf. Ernest L. Bogart, *War Costs and Their Financing* (1921). See also Charles Gilbert, *American Financing of World War I* (1970); for the specific activities of the Treasury, see *The Annual Reports of the Secretary of the Treasury;* William G. McAdoo, *Crowded Years, the Reminiscences of William G. McAdoo* (1931); and *American Year Book,* 1917, 1918, 1919.

Page 228

For European experience and precedents in the United States, see Paul Einzig, *World Finance, 1914–1935* (1935).

Pages 229–231

The key men in Congress were Claude Kitchin of North Carolina, majority leader of the House and chairman of the Committee on Ways and Means, and F. M. Simmons, also of North Carolina, chairman of the Senate Committee on Finance. See Alex M. Arnett, *Claude Kitchin and the Wilson War Policies* (1937), and Fred J. Rippy, ed., *Furnifold M. Simmons, Statesman of the New South, Memoirs and Addresses* (1936). For McAdoo's meeting with congressional leadership, see *New York Times,* April 8, 1917, I, p. 1; for the congressional debates, see *Congressional Record,* 65th Cong., 1st sess., pp. 626, 640, 690, 746–747, 750, 757, 765–769.

Pages 231–234

For the first tax measure, see House Report, No. 45, 65th Cong., 1st sess.; *Congressional Record,* 65th Cong., 1st sess., pp. 2303, 2343, 2712–2777, 5963–5964, 5971, 6245–6246, 6270–6288, 6503, 6538–6561. The Senate Committee's own amendment providing for an excess profits tax passed 71 to 7. Bankhead, Borah, Gronna, Johnson, La Follette, Underwood, and Vardaman voted nay. *Ibid.,* pp. 6854–6856, 7633. See also *Nation,* 105 (September 6, 1917), 249; *New Republic,* 12 (September 15, 1917), 175; *Cleveland Press* in the *Literary Digest* (October 13, 1917), p. 14.

Pages 234–235

For conditions creating uncertainty in the investment market, see *Congressional Record,* 65th Cong., 2d sess., pp. 2778–2781; For the War Finance Corporation and the Capital Issues Committee in general, see *Reports of the Secretary of the Treasury,* 1917, 1918, and 1919;

Woodbury Willoughby, *The Capital Issues Committee and War Finance Corporation* (1934), pp. 16–21, 65; *American Year Book,* 1918 and 1919.

Pages 235–237

For the legislation, see *Congressional Record,* 65th Cong., 2d sess., pp. 2605, 3041, 3050, 3081–3083, 3096, 3141, 3842. The three senators opposed were Harding (Rep.) from Ohio, Hardwick (Dem.) from Georgia, and Sherman (Rep.) from Illinois. *Ibid.,* p. 3151.

Pages 237–238

Report of the War Finance Corporation, House Document No. 1387, 65th Cong., 3d sess.; *Report of the Capital Issues Committee, House Document* No. 1485, 65th Cong., 3d sess. (December 3, 1918).

Pages 238–248

The following monographs are basic sources for several of the topics covered within this section: Zechariah Chaffee, Jr., *Free Speech in the United States* (1941); Donald Johnson, *The Challenge to American Freedoms; World War I and the Rise of the American Civil Liberties Union* (1963); Charles Kellogg, *NAACP: A History of the National Association for the Advancement of Colored People* (1967); H. C. Peterson and Gilbert C. Fite, *Opponents of War, 1917–1918* (1957); and Harry N. Scheiber, *The Wilson Administration and Civil Liberties, 1917–1921* (1960). I also made extensive use of the annual reports of the Attorney General.

Pages 238–240

For Wilson's attitudes, see Link, *Wilson: Confusions and Crisis, 1915–1916* (1964), p. 36; and John M. Blum, *Joe Tumulty and the Wilson Era* (1951). For the position of the General Staff, see *Report of the Chief of Staff,* 1915 and 1916; for George Creel, see *How We Advertised America* (1920). For the educational program of the CPI, see Lewis P. Todd, *Wartime Relations of the Federal Government and the Public Schools, 1917–1918* (1945).

Pages 240–242

For the Wilson quotations, see Johnson, *The Challenge to American Freedoms,* p. 54. On the Espionage Act, see *Congressional Record,* 65th Cong., 1st sess., pp. 3144, 1816, 1819, 1841, 3145. The *New York Times* is quoted in Ray Stannard Baker, *Woodrow Wilson: Life and Letters,* 8 vols. (1927–1939), VII, 51. In the House also, an overwhelming number of Republicans opposed the censorship section while the Democrats almost equally overwhelmingly supported it. See *House Report,* No. 30, 65th Cong., 1st sess.; and *Congressional Record,* 65th Cong., 1st sess., pp. 831 et seq., and 2269–2270. For enforcement, see *Literary Digest,* 54 (April 7, 1917), 968, and 55 (September 1, 1917), 10; *Con-*

gressional Record, 65th Cong., 1st sess., p. 7020; Todd, *Wartime Relations of the Government and the Schools,* pp. 71–85.

Pages 242–243
On conscientious objection, see *Survey,* 26 (April 1, 1916), 37, and (April 22, 1916), 95–96; Beaver, *Baker,* pp. 231–233; Norman Thomas, *The Conscientious Objector in America* (1923).

Pages 243–246
The most comprehensive work on black people in World War I is Emmett J. Scott, *Scott's Official History of The American Negro in the World War* (1919); for statistics, see pp. 66–74. In 1918, 3,203 blacks were in the regular navy and an additional 2,000 in the naval reserve. *Report of the Secretary of the Navy,* 1918, p. 453. For statistics on lynching, see *World Almanacs;* for data on black workers in the South and conditions in the North, see J. H. Dillard, ed., *Negro Migration in 1916–1917* (1919); for comments on migrations, see *Literary Digest,* 54 (June 23, 1917), 1914. For the *Chicago Tribune* quotation, see *Literary Digest,* 44 (June 23, 1917), 1914. On attempts to improve relations, see *Report of the Secretary of Labor,* 1918, pp. 111–113; and *ibid.,* 1919, pp. 132–133. On Wilson's reluctance, see Beaver, *Baker,* pp. 228–230, and Jane L. and Harry N. Scheiber, "The Wilson Administration and the Wartime Mobilization of Black Americans, 1917–1918," *Labor History,* 10 (Summer 1969), 433–458.

Pages 247–248
On the Trading-with-the-Enemy Act, see *Congressional Record,* 65th Cong., 1st sess., p. 7421. Only one record vote was taken in either house: in the Senate on the final vote, Cummins of Iowa, France of Maryland, Johnson of California, Kirby of Arkansas, Norris of Nebraska, and Watson of Georgia voted nay. On censorship, see James R. Mock, *Censorship,* 1917 (1941); Report of the Postmaster General, 1918; Donald O. Johnson, "Wilson, Burleson, and Censorship in the First World War," *Journal of Southern History,* 28 (February 1962), 46–58. Burleson's quotation is in Scheiber, *The Wilson Administration and Civil Liberties,* p. 32; see also Baker's *Woodrow Wilson,* VII, 165. On the Sedition Act in Congress, see *Congressional Record,* 65th Cong., 2d sess., pp. 6056–6057, 6186.

Pages 248–250
For food statistics, see *Historical Statistics . . . to 1957,* p. 126. Basic sources for this chapter are William C. Mullendore, *History of the United States Food Administration, 1917–1919* (1941), and Herbert Hoover, *The Memoirs of Herbert Hoover; Years of Adventure, 1874–1920* (1951); *Reports of the Secretary of Agriculture* provides data about agricultural production. For Hoover's appointment, see Charles Seymour, ed., *The Intimate Papers of Colonel House* (1928), III, 16–17; Baker, *Woodrow Wilson,* VII, 5.

Page 250

For the activities of the Department of Agriculture, see *Report of the Department of Agriculture,* 1917; F. L. Allen, "The Council of National Defense Systems," pp. 28ff.

Pages 251–252

The quotations from the press are in *Literary Digest,* 55 (August 1, 1917), 9. The congressional debates are significant; see, for example, *Congressional Record,* 65th Cong., 1st sess., p. 5922. For Wilson's opposition to a board, see Baker, *Woodrow Wilson,* VII, 191 and 199. For the vote in the Senate, see *Congressional Record,* 65th Cong., 1st sess., pp. 5766–5767, 5926–5927. The negative votes were France of Maryland, Gronna of North Dakota, Hardwick of Georgia, Hollis of New Hampshire, La Follette of Wisconsin, Penrose of Pennsylvania, and Reed of Missouri. See also Paxson, II.

Page 252.

For the activities of the Food Administration, see also William R. Johnson, "Herbert Hoover and the Regulation of Grain Futures," *Mid-America,* 51 (July 1969), 155–174; Frank M. Surface, *The Grain Trade During the World War* (1928).

Pages 252–254

For the discussion of the price control issue, see Charles W. Baker, *Government Control and Operation of Industry in Great Britain and the United States During the World War* (1921), pp. 94–99, and Tom G. Hall, "Wilson and the Food Crisis: Agriculture Price Control during World War I," *Agricultural History,* 47 (January 1973), 25–46; for the Wallaces, see Russell Lord, *The Wallaces of Iowa* (1947); Frank M. Surface, *American Pork Production in the World War* (1926) and *The Stabilization of the Price of Wheat during the War . . .* (1925); Seward W. Livermore, "The Sectional Issue in the 1918 Congressional Elections," *Mississippi Valley Historical Review,* 35 (June 1948), 29–60, a seminal article. See also Benjamin H. Hubbard, *Effects of the Great War Upon Agriculture in the United States and Great Britain* (1919), pp. 120–126. Finally, check Craig Lloyd, *Aggressive Introvert; A Study of Herbert Hoover and Public Relations Management, 1912–1932* (1972).

Pages 254–259

Much of the data from this section is taken from *Report of the U.S. Fuel Administration,* 1917, and H. A. Garfield, *Final Report of the United States Fuel Administrator, 1917–1919* (1921). The quotation is from the *Final Report,* p. 7. The coal problem is considered in William Notz, "The World's Coal Situation during the War," *Journal of Political Economy,* 26 (June 1918), 567–611, and (July 1918), 673–704; the Federal Trade Commission made a critical study of the coal industry. *Report of the Federal Trade Commission on Anthracite and Bituminous Coal,*

June 20, 1917. For attitudes toward the coal crisis, see *Literary Digest,* 55 (July 7, 1917), 19; *New York Times,* June 28 and 29, 1917; Beaver, *Baker,* pp. 64–65.

Pages 255–256

For Representative Robbins' remarks, see *Congressional Record,* 65th Cong., 1st sess., pp. 5762–5764. On the appointment and philosophy of Garfield, see Notz, pp. 690–694; *Report of the Administrative Division, Fuel Administration, 1917–1919* (1920).

Pages 256–257

For labor relations, see *Report of the Bureau of Labor of the United States Fuel Administration,* January 6, 1919; William Green, "America's Coal Miners on Duty," *American Federationist,* 25 (October 1918), 889–893.

Pages 258–259

An excellent analysis that puts the period of the war in proper perspective is Gerald D. Nash, *United States Oil Policy, 1890–1964: Business and Government in Twentieth Century America* (1968). For oil production, see *Report of Secretary of the Navy,* 1915, pp. 62–63, and 1917, pp. 58–59. Joseph E. Pogue, *Prices of Petroleum and Its Products During the War, U.S. Fuel Administration* (1919), pp. 32–33. For the value of oil products, see *Report of the General Director of the Oil Division,* U.S. Fuel Administration, December 20, 1918, p. 262; for cooperation with the Council of National Defense, see Clarkson, *Industrial America in the World War,* pp. 29, 499–500. On Requa and his program, see *Report of the General Director of the Oil Division,* U.S. Fuel Administration, including Exhibit A; Mark Requa, *The Relation of Government to Industry* (1925).

Pages 259–266

The general works that cover in different degrees of detail the subject of this section in addition to those already cited are: F. H. Dixon, *Railroads and Government: Their Relations in the United States, 1910–1921* (1922); Walker D. Hines (for a time the director general of the railroads), *War History of the American Railroads* (1928); and the most recent and most analytical account, K. Austin Kerr, *American Railroad Politics, 1914–1920: Rates, Wages, and Efficiency* (1968). For a careful administrative study of the railroads, see Kevin Byrne, "The U.S. Railway Administration: An Administrative History," unpub. doctoral diss. (Duke University, 1974). See also William J. Cunningham, "The Railroads under Government Operation . . .," *Quarterly Journal of Economics,* 35 (February 1921), 288–340; the *American Year Book,* 1917, 1918, 1919.

Pages 259–260

For an example of congressional discussion on waterways, see *Congressional Record,* 65th Cong., 2d sess., p. 2513. The entire section on inland waterways is based on *Report of the Chief of Inland and Coastwise Waterways Service to the Secretary of War, 1920* (1920).

Pages 260–261

On trucking, see Report of the Motor Transport Corps in *Annual Report of the Secretary of War,* 1919; Report of the Quartermaster General in *Annual Report of the Secretary of War,* 1917, pp. 313–318. For the statistics on trucks, see National Automobile Chamber of Commerce, *Facts and Figures of the Automobile Industry,* 1921; cf., figures in *Final Report of the War Industries Board,* pp. 769–773. See also George W. Grupp, *Economics of Motor Transportation* (1923), p. 375. For the compliment to the industry, see *American Year Book,* 1918, p. 604. On highways, see *Report of the Secretary of Agriculture,* 1918, pp. 40–41 and 1919, pp. 394–395.

Pages 262–264

For freight revenues, see *Historical Statistics . . . to 1957,* p. 431; *American Year Book,* 1915, p. 540. For the hearings, see *Interstate and Foreign Transportation,* Hearings before a Joint Subcommittee on Interstate and Foreign Commerce, Congress, Pursuant to . . . [S. J. Res. 60] . . . November 20, 1916–[December 19, 1917]; Minority Report of House Committee on Interstate and Foreign Commerce, in *House Report,* No. 294, pt. 2, 65th Cong., 2d sess.

Pages 264–266

Wilson's proclamation is quoted in Hines, pp. 245–247. Press comment from the *Literary Digest,* 55 (December 22, 1917), 7–8, (December 29, 1917), 112, and 56 (January 5, 1918), 7. For railroad legislation, see *Congressional Record,* 65th Cong., 2d sess., pp. 2198–2199, 2267, 2434, 2202–2208, 2436, 2336–2337, 3500. See also the Minority Report, Senate Committee on Interstate Commerce, *Report* No. 246, pt. 2, 65th Cong., 2d sess.

Aaron A. Godfrey, *Government Operation of the Railroads: Its Necessity, Success, and Consequences, 1918–1920* (1974) came out too late to be used in writing this section. Godfrey's general conclusions were that the Railroad Administration met the needs of the emergency successfully, but did not fulfill the "extravagant predictions" for economies that McAdoo and others expected from unification under government control.

Pages 266–277

General scholarly works on shipping during World War I are few although government documents are rich in source material. See especially *Report of the War Trade Board and the U.S. Shipping Board.* Paxson and Soule put the Shipping Board and the War Trade Board in context, and for the politics of shipping, see Jeffrey J. Safford, "The United States

Merchant Marine and American Commercial Expansion, 1860–1920,"
unpub. doctoral diss. (Rutgers University, 1968). See also *American
Year Book* 1914–1919 for comprehensive articles and detailed statistics.

Page 267-270

For the shipping losses and means of trade control, see Arthur S. Salter,
Allied Shipping Control; An Experiment in International Administration
(1921), pp. 12, 102–108, 354, 356. On Vance McCormick, see *New York
Times,* June 17, 1946. For the *New York Tribune* quotation, see *Literary
Digest,* 55 (October 27, 1917), 7–9.

Pages 270-272

For commentary on the membership of the Shipping Board and the
controversies that developed, see *New York Times,* December 23, 1916;
January 28, 1917; April 29, 1917, Section VI; June 9, 1917; and July
17, 1917; Bernard N. Baker, "The Importance of an American Merchant
Marine," *Annals of the American Academy . . . ,* 60 (July 1915), 52–57;
Joseph B. and Farnham Bishop, *Goethals, Genius of the Panama Canal;
A Biography* (1930), pp. 274–278, 287–293, 305–312, 329–364. U.S.
Senate, Committee on Commerce, *Hearings on . . . U.S. Shipping Board,
Emergency Fleet Corporation,* December 21, 1917, 75th Cong., 2d sess.,
I, 1065–1069, 1097–1117, 484–514, 11–15; *Literary Digest,* 54 (June 9,
1917), 1768; U.S. Congress, *House Report,* No. 1399, 66th Cong., 3d
sess., p. 4; *Congressional Record,* 65th Cong., 1st sess. (May 18, 1917),
pp. 1645, 2512–2513, 2519–2527, 3540, 3550, 3278; for Denman's
statement, see *ibid.,* pp. 6051–6054; and for Wilson's request for Denman's
resignation, see *Congressional Record,* 65th Cong., 1st sess., p. 6053.

Pages 272-273

For the accomplishments of the Shipping Board under Denman, see
New York Times, July 25, 1917; "A Great American Mercantile Marine
for the War Emergency," *Current History,* 7 (1917), 17–20; D. H. Smith
and Paul V. Betters, *United States Shipping Board; It's History, Activities
and Organization* (1931), p. 71; Edward N. Hurley, *The Bridge to France*
(1927), p. 41; *Hearings . . . U.S. Shipping Board,* I, 1103–1104; *House
Report,* No. 394, 65th Cong., 2d sess., pp. 15, 19.

Page 273

On Hurley, see *Literary Digest,* 57 (April 6, 1918), 70; Hurley, *Awakening of Business* (1916). Hurley worked successfully with Goethals'
successor Admiral W. L. Capps. See also *Current Opinion,* 63 (November
1917), 306–307; *Hearings . . . U.S. Shipping Board,* I, 16–17.

Pages 273-275

On Hurley's policies, see *New York Times,* August 5, 1917; Hurley,
The Bridge to France. On standardization, see Bishop, p. 344; Edwin
Wildman, "Edward N. Hurley—Shipbuilder to Uncle Sam," *Forum,* 59

(April 1918), 411–423; on Hog Island, see "The World's Greatest Ship-yard," *Current History,* 8 (1918), 23–24; U.S. Senate, Committee on Commerce, *Hearings . . . U.S. Shipping Board,* 65th Cong., 3d sess., pt. 4, p. 40. For Vardaman's attack, see *Congressional Record,* 65th Cong., 3d sess., pp. 4852–4854, and for the defense, see *Hearings . . . U.S. Shipping Board,* 65th Cong., 3d sess. (January 30, 1919), pt. 8; see also William N. Thurston, "Management-Leadership in the United States Shipping Board, 1917–1918," *American Neptune,* 32 (July 1972), 155–170.

Pages 275–276

On Schwab, see Hurley, *The Bridge to France,* pp. 138–141; *New York Times,* July 5 and 6, 1918. On the importance of Edwin Gay, see Soule, *Prosperity Decade,* p. 32; Hurley, *The Bridge to France,* pp. 108–109; Clarkson, pp. 200–201.

Pages 276–277

For final conclusions and statistical summary of the activities of the U.S. Shipping Board, see U.S. Senate, Document No. 210, 65th Cong., 2d sess.; U.S. Shipping Board, *Fifth Annual Report;* U.S. Senate, Committee on Commerce, *Hearings on . . . the U.S. Shipping Board,* 65th Cong., 3d sess., pp. 3–51; *Report of Director General Charles Piez to Board of Trustees of Shipping Board Emergency Fleet Corporation,* April 30, 1919.

Pages 277–291

Although the usual references to Clarkson, Livermore, Soule, and Paxson apply for the War Industries Board, that agency has also had scholarly treatment in depth. A critical, yet authoritative general study is Robert D. Cuff, *The War Industries Board.*

Pages 277–279

Quotation from the *London Times* is in Charles W. Baker, *Government Control and Operation of Industry in Great Britain and the United States during the World War* (1921), p. 31. The early complications of industrial mobilization are described in Robert D. Cuff, "Bernard Baruch: Symbol and Myth in Industrial Mobilization," *Business History Review,* 43 (Summer 1969), 115–133; Melvin I. Urofsky, *Big Steel and the Wilson Administration; A Study in Business-Government Relations* (1969); Beaver, *Baker,* p. 71; Edward M. Coffman, "The Battle Against Red Tape: Business Methods of the War Department General Staff, 1917–1918," *Military Affairs,* 26 (Spring 1962), 1–10; Paul A. C. Koistinen, "The 'Industrial-Military Complex' in Historical Perspective: World War I," *Business History Review,* 41 (Winter 1967), 376–403; Joseph Henry Foth, *Trade Associations, Their Services to Industry* (1930), pp. 3–35; Cuff, "Woodrow Wilson and Business-Government Relations during World War I," *Review of Politics,* 31 (July 1969), 385–407.

Pages 279–280
On Baruch, see also Bernard Baruch, *Baruch: The Public Years* (1960), pp. 1, 21–23, 38–39; Curtice N. Hitchcock, "The War Industries Board: Its Development, Organization, and Functions," *Journal of Political Economy,* 26 (June 1918), 545–566.

Pages 280–281
For the events leading up to the establishment of the War Industries Board, see also Daniel R. Beaver, "Newton D. Baker and the Genesis of the War Industries Board, 1917–1918," *Journal of American History,* 52 (June 1965), 43–58.

Pages 281–282
For the complex government-business relations which developed under the War Industries Board, see especially Cuff, *The War Industries Board* and also "A 'Dollar-a-Year Man' in Government: George N. Peek and the War Industries Board," *Business History Review,* 41 (Winter 1967), 404–420; cf. Koistinen.

Pages 282–284
For the growing criticism of the board and the counterattack, see Beaver, "Baker and the War Industries Board," pp. 51–54; Edward M. Coffman, "The Battle Against Red Tape," *Military Affairs,* 26 (Spring 1962), 1–10; Koistinen, pp. 396–398; Urofsky, *Big Steel and the Wilson Administration,* pp. 212ff.

Page 284
For the letter appointing Baruch, see Wilson to Baruch, March 4, 1918, in Clarkson, pp. 49–50.

Pages 285–286
On price control, see Simon Litman, *Prices and Price Control in Britain and the United States during the World War* (1920), pp. 203–205.

Pages 286–287
On priorities and commandeering, see Randall B. Kester, "The War Industries Board, 1917–1918: A Study in Industrial Mobilization," *American Political Science Review,* 34 (August 1940), 655–684.

Pages 287–289
On controversies between business and the War Industries Board, see Baruch, *The Public Years,* pp. 59–79; Urofsky, *Big Steel and the Wilson Administration,* pp. 207–216. On industrial conservation, see Baruch, *The Public Years,* p. 73.

Pages 289–291
On the question of conversion, see Arthur Fontaine, *French Industry During the War,* abridged ed. (1926), p. 282; Leonard P. Ayers, *The War with Germany: A Statistical Summary,* 2nd ed. (1919), pp. 66–67, 71,

80, 81, 88, 95; for the details on ordnance, see Report of the Chief of Ordnance, 1919, pp. 3871–3872, 3911–3915; *ibid.,* 1918, p. 1052; Robert D. Cuff, "A 'Dollar-a-Year-Man' in Government: George N. Peek and the War Industries Board," *Business History Review,* 41 (Winter 1967), 404–420.

For a summary of the still unresolved question of the role of the General Staff, see Edward M. Coffman, *The War to End All Wars: The American Military Experience in World War I* (1968), pp. 165–167; Beaver, Baker, chaps. 6 and 7; Edward M. Coffman, *The Hilt of the Sword: The Career of Peyton C. March* (1966); Baruch, *Public Years,* pp. 72–73.

Pages 291–292

Basic sources for this section are the annual reports of the secretary of labor, Don D. Lescohier and Elizabeth Brandeis, *History of Labor in the United States, 1896–1933, Working Conditions* (1935), and more specifically Gordon S. Watkins, *Labor Problems and Labor Administration in the United States During the World War* (1920); Samuel Gompers, *American Labor and the War* (1919); and John S. Smith, "Organized Labor and Government in the Wilson Era, 1913–1921: Some Conclusions," *Labor History,* 3 (Fall 1962). The Wilson quotation is from the *Annual Report of the Secretary of Labor,* 1918, p. 11; the data on wages and prices is from the *Final Report of the Commission on Industrial Relations,* I, 30–31; *Bulletin of the U.S. Bureau of Labor Statistics,* No. 270, pp. 44–47; 62, 66, 463–464; Paul H. Douglas, *Real Wages in the United States, 1890–1926* (1930), p. 116.

Page 292

The detail on employers' organizations and Massachusetts is from *American Year Book,* 1916, pp. 428–438, and *ibid.,* 1917, p. 426.

Pages 292–294

On cantonments, see *Report of the Secretary of War,* 1917, pp. 27–35; Alexander M. Bing, *War-time Strikes and their Adjustment* (1921), pp. 20–21. For the efforts to solve labor problems, see also John R. Commons and John B. Andrews, *Principles of Labor Legislation* (1927), pp. 151–154; *Report of the Commission of Mediation and Conciliation, 1913–1919,* pp. 5–25.

Pages 294–297

On agricultural labor and women, see the Official Bulletin of the Department of Labor, January 24, 1918; and especially F. L. Allen, "Council of National Defense"; and also *New York Times,* February 4, 7, March 5, 10, 13, and 30, 1917.

Pages 297–302

On Gompers and the development of governmental labor policy, see Samuel Gompers, *Seventy Years of Life and Labor; An Autobiography*

(1943), p. 354; Frank L. Grubbs, Jr., *The Struggle for Labor Loyalty: Gompers, The AF of L, and the Pacifists, 1917-1920* (1968); Bernard Mandel, *Samuel Gompers; A Biography* (1963); *Literary Digest*, 54 (June 16, 1917), 1838; Report of the War Labor Conference Committee to the Council of National Defense, December 20, 1917, in *Bulletin 287 of Bureau of Labor Statistics;* Memorandum of Advisory Council to Secretary of Labor, January 19, 1918, and statement of John Lind . . ., both in Report of War Labor Conference Board, *Bulletin 287 of Bureau of Labor Statistics;* Henry F. Pringle, *The Life and Times of William Howard Taft* (1939), II, 915-925. *National War Labor Board: A History of its Formation and Activities . . ., Bulletin 287 of Bureau of Labor Statistics;* Abraham L. Gitlow, *Wage Determination Under National Boards* (1953), pp. 110-111.

Pages 302-303

On the IWW, see Melvin Dubofsky, *We Shall Be All; A History of the Industrial Workers of the World* (1969).

8

National Power and Demobilization, 1900-1919

The previous chapter ended almost in the middle of a sentence in a way that might be considered symbolic of the theme of this book: the build-up of national power to unprecedented heights and then collapse. The present chapter is designed to review some of the complexities leading to the development of national power prior to involvement in the First World War; to suggest the complex forces leading to the even greater centralization during the war; and to contrast the appearance of victory in 1918 with demobilization in 1919.

Prohibition

Although the temperance crusade had played a lively role in American politics for generations at the local and sometimes at the national level, its tempo had changed dramatically during the war years. The dries, mobilized by such organizations as the Antisaloon League and the WCTU, supported by Evangelical churches such as the Baptists and Methodists, rural more than urban, middle class more than working class, rallied for a final campaign. This campaign was no longer designed to educate or to move gradually from areas where support for temperance was pervasive to those where it was uncertain. The intent was for the federal government representing a substantial percentage of the population to coerce another substantial percentage of the population into accepting prohibition. As the *Antisaloon Yearbook* put it in 1911, "This battle is not a rose-water conflict. It is war—continued, relentless war."

As war, it became an increasingly single-minded effort whose principal advocates became less concerned with other reforms of the era. Yet it remained one of the most politically explosive issues of the day. President Wilson worried about it. He saw it as a "social and moral" issue which could play hob with party politics. He favored local option and never supported national prohibition. Yet by skillful politics the dry forces won an impressive series of victories in Congress as the war created a psychological climate favoring restrictions on the use of grain for manufacturing alcoholic beverages and encouraging sobriety among workers and soldiers. In December 1917 Congress sent the Eighteenth Amendment to the states for ratification. To the amazement of its opponents, the dry forces again demonstrated their influence on state legislatures and the popular appeal of the issue when thirty-six states ratified the amendment within fourteen months and forty-five within sixteen months. By this amendment and by the Volstead Act which implemented it, "the manufacture, sale, or transportation of intoxicating liquors within, the importation thereof into, or the exportation thereof" from the United States was forbidden.

This extraordinary success of pressure politics represents one of the most extreme examples of the extension of national power. At the same time it points to the complex forces which were at work in the early twentieth century leading to that extension. To millions of evangelical Protestants, drinking alcohol was a sin; and to millions of people prohibition was a reform, much more than a question of personal morals: drunkenness was an evil which affected families and children, caused industrial accidents, and led to absenteeism. To some, moreover, prohibition was supportable because it represented an attack upon the saloon, the stronghold of the corrupt political boss, the outlet for the liquor interests which subverted legislatures and fought women's suffrage. Perhaps psychological factors were involved if the prohibition crusade is viewed as a clash of rural versus urban values or even as a threat to the Anglo-Saxon Protestant middle class by the Roman Catholic immigrant. Undoubtedly too politics was involved as the aspiring office-seeker took the political temperature and calculated the political clout of the Antisaloon League and the WCTU.

Domestic Reform

The conclusion that federal power should be invoked to solve a problem which had not been solved by voluntary or local or state action was fully in accord with the mood of the twentieth century. The idea that people could live happily in "a society of island communities," as Robert Wiebe has pointed out, was rapidly breaking down. Technological developments in transportation and communication, industrialization, urbanization, internal migration, and immigration had created conditions which provoked somewhat comparable responses throughout the world. Educated elites produced new psychology, new educational theories, new anthropology, new economics, new philosophy, new political and legal theories. Many of these new departures in theory had practical applicability to the conditions in which people lived or the ways in which they made their living.

Most of them had abandoned the pessimism implicit in philosophies of laissez faire and were arguing that people through institutions such as the school and the state could solve these problems.

In spite of lip service to laissez faire, to be sure, Americans had not hesitated to use state or even the federal governments to solve particular problems in the nineteenth century. Such problem-solving simply had meant increasing power here and there. It did not require any fundamental change in the political or economic system. In fact none of the radical movements calling for revolutionary change ever won sufficient popular support in the United States to make revolution a viable alternative. IWW's, idealistic in their goals, extreme in their rhetoric, clumsy in their techniques, failed to capture the labor movement. The socialists had the best chance, and some argue that had it not been for the division caused by the war and the repression that accompanied and followed the war, socialism might have succeeded in the United States at least as much as it had in Britain or France. The contention, however, is questionable. American socialists were hopelessly split even before the war. Although Gompers aimed at a new society based upon the power of the workers, he and most of the trades unions rejected socialism; and the legislative programs of Roosevelt, Taft, and Wilson seemed to offer more attractive alternatives than socialism to those who voted.

Most Americans who favored change to meet the challenges of the twentieth century, then, apparently hoped to reform and to strengthen the system, not abandon it. Even businessmen, in popular myth the personification of laissez faire, were turning to government to protect their interests. Yet their interests were almost as varied as businesses and businessmen. Some of them, fearing consolidations as a threat to competition, looked to government to break those consolidations up. Others, thinking that efficiency and stability were more important than cutthroat competition, called for "the new competition" in which businessmen or trades associations would work with the government in developing codes of fair trade practices. Similar differences within the business community on questions such as railroad regulation, banking, control of the sale of food and drugs, taxation, and tariffs provided the basis for alliances with consumer organizations, which saw in state and nation the regulatory power necessary to provide price and tax structures and standards of products that would protect the consumer.

Consumer groups found even closer allies in organizations interested in particular reforms or in the protection of underprivileged groups. The Women's Trade Union League, the American Association for Labor Legislation, the National Child Labor Committee, and many others were advocating legislation which would ensure social justice. At times, such aims clashed with businessmen who were calling for reforms to promote order, economy, and efficiency, but the conflict in goals demonstrates the complexity of the politics of reform rather than hypocrisy on the part of the reformers.

Any reform that required the increase of national power inevitably became involved in politics of the most intricate kind at various levels. A demand for reform usually began with local agitation and then might eventually lead to controversies over state's rights or conflicts in jurisdiction between state and federal agencies. It certainly would involve representatives and senators, most of whom were from rural areas and small towns, only gradually adjusting to the realities of the twentieth century and to whom a billion-dollar federal budget was inconceivable. These legislators were besieged by a bewildering number of pressure groups and were led by committee chairmen or party leaders whose political experiences and governmental philosophy were rooted deeply in the nineteenth century.

Under such circumstances, executive leadership was of primary importance, and the expansion of federal power during the administrations of Roosevelt, Wilson, and even McKinley and Taft was a testimony to their effectiveness. In most instances, it is true, their principal achievements were compromises and some of them were at one time or another, in whole or in part, supported by businessmen or business organizations. Yet such support does not necessarily prove that the changes brought about were not designed to right a wrong or serve the national interest.

Foreign Expansion and War

Coincidentally with the increase of national power in domestic affairs occurred an expansion of American interests overseas, a more frequent involvement in controversies with other nations, and a consequent strengthening of American power in international affairs. While a cobweb of factors—political, economic, strategic, ideological, psychological—turned the nation's attention outward, Theodore Roosevelt added distinction to the years after the Spanish-American War in foreign as well as in domestic affairs. Roosevelt had acquired a positive notion of the position of the United States in the world and was determined to develop sufficient military power to earn the respect of other world powers. Although a small warrior cult together with several active pressure groups supported Roosevelt's expansionist tendencies, no industrial-military complex influencing governmental policy existed before the First World War. Although a few congressmen and senators took the well-being of the services very seriously, congressmen in general were undoubtedly influenced more by constituents who did not seem to be particularly concerned with foreign affairs. Moreover differences within and between the services made almost impossible a united front in proposing a defense program. In spite of these obstacles, however, skillful leadership on the part of Roosevelt, Taft, Elihu Root, as well as some of the military leaders and congressmen resulted in a significant modernization of the military services. Fundamental changes were made in organization, in training, in armament, and in strategic considerations, and expenditures of the War Department increased from $112.2

million to $202.1 million between 1902 and 1913 and of the Navy Department from $67.8 million to $133.2 million.

Woodrow Wilson, though not the warrior type of Theodore Roosevelt, was not an anti-imperialist. Although he questioned Roosevelt's impatient maneuverings in acquiring the Isthmus of Panama, he generally supported overseas expansion and consistently stood on the principle that overseas trade was a national right mutually advantageous to all. One unifying theme in his foreign and domestic policies was the consistency with which he favored actions that would encourage or protect foreign trade. Even in the years when he was preaching the New Freedom, he was urging the extension of trading frontiers abroad and the development of federal policies and institutions that would support such an expansion. To him the historic principles of the Open Door and Freedom of the Seas were more than merely idealistic platitudes. They were practical and necessary bases for an expanding economy. What is more, they could be defended on moral grounds. What, indeed, were the moral alternatives to principles which called for equality of treatment for all?

Wilson's views on trade and American interests in a liberal world order were important factors in propelling the United States into the First World War. This war required an unprecedented concentration of national power as congressmen gritted their teeth and appropriated more funds than had ever been appropriated before. They conscripted military fighting forces, legislated controls over food, fuel, shipping, and civil liberties; they authorized the government to take over the telephone, telegraph, and railroad systems and to go into the business of building ships; they gave sweeping legislative support to presidential war powers, and watched the president use them in setting up institutions to control industry, influence prices, and stabilize labor conditions; they even decided what people could not drink; they increased tax rates to unprecedented heights and supported bond drives that carried federal emissaries seeking funds throughout the nation.

The victory loan drive of April 1919 brought previous campaigns to a triumphant climax. Motion picture stars and decorated veterans toured the country; 100,000 clergymen "delivered liberty loan sermons"; salesmen received 85,000 captured German helmets as prizes; flying aces gave aerial demonstrations"; the rallying cry was to "finish the job."

In comparison with prewar experiences, the problem of federal finances was almost overwhelming. The Treasury had sold billions of dollars worth of certificates of indebtedness. These short-term certificates were used essentially to pay for the costs of the war to the United States, a cost which ran at the rate of $42.8 million a day from July 1, 1917, to June 30, 1919. The daily cost for Great Britain, France, and Germany ran somewhat more than $32 million for each country. The liberty and victory loans amounting to about $21.5 billion and the internal revenue and tariff collections of the period (1917–1920) amounting to about $13.5 billion were used to pay back these short-term loans. In other words, counting the year 1920, about 36 percent of the war was paid for by taxation. If the year 1920 is excluded from the calculation, the figure is about 25 percent. Wilson and McAdoo fought for additional taxes, particularly a "real war-profits tax" in 1917, but Congress did not oblige until February 1919 with a bill that would effect revenue only in 1920. About $9.5 billion of the total went to the Allies, the notorious war debts which were to be a source of irritation for many years to come.

Although the Federal Reserve experts at the time and recent critics have questioned the Treasury's policies as being short-sighted and inflationary, other belligerents fared less well. In Britain, for example, current taxes paid for about 20 percent of the war's costs; in Germany, the figure was less than 2 percent. Britain likewise experimented with the bank rate, immediately jumping it to the "fantastic rate of 10 percent," but, according to one critic, no government really had a plan, and the "way in which note issue, public debt, and the purchasing power of consumers increased amounted to a complete leap in the dark."

To social justice reformers also the war was a leap in the dark. To some, war signaled the death knell of hopes for reform. To those especially who considered the Progressive party as the most promising instrument of reform, these fears had substance, as the Progressive party collapsed. Even more when the United States entered the war, they envisaged the war effort as threatening labor standards, so grudgingly obtained, and abridging civil liberties in the name of national security.

Yet the emotionalism and enthusiasm for the war effort captured probably a majority of the social reformers. Jane Addams, Lillian Wald, Randolph Bourne, and other dedicated pacifists could not see that any indirect results of war could justify its horrors. Others, however, accepted Wilson's eloquent call for a war to make the world safe for democracy. They gloried in new agencies partially staffed with social workers and college professors. John Dewey, Herbert Croly, Walter Lippmann, delighted with the mobilization of industry and of transportation and communication, said good-by to laissez faire and praised the new day of national power and government planning. They saw how the war inaugurated federal housing projects in which those who had been denouncing the blight of the slums as well as those who were professional urban planners were involved. They thought that the inauguration of social insurance schemes for the military might provide precedents for civil life and that the publicity given to sanitation and disease in the military camps might shock the public into an awareness of the seriousness of the problems elsewhere. For many women the war brought a new day. Their activities with the Red Cross overseas, their contributions in industry recognized by the establishment of the Women's Bureau in the Department of Labor, and the stimulation that these services gave to the women's suffrage movement culminated in the passage of the Nineteenth Amendment. The war helped to persuade even Wilson, who at first had opposed women's suffrage and then had urged that it should be left up to the states, that women had earned the right to vote.

The war likewise was a landmark in the history of race relations. The sad plight of black people in northern cities had stirred the consciences of an increasing number of social workers during the first decade of the century and had contributed to the founding of the NAACP and the Urban League. These organizations, however, had had little influence on federal policy. Roosevelt's position on race was outspoken but ambivalent, and black leaders never forgot how he had undercut those at the convention of the Progressive party in 1912 who had wanted to recognize black party workers in the South. Wilson's position was even less acceptable to most black leaders. He never completely lost the conventional attitude of the stereotyped southern patrician, and federal segregation increased during his administration.

Then came the war. It led to no Utopia for blacks. Segregation in the services continued. Migrations north and into the cities did not eliminate discrimination in jobs and housing. Racial friction led to riots, and lynchings reached a peak. Yet for the first time since Reconstruction, the federal government took halting steps to meet some of the challenges posed by the black citizen. As W. E. B. Du Bois put it in September 1918, "Since this war began we have won: Recognition of our citizenship in the draft; One thousand Negro officers; Special representation in the War and Labor Departments; Higher Wages and Better Employment; Abolition of the Color line in railway wage; Recognition as Red Cross nurses; Overthrow of segregation ordinances; a strong word from the President against lynching."

While reformers were attempting to use the war to achieve their social goals, economic mobilization led to the development of what at least one writer has called an industrial-military complex. Although it was quite different from that of the 1950s and 1960s, there was, in fact, no alternative to groping and conscious collaboration between industry and government since there were few civil servants or independent professionals qualified to take responsible positions in managing the economy. Industrialists understood their industries; shippers understood shipping; railroad men understood railroads; and it was to these men that the administration and the Council of National Defense turned to find the administrators who would direct the mobilization effort. They were men of varied background, usually chosen because they held key positions in a trades association or because they were recommended by the Chamber of Commerce. Under the circumstances conflicts of interest were built into the system; yet to some extent a type of conflict of interest was in accord with that attitude of mind both in business and government which called for a new competition based upon order, stability, and cooperation rather than the struggle for existence and the survival of the fittest.

A substantial number of congressmen and businessmen, moreover, saw the war as an opportunity to strengthen the postwar position of the United States in world affairs at the expense of European countries weakened by their all-out efforts to survive. Undoubtedly Wilson himself envisaged using American economic and financial power made supreme by the war as a means of persuading other world powers to conform to a liberal world order. Thus the Tariff Commission, authorized in 1916, reinforced by the Webb-Pomerene Act in 1918 and the Edge Act in 1919, made possible trade negotiations and special concessions to American industries and bankers which would support American penetration of overseas markets.

Although the war strengthened the position of corporate capitalism and resulted in large profits for some corporations, there was little or nothing conspiratorial about these developments. There was a great deal of confusion about them. The men in government service were in most instances patriotic men whose primary purpose was to win the war as quickly as possible. Although cooperation seemed to be the principal aim in the relationship between the agencies and business, this aim did not prevent tough talk and tough action on the part of the bureaucrats when businesses seemed to be taking action contrary to the war effort. Moreover the experiences of business leaders on the wartime agencies persuaded many of them that a continuation of comparable agencies in peacetime would be a very good thing indeed.

In the case of the National War Labor Board, even Taft hoped that such an institution could be continued after the war. His experiences taught him, as he himself admitted, that the classic views of Adam Smith did not have all the answers. Experiences of the war years were particularly poignant to operators in coal and oil and the leaders of the United Mine Workers. As the Fuel Administration was preparing to dissolve at the end of the war, Administrator Garfield invited representatives of labor and management to a conference in February 1919 on the future of the industry. Seven leading operators, both union and nonunion, from the National Coal Association and six officials from the United Mine Workers attended. Without exception, these representatives warned against returning to prewar days, decried unrestrained competition, and called for cooperation. And Harry N. Taylor, president of the National Coal Association, talked about the need for a fair wage for labor, a fair return for capital but with the public protected, and standards of safety to protect the miners.

Apparently with complete unanimity the conference agreed on the need for some sort of advisory governmental commission that would lead in providing industrial cooperation and fair labor relations. In an optimistic mood the conferees recommended that President Wilson be sounded out on a proposal for such a commission. By the time the proposal reached the president a few weeks later, it had been expanded to include an advisory industrial cabinet representative of labor and management of all leading industries.

Within a few months, however, the momentum was lost. Although Wilson seemed to favor the proposal, the league controversy and differences among his advisers led to the disappearance of the plan. According to Garfield writing in 1921, "Had this plan been put into effect as the President intended prior to his return from Paris, there is every reason to believe that the spirit of friendly cooperation would have continued, that there would have been no strike in the coal mines nor upon the railroads. . . . But we have failed, and the failure is not due to the President, but to those who exercised the powers of administration" during his illness.

Control of Transportation and Communication

Perhaps the most extended controversy over the expansion of national power involved those industries, such as the railroads, which were taken under direct federal control. In 1919, President Charles E. Mitchell of the National City Bank insisted that "the American people paid $864,000,000 more in rates for inferior service and were taxed $210,000,000 in addition." He insisted that any savings made were infinitesimal as compared to a deterioration of service and an "alarming" condition of railroad finance. In 1924, the "net cost" of federal control of railroads, express, coastwise shipping, and inland waterways was officially recorded as $1,123,500,000. Such statistics and reports that equipment and property had seriously deteriorated under government control supported those who were convinced of the "inevitable weakness of any system of Government operation or Government ownership." As Senator James Watson of Indiana put it, "Those of us who prophesied evil, weakness, inefficiency, and incompetency when these lines were taken over have had our prophesies fulfilled."

However, these hostile analyses do not adequately consider the extraordinary conditions of 1918 and 1919. Federal operation began with unparalleled congestion at a time when the East was afflicted with one of the worst winters on record. Subzero temperatures and blizzards strained maintenance operations as they had rarely been strained before; the coal famine, increased prices and wages all led to unprecedented costs. None of these problems would have been removed under private operation.

In spite of these conditions, the Railroad Administration performed effectively in 1918. Unification, standardization, and coordination of facilities, personnel, equipment, and routes were effective; accounting and statistical procedures were simplified; congestion was relieved; freight service improved, and troop trains proceeded to their destination with comparatively few accidents. One of the principal complaints of the railroads was that their equipment was not returned to them in good repair in spite of guarantees that it would be returned in as good condition as when taken over. Actually, the railroads had been doing little to maintain their equipment when federal control began, and the Railroad Administration had spent about twice as much in maintenance as had the railroads before the war. The railroad properties were not being fully maintained, but an economy-minded Congress was simply not providing enough money. Thus the administration did its best and left it up to the railroads to prove that their equipment was in worse condition than when it was taken over. At the same time, the administration conducted itself with little evidence of partisan or regional discrimination, maintained good labor relations, and made no effort to hide critical statistics.

By the end of the war, the principal means of transportation and communications were under federal control. In May 1918, the Director General had encouraged the four principal express companies—the Adams, American, Wells-Fargo, and Southern—to combine under the name of the American Railway Express Company. On November 16, 1918, the president added this company to the jurisdiction of the Railroad Administration—along with the internal waterways and Atlantic coastal shipping. By this time Congress had authorized the president to take over the telephone, telegraph, and marine cable industries, and on July 22, 1918, he had officially assumed control of the telephone and telegraph systems and, on November 2, the submarine cable. Wilson assigned the responsibility of administering these properties to Postmaster General Burleson, and Burleson took over enthusiastically, but early in 1919 he raised wages of personnel and shortly thereafter in April 1919 he raised both telephone and telegraph rates. Other changes stirred up the critics. The Democratic *New York World* reminded its readers that in January Burleson had promised better service at lower costs and pointed out that the president of Postal Telegraph had promised to "carry on the telegraph business at the old rates at once" if the lines were returned. Opponents of government ownership expressed delight at what they considered Burleson's failure. "He has done his little bit," editorialized the *Portland* (Oregon) *Telegram,* "to check one phase of radical socialism." Even Representative James B. Aswell of Louisiana who had introduced the wire-control bill in July 1918 apologized for the increase in rates, and saw this as indicative of a failure of government control or ownership. Aswell could not believe that Burleson was responsible but blamed "thoroughbred Republicans kept in office by the Democratic Administration."

Obviously there were as subtle issues involved in the communications controversy as was the case with the railroads. Republicans were eager to find issues for the election of 1920, and a Wilson associate provided a good target. Moreover state commissions may have had as much interest in telegraph-telephone regulation as in railroads, and wanted to get their prewar powers back. The Corporation Commission of Oklahoma denounced higher rates of federal inefficiency and called for return to private owners; the Nebraska State Railway Commission, the Kansas Commission, the New Mexico Corporation Commission, the North Carolina Corporation Commission, and the North Dakota Board of Railway Commissioners all urged the return to private operation with the implicit understanding that state regulation would take over. The rising storm came to a climax in a letter to Wilson from the National Association of Railway and Utilities Commissions urging an end to government control before June 30.

Burleson surrendered and surprised even his friends late in April 1919 by urging the president to return the cable lines and the telephone and telegraph lines to their owners as soon as practicable. The president complied, but urged legislation which would provide for the coordination and unification of the telephone and telegraph lines, their operation by private companies under the regulation of the Interstate Commerce Commission and a special, representative tribunal to hear labor disputes.

Burleson's footwork was fast, and he arranged for the return of the lines to their private owners in June more than a month before Congress had repealed the law authorizing the president to take over the lines.

The controversies over the disposition of the telephone and telegraph lines after the war were comparatively mild when compared with bitter debates over what was to happen to the railroads. The conflicting pressures of "railroad politics" saw little diminution when the war ended. Although some of the shippers and perhaps some of the state and national commissioners might have wished to return to the prewar regulatory system, their's was a minority position. Even the most individualistic prewar operators seemed to be demanding a system which would provide greater efficiency, order, stability, and unity.

Although most railroad operators were unfavorable to federal control, those who became a part of the Railroad Administration became its most ardent defenders. Walker Hines, for example, chairman of the board of the Atcheson, Topeka, and Santa Fe, who had served as assistant to the director from the beginning of the administration and succeeded McAdoo as director in January 1919, considered federal control under circumstances comparable to World War I "imperative." Regional directors of the administration, such as A. H. Smith, president of New York Central, C. H. Markham, president of the Illinois Central, Hale Holden, president of the Burlington, and B. F. Bush, president of the Missouri Pacific all considered federal control effective. In the Senate, on the other hand, Senator Cummins worked out an elaborate scheme that would promote efficiency by substituting a transportation board for the state and national commissions, a change not popular with the commissions and a great many of the shippers. And the railroad labor unions endorsed a moderate program of nationalization proposed by their general counsel, Glenn Plumb. Finally in 1920, Congress approved a compromise—the Transportation Act of 1920—which returned prewar regulatory powers to the Interstate Commerce Commission, established a Railway Labor Board to resolve labor disputes, and recognized the possible need for greater consolidation of the lines. The Transportation Act of 1920 thus became another landmark in the history of Congress' carrying out its constitutional role of regulating commerce in the shape of interstate railroads.

Control of the Military

By the time the war ended, centralized power in the United States was symbolized by Wilson's victory in Congress which made him commander in chief in fact as in name. He had defeated those elements in Congress which had proposed to limit his authority by establishing a special war committee. He had succeeded even though a number of his own congressional leaders opposed him. When Congress approved the Overman Act in April 1918, it had approved such sweeping powers for the president that Senator Brandegee of Connecticut could with some truth say, "If any power, constitutional or not, has been inadvertently omitted from this bill, it is hereby granted in full."

This sweeping power was important not only for what it meant to mobilization at home, but for what it meant to fighting the war abroad. There simply was no precedent in the United States for coordinating the kind of war that was being fought. For the first time, the nation was fighting a huge land war overseas in conjunction with Allies. The American navy had to transport hundreds of thousands of troops and thousands of tons of supplies across three thousand miles of ocean and in so doing had to fight submarines both with surface convoys and with an unbelievable submarine mine barrage of the North Sea.

The American army was called upon to play an even more decisive role. From the time the United States entered the war until a few months before the armistice, French and British military leaders were calling for more and more American troops. By June 1918 they had convinced General John Pershing, the commander of the American Expeditionary Force in France, that 100 divisions, probably around 5 million men, would have to be on the battlefields of France by July 1919. This fantastic figure was substantially larger than the combined Allied armies then on the western front and would make the United States the strongest military power in the world.

Wilson reluctantly approved an eighty-division program, but he may well have done so with his tongue in his cheek since he knew that such a program might require production that would exceed the capacity of the country. In any case confusion existed as to what the eighty-division program meant in terms of manpower commitments, and as late as October 1918, Secretary of War Baker was in France apparently trying to find out. By this time, however, the fortunes of war had changed, and Supreme Allied Commander Ferdinand Foch admitted that forty American divisions would suffice to win the war. Actually forty-two divisions arrived in France, and twenty-nine went into action.

The inability to decide what force was needed to win the war reflected the institutional weakness and confusion in command theory which characterized American military policy in the first two decades of the twentieth century. The organizational framework created by Root and Roosevelt in the first years had suffered tensions and setbacks for the next dozen years; but finally the demands of the First World War provided the experiences that were to make possible a much more effective use of military power during World War II.

Wilson, however, did not want to be the kind of commander in chief that Franklin Roosevelt aspired to be twenty-five years later. Wilson drew a fine line, of his own definition, between "policy," which he saw as his responsibility, and military functions, which he saw as the responsibilities of professional army and navy personnel. Only when seemingly insoluble differences developed over military questions was he willing to intervene as commander in chief. In the case of the western front, for example, he saw to it that a strong man, General Pershing, was appointed commander of the American Expeditionary Force, and then he left it to Pershing to make the key decisions. Wilson continued to endorse the principle of leaving key military decisions to men in the field even when Marshal Ferdinand Foch was appointed Supreme Allied Commander in April 1918. Wilson had long favored unity of command, and he informed Pershing that although military decisions could still be made in the field, Foch had become the supreme commander.

Wilson was apparently so convinced of the importance of not interfering with commanders in the field that he saw no need of a strong chief of staff at home to coordinate the entire military effort. He assumed that his friend Baker as secretary of war could provide the necessary liaison between Pershing and mobilizers in the United States. Once Pershing arrived in France, however, his cables demanding men and supplies came so rapidly that the machinery broke down and endangered the entire war effort. Political pressures, if for no other reason, demanded strong leadership at home as well as abroad.

The appointment of Peyton March as chief of staff in March 1918 was an important landmark in the history of American military power. March's ruthlessness shocked some, but within weeks he had assumed control over the bureaus, and was forcing the armchair colonels to burn the midnight oil. He carried on a running feud with Pershing, but he set the army's house in order, and as George Marshall, a colonel on Pershing's staff, later commented, considering "the inevitable confusion incident to coordinating industries in the United States, training, shelter, and shipping, it is surprising that the demands from the AEF were met to the extent they were." March's personal success in carrying out his mission led in August 1918 to the even more important symbolic recognition of his office in a general order which stated that "the chief of staff by law takes precedence over all the officers of the Army."

Wilson's concept of the role of commander in chief may not have provided the most efficient organization. He did not arrive at the concept, however, thoughtlessly or merely because of his distaste for war. In the last analysis the explanation boiled down to a question of goals and power.

Wilson had certain idealistic goals—a liberal, democratic world order where trade might move without discrimination and where peaceful relations would be secured by the League of Nations. In the early months of America's participation, he did not have the power to obtain guarantees for these goals, and he was determined not to get involved in negotiations which might require concessions. By the end of the war, he envisaged the United States with a navy second to none, with the greatest army in the world, and with England and France, as he put it "financially in our hands." Then, he said, "we can force them to our way of thinking." According to Ernest May, "He evaded duty as commander in chief in order to do his larger duty as president of the United States."

Demobilization

The armistice of 1918 came as the military and industrial power of the United States was only in an early stage of mobilization. Yet the twenty-nine divisions together with financial and logistical support and clever Wilsonian diplomacy had tipped the balance against the tired Germans.* At that time, the army had almost four million men under arms, a huge navy building program had been authorized, and the economy was only beginning real war production. Within two months almost one million men had been discharged; in another six months, almost three million men had returned to civilian life; and the debate was under way as to what kind of peacetime army the United States was to have.

Even within the army and the navy differences existed as to the nature of the peacetime forces, but all notions of universal military service and a navy second-to-none had to give way to peacetime realities. The army had to accept a compromise which among other things authorized a regular force of no more than 288,000 men, provided for a reserve officers training corps, and left the National Guard as the principal source of reserve fighting power. That compromise provided the structure for the army until World War II. In much the same way the Washington Conference in 1922 set the limits to naval expansion.

Equally swift and even more haphazard demobilization took place on the economic front. Wilson, absorbed in making plans for the future of the world and physically exhausted, had made no plans for his own country and received little help from the Council of National Defense. In fact no centralized direction existed. Within a year of the armistice, the War Industries Board, the Food Administration, the Fuel Administration, and the War Trade Board had closed their offices. In 1920, the Railway Administration, supported by the Transportation Act of 1920, returned the roads

---

*Casualty figures for Americans included 53,402 battle deaths, 63,114 deaths from other causes, and 204,002 "wounds not mortal."

to private ownership, and by the Merchant Marine Act of 1920 Congress ordered the liquidation of the Shipping Board. Moreover the high hopes of those on the National War Labor Board for continuing machinery to adjust labor disputes collapsed with the disappearance of the board itself and the bitter strikes of 1919.

Although demobilization took place chaotically and sometimes disastrously, experiences survived the wreckage. When depression was threatening the destruction of the American economy, veterans of the financial crises of the First World War persuaded President Hoover to revive the War Finance Corporation, and under the name of the Reconstruction Finance Corporation, it became his principal agency in bolstering staggering industries and financial institutions. When Franklin Roosevelt became president, his experiences as assistant secretary of the navy undoubtedly led him to liken the fight on the depression to wartime mobilization, and he brought in numerous people with experiences in the wartime agencies to fill slots on newly created agencies of the New Deal. Even one of the relatively minor agencies of the war, the Capital Issues Committee, provided data that could well have foretold one of the most controversial agencies created in the early 1930s. That committee soon after its formation became depressed by fraudulent practices in the sale of securities. State regulation could not touch those enterprises operating in other states, and the committee estimated that at least $500 million annually was being "invested" in "fraudulent or worthless stocks." In Britain, the committee pointed out, regulation of security issues had "existed in some form since 1862." The principles upon which the committee worked were to disapprove obviously unsound enterprises because they would "encourage economic wastes," and to urge the postponement of enterprises perfectly acceptable in peacetime but not necessary in wartime. Without coercive power, however, appeals to the patriotism of some promoters were in vain. Thus a considerable traffic developed in fraudulent stocks, particularly with a gullible public holding liberty bonds.

Schools of stock sellers were established for the sale of fraudulent stock. They were in great demand and were making good money—one report indicated a minimum of $300 per week. Sales people in one school were informed that "there never was a time when all the suckers had the money they have at present." Such actions persuaded the committee that "the Federal supervision of security issues, here undertaken for the first time, should be continued by some public agency . . . in such a form as to check the traffic in doubtful securities, while imposing no undue restrictions upon the financing of legitimate industry. It would be fifteen years before Congress would follow the advice of this Capital Issues Committee. The War Finance Corporation, however, continued to play a role in the early twenties, and then had a reincarnation in 1932 as the Reconstruction Finance Corporation.

Dream, Reality, and Some Disillusionment

Had there been no war, the base still would have been firmly laid for the extension of national power over the economy. No philosophical theory or blueprint for this extension, except perhaps in the Progressive platform of 1912 or the Democratic platform of 1916, existed. Each extension of federal power had been a response to different demands frequently from different people or from different groups and for a variety of reasons. Yet executives and Congresses had established powers to regulate numerous aspects of the economy; to protect natural and human resources; to tax individuals and corporations both to raise revenue and to redistribute income; to provide subsidies, loans, and all kinds of information; and to manage the currency and furnish a banking structure that would serve all the people.

In spite of the enormous increase in the powers of the federal government between 1900 and 1919 presumably to benefit its citizens—no utopia had been created. Industrial workers were earning higher real wages and were apparently able to maintain a higher standard of living, and farmers were probably better off than they had ever been before. Yet the distribution of personal income which was completely out-of-joint in 1910 was equally so in 1918 and worse in 1921.* Millions of families were living in poverty, and many farmers led a precarious existence as the number of owners becoming tenants continuously increased by more than 20 percent between 1900 and 1920. More confusing was the use to which federal power could be put. Even those who had supported increased government regulation and increased government services as solutions to the nation's ills were increasingly aware that institutions created with a certain purpose could be subverted by those who controlled the institutions, and that there was a danger that state power could be used to suppress personal freedom, particularly in wartime. In fact all belligerents during the First World War had passed laws providing for the internment of people suspected of aiding the enemy, for censorship of information that might aid the enemy, and for suppression of activities that might produce defeatism. In the United States the president recommended and Congress approved sweeping acts presumably to prevent subversion and to protect the national security. Yet these enactments and the ways in which they were enforced reflected attitudes and fears that only indirectly related to security in the military sense. Racial tensions culminating in riots and a mass movement showing support for the black nationalism of Marcus Garvey, Jewishness emerging as Zionism, and the self-assertion of ethnic groups not willing to submerge themselves in the melting pot threatened the stereotype of American cul-

*An estimate of the National Industrial Conference Board showed the top tenth received 33.9% of the national income in 1910, 34.5% in 1918, and 38.2% in 1921. The lowest tenth were receiving 3.4%, 2.4% and 2%. *Studies in Enterprise and Progress* (1939), p. 125. For standard of living, see *Family Budgets of Wage Earners* (1921), p. 67.

ture. Labor unrest no longer subject to the benevolent controls of the National War Labor Board both challenged the leadership of the AFL and demanded union recognition and better working conditions from unwilling employers. Always in the background loomed the mysterious threat of the Bolsheviki. Enforcement of the Espionage and Sedition acts fitted in with the emotionalism of the times, and federal courts did little to restrain the use of federal power to abridge civil liberties.

A constitutional guarantee of free speech is not absolute. Even in peacetime, it does not protect a person who directly urges another to perform an illegal act, who libels or slanders another, or who incites a riot. Moreover censorship has been generally accepted in wartime in those battle areas actually under control of the military. The problem is to determine how much restraint on speech in wartime is legitimate. To some extent such a determination depends upon the whim of a judge, but the judge must grapple with the essential question of "what is the test of criminality." According to Zechariah Chafee, a leading authority on civil liberties, the two most difficult questions regarding limitations on speech are the doctrine of indirect causation "under which words can be punished for a supposed bad tendency long before there is any probability that they will break out into unlawful acts" and "the doctrine of constructive intent, which regards the intent of the defendant to cause violence as immaterial so long as he intended to write the words."

Judge Learned Hand of the South District of New York attempted to repudiate the principle of "the remote bad tendency" in the case of the *Masses Publishing Co.* v. *Patten* in 1917. The postmaster general had excluded the *Masses,* a monthly "radical" journal, from the mails because of its attacks upon the war effort. The publisher asked Hand to "enjoin the postmaster of New York" from its action. Hand granted the injunction while admitting that "political agitation . . . may in fact stimulate men to the violation of law." Hand concluded that "to assimilate agitation, legitimate as such, with direct incitement to violent resistance, is to disregard the tolerance of all methods of political agitation which in normal times is a safeguard of free government."

The circuit court reversed Hand's decision. It upheld the authority of the postmaster general, ruling that an accused should be judged guilty "if the natural and reasonable effect of what is said is to encourage resistance to the law." In short, the circuit court accepted the principle of the "remote bad tendency." The judges also inferred intent "from the existence of the indirect injurious effect."

This decision, being one of the earliest tried under the Espionage Act, became a precedent. Conviction after conviction followed. One notorious case involved a moving picture entitled *The Spirit of '76,* a story of the American Revolution which showed atrocities committed by British soldiers. The district attorney of Los Angeles charged the producer of the film with violating the Espionage Act. The district judge sentenced the producer to imprisonment for ten years and a fine of $5,000 on the grounds of questioning "the good faith of our ally, Great Britain."

Not until 1919 did any of the cases first prosecuted in the district courts reach the Supreme Court. The first of these cases *Schenck* v. *United States* tested the constitutionality of the Espionage Act. Schenck and his associates had mailed directly to young men about to be drafted leaflets denouncing the Selective Service Act and urging them to resist the draft. Convicted in the district court of violating the Espionage Act, the defendants appealed, claiming that the enactment violated the freedom of speech provision of the Bill of Rights. A unanimous Court upheld the conviction and the constitutionality of the act based upon a nation's war powers. Associate Justice Oliver Wendell Holmes, Jr., however, included in the decision a definition of freedom of speech, comparable to that of Learned Hand, which has since assumed the sanctity of constitutional doctrine:

> We admit that in many places and in ordinary times the defendants
> in saying all that was said in the circular would have been within
> their constitutional rights. But the character of every act depends
> upon the circumstances in which it is done. . . . The question in
> every case is whether the words used in such circumstances are of
> such a nature as to create a clear and present danger that they will
> bring about the substantive evils that Congress has a right to prevent.
> It is a question of proximity and degree. When a nation is at war
> many things that might be said in time of peace are such a hindrance
> to its effort that their utterance will not be endured so long as men
> fight and that no court could regard them as protected by any con-
> stitutional right.

A second case, that of *Abrams* v. *United States,* tested the constitutionality of the amendment to the Espionage Act, known as the Sedition Act. The defendants in this case had thrown leaflets out of a window at the corner of Houston and Crosby Streets in New York City in August 1918 urging workers engaged in war production to strike as a demonstration against sending an American expeditionary force into Russia. A federal district court convicted the defendants of violating the Sedition Act; they promptly appealed; and a majority of the court upheld the conviction on the grounds of intent to incite disaffection "at the supreme crisis of the war." By this time Holmes had been converted to a much more libertarian interpretation of the First Amendment and supported by Wilson's appointee, Brandeis, dissented. Holmes' eloquent dissent admitted that "persecution for the expression of opinions" was logical. "But," he went on,

> when men have realized that time has upset many fighting faiths,
> they may come to believe even more than they believe the very
> foundation of their own conduct that the ultimate good desired is
> better reached by free trade in ideas—that the best test of truth is
> the power of the thought to get itself accepted in the competition of

the market. . . . That at any rate is the theory of our constitution.
It is an experiment as all life is an experiment. Every year if not
every day we have to wager our salvation upon some prophecy based
upon imperfect knowledge. While that experiment is part of our system, I think that we should be eternally vigilant against attempts to
check the expression of opinions that we loathe and believe to be
fraught with death, unless they so immediately threaten immediate
interference with the lawful and pressing purposes of the law that an
immediate check is required to save the country.

The Loss of National Leadership

Rarely, if ever, has there been such a tragic and anticlimactic period in the
history of the United States as those months immediately after the war. It
calls for comparisons with the "critical period" of the 1780s and the
"reconstruction" of the 1860s and 1870s. With the armistice came a
chaotic demobilization, the Red Scare added to the tensions, and national
leadership was lacking. Politics, which had never been adjourned during
the war, was in disarray. The Republicans, still the majority party, had
partially recovered from the progressive exodus of 1912 and had won control of both houses of Congress in 1918. The coalition which had reelected
Wilson in 1916 was breaking down. For almost two years there was no
president of the United States.

The chaotic quality of these two years demonstrated how important
executive power had become in maintaining stability in twentieth-century
society. The collapse of the executive provided a vacuum in which some of
the same power struggles that had characterized the period before and
even during the First World War broke out with renewed intensity. Although these had not been class struggles in the Marxian sense, radical
groups such as the socialists and IWW's, and even in a somewhat more
guarded way Samuel Gompers and his followers, preached that doctrine.
In so doing they aroused enough consternation to be considered a continual threat to the status quo. Indeed the fear of radicalism at times persuaded
the traditionally minded political parties and alert politicians to choose
their issues in a way that would win support from those who might otherwise be attracted by the radical appeal.

While on the one hand the radical threat to the capitalist system was
raising the specter of revolution, on the other the development of corporate
power both in industry and finance raised far-reaching questions as to
whether concentrated economic power could serve the best interests of
society as a whole. Although the bogey of monopoly played an important
political role, it is uncertain how much actual control the great industries
or finance capitalists had over the economic system. Farm organizations,
labor unions, antimonopoly groups, and numerous other consumer organizations developed countervailing power, first on the local level and then in

party conventions and in Congress. Congress, particularly the Senate in the first years of the century, seemed to be susceptible to business influences, and had there been a business monolith, the subordination of national politics to corporate capitalism might have been significant. There was, however, no such business monolith. All sorts of differences existed depending upon region, size, or type. Nonetheless, even though the merger movement may have failed to win control of the economy, as Gabriel Kolko insists, the "larger interests" undoubtedly prevail when there is competition between small business and big business.

A lack of unity also characterized other sectors of the economy. In spite of the predominantly rural background of many of its members, Congress appeared less susceptible to the farmers' needs than were the state legislatures. No such political pressure group as the American Farm Bureau Federation existed before the First World War, and an agrarian bias of many congressmen was rarely sufficient to combine divers interests such as those of southern cotton with those of western wheat. The influence of labor organizations upon national policy was probably even less than that of the farmer. Most congressmen would probably have considered any fraternizing with labor leaders socially unacceptable. Labor as a political power bloc provided only an insignificant threat. The AFL was the strongest force in the labor movement, but that federation represented only a small fraction of the workers and it certainly could not deliver the labor vote. Only occasionally as in the case of the anthracite coal strike of 1902 and the railroad strike of 1916 did the organized workers show their potential economic power and gain significant concessions which were essentially political.

The war increased the political power of both corporate capitalism and the wage earners, both organized and unorganized. Here the all-consuming goal was to win the war. The unprecedented demand for workers at a time when many of them were being conscripted for military service resulted in official support for labor's demands and an institutional protection for high standards including the rights to organize and bargain collectively. Likewise, unprecedented demands upon a hitherto uncatalogued economy seemed to offer no alternative but to bring industrialists into strategic positions created to keep the economy functioning and to cooperate with representatives of key industries.

The war did provide precedents for greater cooperation between the government, the armed services, and industry. Neither attempts to modernize the military services prior to the First World War nor the streamlining of the services brought about by the demands of the war effort produced a military power bloc. However the procedures worked out by trial and error between the military services and the War Industries Board had a long-range effect of demonstrating the mutual advantages of military-industrial cooperation. By the end of the war the prestige of the military was high, and through selective service its influence had been felt in every community in the land. Yet this prestige barely survived the armistice. Superpatriotism, it is true, provided a stimulus for the Red Scare, but it was not sufficient to combat the pacifism and the drive for economy that put severe limitations on the size of the army in the National Defense Act of 1920 and of the navy in the Washington Conference of 1922. The ideas of military-industrial cooperation, however, had become firmly fixed and continued to influence military policy in the 1920s and the 1930s.

Through the period from 1900 to 1919, Congress played a key role in authorizing fundamental change. The pervasive problems caused by industrialization, urbanization, personal mobility, and technological invention had thrown new responsibilities on the federal government. Pressure groups of all kinds were competing with local constituencies and with party loyalties in winning over senators and representatives to support various issues. It is rarely clear what influences persuade congressmen to vote as they do. A basic assumption must be that most of them are conscientious, do their homework, and vote as they do for reasons of party or personal preference. Pressure groups, particularly coalitions of consumers, at times undoubtedly provide the decisive influence; yet rarely does such an influence alone suffice. In the case of women's suffrage, for example, previously undecided congressmen may have been influenced as much by the contribution of women to the war effort as by pressure groups and demonstrations, as they looked forward to the next election and voted for the Nineteenth Amendment. Even the passage of the Eighteenth Amendment, supported by the Antisaloon League, one of the most effective pressure groups in the nation's history, was aided by the particular conditions caused by the war.

An even more important source of power was the office of the executive. Tensions inevitably exist between congressional power and presidential power, and these tensions become particularly abrasive during the administrations of strong presidents. Strong presidents such as McKinley, Roosevelt, and Wilson were determined not only to execute the laws passed by Congress but to propose them and provide legislative guidance for them. Moreover they consciously shaped the course of their administrations by the ways funds were spent in executing the laws and by the types of appointments which were made.

The president and his vice president are the only officials chosen by the national electorate. He and his bureaucracy are the ones most capable of performing the task of referee by rising above regional interests and pressure groups and acting for the nation as a whole. Yet even presidents, and certainly their appointees, are impressed by power, and, as Robert Wolff has pointed out clearly, important interests frequently do not have power. In 1919, for example, some 250,000 American Indians, 170,000 Orientals, 10 million blacks, an uncertain percentage of the 18 million foreign-born, 2.5 million tenant farmers, and the uncounted numbers in poverty did not have "the power" and as interests were rarely adequately represented. As E. E. Schattschneider has said, "The flaw in the pluralist heaven is that the heavenly chorus sings with a strong middle class accent."

In spite of the fact that these interests did not have the power, they posed a threat to the security of the status quo at a time when demobilization was proceeding without plan; when revolutions were occurring abroad; when mutters of radicalism were being heard at home; when labor was disillusioned and striking because wartime labor power seemed to have collapsed while corporate power seemed stronger than ever; indeed when the whole economy seemed to be out of joint; and when the Red Scare had begun. Would a strong president have been able to maintain perspective, stand above these pressures and conditions, and bring about a more orderly demobilization? Chance made impossible an answer to that question:

Woodrow Wilson, as a college professor in the 1890s, had been one of the world's leading authorities on public administration. He had served as president of Princeton, as governor of the state of New Jersey, and as president of the United States. In all these posts, he had demonstrated unusual administrative skills and had pushed through innovative programs by skillful negotiation, compromise, and leadership ability. Yet the last years in all three of these posts were unhappy ones for him, clouded with personal failure.

Throughout his career, indeed from his school days, he had fought periodic physical ailments. Prior to 1896, the most irritating of these ailments were probably psychosomatic. In 1896, however, he began to lose the use of his right hand; so, characteristically, he disciplined himself to write with his left hand. In 1906, he awoke one morning blind in his left eye, a disability from which he never completely recovered. Apparently he was suffering from high blood pressure and from "occlusive disease of the internal carotid artery, the major supplier of blood to the brain." This disease apparently affects people differently but may lead to a change in behavior depending upon particular circumstances and the personality of the afflicted individual. At this time one doctor suggested that Wilson give up active work. Again characteristically he refused, but he did change his routine—more rest, fewer personal contacts, more secretarial help, less mingling with crowds. His affliction continued, however, to be sufficiently serious to cause one neurologist to predict, when Wilson was elected president, that he would not complete his term. He was plagued by frequent, blinding headaches as well as continual bouts with undefined illnesses which he usually called "colds." While in Paris in April 1919, he became seriously ill, an illness probably caused by a blood clot on the brain. The change in behavior at this time was marked—more irritability, more intolerance of other people's views, delusions about what was going on around him. In September and October 1919, he became progressively worse, and on October 2, a debilitating stroke occurred. From then until

March 1921, Wilson was president in name only, living in the delusion that he had not lost his capacity to govern and yet unable to provide the leadership that had served him so well in Princeton, in the governor's chair, and in Washington from 1913 to 1918.

Bibliography

Pages 317–338

This chapter is obviously based on a mélange of numerous ideas contributed by others previously cited. On the question of power, I found the comments of Richard Gillam in his anthology, *Power in Postwar America; Interdisciplinary Perspectives on a Historical Problem* (1971), particularly helpful.

Pages 317–318

On temperance and prohibition, see previous references for Chapter 3, pp. 25–30 and particularly Lewis L. Gould, *Progressives and Prohibitionists: Texas Democrats in the Wilson Era* (1973); Richard L. Watson, Jr., ed., *Bishop Cannon's Own Story: Life as I Have Seen It* (1955), chap. VI. The quotation from *The Antisaloon Yearbook* is in Joseph R. Gusfield, *Symbolic Crusade; Status Politics and The American Temperance Movement* (1965), p. 107; Wilson's attitude is brought out in John Blum, *Joe Tumulty and the Wilson Era* (1951), pp. 148–149.

Page 318

Robert Wiebe's thesis is brought out most clearly in *The Search for Order, 1877–1920* (1967).

Page 319

On the socialists, compare James Weinstein, *The Decline of Socialism in America, 1912–1925* (1967) with Michael Bassett, "The Socialist Party of America, 1912–1919; Years of Decline," unpub. doctoral diss. (Duke University, 1964).

Page 321

On Wilson's attitude toward trade, I have obviously borrowed heavily from Martin J. Sklar, "Woodrow Wilson and the Political Economy of Modern Liberalism," *Studies on the Left,* 1 (1960), 17–47, and N. Gordon Levin, Jr., *Woodrow Wilson and World Politics; America's Response to War and Revolution* (1968).

Pages 321–322

For the victory loan drive, see *Report of the Secretary of the Treasury,* 1919, pp. 70–71. Statistics on costs of the war are confusing and contradictory in part because of the difficulty of determining what periods are covered. See Charles Gilbert, *American Financing of World War I*, pp. 72–73, 222–223; Paul Studenski and Herman E. Krooss, *Financial History of the United States*, pp. 291–300; and Paul Einzig, *World Finance*, pp. 31, 47.

Pages 322–324

On the views of progressives about war, see Allen F. Davis, "Welfare, Reform and World War I," *American Quarterly*, 19 (Fall 1967), 516–533. On black people, see previous chapters, but note especially Gilbert Osofsky, "Progressivism and the Negro: New York, 1900–1915," *American Quarterly*, 16 (Summer 1964), 153–168. For the goals of American trade, see Carl P. Parrini, *Heir to Empire: United States Economic Diplomacy, 1916–1923* (1969).

Pages 324–325

For Taft's position, see Henry F. Pringle, *The Life and Times of William Howard Taft*, II, 915–925. For the hopes of the Fuel Administration, see *Final Report of the U.S. Fuel Administration*, pt. 2, 1917–1919. Also *New York Times*, August 27, 1919, p. 19.

Pages 325–327

For the accomplishments of the Railroad Administration, see Kerr, *American Railroad Politics*, pp. 119–122; *American Year Book*, 1918, pp. 364–365, 570–572; 1919, p. 350; Hines, *War History of American Railroads*, pp. 30–41, 216, 239, 269–275; Dixon, *Railroads and Government* . . . pp. 135–136, 160–161, 190–197; *Literary Digest*, 61 (April 19, 1919), 140–141; (September 6, 1919), p. 134; *Congressional Record*, 66th Cong., 1st sess., pp. 921ff.; Cunningham, "Railroads under Government Operation . . .," I, 309–340, and II, "From January 1, 1919–March 1, 1920," *Quarterly Journal of Economics*, 36 (November 1921), 47–57.

Page 326

For express companies and coastwise shipping, see *American Year Book*, 1918, pp. 58–59, 562.

Pages 326–327

For telephone, telegraph, and cables, see *Report of the Postmaster General on the Supervision of the Telegraph, Telephone, and Cable Properties*, October 31, 1919, *Sen. Doc.*, No. 152, 66th Cong., 1st sess.; *Annual Report of the Postmaster General*, 1919, pp. 22–23, and 1920, pp. 13–14; *Final Report of the Postmaster General on the Telephone, Telegraph, and Cable Companies* . . ., February 23, 1921, *Sen. Doc.*, No. 415, 66th Cong., 3d sess.; *Literary Digest*, 61 (April 19, 1919), 14–15; Committee on Interstate and Foreign Commerce, June 16, 1919, to Repeal the Telephone and

Telegraph Act, *House Report,* No. 45, 66th Cong., 1st sess.; *American Year Book,* 1919, pp. 40–42.

Pages 328-331

The Brandegee quotation is from Frederick L. Paxson, *American Democracy and the World War,* II (1936), chap. X. The military story of the war is told in Edward M. Coffman, *The Hilt of the Sword: The Career of Peyton C. March* (1966) and *The War to End All Wars; American Military Experience in World War I* (1968); Harvey A. DeWeerd, *President Wilson Fights His War; World War I and American Intervention* (1968); and S. L. A. Marshall, et al., *The American Heritage History of World War I* (1964). For a thoughtful treatment of Wilson as Commander in Chief, see Ernest R. May, "Wilson," in May, ed., *The Ultimate Decision: The President as Commander in Chief* (1960). On demobilization, see Paxson, vols. II and III, and especially Robert K. Murray, *The Harding Era: Warren G. Harding and His Administration* (1969), chap. III (footnote 3 gives a useful bibliography for demobilization).

Page 331

A brief treatment of the heritage of the war in later administrations is William E. Leuchtenburg, "The New Deal and the Analogue of War," John Braemen, et al., ed., *Change and Continuity in Twentieth Century America* (1964), pp. 81–143. For the Capital Issues Committee, see *Report of the Capital Issues Committee, House Doc.,* No. 1836, 65th Cong., 3d sess. For the reincarnation of the War Finance Corporation, see Gerald D. Nash, "Herbert Hoover and the Origins of the Reconstruction Finance Corporation," *Mississippi Valley Historical Review,* 46 (December 1959), 455–468.

Page 332

To get some idea of comparative income distribution is difficult. In addition to references in the note in the text, see Wesley C. Mitchell, et al., *Income in the United States; Its Amount and Distribution 1909-1919,* 2 vols. (1921–1922). Richard Abrams, "The Failure of Progressivism," in Richard Abrams and Lawrence Levine, *The Shaping of Twentieth Century America, Interpretive Essays,* 2nd ed. (1971), pp. 207–224.

Pages 332-335

On the Red Scare, see Robert K. Murray, *Red Scare; A Study in National Hysteria, 1919-1920* (1955); Stanley Colben, *A. Mitchell Palmer: Politician* (1963) and "A Study in Nativism: The American Red Scare of 1919-1920," *Political Science Quarterly,* 74 (March 1964), 52–75; Paul L. Murphy, "Sources and Nature of Intolerance in the 1920's," *Journal of American History,* 51 (June 1964), 60–76. On the constitutional questions of free speech, see Chafee, *Free Speech in the United States,* especially,

pp. 8, 23–24, 46, 50, 81, 108–140; Petersen and Fite, *Opponents of War,*
pp. 92–93; Alfred A. Kelly and W. A. Harbison, *The American Constitu-*
tion, p. 666. On the subject in general in the twentieth century, see
William Preston, Jr., *Aliens and Dissenters; Federal Suppression of Radi-*
icals, 1903–1933 (1963). Holmes was clearly wrestling with the meaning
of free speech in 1919. See also Fred D. Ragan, "Justice Oliver Wendell
Holmes, Jr., Zechariah Chafee, Jr., and the "Clear and Present Danger
Test for Free Speech; The First Year, 1919," *Journal of American History,*
58 (June 1971), 24–25; see Seward P. Livermore, *Politics is Adjourned*
for evidence that politics clearly was not adjourned on this question
during the war or immediately thereafter.

Pages 338–339
   References on Wilson's physical ailments can be found in the multi-
volume, magnificent edition of *The Papers of Woodrow Wilson* edited
by Arthur S. Link, but the concluding pages on Wilson's health are
based substantially on Edwin A. Weinstein, "Woodrow Wilson's Neuro-
logical Illness," *Journal of American History,* 57 (September 1970),
324–351.

Index

Aaron, Daniel, 60
Abbott, Grace, 85
Abrams v. *United States*, 334–335
Acres of Diamonds, 45
Adams, Herbert Baxter, 151
Adams, Herbert Carter, 39, 41
Adams, Samuel H., 62, 126
Adams Express Co., 326
Adamson, William C., 125
Adamson Act, 197, 262
Addams, Jane: founds Hull House, 43; and Dewey, 52; and settlement houses, 64; on prohibition, 73; and conservation, 74; and NAACP, 80; and Roosevelt, 144, 146; and labor, 168; and child labor, 200; and election of 1916, 208; and the war, 219, 322
Advisory Commission to Council of National Defense, 221, 263, 278–281, 297
Aeronautics Advisory Committee, 3
Agricultural Appropriations Bill of 1906, 126
Agriculture: wheat production, 9; developments in, 20–22, 165–166; government support of, 21, 198–199; during the war, 249–254
Agriculture, U.S. Department of: functions of, 24; under James Wilson, 166; under Woodrow Wilson, 198–199
Ainsworth, Fred C., 186

Airplanes: Wright brothers', 2; military development of, 186–187
Alabama, populism and progressivism in, 77
Alaska: seal fisheries in, 138; coal lands in, 140
Aldrich, Nelson W.: as leader of Senate, 100; and Roosevelt, 106; on pure food and drugs, 125–126; and income tax, 138; retirement of, 141
Allied Blockade Committee, 269–270
Allison, William B.: characteristics of, 100; and Roosevelt, 106; and pure food and drugs, 125
Altgeld, John Peter, 36, 52
Amalgamated Assn. of Iron, Steel, and Tin Workers, 13
Amalgamated Copper Co., 6
American Alliance for Labor and Democracy, 298
American Asiatic Assn., 170
American Assn. for Labor Legislation, 297–298, 319
American Automobile Assn., 199
American Bankers Assn., 166
American Committee on Social Insurance, 167, 168
American Defense Society, 283
American Economics Assn., 39–40
American Expeditionary Force, 328–330